CRITICAL THINKING IN PSYCHOLOGY AND EVERYDAY LIFE

CRITICAL THINKING IN PSYCHOLOGY AND EVERYDAY LIFE

A GUIDE TO EFFECTIVE THINKING

D. Alan Bensley

Frostburg State University

worth publishers
Macmillan Learning

New York

Vice President, Editorial, Social Sciences and High School: Charles Linsmeier
Program Managers: Daniel McDonough, Christine Cardone
Assistant Editor: Melissa Rostek
Editorial Assistant: Un Hye Kim
Marketing Manager: Kate Nurre
Marketing Assistant: Morgan Ratner
Executive Media Editor: Noel Hohnstine
Assistant Media Editor: Nik Toner
Media Production Manager: Joseph Tomasso
Director, Content Management Enhancement: Tracey Kuehn
Managing Editor: Lisa Kinne
Senior Content Project Manager: Vivien Weiss
Senior Workflow Supervisor: Susan Wein
Photo Editor: Sheena Goldstein
Director of Design, Content Management: Diana Blume
Senior Design Manager: Blake Logan
Interior Designer: Patrice Sheridan
Art Manager: Matthew McAdams
Composition: Lumina Datamatics, Inc.
Printing and Binding: LSC Communications
Cover: Clive Watts/Alamy

Library of Congress Control Number: 2017940132
ISBN-13: 978-1-319-06314-6
ISBN-10: 1-319-06314-4

Printed in the United States of America
First printing

Worth Publishers
One New York Plaza
Suite 4500
New York, NY 10004-1562
www.macmillanlearning.com

This book is dedicated to the memory of my parents, Don and Irene Bensley,
who fostered in me a love of learning and critical thinking.

ABOUT THE AUTHOR

D. Alan Bensley is a cognitive psychologist who received his BA from Grinnell College and his MS and PhD degrees from Rutgers University. He is a full professor of psychology at Frostburg State University and has taught critical thinking for more than 20 years. His first textbook, *Critical Thinking in Psychology: A Unified Skills Approach,* was published by Brooks-Cole in 1998. Dr. Bensley has numerous published articles on improving critical thinking, learning outcomes assessment, and psychological misconceptions. He is the past coordinator of critical thinking assessment at Frostburg University and is the current learning outcomes assessment coordinator for his department. His outside interests include a fascination with what science tells us about the world and what science fiction says about what the world might be like in the future.

BRIEF CONTENTS

CONTENTS

CHAPTER 1   INTRODUCTION TO CRITICAL THINKING IN PSYCHOLOGY AND EVERYDAY LIFE   1

CHAPTER 2   DEDUCTIVE REASONING, PREDICTION, AND MAKING ASSUMPTIONS   27

CHAPTER 3   INDUCTIVE REASONING IN PSYCHOLOGY AND EVERYDAY LIFE   49

CHAPTER 4   CRITICAL THINKING AND SCIENTIFIC REASONING   73

CHAPTER 5 PSEUDOSCIENCE, SCIENCE, AND EVIDENCE-BASED PRACTICE   103

CHAPTER 6 ERRORS IN ATTENTION, PERCEPTION, AND MEMORY THAT AFFECT THINKING   135

CHAPTER 13   CRITICAL THINKING IN CLINICAL REASONING AND DIAGNOSIS   321

CHAPTER 14   LANGUAGE, WRITING, AND CRITICAL THINKING   357

PREFACE FOR STUDENTS

As a psychology student, you are curious about why people behave and experience the world the way they do. You may have wondered whether people are basically selfish, or may have asked yourself, "Do I see the world the way it really is?" You may have heard of people being falsely imprisoned for crimes they did not commit based on eyewitness testimony. Do people make eyewitness memory errors that regularly lead to the conviction of innocent people? What causes people to behave so aggressively toward each other and commit murder, terrorist acts, and genocide in so many parts of the world? You may have wondered why some people maintain unusual beliefs, such as having been in contact with aliens from other planets. Why do others continue to believe in conspiracy theories that have been discredited, such as the belief that the U.S. government was behind the September 11, 2001, attacks on the World Trade Center and the Pentagon? These are some of the fascinating and important psychological questions discussed in this textbook.

Critical Thinking in Psychology and Everyday Life shows how a scientific, critical thinking approach can be effective in addressing psychological questions and discusses other questions that straddle the boundary between science and nonscience. What does science have to say about whether some people have special psychic abilities, such as being able to "see" the future? Can people use their minds to move objects without any physical aid? Do ghosts exist? You may have heard of near-death experiences in which a patient sees herself looking down at her body on an operating table. Does the mind actually leave the body during an out-of-body experience? You may be surprised to learn that we are tantalizingly close to a scientific answer to this last question (see Chapter 7).

This textbook seeks to engage you in a serious search for answers to these fascinating questions using what psychologists and other scientists know about how to think effectively. It is a guide for how to separate fact from speculation and true claims from misconceptions and misinformation. It can also help you learn to avoid the many thinking errors and biases people often demonstrate. Furthermore, you can use what you learn here to think more effectively about information in your other courses and on the Internet.

Perhaps your interest in psychology is focused more on how to help people with their problems. But help is not helpful if it is not really effective. Chapter 5 examines how to identify effective treatments and avoid ineffective ones that some people nonetheless claim are effective. Chapter 13 discusses how to diagnose psychological disorders and how to avoid the errors in reasoning about people's problems that even clinicians make. Together, these chapters can guide you toward more effective ways to help others.

Finally, what you get out of this book will largely depend on what you put into studying and practicing the ideas found in it. You should complete the exercises and answer the questions in each chapter, reflecting on the feedback you get as you progress through the textbook. Critical thinking is effortful thinking, but it is worth the effort and can ultimately help you think more effectively about questions in psychology and everyday life. Enjoy the journey as you learn how to think like psychologists when they do their best thinking.

PREFACE FOR INSTRUCTORS

OVERVIEW OF THE TEXTBOOK

Critical thinking (CT) is more important than ever before. In the sea of information we swim in daily, we encounter misinformation, fake news, scientific findings that seem to reverse, and treatments that do not work but which are nevertheless peddled enthusiastically. Unfortunately, students are often ill-equipped to critically evaluate this information. Accordingly, the primary purpose of this CT textbook is to improve the ability of psychology students to think effectively about psychological questions and to apply their knowledge and skills to thinking about everyday issues.

Because CT is multidimensional and requires the right skills, dispositions, metacognition, and relevant knowledge, the instruction in this textbook explicitly targets all these components for improvement. Given the complexity of CT, it can be derailed in multiple ways. Some people may lack CT skills, such as the ability to draw well-reasoned conclusions, and may be prone to a variety of thinking errors. Others may lack a CT disposition, such as an appropriately skeptical attitude; as a result, they might gullibly accept a claim without adequate evidential support. Still others who lack knowledge may fall prey to psychological misconceptions, such as the belief that the full moon makes people behave abnormally. Finally, individuals with a metacognitive deficit may not even be aware that they lack skills, knowledge, or the disposition to think critically; as a result, they may not recognize the need to take steps to improve their thinking. *Critical Thinking in Psychology and Everyday Life* takes a comprehensive approach, both instructing students how to engage in good reasoning while also seeking to eliminate their misconceptions, reduce their biases, and correct their thinking errors.

Psychology has much to say about good thinking and how to draw reasonable conclusions about psychological questions. This book applies the research on thinking and uses ideas from cognitive psychology, social psychology, abnormal/clinical psychology, and research methodology to present the discussion of critical thinking and scientific thinking. In addition, the book addresses questions related to many of the major areas in psychology covered in general psychology courses. As long as instructors first use Chapters 1–4, they can pick specific chapters they wish to use to supplement their course with discussions of topics relevant to specific areas of psychology. Because of its somewhat modular organization, it can be used flexibly, as discussed further in the Instructor's Manual.

One strategy for teaching students to think critically about content is to pose fascinating and controversial psychological questions as topics for CT analysis while at the same time explicitly teaching students how to engage in this analysis. For example, the textbook discusses whether UFOs are the spaceships of aliens, whether some people have paranormal powers, whether eyewitness memory is accurate, whether the 9/11 attacks were part of a U.S. government conspiracy, whether the best way to persuade terrorists to modify their extremist behavior is to help them reconnect with their families, as well as many other topics students usually find fascinating.

Chapters also include many real-world examples, such as the gullibility of investors who accepted Bernie Madoff's claims that he could make them rich, but ended up losing their life savings instead—an illustration of the consequence of lacking a skeptical attitude. Many more everyday judgment errors are highlighted in the chapters on superstition, judgment, and motivated reasoning. Examples include discussions of why a dentist spent $32,000 for John Lennon's decayed molar and how AIDS patients in sub-Saharan Africa continue to use the traditional cures of witchdoctors alongside more effective, evidence-based, medical treatments available today.

APPROACH AND ORGANIZATION

The guiding theory of CT instruction used in the book is an approach called *direct infusion*. Based on extensive research on CT instruction across the curriculum (e.g., Abrami et al., 2008; Mayer, 2004) and on our research on CT instruction in psychology (e.g., Bensley & Murtagh, 2012; Bensley & Spero, 2014), direct infusion is an effective form of explicit CT instruction. It combines elements of direct instruction and the infusion of CT skill instruction into regular subject matter instruction within a course or as part of topical coverage in a subject. Specifically, in direct infusion instructors explicitly identify the CT skills to be acquired, and then guide students in the use of CT rules and principles to enable thinking effectively about subject matter. Improving students' ability to think critically requires the right practice and feedback. The exercises and formative assessments encourage metacognitive awareness for improving future performance. For a more detailed discussion of direct infusion, see Bensley (2011).

At the beginning of each chapter, the first of several **Practice Thinking** (PT) exercises is a list of "What Do You Think?" questions designed to engage students in thinking about the psychological ideas noted therein and to reflect on their beliefs. At the end of each chapter, the same questions are asked in the "What Do You Think **NOW**?" section, this time designed to engage students in reflecting on how their ideas and beliefs have changed after thinking critically about the questions. This practice promotes improvement in metacognition because the questions focus on psychological misconceptions that are corrected through the discussion of the chapter. More explicit discrepancies between students' knowledge and their beliefs in relation to the evidence-based findings are presented in the chapter. Answers to the PT exercises that provide feedback are available in the Instructor's Resources to share with students after they have had the opportunity to complete the PT exercises.

Incorporated into the activities and exercises are many everyday, real-world examples of thinking errors and fallacies. For instance, the thinking error of hasty generalization is illustrated by the case of the CNN journalist who reported that the Supreme Court had declared the Affordable Health Care Act (ObamaCare) unconstitutional, when in fact the reporter had read only the first page of the decision, sacrificing accuracy for speed. The thinking exercises in the book give students practice in identifying other thinking errors introduced in the chapters.

PEDAGOGICAL FEATURES AND ANCILLARY MATERIALS

In addition to CT exercises, the textbook employs other pedagogical features. For example, the **chapter learning outcomes** have been written in the form recommended by research on writing learning objectives (Osborn, 1973) to help students target the important skills they should develop. To scaffold and make more explicit the information that is important for CT, the book contains additional tables that summarize how to execute different thinking skills, how to understand the strengths and weaknesses of different kinds of evidence, and how to recognize and correct different kinds of thinking errors.

Critical Thinking in Psychology and Everyday Life also illustrates CT concepts and skills using basic diagrams of arguments, figures that depict important examples and ideas, and pictures that engage students in the important ideas—all of which are closely aligned with points made in the textbook. Important terms are highlighted and defined the first time they are used, and each chapter concludes with a summary of the important concepts, CT skills, misconceptions, and thinking errors. A set of review questions that address important concepts are found at the end of each chapter.

To further supplement and engage students, other activities encourage students to use the knowledge and skills they are developing to perform interesting CT tasks. These activities can be used in class discussions. One such activity accompanies the emotion and motivated reasoning chapter; it deals with the mass delusion arising from the War of the Worlds radio broadcast and asks students to analyze the phenomenon from different perspectives. The presentation in Chapters 2 and 4 is supplemented with activities for analyzing the case of Charles Whitman, the mass murderer who, after murdering his wife and mother, killed 14 people from atop the University of Texas Tower. A third activity is especially appropriate for instructors using the textbook in the psychology capstone course. It is designed to help students create and critically evaluate a plan for using their knowledge of psychology and their CT skills in a simulation of a real-world activity. It encourages students to develop evidence-based solutions to problems they would likely encounter—a skill they can apply in their future life after college.

Finally, to support instructors' teaching and students' learning of the material, I have constructed lecture slides for each chapter that use pedagogical features of the textbook and encourage student engagement. The lecture slides track closely the content of chapters. In addition, they contain optional activities to support in-class practice of CT skills that supplement the textbook presentation.

ASSESSMENT MATERIALS

To evaluate the effectiveness of the direct infusion approach to CT instruction used in teaching with the textbook and to assess the various aspects of CT, we developed three sets of assessment materials. The first set, called Practice Thinking exercises (introduced earlier), are in-chapter exercises designed to help students self-assess their development of knowledge and skills as they progress through each chapter. The exercises target CT skills for argument analysis, critical reading, evaluation of information on the Internet, clinical diagnosis and reasoning, distinguishing science from pseudoscience, identifying thinking errors, recognizing psychological misconceptions, and critical writing. Consult the Instructor's Manual for more information about using them.

The second set of assessment materials is a test bank that can be used to construct tests and quizzes for chapters and units. The test bank includes formative assessment questions that align well with test and quiz questions and can prepare students for taking chapter quizzes and unit tests that instructors may customize for their courses.

The third set of assessment materials is an independent battery of other tests and measures called the Critical Thinking in Psychology Assessment Battery (CTPAB). The various CTPAB tests and measures can be used for summative assessment of both a CT course and psychology programs at large. Specific tests and measures of the CTPAB are designed to assess the various aspects of CT—including CT skills for reasoning, CT dispositions, and metacognition—as well as the failure to think critically, such as measures of psychological misconceptions, pseudoscientific beliefs, and other unsubstantiated beliefs. This third set of assessment measures is currently in development at Worth Publishers/Macmillan Learning. Those instructors and departments interested in reviewing or inspecting the CTPAB for assessment should contact Matt Wright (matt.wright@macmillan.com) for more information.

These assessment materials are available for use along with the textbook and are described more fully in the Instructor's Manual and Test Manual that accompany *Critical Thinking in Psychology and Everyday Life*.

ASSESSMENT STUDIES

To better understand the CT of our students and our assessment measures, we have conducted numerous empirical studies on the instructional techniques and materials, as well as on the assessment measures themselves. Research findings indicate that the measures studied have acceptable reliability and validity in the samples tested (e.g., Bensley, Lilienfeld, & Powell, 2014; Bensley et al., 2016). Other studies have consistently supported the effectiveness of the direct infusion, CT instructional approach (e.g., Bensley et al., 2010; Bensley et al., 2016; Bensley & Spero, 2014). For more information on the assessment studies research, see the Test Manual that accompanies the textbook.

ACKNOWLEDGMENTS

First, I wish to thank the following reviewers, who did a careful and thorough job in providing feedback on the textbook manuscript and provided many insightful comments:

Arno R. Kolz, Manhattan College
Jeffrey Eiseman, University of Massachusetts
Kathryn Saulsgiver, Rowan University
Laura M. Juliano, American University
Lawton K. Swan, University of Florida
Marianne Wilson, California State University–Bakersfield
Michael Granaas, University of South Dakota
Michael Tagler, Ball State University
Robert Guttentag, University of North Carolina at Greensboro
Yasmine Kalkstein, Mount Saint Mary College

I am especially grateful for the sage advice and expert guidance of my two editors at Worth, Christine Cardone and Daniel McDonough, as well as the careful oversight of Shani Fisher and Matt Wright, and the able assistance of editorial team members Melissa Rostek, Nik Toner, and Un Kim. I am very appreciative of the excellent work of the Worth production team, which includes Vivien Weiss, Sheena Goldstein, Naomi Kornhauser, and copy editors Jill Hobbs and Barbara Curialle.

Thanks to my wife, Nancy Bensley, for her critical thinking and insightful comments about so many things. Thanks also to my daughter, Kaitlin Bensley, for her fine graphic design work in Chapter 8.

I would also like to thank my graduate research assistants, who helped with learning outcome assessment research, including: Allison Bates, Vanessa Rowan, Deborah Crowe, Rachel Spero, Crystal Rainey, Krystal Rowan, and Florent Grain. Thanks also to Crystal Church and Lennon Ingram, who helped a great deal with references, as well as to Rhonda Hensel and Kathy Showalter of the Lewis Ort Library Interlibrary Loan Service for helping me obtain articles and books not directly available in the University of Maryland system. I am grateful to Randy Galliher and Karen Lancaster and the other helpful staff at the Frostburg State University Printing Services for the photocopying of the manuscript they have done for my students for several semesters. Thanks to Debbie Koon, our able administrative assistant, who has so much useful information about how things work.

I would also like to thank colleagues who have supported me in my work with critical thinking. For example, several members of the Frostburg State University Department of Psychology have supported my efforts to improve the critical thinking of our students. Thanks to the late Chrismarie Baxter for suggesting that I teach a senior capstone course on CT and for encouraging me to develop CT assessment measures. Thanks to my department, in general, for having the foresight to develop a CT course for beginning students. My colleagues Michael Murtagh, Jennifer Flinn, and Paul Bernhardt, in particular, have made considerable contributions to our learning outcomes assessment research, and I thank them for their help. Outside of my department, I wish to thank Scott Lilienfeld, whose work with misconceptions and pseudoscience has inspired me and whose collaboration on misconceptions research I greatly appreciate. Lastly, I thank Jane Halonen, who many years ago first encouraged me to write a CT textbook and later to develop CT assessment measures.

INTRODUCTION TO CRITICAL THINKING IN PSYCHOLOGY AND EVERYDAY LIFE

LEARNING OUTCOMES

After studying this chapter, you should be able to:

1. Explain what critical thinking is and why it is important.

2. Display working knowledge of important terms such as *claim, evidence, argument, counterargument,* and *conclusion.*

3. Distinguish arguments from non-arguments and facts from opinions and inferences.

4. Recognize some common thinking errors and psychological misconceptions.

WHAT DO YOU THINK?

Bettmann / Getty Images

FIGURE 1.1 Paracelsus popularized the misconception that the moon causes "lunacy."

A good first step in thinking critically about important questions is to find out what you think. Each chapter of this book begins by asking what you think about the fascinating and important questions discussed in that chapter. Critical thinking (CT) is a useful approach to answering such questions because it provides the means to reason effectively about them. For example, people have long connected changes in the moon, stars, and planets with behavior. In the sixteenth century, the Swiss physician Paracelsus proposed that the moon made people "crazy" (see Figure 1.1). The words lunatic and lunacy, derived from luna, the Latin word for "moon," reflect this supposed lunar influence on the mind.

In one study of mental health professionals, nearly 81% said they believed in this influence (Owens & McGowan, 2006). One of my students who worked at a mental health facility said staff members were convinced that their clients did behave strangely whenever the moon was full. Likewise, many college students think that the full moon makes people behave abnormally—specifically, 45% in a study by Russell and Dua (1983) and about 40% in a recent study we conducted (Bensley & Lilienfeld, 2015). What do you think about this question and the others listed below? Write your answers now to keep a record of your thinking.

 Practice Thinking 1.1: What Do You Think?

Please explain how you know.

1. Do people tend to behave abnormally during a full moon? _____

   _____

2. Is one theory just as good as another because each is "just a theory"?

   _____

3. Can astrologers accurately predict the future? Should a world leader consult an astrologer to make important decisions? _____

   _____

4. Do opposites attract in romantic relationships? _____

   _____

5. Should I stick with my first answer on a test or should I switch to a different answer? _____

   _____

You may be surprised to learn that there is *no connection* between the phase of the moon and abnormal or deviant behavior—nor between the moon and the murder rate or roughness in hockey games. Neither the number of psychiatric admissions (Kung & Mrazek, 2005) nor the number of suicides (Gutierrez-Garcia & Tusell, 1997) increases during a full moon. How could so many people be wrong about this? Perhaps they are not aware of the many psychological studies that have consistently found no connection. The psychologists James Rotton and Ivor Kelly (1985) reviewed 37 published studies and found no good evidence that any phase of the moon produced an increase in various indicators of deviant or abnormal behavior.

This example clearly shows that although many people may believe something is true, they can still be wrong. In this case, the statements of Paracelsus, the opinion of many college students, and the informal observations of workers at a mental health facility are all at odds with the conclusion drawn by scientific experts and their research. Whom should we believe? A critical thinker would make that decision after carefully evaluating the relevant evidence, or the reasons supporting one conclusion versus another. Evidence comes in various forms, such as the opinions of experts, informal observations, personal experience, and the results of scientific research studies.

How are we to evaluate this evidence when different sources offer support for both sides of an argument? Because this is a psychological question, we should put more trust in the side that is supported by the highest-quality scientific research. Discussion of what makes some types of evidence better than others brings us to the main purpose of this book.

THE PURPOSE OF THIS BOOK

This book's purpose is to help you learn *how* to think more effectively about questions, both in psychology and in everyday life. This is very different from telling you *what* to think or believe. Learning how to think critically about psychological questions is important because it often results in psychologists producing their best thinking. It is also important for you, as a student and citizen, to learn how to draw well-reasoned conclusions because doing so will serve you well throughout life. We live in the "Information Age," wherein we are bombarded with vast amounts of information from the media, online sources, and new scientific research studies. We need critical thinking (CT) to help us sort through, analyze, and evaluate this ocean of information. But what exactly is critical thinking?

WHAT IS CRITICAL THINKING?

Experts have offered many definitions of CT (e.g., Ennis, 1987; Halpern, 1998; Lipman, 1991; Paul, 1993). To simplify, we will examine some of the most important and consistent ideas emerging from attempts to define it. Robert Ennis, a recognized authority on CT, has provided a commonly cited definition that emphasizes the practical aspects of CT: **"Critical thinking is reasonable, reflective thinking that is focused on deciding what to believe or do"** (Ennis, 1987, p. 9). If CT really is practical, then it should help a person decide what to believe or do on a wide range of questions—from personal decisions such as "Should I take this nutritional supplement to help my cold?" to more scholarly questions such as "What is the best theory of depression?"

To decide what to believe or do, a person's thinking should be reasonable, showing a careful consideration of the relevant evidence and examining the reasons for believing or not believing some claim. The word *reasonable* also implies that thinking is sound, logical, and fair. To say that CT is "reflective" means that it involves thinking deeply about things, especially about the quality of one's own thinking. To help us think critically about both scientific and everyday questions, we will use a similar definition of CT: **Reflective thinking involved in the evaluation of evidence relevant to a claim so that a well-reasoned conclusion can be drawn from the evidence.**

Examining the word *critical* can help, too. In everyday language, being "critical" often means being judgmental or making overly negative comments. In contrast, referring to one's thinking as "critical" implies careful evaluation or judgment (Halpern, 2014). The latter sense of the word *critical* reflects its origins in the Greek word *kriterion,* derived from *crites,* meaning "judge" (Beyer, 1995). Notice that *kriterion* is very similar to the English word *criterion,* which refers to an accepted standard used in judging. Critical thinkers use criteria to make reasoned judgments (Lipman, 1991).

CRITICAL THINKING AND SCIENCE

Like critical thinkers, scientists use standards and criteria to make reasoned judgments (Bensley, 2011). Psychological scientists use standards that allow them to evaluate the quality of a study and the amount of support it provides for a theory or hypothesis. In Chapter 13, we will see that clinical psychologists use criteria to decide whether someone suffers from a mental disorder.

Another connection between CT and scientific thinking is that both involve the coordination of theory and evidence (Kuhn, 1993). The kind of evidence that psychologists and other scientists especially value is empirical data, which come from carefully made observations. Psychologists who think critically seek to draw conclusions and make judgments that are consistent with high-quality data. When clinical psychologists take a scientific and critical thinking approach to diagnosis, they make careful, systematic observations of their clients' signs, symptoms, and behaviors, judging how well these fit the criteria for one diagnosis versus another. Learning how to think critically and scientifically requires learning how to use criteria, standards, and rules for evaluating the evidence in one's field.

At this point, you might ask, "But aren't people entitled to their own opinions?" Of course, each of us has our own thoughts, beliefs, and conclusions. That does not mean, however, that one conclusion is just as good as another. When good standards and criteria are applied to evaluate thinking in a particular situation, some ways of thinking can lead to better conclusions than others. To arrive at these better conclusions takes CT, not merely accepting any conclusion that someone else draws.

SOME IDEAS ARE BETTER THAN OTHERS

Unfortunately, people often accept false claims and endorse poor practices without even realizing it. For instance, rather than applying treatments with demonstrated effectiveness, some psychologists use therapies that good scientific research has shown to be ineffective. Certain treatments even harm the people they are intended to help (Lilienfeld, 2007). Learning how to think critically provides the tools to evaluate such claims and avoid dangerous practices.

Along the same lines, some theories can be shown to be better than others. Failing to realize this, sometimes people say, "Oh, it's just a theory"—implying that all theories are inherently flawed and that one person's theory is as good as another's. For example, opponents of Darwin's theory of evolution often say, "It's only a theory," meaning that it can't be proven. Although no scientific theory or hypothesis can technically be proven to be true, some theories like the modern synthesis version of Darwin's theory of evolution have been much better supported than others (Dawkins, 2009). Darwin's theory of evolution assumes that organisms change over time through mutation and natural selection. Those organisms with traits that help them survive long enough to reproduce can pass along these adaptive traits to their offspring, increasing the frequency of adaptive traits.

Darwin's theory is better because it is consistent with more, higher quality, scientific evidence than competing theories. It has been supported by research showing that certain traits become more or less frequent in response to environmental pressures, by research in geology showing that more distantly related organisms tend to be deposited deeper and deeper into older layers of rock, and by research in molecular biology showing that more distantly related organisms share fewer genes (see Coyne, 2009; Dawkins, 2009; Palmer, 2009 for reviews).

More support for the modern version of Darwin's theory comes from the selective breeding of domesticated animals and the relationships with their wild counterparts. For instance, genetic research suggests that all dogs descended from the wolf. Modern dogs can still breed successfully with wolves. Examine Figure 1.2 and ask yourself, "Why do some dogs look more like wolves while others look so different?" At first, the wolves that evolved into dogs were probably those that were willing to get closer to humans so that they could scrounge for food in human garbage dumps (Coppinger & Coppinger, 2002). More of these wolves survived and passed along their genes to their offspring. Then our ancestors used *artificial selection,* a process like natural selection, to breed this group to be less aggressive and to have specific traits.

FIGURE 1.2 All of these dogs are the same species and descended from the wolf. Instead of allowing the dogs to change slowly through natural selection, our ancestors artificially selected (bred) them to have very specific characteristics over the last few thousand years.

Chris Collins/Lithium/AGE Fotostock

Scientists apply good theories, such as modern evolutionary theory, to help them make predictions and explain phenomena. A **theory** is a set of general principles that attempts to explain and predict behavior or other phenomena (Myers & Hansen, 2012). Predictions from a scientific theory tend to be confirmed more often when based on many prior, carefully made observations. No other theory in biology (or in psychology, for that matter) has been so well supported and had so many of its predictions confirmed as modern evolutionary theory (Coyne, 2009). Still, its predictions are not perfect, and it continues to be improved (Gould, 2002).

Isaac Asimov made a similar point when he explained how the theory that the earth is round is superior to the theory that it is flat (Asimov, 1989). The round-earth theory is not completely true: The earth is not perfectly spherical but bulges outward at the equator. However, the round-earth theory is clearly better than the flat-earth theory because predictions made from it are more accurate than those made from the flat-earth theory. Oddly, despite thousands of satellite images revealing the curvature of the earth, some "flat-earthers" still do not accept the better theory. They are demonstrating belief perseverance, the refusal to reject or revise one's faulty belief when confronted with evidence that clearly refutes that belief (Anderson, 2007). Another good example is how "birthers," or people who continue to believe that former U.S. President Barack Obama was not born in the United States (thus making him ineligible to be president), maintained that belief, even after Obama produced his birth certificate showing he was born in Hawaii.

That one theory can be shown to be better than another is important because even people who have not studied psychology use their own informal, often inaccurate, commonsense "theories" to explain behavior and other events (Rips & Conrad, 1989). These popular beliefs are not really scientific theories, but they are sometimes called commonsense psychology (Heider, 1958; Myers & Hansen, 2012). For example, common folk wisdom says "opposites attract," suggesting that people who are very different from each other may be attracted to each other. On the other hand, you have probably also heard it said that "birds of a feather flock together," suggesting that people who are more similar will tend to be attracted to each other (Stanovich, 2010). Many popular Internet dating sites endorse the idea that similarity in couples promotes successful relationships. Other people would argue that being with someone who is different from you keeps the relationship interesting. Both sides can't be right. Psychological research, in general, supports the idea that people who are similar are more likely to be attracted to each other (e.g., Byrne, 1971; Lewak, Wakefield, & Briggs, 1985; Wade & Tavris, 1993). Therefore, the idea that "opposites attract" in interpersonal attraction is a misconception to be abandoned in favor of the notion that people tend to be more attracted to people like themselves.

Sometimes, however, commonsense psychological ideas are correct, such as the idea that studying more leads to better learning and memory. It does (Baddeley, Eysenck, & Anderson, 2015). Critical thinking and good scientific research can help determine which of your ideas are right and which are wrong. The important thing is that learning *how* to think critically can help you decide *what* to think so that you are not stuck with wrong, sometimes dangerous ideas. Unfortunately, considerable evidence suggests that people often do not think critically.

WHY WE NEED TO IMPROVE THINKING

Suppose you are accused of committing a crime and your fate depends on the judgment of 12 jurors. You would hope that the jury carefully and objectively evaluates all the evidence relevant to your case. Unfortunately, Kuhn, Weinstock, and Flaton (1994) found that many of the participants, asked to evaluate the evidence from an actual murder trial, constructed only one story or theory accounting for the evidence in trying to understand the many facts and details of the case. Jury reasoning is an especially demanding task for citizens because they must consider multiple perspectives and coordinate various kinds of evidence with more than one theory. In general, the success of a democracy depends on its citizens making good judgments about the claims made by the media, politicians, and other sources (Glaser, 1985; Paul, 1984).

The world of finance provides many examples of CT failures. Many U.S. citizens have massive credit card debt and do not realize that using a credit card is essentially taking out a high-interest loan (Stanovich, 1994). Likewise, the wishful thinking of investors and the uncritical evaluation of loan applications by lenders led to the savings and loan fiasco of the late 1980s, which cost American taxpayers hundreds of billions of dollars. Another example was the Ponzi scheme of Bernard Madoff, discovered in 2008. In a Ponzi scheme, the schemer makes investment promises that are too good to be true, pockets investors' money, and repays earlier investors with the money from new investors (Greenspan, 2009). Madoff was said to have "made off" with $65 billion of investors' money, including that of actor Kevin Bacon, director Steven Spielberg, and many less well-known individuals.

The failure to think critically is often associated with thinking errors. **Thinking errors** are mistakes in judgment and reasoning that take a variety of forms, as when people fail to follow the rules of logic or misunderstand probability in making judgments. Other thinking errors occur when people use a rule that in some cases leads to a good judgment, but in other cases does not. In each chapter, we will examine different thinking errors and how to handle them.

Thinking errors and the failure to think critically in general often result in misconceptions. A **misconception** is a persistent, mistaken idea or belief that is contradicted by established scientific evidence (Taylor & Kowalski, 2004). **Psychological misconceptions** are sometimes called "myths" about the mind because they are firmly held beliefs about behavior and mental processes that are not supported by psychological research (Lilienfeld, Lynn, Ruscio, & Beyerstein, 2010). Many commonsense psychological theories are misconceptions, such as the idea that the moon causes people to behave abnormally and that opposites attract in romantic relationships.

Another common misconception among students is that staying with your first answer on a test is better than changing an answer. About three-fourths of students agreed that changing one's first response would tend to lower the test score (Balance, 1977; Benjamin, Cavell, & Shallenberger, 1984). Research clearly shows this is a misconception and that students are statistically better off changing their answers (Benjamin et al., 1984; Geiger, 1996). Of course, changing an answer does not work if you are simply guessing. Changing it is more effective if one has good reason to think the initial answer might be wrong (Shatz & Best, 1987). Throughout this book, we examine psychological misconceptions like these, so you can revise your incorrect ideas.

Sometimes, the failure to think critically about scientific questions leads a person to accept pseudoscientific claims. The prefix *pseudo-* means "false." Pseudoscience is an approach that makes false claims and masquerades as real science, discussed at length in Chapter 5. A good example of a pseudoscience is astrology; it might appear to be scientific, but it is neither scientific in approach nor supported by scientific research (Crowe, 1990). The horoscopes that astrologers cast appear to be scientific because they require complicated calculations based on the position of the stars and planets at the time of a person's birth, but the predictions astrologers make seldom turn out and are based on ideas inconsistent with the facts of astronomy, a true science.

You might say, "Why worry about belief in astrology—it's just a harmless pastime." But what if the president of the United States, the most powerful person on the planet, regularly consulted an astrologer to help make important decisions? According to one of his top advisers, the late President Ronald Reagan and his wife Nancy regularly consulted with their personal astrologer to help decide when to make appearances and important speeches, when to have meetings with world leaders, and even what to discuss at those meetings (Regan, 1988). The Reagans' interest in astrology dated back at least to his time as governor of California. He is reported to have chosen to be sworn in for his first term as governor at just after midnight because an astrological reading said it was a propitious time (Donaldson, 1988).

The failure to think critically is related to other mistaken ideas such as superstitions, conspiracy theories, and urban legends that are commonly found in everyday thinking and experience. Another example is belief in paranormal claims such as channeling, the new-age method of contacting spirits. Channeling, like its predecessor spiritualism, is a lucrative business, netting millions of dollars per year for those who serve as channels to communicate with the dead (Kyle, 1995). The confessions of a lifelong medium, M. Lamar Keene, who was on the board of directors of the Universalist Spiritualist Association (the largest of the American spiritualist groups), reveal the extent of fraud involved in such groups. Keene described how a medium with sexual designs on a female client approached her with the promise of special spirit ministrations, and then led her away to a darkened room where he had sexual intercourse with her. Thrilled by the experience, the gullible woman rushed to tell her husband how the spirits had chosen her for this special experience (Leahey & Leahey, 1983). Examples like this suggest the need for CT, but what does the research tell us?

Considerable research evidence suggests that students' thinking skills are not adequate to meet the challenges they face. Many educational reports, including the National Assessment of Educational Progress (NAEP), referred to as the "Nation's Report Card," have argued that the American educational system is failing to teach many of its students how to think effectively and that many students could not solve scientific problems (National Center for Educational Statistics, 2003, 2009).

Langer and Applebee (1987) found that students often have difficulty in persuasive and analytic writing, two kinds of writing that require CT. Using developmental tests of reasoning, McKinnon and Renner (1971) found that only one-quarter of all first-year college students they tested showed the ability to reason logically and abstractly. Although a college education seems to improve CT somewhat, this improvement, although significant, is not substantial (Keeley, Browne, & Kreutzer, 1982; Pascarella & Terenzini, 1991). Moreover, college education may not help improve CT as much as in previous years (Pascarella & Terenzini, 2005). Similarly, Perkins (1985) found that schooling had some impact on students' abilities to reason about everyday questions, but not as much as we would hope for if students had become proficient at CT. Let's examine what it takes to improve thinking.

WHAT IT TAKES TO THINK CRITICALLY

Theory and research on CT suggest that a person must have four things to become a proficient critical thinker (Bensley, 2011; Byrnes & Dunbar, 2014; Ennis, 1987; Halpern, 1998; Perkins, Jay, & Tishman, 1993). These include:

1. Knowledge of reasoning terms, concepts, and rules and how to use them (CT skills)
2. Knowledge relevant to the problem or question (knowledge of topic)

3. Awareness of one's own thinking and how to regulate it (metacognition)
4. The appropriate dispositions for thinking critically (CT dispositions)

To think critically about a psychological question, you should know common terms, concepts, and rules used in reasoning about such questions. These include terms such as *claim, evidence, conclusion,* and *argument,* as well as the rules for reasoning about psychological questions. After you become familiar with these terms, you need to practice using these concepts and rules to acquire CT skills, such as the ability to recognize different kinds of evidence and to evaluate the quality of evidence offered in support of claims.

Reasoning about a specific question, such as whether the moon makes people behave abnormally, further requires the knowledge of important ideas and research related to this question. Thinking is always *about* something. If you do not understand ideas related to a question, you will not be able to use your reasoning skills to think effectively about the topic.

Unless you know when to use your knowledge and skills and whether you are using them correctly in a situation, you will not think effectively. **Metacognition** refers to the awareness and knowledge of one's own thinking that allows a person to regulate that thinking. Critical thinkers think about their own thinking, monitoring their progress on a thinking task to improve the quality of their thinking. Checking your work when answering a question or solving a problem is an example of metacognitive monitoring; subsequent revision of your answer is an example of self-regulation.

Critical thinkers must also be disposed or inclined to use their knowledge and skills to answer questions. They need to have dispositions such as open-mindedness, fair-mindedness, and a skeptical attitude toward unsupported claims. Critical thinking dispositions are attitudes, traits, thinking styles, and motives that make it more likely a person will think critically. Critical thinkers show open-mindedness and fair-mindedness in their willingness to consider and fairly evaluate new ideas that may be very different from their own beliefs; they show a skeptical attitude when they ask "Why?" after someone makes a claim without offering a reason to support it.

Questioning our beliefs and considering views that challenge our own favored beliefs are hard to do. Even famous, scientifically trained people, known for their thinking skills, have sometimes been unwilling to fairly and objectively evaluate evidence that went against their beliefs. Sir Arthur Conan Doyle, the brilliant creator of Sherlock Holmes and a scientifically trained physician, uncritically accepted the ideas of spiritualism, believing that mediums can contact the spirits of the dead during séances (Figure 1.3a). Conan Doyle also believed that fairies

(a)

(b)

FIGURE 1.3 Sir Arthur Conan Doyle was not skeptical of photographs like (a) the one of a "spirit" manifesting itself at a séance or (b) the Cottingsley fairies despite evidence that they were faked. He was not disposed to use his scientific knowledge and reasoning skill to think critically about these questions.

had been photographed in England's Cottingsley Glen (Figure 1.3b). Although experts questioned the authenticity of the photos, Conan Doyle himself did not seriously question them.

Despite the fact that no good scientific evidence then or now supports the ability to contact spirits of the dead or the existence of fairies, Conan Doyle believed in these ideas completely. His uncritical acceptance of spiritualism seems all the more ironic, given that his character Sherlock Holmes was a superb detective noted for his ability to reason well. Despite his gullibility about spiritualism and fairies, Conan Doyle was skeptical of new medical treatments and once solved an actual crime himself. His failure to think critically about the claims of spiritualism was thus not due to his lack of CT skills but to his unwillingness to apply those skills when it came to spiritualism (Bensley, 2006). Clearly, thinking critically requires both dispositions and skills, as the research shows (Taube, 1997).

USING THIS BOOK TO IMPROVE YOUR THINKING

As you read this book, you should begin to question whether your own common-sense psychological "theories" are right. Compare your own ideas with the well-supported scientific theories discussed so that you can revise any incorrect ideas as needed. In many ways, this book is a user's guide on how to think effectively.

Besides helping you eliminate misconceptions, it is designed to help you overcome thinking errors and biases commonly found in everyday living and sometimes even in the thinking of experts. Throughout this book, we examine what scientific research says about how the mind works and how to improve thinking. To learn how people think and form beliefs, we examine many controversial ideas found in urban legends, conspiracy theories, and beliefs about things such as ghosts, out-of-body experiences, extrasensory perception, UFOs, and many other fascinating topics.

Fortunately, research has shown that people can learn how to think more effectively with the right method and practice (see Abrami et al., 2008; Bensley, 2011; Halpern, 1993, 1998 for reviews). This book incorporates these findings in a set of techniques and exercises that should improve CT. In fact, studies have found that after using the approach described in this book, students showed significant improvement in their CT skills and knowledge (e.g., Bensley, Crowe, Bernhardt, Buckner, & Allman, 2010; Bensley & Haynes, 1995; Bensley, Rainey, Lilienfeld, & Kuehne, 2016; Bensley & Spero, 2014).

To help improve your thinking, each chapter contains various Practice Thinking exercises, such as the one below, that target specific thinking skills. As with improving other skills, improving thinking takes practice. Do the exercises as you read the chapters you are assigned. You can further improve your CT by taking an active approach to your learning. Read the material carefully and check your understanding as you go along to make sure you are acquiring the relevant knowledge.

To increase your metacognitive awareness even more, compare your Practice Thinking exercise answers with those found online, carefully reflecting on how to improve any incorrect answers. To become more disposed to think critically, try to be open- and fair-minded when encountering ideas different from your own; consider the other side, but be skeptical of claims that are unsupported. How much you get out of this book will largely depend on your willingness to work at applying these ideas to carefully and objectively examine the quality of your own and other people's thinking.

 Practice Thinking 1.2: Identifying the Components of Critical Thinking

Decide whether each example below involves primarily a lack of CT skill, a CT disposition, or a failure of metacognition. Write the problem with thinking in the space provided and give a reason for your answer.

1. After their psychology lecture on hypnosis, Phillip asked Angie if she thought that hypnosis was a distinct state of consciousness. She said, "Yeah, sure." Then Phillip said, "Didn't you hear the instructor say that research shows it is not different from ordinary waking consciousness? Rather, it simply involves people who tend to get absorbed in imagining what the hypnotist suggests." She said, "I guess I missed that part and wasn't aware of it." _____

   _____

2. Devin was reading in his psychology textbook about the idea that people are right-brained or left-brained. Although the book's review of the research literature concluded that there are differences in the functions of the hemispheres, the idea that people are right-brained or left-brained is an exaggeration and a misconception. Unfortunately, Devin did not know how to evaluate the evidence in the research review and continued to believe in the misconception that people are right-brained or left-brained. _____

   _____

3. Cara read that a positive attitude cannot stave off cancer, contrary to her prior belief. She said, "That information I read is simply not true, and I am sure that having a positive attitude can help prevent and even cure cancer." _____

   _____

WHY DO PEOPLE HOLD FALSE BELIEFS?

Why do people believe that the moon causes abnormal behavior and other false claims unsupported by scientific research? It would seem that knowing the real causes of abnormal behavior would be more useful. Perhaps a believer in lunar lunacy simply does not know there is no connection. It turns out that answering this question is more complex and requires that we make a distinction between how people first acquire a misconception and why they persist in believing a false claim.

People often acquire misconceptions like the lunar lunacy idea because of their tendency to see patterns that are not really there. In later chapters, we discuss how people often seem to be selective in what they perceive, attend to, and remember. They may pay attention to certain information and ignore other information, leading them to find patterns that do not exist. For example, when the moon is full, people may tend to notice that others are behaving abnormally, but they do not look for this abnormal behavior when the moon is *not* full. Once people find a pattern, they tend not to test whether a relationship actually exists or not; but avoiding misconceptions requires active reflection, not passive acceptance of claims.

Psychologists have developed a theory called *dual process theory* that can help us understand the thinking that leads people to accept or reject false beliefs (e.g., Epstein, 2008; Kahneman, 2011; Stanovich & West, 2000). According to one dual process theory called *rational-experiential theory,* people who take a more intuitive-experiential approach in their thinking tend to rapidly respond to questions without deliberation, using their vast knowledge of patterns and experience (Epstein, 2008). This approach, also called *Type 1 thinking,* is what people use when they quickly respond with their commonsense knowledge. If instead, people deliberately analyze and reason about information presented to them, they are taking a more rational-analytic approach (i.e., engaging in *Type 2 thinking*). Although we need and engage in both kinds of thinking, we often tend to rely on the intuitive-experiential approach unless we realize that we need to engage in more effortful, rational-analytic thinking. Can you tell which approach is likely used in answering the following questions?

1. $2 + 4 = $ _____
2. If a bat and ball cost $1.10 and the bat costs $1 more than the ball, how much does the ball cost?
3. What is 27×43?
4. Do people who have been abused often repress their memory of that abuse?

You likely had no trouble answering the first question. Type 1 thinking, which is intuitive-experiential, helped you rapidly answer "6." However, if you rapidly answered the second question "10 cents" (as people often do), then using Type 1 thinking led you to the wrong answer (Fredericks, cited in Kahneman, 2011). The answer is 5 cents (the bat must cost $1.05 for it to cost $1.00 more). Slowing down your thinking and engaging the rational-analytic system would have helped you answer correctly. Clearly, the third problem requires more complex calculations and the deliberate, effortful processing of Type 2 thinking.

If you answered the fourth question rapidly on the basis of what you have heard, as many people do, you likely answered, "Yes" (Bensley & Lilienfeld, 2015). Here again, when Type 1 thinking is deployed, it leads to an incorrect answer. Answering this question correctly requires Type 2 thinking. Careful analysis and reasoning about the scientific evidence relevant to this question will show in later chapters that repressed memory is very rare, if it occurs at all.

For many questions, the intuitive-experiential system works just fine, as when we need to access facts rapidly or make judgments of preferences; but most of the questions we examine in this book require more rational-analytic thinking. Critical thinkers take the time to analyze, evaluate, and question the information they are provided, engaging Type 2 thinking. Critical thinkers do not accept pseudoscientific theories for which there is no good evidence. They remain skeptical of such claims until they are given good reason to believe them. They carefully evaluate the evidence relevant to such claims so that they can draw well-reasoned conclusions about them. Because they seek to reason well and avoid thinking errors, they are less likely to hold misconceptions (Bensley, Lilienfeld, & Powell, 2014; McCutcheon, Apperson, Hanson, & Wynn, 1992).

Practice Thinking 1.3: Identifying the Kind of Thinking Needed

For the first two examples, decide what kind of thinking is most appropriate—Type 1/intuitive-experiential or Type 2/rational-analytic—and then give a reason for your decision. For exercises 3 and 4, describe an example from your own life in which you needed or would need the kind of thinking indicated.

1. You are deciding which kind of candy tastes the best. _____

   _____

2. You are deciding which is the best theory of learning. _____

   _____

3. Type 1: _____

4. Type 2: _____

The next section is intended to help you acquire knowledge of reasoning terms, concepts, and rules.

BASIC TERMINOLOGY

Suppose you are talking with a friend about violence in our society, and she says, "I think people today are very aggressive." In making this statement, your friend has just made a claim. A **claim** is a statement asserting that someone or something has a particular characteristic or property. We treat a claim as if it is either true or false, but not both. In this case, your friend has asserted that it is true that people have the characteristic of being very aggressive.

If, after thinking about it, your friend has accepted as true the claim that people are basically aggressive, we say that she has drawn a **conclusion**, to distinguish it from simply a claim being considered. Conclusions can take a variety of forms, such as judgments, decisions, identifications, diagnoses, and inferences. A person often signals a conclusion by using indicator words, such as "I conclude," "I believe," "I think," or "I have decided." Other expressions signal that a conclusion follows, such as "In conclusion," "Therefore," "Consequently," "Thus," "Hence," "As a result," or "For these reasons." See the Appendix for more indicator words used in the language of argumentation.

In the preceding example, your friend did not use any of these indicator words, but she still might have drawn a conclusion, because in everyday conversations people often do not explicitly distinguish between a claim and a conclusion. Although we hope that conclusions and inferences follow from good reasons, people often make inferences without first showing much reasoning. Sometimes, inferences are more like guesses, suppositions, or simply connections between ideas. For example, Kevin says, "Joan talks about psychology a lot. I suppose she is majoring in psychology." In this case, Kevin is signaling he is not committed to his inference that Joan is a psychology major. He would probably admit he is not sure if it is true. Should you accept people's conclusions merely because they are confident of them?

If you are a critical thinker, the answer should be, "Not unless they have provided good reasons or evidence to support their claims." As mentioned before, evidence refers to a reason or reasons offered in support of a claim or conclusion and can take a variety of forms. One kind of evidence takes into account what most people think, looking for a consensus of opinion or general agreement about some claim. If many people share the same opinion as your friend, this might be a reason (although not a particularly good one) to accept the claim that people today are more aggressive than in earlier times.

Another kind of evidence is a case or example that someone offers to support a claim. For instance, a friend might say that people are basically aggressive because he knew someone who got very angry and then punched someone else.

Or he might quote the statement of an authority or expert on aggression as evidence to support the claim that people are basically aggressive.

Still another type of evidence is a fact that is offered as a reason for accepting a claim. A **fact** is a commonly observed event or statement that is taken as true and not likely to change. Facts are not simply opinions shared by many people but are accepted as true because they can be objectively verified. In science, facts are research findings that are reliably obtained. In biology, it is a fact that organisms evolve. In psychology, it is a fact that people forget things. Scientists often agree on the facts, but they may differ in how they interpret and explain those facts. A fact obtained through good scientific research provides a good reason for accepting a claim. You should note, however, that although we often treat facts and claims as true when reasoning from them in science, this oversimplifies their status in the real world.

Practice Thinking 1.4: Deciding on the "Truth" of Statements

Decide whether the following four statements would be generally considered true (T) or false (F) and label each one accordingly. For each true statement, explain why it is considered true, identifying it as true because it is either an accepted definition or a fact supported by research.

1. Critical thinking dispositions are attitudes, traits, thinking styles, and motives that make it more likely a person will think critically. _____

    _____

2. The more you study, the more you will tend to learn. _____

    _____

3. The full moon causes people to behave abnormally. _____

    _____

4. When taking a test, it is better to stick with your initial answer. _____

    _____

5. What is a true statement or fact that you know? How do you know it is true?

    _____

Returning to the conversation about violence and examining your friend's statement more closely, you can see that your friend has only made a claim, offering *no* evidence to support it. Perhaps your friend simply forgot to provide a reason. Or perhaps the claim is simply your friend's opinion. In either case, your friend has *not* made even a basic argument, and you should *not* be persuaded by what she has said. We define a basic **argument** as offering a reason or evidence in support of a claim or conclusion. Often, when we hear the word *argument* in everyday conversation, we think of people yelling at each other in a heated dispute. This is not what we mean; rather, in making an argument, the critical thinker provides both a claim or conclusion and evidence to support it.

Figure 1.4 shows the difference between a simple claim and a basic argument. Figure 1.4a makes the important point that someone who is not supporting a claim with a reason is not making a basic argument. Likewise, someone who accepts a claim without a reason is drawing an unsupported conclusion. Critical thinkers don't just make claims—they make arguments (Figure 1.4b). Moreover, they base their conclusions on reasons.

The next time someone makes a claim about something important without offering a reason, as shown in Figure 1.4a, ask, "Why do you think that?" When one of your teachers asks what you think, don't just state an opinion. Instead, support your claim with a good reason, as shown in Figure 1.4b. Teachers who emphasize CT appreciate this kind of answer.

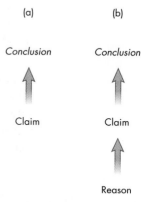

FIGURE 1.4 (a) An unsupported claim, often just someone's opinion, becomes a conclusion when it is accepted. (b) A basic argument in which a claim is supported by at least one reason.

Practice Thinking 1.5: Distinguishing Arguments From Non-arguments

Read each of the following statements and write "Yes" if it is a basic argument or "No" if it is not. For each, explain your answer.

1. The storage capacity of short-term memory is 7 ± 2 bits of information.

    _____

2. Because Mary felt very anxious just seeing a picture of a snake, her behavior therapist decided she had a phobia (irrational fear) of snakes.

    _____

3. After observing many young children trying to solve a problem, the developmental psychologist concluded that only older children and adults could solve the problem.

   _____

4. Emotions are motivated states associated with subjective experiences such as feelings, expressive behaviors such as smiling, and physiological changes such as increased heart rate.

   _____

5. John Watson, a founder of behaviorism, said that science requires observation of events that can be verified but that mental states are not directly observable. Therefore, psychologists should study only observable behavior and not mental states.

   _____

6. Kyle said, "I consulted my horoscope for today, and the astrologer said I will come into some money, so I'm going to look around for opportunities to make some."

   _____

When you are trying to decide whether an argument has been made, it often helps to first locate the conclusion. Consult Appendix A to help find indicator words that signal a conclusion and other parts of arguments. For example, in Practice Thinking 1.5 statement 5 above, the word *therefore* indicates the point at which a conclusion follows. Next, find a reason or premise supporting the conclusion you found. Statement 5 also contains a reason, so together they make an argument. In statement 2, the word *because* signals that a reason has been provided and connects this reason to a conclusion. Statement 2 contains both a reason and a conclusion, making it a basic argument. Statements 1 and 4 do not contain both a reason and a conclusion and thus are not arguments. The indicator words for identifying parts of arguments can be helpful, but proceed carefully. Simply using a word like *because* without providing a reason does not make an argument (Fawkes, 2003).

Well-formed arguments found in discussions of psychological questions, debates, jury trials, and in some everyday situations are much more elaborate than the basic arguments we have examined so far. One important difference is that evidence is presented on more than one side of a question. In such exchanges, after one side has presented supporting evidence, the other side presents evidence supporting a position that is inconsistent with the first position. This counterclaim and corresponding evidence that run counter to or disagree with the first claim are referred to as a **counterargument**.

For instance, suppose you are discussing who was the most ruthless dictator in all of history. One person offers, "I believe it was Adolf Hitler, because his actions started World War II and contributed to the extermination of six million Jews in the Nazi concentration camps." A second person responds with the counterargument, "Yes, Hitler was brutal, but what about Joseph Stalin, who ruled Russia and the Soviet Union with an iron fist from 1923 to 1954? He murdered as many as six million of his own countrymen with whom he disagreed. Through neglect, his assignment of people to starvation camps, and his failure to prepare for the war against Hitler, a total of 24 million more people died."

Research suggests that finding and making counterarguments is a hard skill to acquire (Voss & Means, 1991). Children acquire skills of argumentation in stages; the ability to recognize and use counterarguments develops relatively late (Coirier & Golder, 1993). Other research suggests that students tend not to offer counterarguments when they should (Voss & Means, 1991). A study of juror reasoning showed that some participants acting as jurors considered only one position in an argument from an actual trial (Kuhn, Weinstock, & Flaton, 1994). This suggests we should practice identifying and using counterarguments.

 ## Practice Thinking 1.6: Identifying a Counterargument

Suppose two students are discussing whether or not people are basically selfish (discussed at length in Chapter 10). After reading the students' discussion, write the claim of the main position and the evidence supporting it, and then write the counterclaim made in the counterargument, along with the evidence supporting it.

Jake says, "People are not basically selfish; plenty of examples show this. There's the case of Lenny Skutnik, a bystander at the scene of a plane crash in the Potomac River in the middle of winter, who imperiled his own life by repeatedly diving into the frigid waters to save some of the passengers." Gina replies, "What about people who help others for selfish reasons? I heard that Abraham Lincoln ordered his carriage to stop to save some drowning pigs so he could avoid having a guilty conscience over the matter."

Claim: _____

Evidence: _____

Counterclaim: _____

Counterevidence: _____

IDENTIFYING AND CORRECTING THINKING ERRORS

Now that you have learned about arguments, you may better appreciate how thinking and arguments can go wrong—thinking errors. One basic rule is that we should argue from true statements, knowledge that we possess, and high-quality evidence to draw well-reasoned conclusions. One kind of thinking error that clearly violates this basic rule is called argument from ignorance or possibility.

TABLE 1.1 Summary of Thinking and Argumentation Errors

Name	Description	How to Fix or Avoid It
Failure to make an argument	Making a claim without providing a reason or evidence to support it, especially when a reason has been requested	Provide a reason or evidence to support a claim; ask "Why?" if no reason is provided.
Argument from ignorance or possibility	Claiming a conclusion is true because we don't know for sure whether it is false or simply has not yet been proven to be untrue, in which case it is possibly true	Draw conclusions based on facts and knowledge, not on ignorance; search for positive evidence to support a new claim.
Belief perseverance	Not revising one's belief or conclusion when good reasons have clearly shown the belief or conclusion to be wrong	Consider the other side or alternative positions and explain how the alternative belief could be true.

It occurs when someone concludes something is true because it is possible that it is true or because it is not yet known to be false. For example, in response to a discussion of the lack of good evidence that Bigfoot exists, someone says, "Scientists have not been able to conclusively prove that Bigfoot does not exist; therefore, it probably does exist somewhere." This is a thinking error because it is illogical to conclude that something exists when there is a lack of evidence for it. See Table 1.1 for a summary of the thinking errors discussed in this chapter.

 Practice Thinking 1.7: Recognizing and Fixing Thinking Errors

In the space that follows, write the thinking error in each example and then explain how to fix it.

1. Brad said, "I am certain that UFOs are spaceships carrying alien beings from other worlds and that they have come to Earth already. After all, scientists have not yet proven that UFOs are not alien spaceships."

    Thinking error: _____

    How to fix it: _____

2. Megan told Rob, "I read a literature review in which a psychologist cited many scientific studies showing that people are more attracted to people who are similar to them. Apparently, the idea that 'opposites attract' in romantic relationships has little scientific support." Rob replied, "I don't believe it. I'm very attracted to my girlfriend—and she has very different interests from me."

    Thinking error: _____

    How to fix it: _____

3. Taylor said, "It's clear that human activities are contributing to the warming of the planet."

    Thinking error: _____

    How to fix it: _____

SUMMARY

Many examples from everyday life, such as Ponzi schemes and scams, show the need for improved thinking. Likewise, research on thinking often shows that people are deficient in their reasoning. People use commonsense theories, often acquired from their culture and personal experience, to explain behavior and mental processes without considering the evidence in support of those theories. In contrast, critical thinkers and scientists evaluate the quality of the evidence relevant to a claim in order to draw well-reasoned conclusions from it. Critical thinkers realize that some theories are better than others. Specifically, theories are better when the predictions they make are confirmed and supported by high-quality evidence.

Becoming a critical thinker requires knowledge of reasoning terms and rules, as well as the skills to use them. For example, a critical thinker knows that an argument is a claim/conclusion along with evidence supporting it and can distinguish an argument from a non-argument. As with other skills, improving thinking takes effort and practice. It also takes relevant knowledge about the questions being investigated as well as metacognitive reflection or awareness of one's own thinking. Critical thinkers are disposed to use their skills when appropriate. They are open to new ideas and fair-minded in evaluating them but are also skeptical in that they question new ideas and seek evidence when none has been offered.

Critical thinkers also learn to recognize pseudosciences, such as astrology, and misconceptions, such as "lunar lunacy." Pseudoscience may look like real science, but it is false science and only appears to use the scientific method to arrive at its conclusions. Misconceptions are mistaken ideas that people endorse but that are not supported by good evidence. People who reason from misconceptions draw conclusions that will likely be in error.

Critical thinkers learn to identify and counter the many logical and other thinking errors people make. For instance, people may fail to offer evidence to support a claim or may accept a claim without a good reason supporting it; the critical thinker asks for a reason when none is offered. People sometimes argue from ignorance or possibility, accepting something as true because a lack of evidence has not shown it to be false, but the critical thinker argues from evidence that exists. People also show belief perseverance when they continue to believe unsupported claims, even though good evidence has contradicted their beliefs; critical thinkers align their beliefs with well-reasoned arguments based on high-quality evidence.

Practice Thinking 1.8: WHAT DO YOU THINK **NOW**?
Please explain how you know.

1. Do people tend to behave abnormally during a full moon? _____
   _____

2. Is one theory just as good as another because each is "just a theory"?
   _____

3. Can astrologers accurately predict the future? Should a world leader consult an astrologer to make important decisions? _____
   _____

4. Do opposites attract in romantic relationships? _____
   _____

5. Should I stick with my first answer on a test or should I switch to a different answer? _____
   _____

REVIEW QUESTIONS

1. How is CT defined?
2. Are certain ideas better than others? Are certain theories better than others? Is a certain type of thinking better than another?
3. What is an opinion? When is an opinion a problem for CT?
4. What is evidence? What is its place in CT?
5. Why is CT important? Why do we need it?

6. From a psychological perspective, what does it take to become a critical thinker?

   - What are CT skills?
   - How is knowledge of a subject needed to think critically about a topic?
   - How and why are metacognitive monitoring and self-regulation needed for CT?
   - What are CT dispositions, and why are they needed?

7. What are obstacles to CT?

   - What are thinking errors? Failing to make an argument? Arguing from ignorance? Belief perseverance?
   - What are misconceptions?
   - What is pseudoscience? Does the evidence support a belief in astrology?
   - Why do people persist in believing false theories? What does dual process theory say?
   - Compare intuitive-experiential thinking to rational-analytic thinking.

8. What are the basic CT terms?

   - What is an assertion or claim? Compare it with an opinion and a hypothesis.
   - What is a fact?
   - What is a basic argument? Can you distinguish an argument from a non-argument?
   - What is a counterargument? Can you find a counterargument in a discussion?

9. What psychological misconceptions were discussed in this chapter?

DEDUCTIVE REASONING, PREDICTION, AND MAKING ASSUMPTIONS

LEARNING OUTCOMES

After studying this chapter, you should be able to:

1. Distinguish deductive and inductive reasoning.

2. Recognize assumptions and show how they affect conclusions.

3. Use deductive reasoning to make predictions.

4. Recognize some common thinking errors and psychological misconceptions.

WHAT DO YOU THINK?

We use our thinking to make decisions, judge the quality of products, predict the future, and draw conclusions about life's important questions, such as whether or not to go to war. But how certain can we be that our thinking has led us to a good conclusion or decision? In 2003, many people in the United States were sure that Saddam Hussein, the dictatorial leader of Iraq, was stockpiling weapons of mass destruction (WMDs). Although United Nations weapons inspectors had not found such weapons in Iraq, many people assumed that Saddam had WMDs because he had stockpiled them and used them in the Iran–Iraq War. The George W. Bush administration convinced the U.S. Congress that Saddam did indeed have WMDs, and the U.S. government authorized an invasion that toppled his government within three weeks. Although the war continued for eight more years, resulting in the deaths of more than 4,000 Americans and at least 110,000 Iraqis, no one ever found any WMDs (National Commission on Terrorist Attacks Upon the United States, 2004). How could so many people be so certain and yet so wrong? These examples raise questions about our ability to be certain about what we think we know.

Practice Thinking 2.1: What Do You Think?

Please explain how you know.

1. Can I be certain about a conclusion I draw? Or is there always some uncertainty?

   _____

2. Does improving the self-esteem of students improve their grades and test scores?

   _____

3. Does "blowing off steam" or venting anger help reduce it and prevent aggression?

   _____

4. Is profiling of suspects effective in identifying perpetrators?

   _____

In this chapter, you will see that a particular kind of reasoning, called *deductive reasoning,* can lead to logical certainty but that another kind of reasoning, called *inductive reasoning,* cannot. In fact, our everyday thinking and scientific reasoning usually involve uncertainty.

KINDS OF REASONING

The critical thinker uses the basic tool of reasoning to come to a conclusion. Psychologists and thinkers in all disciplines use reasoning to help them think more clearly about the questions they ask and to advance the state of their knowledge. Reasoning is a powerful tool in this inquiry process because it prescribes conventional ways for us to use language so that arguments can be communicated clearly and analyzed consistently and effectively. In particular, it provides us with rules for relating evidence to conclusions.

Two types of reasoning commonly used in psychology and other sciences are inductive and deductive reasoning. In **inductive reasoning,** we often reason from specific cases to a general principle, such as a theory or hypothesis. For example, the great nineteenth-century French neurologist Pierre Paul Broca made repeated observations on people with damage to the left hemisphere of the brain; he generalized from these cases that if the damage was to a specific area in the frontal lobe, as shown in Figure 2.1, the people would have difficulty speaking. For instance, one patient with damage

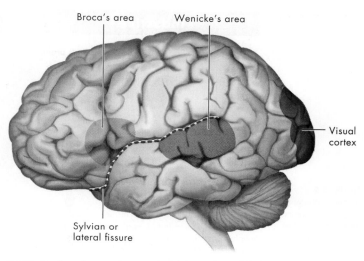

FIGURE 2.1 Broca's area, shown in the left hemisphere of the brain, allows for speech production and is part of a language circuit with Wernicke's area that allows for language comprehension.

to this area was referred to as "Tan" because no matter what he tried to say, it came out "tan" or "tan-tan" or "tan-tan-tan."

Generalizing from these cases and others studied earlier by Marc Dax, Broca used inductive reasoning to support a theory of speech production. The theory stated that because this area in the frontal lobe (later named Broca's area, in his honor) regulates speech production, damage to it would produce a disturbance in speaking (Broca, 1966). The left side of Figure 2.2 illustrates how specific cases of Broca's area damage in which speech is disturbed lead to this conclusion (generalization). A major use of inductive reasoning in science is the justification of a general rule or theory.

In **deductive reasoning,** we often proceed in the opposite direction, from the general theory to the specific case. For example, a psychologist may reason deductively from the general principle of Broca's theory to a specific case, such as Bill's, shown on the right side of Figure 2.2. We can use deductive reasoning to reason from a general theory to make a prediction about a case. Notice that on the right side of Figure 2.2, deductive reasoning starts with a theory, proceeds to a specific case, and concludes with a prediction about that specific case. In contrast, the left side of Figure 2.2 shows that inductive reasoning starts with specific cases of brain damage and then leads to a generalization, Broca's theory. Each kind of reasoning has somewhat different applications and rules, but both *use evidence to draw conclusions about claims*. In this chapter, we focus on the process of deductive reasoning; in Chapter 3, we explore inductive reasoning more closely.

Inductive	Deductive

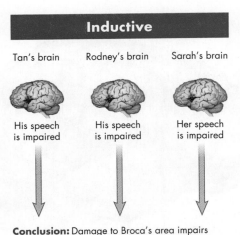

Tan's brain   Rodney's brain   Sarah's brain

His speech is impaired   His speech is impaired   Her speech is impaired

Theory: If people have damage in Broca's area, then speech production will be impaired.

Bill's brain has damage in Broca's area

FIGURE 2.2
A comparison of how inductive reasoning (*left*) and deductive reasoning (*right*) proceed.

Conclusion: Damage to Broca's area impairs people's speech production. (Broca's theory is a generalization from specific cases.)

Conclusion: Therefore, Bill's speech production will be impaired. (This is a specific prediction from a general principle.)

CONDITIONAL DEDUCTIVE ARGUMENTS

Scientists often use deductive reasoning to make predictions and test theories. From theories, they deduce predictions of the results of experiments and case studies in the form of conditional (if–then) deductive arguments. The conventional form of a conditional (if–then) argument has at least three statements; the first two statements, called the premises, set the conditions for the third statement, called the *conclusion,* to be true. The first statement, or major premise, is divided into two parts: The first part, called the *antecedent,* is often preceded by "if." The second part, called the *consequent,* as its name suggests, is often preceded by "then." After the minor premise comes the final statement or conclusion, often signaled by a word such as "therefore." Table 2.1 illustrates the parts of a conditional deductive argument using Broca's theory to make a prediction about the specific case of Bill.

TABLE 2.1 **A Conditional Deductive Argument Using Broca's Theory to Make a Prediction**

	Antecedent	Consequent
Major premise	If Broca's area is damaged . . .	then speech production will be impaired.
Minor premise	Broca's area in Bill's brain has been damaged.	
Conclusion		Therefore, Bill's speech will be impaired.

The first or major premise in Table 2.1 is a general statement of Broca's theory in if–then form. The second or minor premise asserts that the antecedent is true for the specific case of Bill. The conclusion states that a specific form of the consequent (Bill's speech will be impaired) follows from the specific form of the antecedent in the minor premise. This shows how deductive reasoning proceeds from a general (major) premise to a specific conclusion.

 Practice Thinking 2.2: Distinguishing Induction From Deduction

1. A neuroscientist is using a new biochemical test to study schizophrenia, a severe mental disorder involving thought disturbances such as hallucinations and delusions. He observes several people who have normal levels of a brain chemical called dopamine, as well as several who have too little dopamine. Those with normal levels are not schizophrenic and those with low levels tend to be schizophrenic. The brain scientist reasons from these specific cases to the general theory that too much dopamine is related to people having the symptoms of schizophrenia. This is _____ reasoning.

2. If Wernicke's area is damaged, then problems in comprehending language will occur. When a sample of 30 people with damage in Wernicke's area is tested for their understanding of a passage read to them, their comprehension of sentences will be impaired. This is _____ reasoning.

WHAT IS A SOUND DEDUCTIVE ARGUMENT?

The argument in Table 2.1 is a sound argument because of the following:

1. It follows correct logical form (it is valid).
2. Both premises are true and lead to a true conclusion.

If it is true that speech production is impaired when Broca's area is destroyed and if Broca's area in Bill's brain is destroyed, then it *must be true* that Bill's speech will be impaired. When a true conclusion must necessarily follow from true premises, we say that it is **valid**. The valid form in the above argument is called "asserting the antecedent" because the antecedent of the first general premise is restated in specific form in the second premise. When the antecedent has been asserted and when both premises are true and a true conclusion has been drawn, then the argument is valid and sound.

Let's examine another example of how to use deduction to reason from a definition—this time about one of the most challenging problems confronting us, human aggression. Social psychologists define human aggression as "any behavior directed toward another individual with the immediate intent to cause harm" (Anderson & Bushman, 2002, p. 28). Let's begin by turning this definition into a conditional deductive argument, using the example of Mike insulting Rob.

> If a person behaves toward another person with the intention of harming the other person, then that person is showing aggression. Mike said to Rob, "You wear the ugliest clothes. Nobody dresses like that!"

Can you conclude in this example that Mike is showing aggression? Yes, because he has directed a harmful comment toward Rob, apparently intending to make Rob feel bad. The conclusion would be valid because the second premise seems to assert the antecedent, and the argument would be sound because if the first two premises are true, the conclusion is true.

What if, instead, Mike privately said to his friend Emma, "Rob wears the ugliest clothes. Nobody dresses like that!" We might now conclude that this was gossip without the intention to harm Rob and thus not an example of aggression. However, if Mike said this, knowing that Emma would repeat it to other people, his intent still might have been to harm Rob. Then the conclusion that this is aggression would again be true. Notice that our conclusion depends on what we assume Mike's intent was.

USING DEDUCTIVE REASONING TO MAKE PREDICTIONS

We can use conditional deductive reasoning and the correct logical form of asserting the antecedent to make scientific predictions. The "if" part introduces some condition that, when it is present beforehand (i.e., is an *antecedent*), leads to some specified result or *consequent* event. In other words, the antecedent predicts the consequent. So, given Broca's theory, *if* Broca's area in Bill's brain has been destroyed, *then* Bill's speech will be impaired.

Conditional deductive reasoning allows researchers to test general theories by making specific predictions from them in the form of if–then statements. Specific predictions made from a general theory are often referred to as *hypotheses*. We hypothesize about or predict what will happen if certain conditions are present. For example, from the general theory that more practice or study time leads to better learning, we could hypothesize that *if* you study the material in your psychology course, *then* you will do better on your next exam (than if you had not studied for this test of your learning).

We can also use conditional deductive reasoning to make predictions about the outcomes of experiments designed to test hypotheses deduced from general theories. We could, for example, make a prediction about two groups with different amounts of study time, once again testing the theory that amount of practice affects learning. Suppose that one group of subjects studied a list of words for 10 minutes and another group studied the list for 5 minutes. What might we predict about the recall of the list of words by each group? Given that practice improves learning, we would predict that if one group studied for 10 minutes and a second studied for 5 minutes, then the group that studied for 10 minutes would recall more words than the group that studied for 5 minutes.

Sometimes, scientists generate hypotheses from competing theories and then test to find out which theory is better. A good example of this is the difference between social learning theory and the drive theories of aggression, which make very different predictions. The *social learning theory* of aggression by Bandura and Walters (1959) states that people learn how to behave in a particular way by observing other people engage in those behaviors. For instance, individuals who observe others behaving aggressively will themselves tend to behave more aggressively, like the models they observe. Social learning theory also assumes that whether or not the observer engages in an observed aggressive behavior depends on whether the person observes the model being rewarded or punished for the aggressive behavior (Bandura, 1977). If the observer sees the model being rewarded for engaging in the aggressive act, such as appearing to enjoy it or simply not being punished for it, then the observer will tend to engage in the observed aggression. Punishment produces the opposite effect.

In a famous experiment, Bandura and Walters (1959) randomly assigned one group of preschoolers to observe an adult behaving aggressively toward an inflated Bobo (punching bag) doll and another group to simply observe an adult who displayed no aggression. They led both groups to another room filled with attractive toys and, after a few minutes, told the children they could no longer play with the toys because the experimenter had to pick them up for some other children. The researchers then escorted the children to another room with the Bobo doll. As shown in Figure 2.3, children who observed the adult model behave aggressively imitated more of the aggressive acts than did those in the control group.

Courtesy Albert Bandura

FIGURE 2.3 The boy and girl are imitating the adult model's interaction with the Bobo doll, just as social learning theory would predict.

Before reading the answer that follows, use social learning theory to predict in if–then form how aggressive each of the following two groups would be: one that observed a hockey game and another that observed a swim meet. *Answer:* "We expect, on the basis of social learning theory, that if one group watched a hockey game and another watched a swim meet, then the group that watched hockey would behave more aggressively than the group that watched swimming."

In contrast, another theory of aggression called *drive theory,* offered by Lorenz (1966), makes a very different prediction. Drive theory proposes that humans have evolved an instinctual drive for aggression. Because humans have few mechanisms to keep their aggressive drive in check, aggressive drive can build up to dangerous levels and then be released in violent behavior. However, dangerous aggressive drive can be vented or released before an individual becomes violent if that individual observes certain types of events, such as a competitive sporting event. This is consistent with Freud's concept of catharsis and the popular view that when you get angry, it is best to "blow off steam" or vent your anger. For example, in the movie *Anger Management,* a psychotherapist (played by Jack Nicholson) suggests that his perpetually irate client (played by Adam Sandler) throw dodgeballs at schoolchildren to reduce his anger.

Now before reading the answer that follows, make a prediction based on drive theory, using the same two treatment groups and putting it in if–then form. *Answer*: "On the basis of drive theory, we expect that if one group watches a hockey game and another watches a swim meet, the group that watched the hockey game would behave no more aggressively (and perhaps even less aggressively) than the group that watched the swim meet."

What does the research show? Two studies have tested both of these hypotheses at once; the results supported social learning theory and contradicted drive theory. Arms, Russell, and Sandilands (1979) asked sports spectators to rate their hostility before and after viewing professional wrestling, hockey, or swimming. They found, in general, that hostility increased after watching wrestling and hockey but not after watching swimming.

Another experiment by Ebbesen, Duncan, and Konecni (1975) tested aerospace workers who had just been laid off, assigning them to three different conditions of verbal expression of their anger. In a first session of exit interviews, they induced the workers to verbally express their anger toward the company, their supervisor, or themselves. When the workers were later asked to direct their anger either toward the same or a different target, Ebbesen and colleagues found that workers who directed their verbal aggression toward the same target had significantly higher ratings of aggression than workers who directed their anger toward a different target. Social learning theory would predict that verbal expression of aggression would disinhibit the workers' later expression of aggression toward the same target, whereas drive theory would predict that the aggression would decrease after the workers had expressed or vented the first time. Which prediction turns out to be accurate?

Considerable research has supported social learning theory, not catharsis. Social learning theory is important because of its implications for the potentially dangerous effects of observing violence in the media, which has been consistently shown to be related to aggression (Friedrich-Cofer & Huston, 1986). Playing violent video games has sometimes been linked to subsequent aggressive behavior (Anderson et al., 2010), but not always (Ferguson, 2015). Thus, predictions deduced from social learning theory about the aggressive behavior of children after observing violence on TV would more likely be accurate than predictions about what happens after children play video games.

In contrast, numerous studies have shown that catharsis, or venting aggression, leads not to a reduction in aggressive behavior but rather increases it (e.g., Bushman, Baumeister, & Stack, 1999; Geen, Stonner, & Stope, 1975). Although 63% of college students believe that "blowing off steam" is a good way to reduce aggression (Brown, 1983) and many sports enthusiasts believe that watching a violent sport reduces aggression (Wann et al., 1999), the research reviewed shows otherwise. Why, then, do people hold the mistaken belief that catharsis reduces aggression? This may be due to a misinterpretation of their personal experience. People sometimes report feeling less angry after venting and show reduced heart rate after aggression, but catharsis does not reduce later aggressive behavior—it may even increase it (Verona & Sullivan, 2008).

The results from the research we reviewed are more consistent with social learning theory, so predictions from it are more likely to be accurate than those deduced from the drive and catharsis theories. One important implication of this conclusion is that therapists should not encourage their clients, especially if they are children, to vent their aggression (Schaefer & Mattei, 2005); rather, they should help their clients learn to control it.

Like all theories, social learning theory could be improved by testing predictions under different conditions. Newer versions of the theory, sometimes referred to as *social cognitive learning theories,* emphasize cognitive factors (e.g., background knowledge of situations) that are associated with aggression to help explain what happens when a person observes aggression (Saleem, Anderson, & Gentile, 2012). For example, merely seeing a weapon can prime, or activate, knowledge of aggression (Anderson, Benjamin, & Bartholow, 1998), and so can the anticipation of watching a violent movie (Leyans & Dunand, 1991). Social cognitive learning theories are powerful in that they predict conditions not only for antisocial behaviors like aggression but also for prosocial or beneficial behaviors such as helping (Saleem et al., 2012). According to social cognitive learning theory, if a person observes another person helping, then the observer will be more likely to help someone else.

Practice Thinking 2.3: Generating Hypotheses Through Deduction

1. Make an if–then prediction from social cognitive learning theory about whether each of two different groups will help a middle-aged person in trouble. Assume that one group of participants first observes a man help an elderly woman carry packages across a busy street and that the other group first observes the same elderly woman cross the street without any help.

   If _____,

   then _____.

2. Make another prediction about two groups that is based on a different scientific theory.

   If _____,

   then _____.

FALLACIES AND THINKING ERRORS

Asserting the antecedent is the valid form, but what would happen if we instead asserted the consequent? Look at the invalid form of this argument in Table 2.2.

TABLE 2.2 **An Invalid Deductive Argument Showing the Fallacy of Asserting the Consequent**

	Antecedent	Consequent
Major premise	If Broca's area is damaged . . .	then speech production will be impaired.
Minor premise		Bill's speech is impaired. (*Consequent is asserted.*)
Conclusion	Therefore, Broca's area in Bill's brain has been damaged.	

Does asserting the consequent ("Bill's speech is impaired") necessarily lead to the conclusion that Bill has damage to Broca's area? No, this conclusion does not necessarily follow from the major premise and is invalid. It could be that Bill's speech problem is due to another cause such as a developmental disability, or a speech problem such as stuttering. Asserting the consequent is an example of a logical fallacy, or a thinking error associated with deductive reasoning that leads to an invalid argument. Deductive reasoning is sometimes called *formal reasoning* because of this emphasis on using valid forms and formal logic.

Asserting the consequent may occur when people are influenced by a common thinking error called belief bias. People show belief bias when they use their prior knowledge or belief rather than logic to draw a conclusion. They may judge an invalid conclusion to be valid because their background knowledge makes the conclusion seem plausible or believable, instead of analyzing the argument's validity. Analyze the following argument to see how this happens.

Major premise: If people smile, then they are happy.

Minor premise: Jenny has just won the lottery and is happy.

Conclusion: Therefore, she is smiling.

If you thought this conclusion was valid and true on the basis of your knowledge that someone who won a large amount of money would be happy and tend to smile, then you are wrong. This argument is invalid because the consequent has been asserted. Belief bias apparently led you to fall for this logical fallacy. Although Jenny might be happy, it is not necessarily true that she is smiling. Maybe Jenny has damage to the muscles in her face preventing her from smiling. Or maybe she is hiding her happiness so that her greedy relatives do not find out she has won the lottery. In formal (deductive) reasoning, we have to follow the correct logical form of asserting the antecedent—even if it goes against our belief.

Other fallacies called *fallacies of informal logic* are associated with inductive and informal reasoning (Risen & Gilovich, 2007). In Chapter 1, we learned about a common informal reasoning fallacy called *argument from possibility or ignorance,* which occurs when someone concludes something is true because it is possible that it is true or because it is not yet known to be false. For instance, in response to a discussion of the lack of good evidence that Bigfoot exists, someone says, "Scientists have not been able to prove conclusively that Bigfoot does not exist; therefore, it probably does exist somewhere." This is a fallacy because it is illogical to conclude that something exists when there is a lack of evidence for it.

Argument from possibility or ignorance is related to another problem in argumentation called shifting the burden of proof. When a person makes a new claim, it is his or her responsibility to present evidence in support of it—the claimant has the burden of proof. When Charles Darwin first proposed his theory of evolution in 1859, the burden of proof was on him to provide evidence in support of it. In the last 150 years, a massive amount of high-quality evidence has consistently supported Darwin's theory (Dawkins, 2009; Palmer, 2009), so the burden of proof has since shifted to the other side. Despite this, creationists still sometimes say that scientists have not been able to prove conclusively that evolution occurs or to explain how life first started, so they claim that evolutionary theory is false. This strategy shifts the burden of proof away from the opponents of evolutionary theory, who claim that because scientists have not been able to explain everything that needs to be explained, evolutionary theory is wrong. The creationists do not accept that the burden of proof is now on them to offer reasonable explanations supported by high-quality evidence. Arguing from ignorance goes against the CT goal of making arguments from knowledge and the best evidence available.

Another common error in reasoning and argumentation is circular reasoning, in which the conclusion "circles" back to the initial premise. It simply restates in the conclusion what was initially asserted or stated as a reason. When a person reasons to a conclusion that is simply a restatement of the information offered in support of the conclusion, the reasoning goes nowhere (i.e., it just goes in circles) and does not advance our knowledge. The following argument provides an example.

Human aggression involves the intention to harm another person.

Therefore, aggressive people deliberately try to hurt other people.

If you accept the first statement as true, then the conclusion is true—but the argument simply circles back to the first premise, restating the conclusion without offering a different reason to support it. Human aggression is aggression in people, and intentional harming is deliberately hurting other people. Politicians often use circular reasoning to get people to agree with their conclusion without actually providing a real reason to support their conclusion, as shown below.

The presidential candidate said, "I am the most popular candidate with the highest numbers in the polls. Because my numbers are so high, I am the one that most people say they want to vote for."

The candidate's conclusion that he is the one whom most people say they want to vote for is simply a restatement of the claim that he is the most popular candidate with the highest poll numbers. Having the highest poll numbers is not really a reason but rather a way to say he is popular. You should avoid circular reasoning because it does not usefully advance new arguments.

MAKING ASSUMPTIONS AND ARGUING FROM A PERSPECTIVE

The weatherman says it is going to rain tomorrow, and you conclude that you should bring your umbrella. When you decide to bring your umbrella, you have assumed that the weatherman is knowledgeable, a good forecaster, and not going to lie to you about the forecast. We make assumptions all the time without thinking much about them. Most of the time, this causes no problems. Other times, unless we deliberately question our assumptions, something we did not consider can have disastrous effects. Suppose the forecast was for rain and you assumed that the temperature would remain stable. Then it dropped rapidly, turning the rain into freezing rain. This assumption could lead to an accident.

Questioning assumptions in arguments is important, too, because people often make assumptions when they make arguments, leaving out important information that needs to be considered. In this context, we can define an assumption as a premise that is omitted, and it is taken for granted that this premise is true (Reese, 1980). When assumptions have not been explicitly stated in arguments, they leave gaps in those arguments. Finding assumptions is important in order to fully evaluate arguments. Unfortunately, research suggests that, like other people, college students are not very good at identifying assumptions in arguments (Keeley, 1992).

We are most concerned about identifying assumptions that are unwarranted. An unwarranted assumption implies that something is true that has not been justified or supported by a good reason. It can lead to a wrong conclusion when taken for granted. A familiar example of an unwarranted assumption is the *stereotype* (Bassham, Irwin, Nardone, & Wallace, 2005). In this case, people assume that all the individuals of a certain group share the same characteristic. To illustrate, examine the following incomplete argument to find the missing premise and unwarranted assumption. It helps if you first find the conclusion and look for the major and minor premises. Is a premise missing that affects the conclusion?

Terrence was a first-string football player in high school, so when he gets to college and plays, he will not get good grades.

We see that the major premise is missing and makes an assumption:

Major premise: Football players are poor students.

Minor premise: Terrence will play football in college, as he did in high school.

Conclusion: So Terrence will not get good grades in college.

The missing premise that football players are poor students makes an unwarranted assumption and reveals a stereotype. In fact, one of my all-time best students played football all four years of college. My counterexample shows this assumption is unwarranted and false.

Just as stereotypes can provide the basis for making unwarranted assumptions in arguments, so can commonsense beliefs and psychological misconceptions. Analyze the following argument to see if you can find the unwarranted assumption.

The teachers and principals of a school system sought to improve the test scores of all their students by raising students' self-esteem. During the entire school year, teachers and principals conscientiously implemented strategies to improve students' self-esteem. At the end of the year, they observed no improvement on any achievement tests students took. They concluded that self-esteem did not improve their students' test scores.

You could have made several assumptions that would lead to the conclusion being false. For example, you might have thought that the educators assumed that teachers knew how to use effective strategies to improve self-esteem, but they did not. Or perhaps they assumed a year was enough time to show improvement in self-esteem and test scores, but it was not.

A more fundamental unwarranted assumption is revealed when we put in the missing major premise: "If educators improve the self-esteem of students, their test performance will improve." It turns out that this widely held belief about self-esteem is a misconception that convinced many educators in the 1980s to try to improve academic performance by improving students' self-esteem. Their assumption was shown to be unwarranted when no substantial increase in student achievement was observed. Although it is true that better students tend to have higher self-esteem than poorer students, this does not necessarily imply that raising students' self-esteem will improve their academic skills, just that they'll feel better about themselves.

This example also reveals an important power of the scientific approach. Like CT, it allows us to systematically test our assumptions. In the above example, although educators made an unwarranted assumption, they were able to find out that their assumption was unwarranted. In fact, their conclusion is consistent with other findings about self-esteem (Forsyth, Lawrence, Burnette, & Baumeister, 2007).

Finding assumptions in arguments can help us identify the perspective a person takes, too. Perspective is the way a person views or approaches a question, providing a framework within which he or she thinks. Knowing someone's perspective can help us better understand the context of the person's thinking. To illustrate, let's look for assumptions made in a conditional argument about the psychoanalytic notion that people repress, or push, unpleasant memories out of conscious awareness and then cannot remember them. This notion further assumes that children may experience a trauma that they repress for periods of time.

> If a person has a traumatic experience as a child, then he or she will not be able to recall it later. Tina vomited in front of her third-grade class. When asked about the experience as an adult, she could not recall it.

Without being told the perspective taken, we can recognize that this argument is based on psychoanalytic theory. From this perspective, the argument appears to be sound. Furthermore, the argument is valid because it follows the valid form of asserting the antecedent. Recall that when a deductive argument has valid form and all its premises and conclusion are true, then it is sound, and the true conclusion must logically follow. According to psychoanalytic theory, the argument assumes that vomiting in front of class as a child *is* a traumatic experience. But suppose this assumption is unwarranted, and Tina's vomiting was not traumatic. Then this premise would not be true. Perhaps Tina did not find the experience to be traumatic because several children in her class had already gotten sick and the other students felt sorry for her. Unless we questioned this assumption, we might mistakenly conclude that Tina did not recall her experience because it was traumatic.

Another way the conclusion of this argument is false is that the major premise from psychoanalytic theory is false. High-quality research studies have failed to experimentally demonstrate repressed memory (Holmes, 1995). Although sexual abuse is far too common, repressed memories of abuse have been hard to document and occur very seldom.

Perhaps taking a different psychological perspective, one that makes different assumptions about why people forget, could better explain why Tina could not recall the experience. For instance, many cognitive psychologists assume that people are information processors who encode, store, and retrieve information as part of remembering. Cognitive research has shown that the more time that has passed since an experience occurred, the less people tend to remember it. People often forget much of an experience or may be unable to retrieve it from memory at all. From the cognitive perspective, the conclusion is true, but it does not make an unwarranted assumption because it assumes correctly that memories fade over time and that is why Tina could not recall the early memory.

The various subfields of psychology provide different perspectives and frameworks that help us more completely understand complex constructs, such as aggression. For example, psychologists studying personality know that having traits such as irritability and impulsivity make it more likely that someone will be aggressive (Gvion & Apter, 2011). Cognitive neuroscientists help us understand the parts of the brain that become active when a person experiences emotion, as we will discuss in Chapter 9.

Practice Thinking 2.4: Identifying Assumptions in Arguments

To give yourself practice, find the assumption or assumptions made in each argument below.

1. Jerry could not recall the new phone number from memory because he did not recite the number to himself after it was briefly announced. If people do not mentally rehearse or repeat new information to themselves, then they will not be able to store and later retrieve the information from memory.

   What theoretical perspective is assumed? _____

   _____

2. If teachers clearly communicate their expectations about how to succeed, then students will be more successful. Katie tried very hard to raise her grade in Spanish, but she did not understand her teacher's expectations, so Katie ended up with a D.

   Anything else assumed that might account for Katie getting a D? _____

   _____

3. Cities using advanced scientific techniques to solve crimes are better at solving violent crimes than cities that do not. Our city uses the method of criminal profiling to solve crimes. Our city should have a higher rate of solving violent crimes than cities that do not use as many scientific techniques.

What unwarranted assumption is made in this argument? _____

_____

Table 2.3 summarizes four thinking errors to help you recognize examples of them and know how to deal with them. In your review, think about how they are related to other CT concepts. Notice how these thinking errors are often violations of good CT practices, such as using valid forms in deductive arguments.

TABLE 2.3 Summary of Thinking and Argumentation Errors

Name	Description	How to Fix or Avoid It
Asserting the consequent	A fallacy in conditional deductive reasoning that typically occurs when the "then" part is asserted in the second premise	Assert the antecedent or the "if" part of the major premise in specific terms in the second premise.
Unwarranted assumption	Taking for granted that a premise or statement is true that has not been justified or supported by a reason	Find assumptions and make them explicit so that they can be examined and tested; make sure all are supported.
Shifting the burden of proof	Shifting responsibility to the other side to show that your position is wrong when you have not yet provided sufficient evidence to support your side	Assume responsibility for providing support for your unsupported claim to avoid making an argument from ignorance.
Circular reasoning	Reasoning to a conclusion that is simply a restatement of the information in the premises	Offer reasons that actually support and do not simply restate the conclusion.

Practice Thinking 2.5: Recognizing and Fixing Thinking Errors

In the space that follows, write the thinking error in each example and then how to fix it.

1. Human aggression is behavior that is intended to cause harm. Therefore, aggressive people behave in ways that show they are deliberately trying to inflict harm on other people.

    Thinking error: _____

    _____

    How to fix it: _____

    _____

2. Lindsay said, "Scientists have not been able to show that Bigfoot or Sasquatch does not exist, and until they do, I am going to believe it exists. They ought to prove to me that Bigfoot doesn't exist."

    Thinking error: _____

    _____

    How to fix it: _____

    _____

3. If UFOs exist, then people will observe them. Olivia and her friends reported that they saw a UFO; therefore, UFOs exist.

    Thinking error: _____

    _____

    How to fix it: _____

    _____

4. Steve and Jim took turns choosing players for a pickup basketball game at the park. Neither Steve nor Jim knew any of the other guys. Steve decided to choose guys who looked older for his team, but he was surprised when his team lost to Jim's younger-looking team.

Thinking error: _____

_____

How to fix it: _____

_____

5. The presidential candidate said that because so many people were out of work, the unemployment rate was high. Then he said that he was the one who had the best comprehension of how the economy worked because he understood it better than the others.

Thinking error: _____

_____

How to fix it: _____

_____

SUMMARY

This chapter introduced two kinds of reasoning: inductive and deductive. Inductive reasoning has been described as reasoning from specific cases and events to a general rule or principle, such as a theory. Deductive reasoning often involves reasoning from a general rule or principle to a specific case or event.

Thus, deductive reasoning is useful in moving from a theory to a prediction, in reasoning from a definition to an example, and in analyzing some formal arguments. It does so by providing rules for deciding whether arguments are sound. To be sound, an argument must follow valid form, which is asserting the antecedent in a conditional (if–then) argument. Second, when all of the premises are true in a valid conditional argument, then a true conclusion must necessarily follow in a second deductive argument. So deductive reasoning allows us to draw conclusions with certainty because a true conclusion must be obtained under these special conditions. However, many everyday arguments, as well as those that psychologists often make, are more like inductive arguments that involve much more uncertainty, as discussed in Chapter 3.

You should also note that making assumptions that are unwarranted can lead to a wrong conclusion in both inductive and deductive arguments. An unwarranted assumption is something that is taken for granted to be true in an argument but has not been justified or supported by a good reason. Stereotypes and preconceptions, based on commonsense beliefs, form the basis for many unwarranted assumptions.

Practice Thinking 2.6: WHAT DO YOU THINK **NOW**?
Please explain how you know.

1. Can I be certain about a conclusion I draw? Or is there always some uncertainty? _____

_____

2. Does improving the self-esteem of students improve their grades and test scores? _____

_____

3. Does "blowing off steam" or venting anger help reduce it and prevent aggression? _____

_____

4. Is profiling of suspects effective in identifying perpetrators? _____

_____

REVIEW QUESTIONS

1. How do inductive and deductive reasoning differ?

2. What is a conditional deductive argument? What is it used for?
   - What are premises?
   - What is a conclusion?
   - What makes a deductive argument valid?
   - What makes a deductive argument sound?
   - Can you make predictions (generate hypotheses) using deduction?

3. What are fallacies, for example, asserting the consequent? How is belief bias related to it?

4. What are assumptions, and can you find them?
   - What is an unwarranted assumption?
   - How are stereotypes related to unwarranted assumptions?

5. What are other thinking errors discussed in this chapter, besides those mentioned in Question 3? How would you deal with them?
   - What is arguing from ignorance or possibility? How is it related to shifting the burden of proof?
   - What is circular reasoning?
   - How do you avoid making unwarranted assumptions?

6. What are the psychological misconceptions discussed in this chapter?
   - Explain how each of the following statements is wrong and describe the correct view. (a) Venting of anger and aggression is a good way to reduce aggressive behavior. (b) Raising students' self-esteem will improve their grades. (c) Criminal profiling is effective in catching perpetrators (see Practice Thinking 2.5, answer 5).

INDUCTIVE REASONING IN PSYCHOLOGY AND EVERYDAY LIFE

LEARNING OUTCOMES

After studying this chapter, you should be able to:

1. Identify the strengths and weaknesses of various kinds of evidence used in everyday inductive arguments.

2. Distinguish between a good and a poor inductive conclusion.

3. Recognize the limits of inductive reasoning.

4. Recognize thinking errors associated with inductive and informal reasoning.

WHAT DO YOU THINK?

Have you ever had a premonition that something would happen before it happened? Afterward, you might have wondered if you had precognition, or the ability to see the future before it happens. This is an example of extrasensory perception (ESP), a general term that refers to psychic abilities involving communication through nonsensory means. The most recent Gallup poll showed that 26% of Americans believe in precognition and 41% believe in ESP (Moore, 2005).

Let's examine an actual case that might suggest precognition is real. In 1977, Lee Fried, a student at Duke University, delivered a sealed envelope to the office of the university's president. Fried said that the envelope contained a letter predicting an important event that would occur the following week and instructed that the letter be opened in one week. At the end of the week, when the letter was read, it said that two jumbo 747 jets would crash, killing 583 passengers—an event that had actually occurred in the past week. Do some people like Lee Fried have precognition?

Practice Thinking 3.1: What Do You Think?

Please explain how you know.

1. Can people who claim to have precognition accurately predict the future?

   _____

2. Can instruction improve students' critical thinking? How do you know?

   _____

3. Does subliminal learning work? For example, would listening to recordings of a foreign-language lesson while you are asleep help you learn that language?

   _____

4. How much should you trust your personal experience in drawing a conclusion?

   _____

Fried later admitted that he was a magician, so it is likely that he secretly replaced the envelope after the plane crash occurred, making it appear as though he had predicted the disaster (Gilovich, 1991) when in fact he hadn't. Numerous newspapers covered the event, but another magician, named James Randi, found only one article that mentioned Fried's confession (Randi, 1977). This suggests that educated people, including reporters who are supposed to recount the facts, can be easily fooled by such trickery. People often readily accept paranormal explanations, such as precognition, rather than first trying to eliminate other, more plausible explanations for unusual events.

A plausible explanation of an event is one that seems reasonable, given what we already know about science and human behavior. Precognition and other types of ESP seem implausible because they violate what we know from physics. We cannot know that a specific event will happen until *after* it happens—causes precede effects. To explain precognition and ESP, we should first look for ordinary, more plausible explanations, such as trickery, because we know humans often deceive each other (Gendin, 1981).

INDUCTIVE REASONING AND ITS LIMITATIONS

At the heart of much of our thinking is induction, whereby we generalize from specific cases, pieces of evidence, and other bits of information. For instance, we may generalize from our experiences with a certain person whom we have repeatedly caught in lies and thus judge that person to be dishonest. More formally, we use inductive reasoning to generalize from many different bits of evidence to draw a conclusion about questions such as the "What Do You Think?" questions.

Whenever possible, scientists reason inductively from evidence obtained in high-quality research studies to decide whether a hypothesis or theory is justified by the scientific evidence. Unfortunately, people in everyday life often use weak evidence that can lead them to faulty conclusions and therefore to maintain beliefs that are wrong. In this chapter, we first examine some of these weaker kinds of evidence, referred to as *nonscientific evidence*. Then we explain how inductive reasoning in science can lead to more accurate and reliable conclusions. Yet inductive reasoning, whether in everyday life or in science, does have some of the same limitations.

To illustrate one such limitation, the great philosopher and psychologist William James used the example of the claim that all crows are black. Our experience might tell us that all crows are black, but finding one exception—just one white crow—would disprove this claim (see www.birds.cornell.edu/crows/white-crows.htm). This example shows that although the evidence in an inductive argument can provide very strong support, it *never proves* that a conclusion is true. We must allow for the possibility that new and better evidence may come along that leads us to a different conclusion. In science, a better-controlled experiment may produce a finding that forces us to change our conclusion. When we see a white crow, we cannot accept as true the conclusion that all crows are black, but we can still generalize and accept the inductive conclusion that *most* crows are black.

NONSCIENTIFIC APPROACHES TO EVIDENCE

Personal experience is a compelling kind of evidence that comes to us though our informal observations of the world and introspections about what has happened to us. People use personal experiences as reasons to support their beliefs and to persuade others that their claims are true. For instance, someone might argue, "I think people are basically unselfish, because one time I had a flat tire, and this guy stopped and helped me change the tire and wouldn't even take the money I offered him." Or someone might offer a personal experience in the form of a testimonial in support of some product or treatment.

Personal experiences can seem quite vivid, compelling, and memorable because they happen to us. We have special mental access to them, but this access is also a source of the difficulties such experiences present. In particular, personal experience is inherently subjective and cannot be directly observed, making it difficult to verify. This becomes problematic when we use personal experience as evidence because perceptions and memories are often inaccurate, distorted, and biased.

Figure 3.1 shows a visual illusion called the *Müller-Lyer illusion.* Many people report that the line segment from *a* to *b* looks longer than the line segment from *b* to *c,* but the lines are equal in length. Each line segment above the ruler spans 3 equal units and so must be equal in length. Yet the line from *a* to *b* still looks longer even though rationally you know the two must be equal.

FIGURE 3.1 Does the length of the line from point *a* to *b* look longer than the line segment from point *b* to *c*? Count the number of units on the ruler below each line. Does your reason tell you something different from your perception?

The compelling nature of our personal experience contributes to the impression that what we perceive is accurate, real, and trustworthy, even when it is not. This approach to personal experience, called **naive realism**, assumes that we experience the world exactly as it is and that our experience directly informs us about what is real (Ross & Ward, 1996). This is reflected in the everyday expressions "Seeing is believing" and "What you see is what you get." Naive realism appears in social judgments, too, as occurred in the early 2000s when many parents, after observing that their young children developed autism shortly after being inoculated, became certain that vaccines had caused the disorder.

Personal experience is associated with a variety of thinking errors and other sources of bias. For example, research has shown that people tend to remember experiences that confirm their prior beliefs (Ross & Ward, 1996) and to weigh more heavily the vivid personal experiences that come readily to mind when they are making judgments (Kahneman & Tversky, 1972). Unfortunately, people are often unaware of the various influences biasing the interpretation of their experience and the cognitive processes underlying their behavior and judgments (Nisbett & Wilson, 1977).

An ingenious experiment by Anthony Greenwald and his colleagues demonstrates people's lack of awareness of their own mental processes and abilities (Greenwald, Spangenberg, Pratkanis, & Eskenazi, 1991). The study tested whether listening to audio recordings that presented subliminal messages led to subliminal learning and whether people's experience of their own learning was accurate. Recordings that include subliminal messages—that is, messages on the recording that cannot be consciously perceived—are believed by some to enhance learning. To test this, two groups of participants listened to different types of subliminal recordings: one group with messages for improving memory and the other group with messages for improving self-esteem. Furthermore, the recordings that each group received were labeled as to which type of message they contained—however, some were correctly labeled while others were incorrectly labeled. In other words, half of the participants who heard the memory messages received a recording correctly labeled "Memory," whereas the other half received a recording labeled "Self-esteem."

Participants were then tested to see whether either type of message and how it was labeled led to objective improvement in their memory ability, as well as whether they thought their memory ability had improved. Participants showed no improvement on the objective memory tests after listening to either type of recording, indicating that subliminal learning does not work. Nevertheless, those participants who had listened to the recordings labeled "memory"—even the ones who had actually listened to self-esteem messages—reported that their memory ability had improved after listening. This shows that participants were unaware of the messages' lack of effect and that their expectation about what would happen biased their personal experience.

People may have the strong impression that their experience is accurate when it is not, and this lack of awareness can lead them to judge that a treatment is effective when it is not. In this case, personal experience may be partly responsible for the common misconception that subliminal learning is effective. People learn much better when they deliberately study new material rather than listen to recordings in their sleep.

Anecdotes are examples, cases, or stories used to illustrate a point and support a claim. Anecdotal evidence often takes the form of "I know a person who . . ." followed by an example or situation that supports some claim (Stanovich, 2010). For instance, to support the claim that people are basically unselfish, one might offer an anecdote about Mother Theresa, who helped others without desiring anything in return.

Although an anecdote can provide a real-world example relevant to a claim that can seem quite compelling, anecdotes have serious limitations as evidence. First, the observations that led to the account may not be observable again. This makes the situation or person described in the account inherently unique. Another limitation is that anecdotes are typically third-person accounts of someone else's experience, situation, or life event. This gives them a secondhand quality because the interpretation of the account depends on the accuracy and completeness of the original observations.

Furthermore, other related events that may have gone unobserved or unreported could be operating in the anecdotal situation, making it very difficult to account for them in any systematic way. Because individual examples vary from situation to situation and there is no way to replicate them or make them comparable, it is not possible to eliminate alternative explanations for them. For instance, suppose the anecdote of a man who gives all of his extra income to charity is cited to support the claim that people are basically unselfish. It is difficult to eliminate alternative explanations for the man's behavior—such as his being motivated to give to others for a tax write-off or his desire to be acclaimed as a philanthropist. For all these reasons, anecdotes provide very weak support in arguments.

Commonsense belief involves offering a consensus of opinion or a popular view as evidence for accepting a claim. When commonsense belief is used as evidence, it often takes the form of "Everyone knows that [such and such] is true," implying that one should draw the same conclusion as everyone else. This idea of going along with the consensus of opinion is sometimes referred to as "jumping on the bandwagon" and gets some of its persuasive power from the well-documented tendency of people to conform (Asch, 1951). Because commonsense belief is based on the perception of what other people believe and have experienced, as well as on other sources of unsystematic observation, it is subject to some of the same limitations as personal experience.

Commonsense belief is also subject to misinterpretation of what is common experience. For example, someone who says, "Everyone knows that people are basically selfish" is supporting this claim by citing common sense or what people generally consider to be true. Of course, just because many people think it is true does not *make* it true, and the person likely did not conduct a poll to determine what most people think. In fact, people often believe that a consensus of opinion is in agreement with their own favored view (Marks & Miller, 1987). Moreover, a majority opinion about selfishness in a competitive country that emphasizes individualism, such as the United States, may be different from a majority opinion in a country such as China that emphasizes the individual less (Levine, 2003). Although commonsense belief may have the advantage of taking into account the opinions of many people, it provides no systematic means for examining and correcting wrong ideas.

Even in our own culture, the term *common sense* has different meanings. You have probably heard someone say, "That's just common sense," implying that anyone who used practical reasoning and everyday experience would come to the same, correct conclusion. This idea should be questioned, however, because as we have already seen when people use their everyday experience and intuitions, it often leads to thinking errors and faulty conclusions. A few years ago, I was called for jury duty. When the bailiff instructed prospective jurors to use their "good, common sense" in considering the case before them, I cringed. I thought to myself, "Research on juror reasoning suggests that many of these prospective jurors may not be able to reason well" (e.g., Kuhn, Weinstock, & Flaton, 1994). The court's instruction to use "good, common sense" presumes that if people just use their everyday experience and practical reasoning, they will reason well about the case. As discussed in Chapter 6, many people believe that eyewitness memory is accurate and provides good evidence when, in fact, it is often unreliable and eyewitnesses are often overconfident in the accuracy of their memory.

Statements of authority are statements made by someone presumed to have special knowledge or expertise. They are frequently used as evidence in both everyday and scientific arguments. For instance, someone may claim, on the basis of writings of some religious authority, that people are generally selfish—yet another religious authority's writings would disagree. Or suppose a highly qualified mechanic tells you what is wrong with your car. You would probably take this as a statement of authority that is based on his extensive experience or training in auto mechanics. When someone makes an appeal to authority, the quality of the evidence provided depends on the degree to which the presumed authority actually has the relevant knowledge and skills. Therefore, because knowledge is becoming increasingly specialized in the modern world, you would not believe the statements of your mechanic if you needed expert advice on a person's behavioral problem. You would more likely believe the statement of a psychologist in that case, especially one who is an expert on the specific behavioral problem. Authority depends on the relevant knowledge possessed.

Using statements of authority as evidence can present difficulties, too, however. For example, a particular statement may be based primarily on unquestioned beliefs from the authority's culture or tradition. Whom are we to believe if authorities disagree? Religious authorities disagree on the meaning of religious texts. Scientists disagree on the interpretation of research findings and theory. Who's right? Simply accepting an incorrect statement of an authority without question or regard for relevant, high-quality evidence may lead us to a wrong conclusion.

Fortunately, standards can be applied to evaluate the statements of scientific authorities. Scientific authority should rest on the quality of scientific theory, research, and practice. In contrast, nonscientific authority and the other kinds of nonscientific evidence summarized in Table 3.1 do not meet the standards of high-quality scientific research (discussed in more detail later)—especially the standard that scientific research must be based on carefully and systematically made observations.

TABLE 3.1 Strengths and Weaknesses of Nonscientific Sources and Kinds of Evidence

Approach	Strengths	Weaknesses
Personal experience Reports of one's own experience (first person) often in the form of testimonials and introspective self-reports	• Tells what a person may have been feeling, experiencing, or aware of at the time • Is often compelling, vivid, and easily identified with	• Is subjective, often biased, and prone to perceptual, memory, and other cognitive errors • May be unreliable because people are often unaware of the real reasons for their behaviors and experiences
Anecdote Story or example, often biographical, used to support a claim (third person)	• Can vividly illustrate an ability, trait, behavior, or situation • Provides a real-world example	• Is not based on careful, systematic observation • May be unique, not repeatable, and not generalizable to many people
Commonsense belief Informal beliefs and folk theories commonly assumed to be true that are used as evidence	• Is a view shared by many, not just a few people • Is familiar and appeals to everyday experience	• Is not based on careful, systematic observation • May be biased by cultural and social influences • Often goes untested
Statement of authority Statement made by a person or group assumed to have special knowledge or expertise	• Can provide good support when the authority has relevant knowledge or expertise • Is convenient because acquiring one's own knowledge and expertise takes a lot of time	• Is misleading when a presumed authority lacks relevant knowledge and expertise or only pretends to have it • May be biased by personal experience and beliefs

Information from Bensley (2010).

Practice Thinking 3.2: Recognizing Kinds of Nonscientific Evidence

For each of the following examples, first identify the claim and evidence supporting the argument being made. Then write the kind of evidence used in the space provided. Finally, using Table 3.1, think of how a limitation associated with that kind of evidence might be a problem for the support it provides in the argument.

1. During World War I, Albert Einstein, the most influential physicist of the twentieth century, wrote letters to Sigmund Freud arguing for peace and against the waste of life in the war. The ideas of the brilliant Einstein should persuade us that war is wasteful.

   Claim/evidence: _____

   Kind of evidence: _____

   Limitation: _____

   _____

2. When asked by the prosecutor what he had seen, the witness said, "I'm sure the defendant is the person who shot the victim. I saw it with my own two eyes."

   Claim/evidence: _____

   Kind of evidence: _____

   Limitation: _____

   _____

3. Dana said that people with intellectual disabilities should not be allowed to attend the same schools as people of normal intelligence because everyone knows those students can't learn to read well.

   Claim/evidence: _____

   Kind of evidence: _____

   Limitation: _____

   _____

4. According to Sigmund Freud and some psychotherapists, people who have been sexually abused as children repress or push the memory of the abuse outside of awareness, so they can't remember the incident as adults. After they talk to a psychotherapist, however, the memory comes back. For example, my friend was sexually abused when she was 4 years old by her stepfather, but she couldn't remember it until she talked to her psychologist when she was 18 years old.

Claim/evidence: _____

Kind of evidence: _____

Limitation: _____

_____

5. Make your own argument based on one of your own beliefs and support it with one of the kinds of evidence in Table 3.1. Then write a limitation to the kind of evidence used in your argument.

Claim/evidence: _____

Kind of evidence: _____

Limitation: _____

_____

INDUCTIVE REASONING IN SCIENCE

In both the case of everyday arguments and scientific reasoning, induction leads to uncertain conclusions, but induction in science has the important advantage of being able to manage the limits of inductive reasoning. Unlike personal experience and informal observation commonly used in everyday reasoning, scientists make careful, systematic observations. Scientists are also more careful in their reasoning about such observations.

Why do people believe in ESP if the scientific evidence fails to support it? One reason is personal experience. Glickson (1990) found that people who have had personal experiences involving the paranormal believed more strongly in ESP than those who did not have such experiences. Another reason is the media's uncritical, even favorable coverage of so-called psychic events, as in the case of the Lee Fried–Duke story. This unbalanced coverage can be problematic because some people accept media sources as credible and authoritative. Television and movies can make these psychic events seem even more real and authentic (Hill, 2011).

As we have seen with the Lee Fried example, plausibility provides a good initial standard for evaluating claims, such as the likelihood that someone really has precognition. But this question can be addressed better through more direct scientific research that investigates claims of ESP. Recently, Bem (2011) provided experimental evidence of precognition, using a new backward prediction technique—but the quality of the studies that produced these findings has been severely criticized (Alcock, 2011), and Bem's original findings were not replicated in a subsequent study (Galak, LeBoeuf, Nelson, & Simmons, 2012). Also, some parapsychologists have used fakery and fraudulent methods in studies that support ESP's existence. In general, better-quality research has not supported the existence of ESP (Alcock, 2011; Milton & Wiseman, 1999).

REASONING INDUCTIVELY ABOUT WHETHER INSTRUCTION CAN IMPROVE CRITICAL THINKING

The inductive argument that follows is based, in part, on literature reviews by various authors who address the question of whether instruction improves students' critical thinking (CT) (e.g., Abrami et al., 2008; Bensley, 2011; Halpern, 1993, 2014). A literature review summarizes and analyzes research studies on a particular subject, often organizing the studies according to the hypotheses or theories that they support or do not support. It contains many basic arguments linked together to make an extended argument supporting one side or the other. The reviewer evaluates the evidence and arguments made to generalize from them and draw an inductive conclusion.

Unlike the typical literature review, the extended argument presented in Table 3.2 contains evidence written in the form of a series of numbered statements followed by a conclusion to help you see how an inductive argument works. Typical literature reviews, more like the ones found in later chapters of this book, are written in essay format with paragraphs. As you read through the following inductive argument in Table 3.2, ask yourself, "What general conclusion should I draw from the evidence?"

TABLE 3.2 **An Extended Inductive Argument on Whether Instruction Can Improve Critical Thinking**

1. A large study of a thinking skills program for schools in Venezuela showed that students improved their abilities to present oral arguments and to answer open-ended essay questions (Herrnstein, Nickerson, de Sanchez, & Swets, 1986).

2. Children instructed in a program called Philosophy for Children have shown improvement in their reasoning (Institute for the Advancement of Philosophy for Children, n.d.).

3. After instruction in a thinking-skills program, students self-reported that their thinking improved (Dansereau et al., 1979).

4. Some studies found that specific instructional variables thought to be related to CT have produced better test performance on the Watson–Glaser Critical Thinking Appraisal (Bailey, 1979; Suksringarm, 1976) and on the Cornell Test of Critical Thinking (Nieto & Saiz, 2008; Solon, 2007).

5. Studies of specific instructional variables thought to be related to CT have shown no increase on the Watson–Glaser test (Beckman, 1956; Coscarelli & Schwen, 1979).

6. After instruction in thinking skills, students have shown significant gains on tests of cognitive growth and development (Fox, Marsh, & Crandall, 1983).

7. Specific programs designed to teach CT for college students have produced significant gains on tests of CT (Mentkowski & Strait, 1983; Tomlinson-Keasey & Eisert, 1977).

8. Specific programs for teaching CT in college showed that students made no significant gains on CT tests (Tomlinson-Keasey, Williams, & Eisert, 1977).

9. Studies of high school students' reasoning skills (Marin & Halpern, 2010) and of college students who received explicit CT instruction (e.g., Bensley, Crowe, Bernhardt, Buckner, & Allman, 2010; Bensley & Haynes, 1995; Bensley & Spero, 2014; Nieto & Saiz, 2008; Solon, 2007) have found that students who received explicit instruction showed more improvement in their CT than did students who did not receive explicit CT instruction.

10. Authors of literature reviews on teaching CT have concluded that explicit CT instruction is effective (e.g., Bensley, 2011; Halpern, 1993, 1998); explicit instruction shows the largest effect size (Abrami et al., 2008).

Conclusion: Certain types of instruction improve students' CT, especially when instruction explicitly targets CT skill development through specific lessons and feedback.

ANALYZING AND EVALUATING AN INDUCTIVE ARGUMENT

To analyze an inductive argument like the one above, we organize each bit of evidence with the claim or conclusion it supports. Then we carefully examine and evaluate the evidence in terms of its quality (how good it is) and its quantity (how much evidence supports one side versus the other). The basic procedure consists of three steps:

1. Identify and understand the claim or question.
2. Organize the relevant evidence under the side it supports, noting its quality and quantity.
3. Draw a well-reasoned conclusion based on the quality and quantity of the evidence.

Memorizing these steps is a good start, but you need to understand how to apply them. To identify and understand the question and identify claims, you must look for clues. The most obvious clues may come from the title, which asks whether CT can be taught—the central question in its most general form. From this comes the claim that CT can be taught and the counterclaim that it cannot. In a well-written critical discussion of such a question, the question and important terms are often defined at the beginning. As the arguments and counterarguments proceed, the claims and question become more refined and specific. For example, statements 9 and 10 propose that explicit CT instruction may be particularly effective.

QUANTITY OF EVIDENCE

How strong an inductive conclusion we can draw depends on the **quantity** of evidence, that is, how much evidence supports or does not support a claim. Quantity of evidence contributes to inductive conclusions in three ways. First, the critical thinker must consider the number of studies and other pieces of evidence that support a theory versus those that do not support the theory. Assuming that the quality of studies is equal, we tend to more readily accept a hypothesis or theory supported by more studies. Because many more studies support the claim that CT can be taught than do not support it, we tend to favor the conclusion that instruction can improve CT.

The second quantity consideration involves taking into account the number of observations a conclusion is based on. Of course, the more observations and research participants sampled, the better—as long as they are representative of the population or larger group from which they are drawn. Randomly selecting subjects from a population is a good way to obtain a representative sample (i.e., one that is similar to the population you are trying to generalize to). Samples as small as 30 to 40 subjects may generalize reasonably well to the population, but larger random samples are preferable. Because the studies are described briefly in this literature review, we would need to check the original studies to find out how large the samples were. Literature reviews themselves are sometimes cited as evidence in support of claims and can add to the quantitative support for a conclusion, allowing us to generalize from the results of a number of studies that produce the same finding.

The third quantity consideration concerns the size of an effect obtained in a single study or sometimes across many studies. Researchers increasingly take into account the size of treatment effects (effect size) to draw inductive conclusions. For example, the review of studies on teaching CT by Abrami and colleagues (2008) showed that CT instruction tended to be most effective (i.e., had the largest effect size) when instructors explicitly taught CT to their students. This kind of review study, called a *meta-analysis,* can provide a quantitative estimate of the size of an effect across a number of studies, but the support it provides also depends on the quality of the studies selected for meta-analysis.

QUALITY OF EVIDENCE

All evidence is not equal in quality, and the quality of evidence is often more important than the quantity. One high-quality piece of evidence can strengthen an argument more than a lot of low-quality evidence would. For example, a true experiment showing objective improvement after CT instruction, such as the one conducted by Marin and Halpern (2011), would provide stronger evidence than a study in which people self-reported that their CT improved after instruction. Also, sometimes nonscientific evidence is proposed, as when people offer testimonials claiming that instruction helped improve their CT. When the type of evidence cannot be identified in a literature review, it often helps to examine the references or the list of studies and other sources cited at the end of the review to determine whether the studies cited were published in peer-reviewed, scientific journals. Peer-reviewed studies tend to be of higher quality because they have met the standards for publication on the basis of judgments of scientists knowledgeable in a field.

Evaluating the quality of studies in literature reviews sometimes requires additional searching to determine the quality of the source. When a research study is cited in a literature review, it is most often a secondary source in which the author of the literature review summarizes, interprets, or comments on the original research done by someone else. In contrast, a primary source is the original source of some information or idea, such as the original publication of a journal article reporting new research results. A literature review showing that CT can be taught can be very persuasive when it is done by an expert on CT, such as Diane Halpern (1993, 1998), because we expect that the expert will know and interpret the relevant research correctly. Unfortunately, sometimes re-reporting information from secondary sources can result in errors that persist as the information is passed along from one author to another when no author has double-checked the original source. Another problem with secondary reporting occurs when TV reporters describe a single, startling finding from a complicated research study in a 30-second sound bite, often ignoring information about the quality of the research or even misinterpreting the findings altogether.

DRAWING A STRONG INDUCTIVE CONCLUSION

The strength of an inductive conclusion depends on the relative quality and quantity of the evidence. The strongest conclusion we can draw is one in which all of the high-quality evidence supports one side of the argument and no good evidence supports the other side. This special case in inductive reasoning whereby all of the evidence supports one side (i.e., all the premises are true and support a true conclusion) is called a *cogent* argument, but this "strongest of strong" arguments is a rare occurrence in psychology.

Often, the best we can do is to draw a strong conclusion, or one that is *very likely* true, based on the evidence provided. In the preceding discussion, we tentatively concluded that the bulk of the good evidence gathered so far supports the conclusion that CT skills can be taught and that little evidence fails to support it. To say that a conclusion is "tentative" means that we cautiously accept the conclusion for now. More good evidence might later accumulate to support the conclusion that instruction does *not* improve CT, but for now we accept that instruction *can* improve CT. Note that even when all of the evidence supports an inductive conclusion, it still might be overturned by better evidence that comes to light later on.

A strong inductive conclusion depends not only on evaluating the quality and quantity of the evidence but also on the relevance of the evidence. One issue is whether all of the relevant evidence has been evaluated. For example, because CT involves dispositions and metacognition, perhaps the review should have discussed whether instruction can improve those aspects, too. In practice, it can be quite challenging to know whether all the relevant evidence has been included in a review and/or whether certain evidence being presented is indeed relevant at all. To deal with this difficulty, reviews, including those in this textbook, often are selective in the studies they incorporate in order to fairly represent the different sides of a question. Your primary job is to evaluate the evidence presented, but you should be aware that some evidence may be more relevant than other evidence. Sometimes, relevant evidence may even be missing.

Another issue with the relevance of evidence concerns *how* relevant the evidence is. Sometimes an arguer includes irrelevant evidence and information to divert attention from the question at hand, hoping to win the argument by creating a smoke screen—mainly to escape refutation from better evidence that might be offered. This thinking error is called the **red herring fallacy,** named after the technique used to train English foxhounds by dragging a bag of red herring (smelly fish) across the fox's trail to cover its scent (Bassham, Irwin, Nardone, & Wallace, 2005). Like the hounds, the critical thinker needs to learn how to follow the relevant evidence and line of reasoning in an argument and not be distracted by information that does not pertain to the discussion.

The red herring fallacy is a favorite of politicians. For example, Senator Swensen says, "Humans are not contributing to global warming—it is a made-up crisis." Senator Olsen counters, "Lots of good scientific research has found that in the last 50 years the earth has shown very rapid, unprecedented increases in both CO_2 levels and global temperatures. And experiments have shown that CO_2 can increase atmospheric temperature." Swensen replies with a red herring: "The earth periodically goes through cycles of cooling and warming." Swensen's last statement is not relevant because the natural cycles of the earth's cooling and warming are more gradual than the rapid change recently observed. Swensen's comment is just an effort to prevent refutation of his claim by Olsen's scientific evidence.

Just because most of the good, relevant evidence supports a tentative conclusion does not mean we can just forget about the negative evidence that does *not* support the conclusion. As critical thinkers, we should try to find a plausible explanation for nonsupporting evidence, that is, a reasonable explanation for why it did not support the conclusion. For instance, a couple of the failures to support the conclusion that CT can be taught can be explained by the idea that improving CT may take very specific and extensive training. For example, Tomlinson-Keasey and Eisert (1977) failed to show any effect of their training program after one year; but Tomlinson-Keasey, Williams, and Eisert (1977) showed a significant effect after two years of training. Although we may have found plausible explanations for why the studies failed to support the conclusion, this does not mean that these studies now support the conclusion.

Sometimes, when the evidence is mixed, we cannot even draw a tentative conclusion supporting one side versus another. A conclusion receives mixed support when some evidence supports one side, whereas other evidence supports the other side(s) without enough good evidence to favor one conclusion over another. In these cases, the best conclusion is that no firm conclusion can be drawn until more research is conducted that could resolve the controversy.

The pattern of the evidence in an inductive argument may also be complex, leading us to qualify or refine our conclusion to be consistent with what most of the good evidence suggests. A **qualified conclusion** is one that is true under certain conditions, that is, when the appropriate qualifications to the general conclusion have been made. Although scientists try to develop theories that are as general as possible, the evidence often indicates that a theory or hypothesis is true only under certain conditions. This indicates the need to qualify a more general conclusion (Garnham & Oakhill, 1994). For instance, our conclusion that instruction can improve CT is best supported by the research showing that explicit instruction is most effective. Stating our conclusion in this specific form, and in a way that is most consistent with the evidence, can help us make more accurate predictions from our theory, as well as guide us in the practical application of our knowledge.

A famous example of how research can reveal the need to qualify a theory comes from research on brain cells. Decades of research suggested that neurons do not reproduce and that we do not acquire new ones during our lives. According to this view, we are born with a large, but fixed, set of neurons that develop during the first years of life, with no new ones added later. This theory was seriously challenged in the late 1990s when researchers showed that new neurons did form in one specific area of the brain, called the *hippocampus* (Gould, Beylin, Tanapat, Reeves, & Shors, 1999). This discovery forced scientists to qualify the general conclusion that no new brain cells are formed to include the assumption that new neurons *do* form in at least one part of the brain.

It is clear from the preceding discussion that drawing a well-reasoned conclusion from all the relevant evidence is complicated. It often requires identifying a variety of nonscientific and scientific evidence and evaluating the quality and quantity of that evidence. It is little wonder that this process is often cut short and people draw a rapid conclusion, often unwarranted by the evidence. This can result in a thinking error called **hasty generalization**, in which people rapidly generalize from the evidence, perhaps not considering all of it or only superficially analyzing and evaluating it before drawing a conclusion. Hasty generalizations are all too common in everyday situations. Have you ever drawn a conclusion about some situation concerning what a friend did, only to discover that you jumped to a conclusion about that friend before getting all the facts? Taking a careful, systematic approach to evaluating all the relevant evidence before you draw a conclusion can help you avoid making a hasty generalization. In upcoming chapters, we will apply this approach to analyzing the quality and quantity of all the relevant evidence to get answers to some fascinating scientific questions.

Another way people sometimes fail to recognize the limits of inductive conclusions is to make a sweeping generalization. The word *sweeping* implies "wide in range." Someone who makes a sweeping generalization draws a conclusion that is too broad or goes beyond an appropriate conclusion from the evidence at hand. For example, although it is appropriate to conclude from the evidence presented in Table 3.2 that instruction can improve CT, it would be inappropriate to conclude that instruction could improve other kinds of thinking, such as creative thinking. That would be a sweeping generalization because the research we examined was related to CT, not to creative thinking.

Table 3.3 summarizes the various thinking errors discussed thus far. But a final note of caution related to the limits of induction is that the scientific research

TABLE 3.3 **Summary of Thinking Errors Highlighted**

Error Name	Description	How To Fix or Avoid It
Naive realism	Believing that what you perceive is really what is there and that what you experience is necessarily very accurate	Look for objective verification of what you perceive, such as from other observers or from data gathered with scientific instrumentation.
Hasty generalization	Drawing a general conclusion before sufficiently considering all the relevant evidence	Look for all of the relevant evidence and determine whether the samples are representative and adequate.
Sweeping generalization	Drawing a conclusion that is too broad or that goes well beyond what the evidence implies; sometimes, this involves overinterpreting a study's findings	Look at the range within which most of the cases and evidence are consistent with the conclusion and do not extend the conclusion beyond those cases to a different situation or group.
Red herring fallacy	Deliberately sidetracking an argument away from the issue at hand by presenting irrelevant information	Follow the line of reasoning; when irrelevant information is presented, point this out and ask the person to return to the issue.

literature shows a "publication bias" about which studies get published. Scientists look for real relationships between variables that exist, not for effects that do not exist. Consequently, failures to show an effect often do not get published, and literature reviews will be biased to contain studies in which an effect was found. This could raise doubt about the existence of negative evidence or evidence not supporting an effect, such as evidence not supporting the conclusion that CT can be taught.

Practice Thinking 3.3: Recognizing and Fixing Thinking Errors

1. Latoya's experiment on college students showed that teaching one group a study strategy significantly improved the group's reading comprehension of a psychology textbook passage, compared with another group that was instructed to use their usual study strategy. Latoya said this shows that the strategy could help math students do calculations, too.

   Thinking error: _____

   _____

   How to fix it: _____

   _____

2. Reporter: "Mr. President, what do you have to say about the unemployment rate, which has risen nationally and in most states to over 10%?"

   President: "The unemployment rate in Maryland is only 5% and in Washington state only 4%. Although it is a problem for some Americans, I have helped raise wages by 4.5% for many people, and the other side is exaggerating the problem to score political points."

   Thinking error: _____

   _____

   How to fix it: _____

   _____

3. Kyle and Emma were discussing an argument they saw two of their mutual friends having. Emma said, "They were really getting into it. I can't believe Michael actually pushed Lauren!" Kyle said, "What do you mean? I was right there and didn't see that." Emma replied, "You must be kidding. I saw it with my own two eyes, plain as day—he pushed her."

Thinking error: _____

_____

How to fix it: _____

_____

4. In 2012, the U.S. Supreme Court ruled on the national health insurance reform legislation nicknamed "Obamacare" (after former President Obama, who initiated it). Many people thought the conservative court would rule it unconstitutional. When the long-awaited decision was distributed to the press, a CNN reporter read the first page of the multipage decision, which seemed to suggest that the Supreme Court had ruled the law unconstitutional. Wanting to get the scoop, CNN announced that the Supreme Court had struck it down as unconstitutional. But the remaining pages of the document made clear that the Supreme Court had decided the law was constitutional after all.

Thinking error: _____

_____

How to fix it: _____

_____

SUMMARY

Inductive reasoning involves generalizing from specific pieces of evidence to a general rule, principle, or conclusion. A good inductive conclusion is tentatively and probably true, but it could always be overturned by new and better evidence.

Consequently, we never prove that something is true through induction, and we are not as certain that our conclusion is true as we can be with deductive reasoning. We can use inductive reasoning to evaluate and justify hypotheses and theories. When we inductively evaluate the evidence in a literature review, we evaluate the quality and quantity of the evidence.

The kinds of evidence used in everyday reasoning do not meet the higher standards of good scientific evidence and show a variety of weaknesses and limitations. In general, nonscientific kinds of evidence are based on nonsystematic and informal observation, whereas scientific evidence is based on careful and systematic observation. For instance, personal experience, although immediate and compelling, is subject to perceptual and cognitive errors and biases. Despite these limitations, people often show naive realism, believing they are accurately perceiving the world as it really is. Anecdotes are stories or examples based on unique, unrepeatable observations that are difficult to generalize from. Commonsense belief is based on the untested beliefs of many people, informally generalized from presumably common experiences. Statements of authority can be problematic when so-called authorities lack relevant knowledge or are biased. Because authority depends on possessing relevant expertise and knowledge, in scientific arguments the statements of scientists who have expertise concerning scientific research on the relevant question are more authoritative than the statements of nonscientists.

Some thinking errors related to inductive reasoning occur from a failure to evaluate relevant evidence. The red herring fallacy occurs when irrelevant evidence or information is offered in order to derail a discussion of the issue at hand. Hasty generalization occurs when a person is too quick to draw a conclusion, failing to examine all of the relevant evidence. In contrast, when making a sweeping generalization, a person generalizes beyond what the evidence supports.

 Practice Thinking 3.4: WHAT DO YOU THINK NOW?
Please explain how you know.

1. Can people who claim to have precognition accurately predict the future?

   _____

2. Can instruction improve students' CT? _____

   _____

3. Does subliminal learning work? For example, would listening to recordings of a foreign-language lesson while you are asleep help you learn that language? _____

    _____

4. How much should you trust your personal experience in drawing a conclusion? _____

    _____

REVIEW QUESTIONS

1. What is plausibility?
2. What is inductive reasoning? Generalization?
3. Compare inductive and deductive arguments in terms of how we draw a conclusion and the certainty of a conclusion in each case.
    -   What is a basic limitation of inductive reasoning (the white crow example)?
    -   Why are inductive conclusions tentative?
    -   Can inductive reasoning *prove* a conclusion is true?
4. What are some nonscientific sources of evidence? Compare them to scientific sources.
    -   What is personal experience? What are its strengths and weaknesses? How is naive realism an issue for personal experience?
    -   What is commonsense belief? What are its strengths and weaknesses?
    -   What is anecdotal evidence? What are its strengths and weaknesses?
    -   What are statements of authority? What are their strengths and weaknesses?
    -   What is science?
    -   What is the difference between scientific and nonscientific authority?

5. How do we analyze and evaluate an inductive argument? What are the three steps involved?

   - What is quantity of evidence?
   - What is quality of evidence?
   - How can you distinguish primary from secondary sources?
   - What is a strong inductive argument? Can we draw a strong inductive conclusion from the review of whether CT can be taught? How do we do this?
     - Why is including relevant evidence important to making a strong inductive argument?
     - What is a qualified conclusion?

6. What thinking errors are associated with inductive reasoning?

   - What is the red herring fallacy? How do you recognize it?
   - What is a sweeping generalization? How do you recognize it?
   - What is a hasty generalization? How do you recognize it?

7. What psychological misconceptions were discussed in this chapter?

4

CRITICAL THINKING AND SCIENTIFIC REASONING

LEARNING OUTCOMES

After studying this chapter, you should be able to:

1. Explain how nonscientific and scientific reasoning differ.

2. Identify the strengths and weaknesses of various methods used as evidence in scientific research and argumentation.

3. Determine whether a cause-and-effect relationship is likely to exist.

4. Recognize the limits of the scientific approach and inductive reasoning.

5. Recognize thinking errors associated with inductive and scientific reasoning.

WHAT DO YOU THINK?

AP Photo

FIGURE 4.1 Poster for Heaven's Gate, a UFO cult, announcing the end of their time on Earth, detailing when group members would meet with aliens from outer space who resided in a different dimension.

In 1997, 39 members of the Heaven's Gate cult committed suicide by drinking vodka laced with cyanide so they could rendezvous with alien beings whose spaceship was approaching Earth behind Comet Hale-Bopp. Figure 4.1 shows one of the cult's posters announcing this event. Cult members believed that if they committed suicide, alien beings from another dimension would open the gates to heaven for them, thereby saving them from Earth's impending destruction. Some members had belonged to the cult for decades, whereas others were fairly new to these strange beliefs. Yet they all decided to commit suicide. Why?

Practice Thinking 4.1: What Do You Think?

Please explain how you know.

1. When people join a cult, do they accept all the cult's beliefs and lose their ability to think critically? How could you find out?

2. Does observing aggressive behaviors in movies, TV, or video games cause a person to behave aggressively? How could you find out?

3. Does having been sexually abused as a child lead to personality problems as an adult and cause the victim to later become a sexual abuser?

4. Can science answer all questions? Why or why not?

In this chapter, we examine how science helps us obtain better answers to these fascinating and important questions than do personal experience, anecdotes, and other nonscientific approaches. As you will see, the methods that scientists use are superior.

COMPARING SCIENTIFIC AND NONSCIENTIFIC APPROACHES

Scientific evidence, unlike the informal and unsystematic observations of nonscientific evidence, is based on careful and systematic observation. For example, scientists who want to conduct rigorous studies of precognition would use carefully controlled experimentation, not informal observation such as that used by some people at Duke University, who mistakenly concluded that Lee Fried could predict the future. This reliance on personal experience provided no systematic way to test the quality of the information obtained. In contrast, because the scientific approach employs rules and strategies for reasoning effectively about carefully made observations, scientists are able to evaluate and even improve the quality of their data.

Science is called an *empirical approach* because of its reliance on verifiable observations, or data that can be shown to have a certain quality. Scientists use scientific standards of evidence, which are rules and principles used to determine higher- versus lower-quality scientific evidence. The sciences show overlap in the standards they use, but each discipline may develop its own specific rules of reasoning (Bensley, 2011). For instance, all the sciences agree on the general rule that theories must be consistent with evidence. Psychologists specify that experiments can better demonstrate cause and effect than other research designs can. They develop even more specific rules for interpreting the data from research instruments and techniques, such as brain-scanning equipment, that provide much more precise data than nonscientific evidence does. Proper use of the rules for reasoning well about carefully made observations gives the scientific approach its power to answer many different questions.

SCIENCE AS AN APPROACH TO KNOWLEDGE AND EVIDENCE

To answer the many questions posed in a particular field, the scientist looks for lawful relations among variables by using specific methods and techniques based on rules for reasoning effectively about data. For example, suppose a social psychologist wants to find out why a person is helpful in one situation but not in another. She would study the variable—helpfulness—under various conditions. A variable is a characteristic or event of interest that can take on different values. In everyday, nonscientific terms, you might imprecisely refer to someone as "selfish" or "helpful." The psychologist would more precisely define the variable of helpfulness, in terms of how many times the research participant was observed to help. Or the researcher might rate the participant on a selfishness scale ranging from 1 = *not at all helpful* to 7 = *extremely helpful*. This illustrates two ways to operationalize, or represent, the variable in terms of methods, procedures, and measurements. Assigning a number to a helpfulness scale is a useful first step in describing a single variable, but it is limited in what it tells us. To validly measure the construct underlying helpfulness, scientists would use other reliable gauges that could provide converging information about it (Grace, 2001).

Understanding something complex, such as helping behavior, requires that we understand the relationships between variables, not just one variable. A **relationship** between variables indicates that the values of one variable change consistently in relation to the values of another variable. Scientists seek to express relationships in precise terms that can be observed. For instance, on average, participants who score low—say, a 2—on the helpfulness scale tend to score higher on the amount of time spent talking about themselves in a 10-minute conversation—say, 8 out of 10 minutes.

Scientists refer to the predicted relationship between two or more variables as a **hypothesis**. More formally, a hypothesis is often deduced from a theory in the form of a specific prediction, as discussed in Chapter 2. It is a claim about what will happen if we assume that some theory is true. For example, from the general theory that people are basically selfish and motivated by self-interest, we might predict that if participants have the opportunity to help someone else in a new situation, they will not help. Hypotheses can also originate from other sources, including personal experience.

A hypothesis typically makes a prediction about one of two types of relationships: (1) an association or (2) a cause-and-effect relation. In an association, sometimes referred to as a *correlation*, the values of two variables are simply related or change together in a consistent way. In a positive association, as one variable increases, the other variable increases along with it; or as one variable decreases, the other variable tends to decrease. For instance, the more helpful people are, the more likely they are to volunteer. Putting this hypothesis in terms of scores on a 7-point helpfulness rating scale, we might say, "We predict that the higher a person's helpfulness rating score, the more often that person will volunteer to help." It is also true in this positive association that the lower the score on the helpfulness scale, the lower the tendency to volunteer—which illustrates that in a positive association, the values of two variables change in the *same* direction.

In a negative association between variables, the values of the two variables consistently change together in the *opposite* direction. Stating this as a correlational hypothesis for a research study, we might say, "We expect that the higher a participant's score on the 7-point helpfulness scale, the less time that participant will spend doing something to benefit himself or herself."

Showing a cause-and-effect relationship takes more than simply showing an association between variables. To show causation, changes in one variable (the cause) must occur *before* changes occur in the other variable (the effect). Consider this causal hypothesis: "If one group studies a list of words for longer than another group does, then the group that studied longer will recall more on a test of the new words." In this hypothesis, how long people study (the cause) must happen before the effect (how many new words they learned). It makes no sense for a causal form of this hypothesis to predict that people will first recall the new list of 30 words and then will study the words for a longer or shorter time. They are not new words if one has already recalled them.

People find relationships between variables in their daily lives, not just in scientific research. But how good are people at assessing whether variables are correlated? Look at the data in Table 4.1, showing the frequency of cases in which an abnormal behavior is either present or not present in relation to the moon's phase (full or not full). Suppose, as shown in cell A, that people working at a mental health facility observed 12 cases in which the moon was full and people behaved abnormally. Do the data in the fourfold table show that the presence of a full moon is related to abnormal behavior?

TABLE 4.1 The Fourfold Table Showing Cell Frequencies		
	Full Moon	**No Full Moon**
Abnormal behavior	12 (Cell A)	6 (Cell B)
No abnormal behavior	6 (Cell C)	3 (Cell D)

Examining the data in Table 4.1, many of the mental health facility staff mentioned in Chapter 1 would likely find a correlation between the full moon and abnormal behavior, concluding that people tend to behave abnormally during a full moon. But they would be mistaken. This thinking error occurs because people tend to notice co-occurrences of events, like those shown in the higher frequencies of cell A, and do not take into account the frequencies in other cells of the table. You are not likely to hear people say, "Hey, there's a full moon tonight, but nobody is behaving strangely!" (Kohn, 1990). This demonstrates how people often fail to take into account the six cases in cell C who are *not* behaving abnormally during a full moon. Nor are people likely to say, "Wow, the patients are behaving abnormally, but there's not even a full moon!" which demonstrates how they tend to ignore the six cases in cell B. We must take these cases into account because they provide evidence that no relation exists. What does the research say about people's ability to analyze data like these?

The research shows that people are not very good at assessing these kinds of associations; they pay too much attention to cell A and neglect the other cells (Smedsland, 1978). This thinking error is called **illusory correlation** because people mistakenly perceive a relationship (correlation) between two variables when none exists. For example, people often find illusory correlations between certain traits and specific groups, leading to the formation of stereotypes that are unfairly applied to individuals. Even professionals sometimes fall prey to illusory correlation, as when clinicians incorrectly diagnose mental disorders by paying attention to co-occurrences of expected features (cell A) and not considering all the information available (Chapman & Chapman, 1967).

Taking a scientific approach to forming and testing hypotheses can help safeguard against illusory correlation and other thinking errors. By systematically making observations that could show whether variables are changing together or not, scientists look at the data in *all* four cells of a fourfold table. In this regard, a good scientific hypothesis is **falsifiable**, or can be shown to be false (Popper, 1959). When scientists think critically, they do not seek to confirm a hypothesis. Instead, they set up their test to also make observations that could *disconfirm* the hypothesis. Then they examine *all* the data—those that support the hypothesis and those that do not. If we were unable to show that a hypothesis was false, how could we ever find out that our hypotheses and theories were wrong and needed correction? In other words, falsifiability allows for self-correction in science (Myers & Hansen, 2012).

For example, the hypothesis "If people study this critical thinking book enough, they will be able to think critically in a new situation" is not falsifiable. Using the qualifier "enough" is not specific and would always allow for other after-the-fact explanations that would prevent it from being disconfirmed. If people studied this book but were not able to think critically in a new situation, we could always say, "They did not study it enough." But what is *enough*? A good scientific hypothesis needs to make a specific prediction.

When scientists conduct a study that supports a theory or hypothesis, they often try to **replicate** the study, attempting to repeat the observations under similar conditions. A positive outcome can provide more inductive support for a theory, but replicating the findings of a previous study never proves the theory is true. If a theory or hypothesis survives even more rigorous testing under conditions that could disconfirm it, then these positive results can strengthen it even more. On the other hand, if a good experiment fails to support social learning theory and this negative finding is replicated with other high-quality studies, eventually we would decide that under some specific condition, the theory is false and should be revised or is even completely wrong and should be rejected. This outcome might disturb some, but it is a fundamental way for us to correct mistaken scientific ideas.

After our discussion of the neglect of negative evidence in illusory correlation, it may not surprise you that people often do not seek evidence that could falsify their own theories when testing them. Once people find a relationship or form a belief, they tend to look for evidence that confirms or supports their favored belief, often ignoring or minimizing evidence that could disconfirm it; this illustrates a thinking error called **confirmation bias**. In one study, Lord, Ross, and Lepper (1979) first asked participants if they favored or opposed the death penalty. Participants were then given the results of two experiments of equal quality, one that supported the idea that the death penalty deterred further crime and another that did not support this claim. Consistent with the effect of confirmation bias, participants rated the results of the study supporting what they already believed as more convincing than the results of the study that disagreed with their position. After they read the results of the study that disagreed with their position, this negative evidence should have made participants less convinced that they were right, but surprisingly, they became even more convinced of their position.

Confirmation bias is a very common thinking error that affects many kinds of judgments (Nickerson, 1998) and that we will examine at various points in this book. For instance, one study of juror reasoning showed that as a trial progressed, prospective jurors tended to bias their interpretation of newly presented evidence to be consistent with whatever their current preference was in terms of the defendant's guilt or innocence (Carlson & Russo, 2001). In another study, party affiliation biased ballot counters to judge ambiguous ballots as votes in favor of candidates in their party (Kopko, Bryner, Budziak, Devine, & Nawarra, 2011). An everyday example is the "toupee fallacy," which shows confirmation bias in people who believe they can detect when a man is wearing a toupee. Whenever these people learn that someone they suspect of wearing a toupee is actually wearing one, this confirms their belief in their ability. But, because they do not systematically check whether other men they think are *not* wearing toupees are actually wearing them, they get a biased estimate of their detection ability (Novella, 2012).

Are scientists immune to confirmation bias? No, but they have strategies for countering it, such as the peer review of research. When a scientist submits his or her research to be accepted for publication, an editor sends the manuscript to experts on the question (the scientist's peers) who evaluate the quality of the research and look for problems and ways the researcher's conclusions could be false. The peer review process is not foolproof, however, and can itself be subject to confirmation bias. Mahoney (1977) asked scientific journal reviewers to evaluate manuscript submissions of studies that were identical except for their results. The reviewers gave higher ratings to the manuscripts with results supporting their own favored theories than to manuscripts with results that challenged their favored views. This, of course, is problematic. Fortunately, peer review still works because others in the scientific community may find fault with a study or will be unable to replicate the findings of the study in question.

Probability is another tool scientists use to decide whether relationships are real or illusory. **Probability** is "the likelihood that a particular event or relation will occur" (Vogt, 1993, p. 178). For instance, to determine how likely a group rated as selfish and a group rated as unselfish will engage in helping behavior, a researcher conducts statistical analyses on some measure of helping behavior. This involves using probability to estimate the likelihood of obtaining some difference between the two groups simply by chance. If the researcher finds a very low probability that the observed difference between the selfish and unselfish groups was due simply to chance (e.g., if the difference would occur by chance fewer than 5 times out of 100), then the researcher concludes it is likely that a real difference in the two groups exists. The researcher declares this difference to be **statistically significant**, or just significant. This significant difference suggests that a real relationship exists between ratings of people's selfishness and their willingness to help, supporting the hypothesis that unselfish people help more. This also helps reduce the probability that any observed difference in the groups was just a random one that might have been simply observed by chance (as in an illusory correlation).

CAUSATION AND THE QUALITY OF SCIENTIFIC EVIDENCE

Different scientific research methods and designs provide evidence that varies in quality. Because the methods of science involve using observation to test hypotheses and to evaluate theories, the quality of the evidence offered by scientific research depends on the ability to collect high-quality data. The best evidence comes from studies in which observations were made with objectivity, without error, and under carefully controlled conditions.

The quality of the evidence provided by scientific research methods also depends on the degree to which a particular method can establish a causal relation between variables. Recall that the goals of psychology as a science are to describe, predict, explain, and control or manipulate behavior. In order to reach the important goal of explaining behavior, we must be able to show the causes of behavior. When we speak of a **cause**, we are referring to something that has produced an effect. A cause precedes the event it produces (the effect). Knowing the cause can help explain why the effect happened (Zechmeister & Johnson, 1992). To better understand how something might be the cause of some behavior, let's look closely at the three **criteria for establishing causation**, shown in Table 4.2. Recall that a criterion is a standard that must be met or a condition that must be present in order to confirm that something is true.

TABLE 4.2	Three Criteria for Establishing Causation
1.	Two events must covary or vary together consistently (covariation).
2.	One event must occur before the other (time order).
3.	Plausible alternative explanations for the covariation must be eliminated.

To illustrate the use of these criteria, let's apply them to the question of whether precognition caused the supposedly correct prediction of the plane crash in the Lee Fried example from Chapter 3. To show that the covariation criterion was met, we would have to demonstrate that Fried's precognitive ability and the predicted event changed together. We would have to prove that when Fried had his premonition, it was systematically related to the crash. The two events *appear* to have occurred close together in time, suggesting that covariation was present. Also, it *appears* that the precognition occurred before the letter was delivered, suggesting that the criterion of time order had been met, although no other verification of this criterion was demonstrated. Finally, Fried's handing over a sealed letter to a public figure suggested that the letter would not be tampered with and that the event could be documented. This *appears* to eliminate the alternative explanation of cheating as the cause of the correct prediction.

A closer examination of the events shows that none of the criteria were actually met. Fried's confession that he was a magician, which implies that he used deception, suggests that the two events that actually covaried were (1) the swapping of the letters and (2) the reading of the new letter, which was presumed to be the original letter with the prediction. But the contents of the letter had been put in the envelope *after* the jumbo jet crashed, so no premonition occurred before the event. Thus, time order was not met. Nor were two plausible alternative explanations eliminated. First, someone should have tried to falsify Fried's claim by checking how many other events he had predicted accurately. Psychics frequently guess, so sometimes their predictions do turn out to be right, simply by chance. The second, much more plausible, explanation someone should've checked before concluding that precognition was the cause is that Fried engaged in trickery. For example, did Fried ever have access to the letter after the crash occurred? Only Fried's word supported his use of precognition, and he later cast doubt on his claim that he had precognitive ability.

It is clear from analysis of this example that it is virtually impossible to demonstrate causation in an anecdote. In fact, only the true experiment, one of the scientific research designs we discuss next, can put us in the position to infer causation.

STRENGTHS AND WEAKNESSES OF RESEARCH METHODS

Various research methods differ in the kind and quality of information they can provide. In particular, they differ in the extent to which they can control extraneous variables and the degree to which causal inferences can be made. Table 4.3 (on page 90) shows the strengths and weaknesses of various commonly used research methods. One important idea in Table 4.3 is that only the true experiment allows the researcher to make causal inference because it's the only method through which all the criteria for causation can be met; the research methods described next do not have that same capability.

A case study provides a detailed description of part of an individual's life, often documenting a person's abilities, traits, symptoms, behaviors, and treatment. Case studies are often used to study the behavior of people in treatment, as well as special individuals with certain traits and abilities. Although covariation of variables can sometimes be shown, it is much more difficult to show that one variable precedes another. It is frequently even more difficult to eliminate other variables that could be having an effect besides the one that is supposed to be the cause. We call these extraneous variables because they are "extra" variables outside the intended focus of our study that could provide alternate explanations for the research findings.

Compared with anecdotes that also often involve a description of a single person in a situation, case studies differ in that the observations are made systematically and are based on recordings of observations, not simply someone's recollection. Although multiple observations can be made of a single person, like anecdotes, case studies still tend to suffer in terms of quantity of evidence.

Survey research involves asking participants multiple questions. Questions can be asked in a mailed or emailed questionnaire or in a face-to-face interview. The main advantage of surveys and questionnaires is that many questions can be asked of many people. Questionnaires are thus economical and versatile and can address a wide variety of topics, traits, and experiences.

But surveys and questionnaires can present difficulties too. Gathering reliable data depends on the wording of the questions, how the participants are selected, and the truthfulness of their responses. In addition, if researchers do not select respondents in a way that makes the sample representative of a population or if many participants do not respond, it will be difficult to generalize validly from those in the sample responding to the population at large. Also, respondents may not be honest in reporting their opinions or may not remember factual information accurately when asked. Although covariation may be shown between one item and another, the other two criteria for causation are typically not met. In particular, it is very difficult to control extraneous variables—such as individual differences in respondents—that could affect how respondents answer.

Further limitations of surveys are that responses to survey questions can be sensitive to placement in the survey, the context in which questions are asked, and the wording and form of a question (Schwartz, 2007). For example, when Schuman and Presser (1981) asked respondents to report what they considered "the most important thing for children to prepare them for life," only 4.6% wrote a response on the order of "think for themselves." Yet when "think for themselves" was put in a list of alternatives, 61.5% of the participants selected it. This finding suggests that asking a question in two different ways can yield wildly different answers. Ironically, it also suggests that when people were asked to think for themselves by generating a response, they tended *not* to answer that "thinking for themselves" was important. However, when they didn't have to think of the response on their own, they more often thought that "thinking for themselves" was important.

Using **field studies** and **naturalistic observation**, researchers collect data in the natural environment, which has the advantage of avoiding the artificiality of laboratory research. Jane Goodall and other primatologists have used naturalistic observation to study chimpanzees in the wild. Developmental psychologists have used it to study the interactions of children in their classrooms using video cameras to record their behaviors for later study. Because observed behaviors are simply part of a stream of behavior, it is difficult to establish the time order of behaviors and nearly impossible to eliminate extraneous variables. Suppose you are observing the selfish and unselfish behaviors of a person in everyday situations. The person may respond to a variety of situational variables, such as rewards for being generous, that also affect the apparently unselfish behavior.

A **participant–observer** study is a type of field study, often used in social psychology and sociology, in which a researcher infiltrates a group to study it without the participants knowing they are being studied. This reduces the reactivity of participants or their tendency to behave a certain way because they know they are being observed. The sociologist Robert Balch became a participant–observer, joining the Heaven's Gate cult to study how new members were recruited and came to accept the group's unusual beliefs (Balch, 1993). This method allowed Balch and his graduate student assistant David Taylor to find out whether new members accepted all of the cult's extraordinary claims when they first joined, thereby losing their ability to think critically about the claims.

Balch and Taylor found that new members were often seekers who focused on a spiritual quest for fulfillment and had been part of other groups with paranormal beliefs. Consequently, conversion to the cult was not dramatic but seemed like the next logical step for some. Other evidence that members had not been brainwashed came from the fact that many converts left the cult soon after joining and that even some longtime members sometimes raised doubts about the group's fundamental beliefs (Balch, 1993; Balch & Taylor, 1977). Although naturalistic observation by participant–observers made these interesting and important findings possible, this method would not allow the researchers to determine the *causes* of cult-member behavior.

Correlational studies seek to find a *quantitative* relationship between two or more variables in which the variables covary, or vary together. As mentioned earlier, positive correlations occur when two variables vary together in the same direction—as when empathy and the willingness to help are positively correlated. A person feeling empathy identifies with and feels what another person is feeling and tends to help more. A negative correlation might be found between empathy and selfishness. As selfishness increases, people tend to feel less empathy. These variables are covarying in the opposite direction.

Obviously, covariation is easy to establish if the two variables are correlated; however, time order is more difficult to show. Although it appears that an individual may first empathize with someone in need of help and then help that person, the relation between the two variables might go in the other direction. It may be that helping another person reinforces feelings of empathy, making helpers feel more connected to the people they have helped.

Correlational studies cannot easily eliminate other plausible alternative explanations, either, because another variable may actually be the cause for change in the two correlated variables; this is sometimes called the *third-variable problem*. Suppose we find a significant correlation between watching violence on TV and subsequent aggression. We might be tempted to conclude that watching violence on TV leads to more aggressive behavior, but what if a third variable, such as "liking to observe violence," leads people to be both more aggressive and to watch more violence on TV? It is difficult, if not impossible, to eliminate this third variable as an explanation in a correlational study. Consequently, correlation does not allow us to infer cause and effect.

THINKING ERRORS IN WRONGLY INFERRING CAUSATION

You may have heard the expression, "Correlation does not imply causation." Inferring that one of two simply correlated variables is a cause of the other is a thinking error called **confusing correlation with causation**. A good example, discussed in Chapter 2, is the misconception in the 1980s that improving self-esteem would improve academic performance. The many attempts to improve students' academic performance by raising their self-esteem were largely unsuccessful. Although self-esteem is modestly correlated with academic achievement, it does not *cause* it (Baumeister, Campbell, Krueger, & Vohs, 2003). Those who perform better in school are simply more likely to feel better about themselves.

Another misconception related to confusing correlation with causation is the popular belief that victims of sexual abuse will necessarily develop personality problems in adulthood and will become abusers themselves. Although sexual abuse is indeed too common and can be very harmful, the research generally does not support that it *causes* people to develop a specific set of personality issues, such as low self-confidence and problems with intimacy and relationships, that victims carry for the rest of their lives (Lilienfeld, Lynn, Ruscio, & Beyerstein, 2010). Rather, the research shows that abused people are generally resilient and able to adjust to the early trauma. In a meta-analysis of many studies of college students, Rind, Bauserman, and Tromovitch (1998) found that although the students' experience of sexual abuse was related to some psychological problems later in life, the correlations were low.

Moreover, research by Salter and colleagues (2003) found that less than 12% of men who had been sexually abused as children later became abusers themselves (Salter et al., 2003). When compared with the approximately 5% of men who were *not* abused but who later committed sexual abuse, the frequency for sexual abuse victims is certainly higher; but it also means that about 88% of sexual abuse victims do *not* become abusers themselves. Salter and colleagues also found that other risk factors were often present in the abusers as children, such as a lack of supervision and having witnessed serious violence among family members, which may have caused the later abusive behavior. This further suggests that although a correlation is present, causation should not be inferred.

Another kind of thinking error about causation, called post hoc reasoning, occurs when people incorrectly assume that something that merely happened to occur before an event was the actual cause of the event. The English translation of *post hoc* is "after this"; it comes from the longer Latin expression *post hoc, ergo propter hoc,* which means "after this, therefore because of this." Both expressions refer to making an unwarranted assumption about time order, specifically that something occurring *after this* other event was caused by it.

To illustrate, suppose you begin taking vitamins and later notice that your concentration is better than before you started taking them. From this, you may mistakenly conclude that the vitamins caused the improvement in your concentration. Looking back at the events, it may seem that taking the vitamin was the first event and led to better concentration, but the two events may be simply coincidental, and the criterion of time order has not been established. Nor have you met the other criterion of eliminating plausible, alternative explanations. You may have expected the vitamins to improve your well-being in general (a placebo effect, discussed in Chapter 5), and you likely did not establish a controlled variable against which to measure any effects. Or what if, during this time, you also exercised more or got more sleep? These could be the actual causes of the perceived change in your concentration. What is needed is a method that allows us to manipulate one variable so that it clearly occurs before the other variable while we also control other potential causes.

TRUE EXPERIMENTS AND CAUSATION

True experiments *do* allow us to make causal inferences because all three criteria of causation can be met. In a true experiment, an independent variable is manipulated—a variable that the researcher wants to demonstrate is the cause of an effect in another variable called the dependent variable. The dependent variable is the measured variable. In psychological research, the dependent variable is almost always some behavior.

For instance, an experimenter could test the commonsense idea that there is strength in numbers. You might expect that if you needed help, you would be more likely to receive it when more people are available to help than when just one person knows of your plight. An experimenter could test this hypothesis by varying the levels of the independent variable in terms of an expectation of how many people the research participants believed were available to help a person in need. He could randomly assign participants to two groups: One group is led to believe that only each of them individually is available to help; a second group is led to believe that others are also available to help.

After manipulating the independent variable, the experimenter then measures the effect on the dependent variable—the willingness to help the person in need. Because these two levels were presented before the dependent variable, the criterion of time order has been met. If the independent variable produces significant differences in the two groups' willingness to help, then the criterion of covariation has also been met. Finally, because of random assignment of participants to the two groups, the experimenter has controlled extraneous variables, such as individual differences in the tendency to help, and has thus met the criterion of elimination of plausible alternative explanations.

Note that true experiments are useful not only for showing causation but also for correcting misconceptions. When Darley and Latané (1968) conducted this experiment on helpfulness, they found that participants who thought they alone were available to help were more likely to provide that help. This revealed the real cause of helping in this situation, contradicting the misconception that someone in need is more likely to receive help when more people are present (as discussed further in Chapter 10).

The goal of the experimenter is to show that it was the independent variable—and no other variable—that had an effect on the dependent variable. Experimental controls help to accomplish this goal, at which point the experiment is said to have internal validity. When internal validity is high, the experimenter is in a good position to show that it was the independent variable and no other variable that caused the changes in the dependent variable. This result is possible because this true experiment was well conducted and controlled for extraneous variables that could have caused the changes in the dependent variable.

However, what if an experimenter tests participants in a way that allows an extraneous variable to bias the results? Returning to our helpfulness experiment, suppose the researcher always tested the group that thought no one else was available to help before testing the group that thought others were available to help? Suppose further that he always tested first the participants who had signed up for the experiment first and thus seemed most eager to assist? This would introduce a confounding variable, willingness to help, an alternate explanation for why participants helped (i.e., other than the independent variable being the reason). How would the experimenter know whether the hypothesis had been supported?

Even if the group members who thought they alone knew the plight of the person were found to help more than the other group, we could not be sure that it was because they thought they alone were available to help. It could be that the group tested first was already more likely to assist because they volunteered first, suggesting greater willingness to help. We say that whether or not anyone else was aware of the plight of the person (the independent variable) was confounded with "time of volunteering/willingness to help." A **confounding** variable is an extraneous variable that varies along with the independent variable and could also plausibly account for the changes in the dependent variable. This threatens the experiment's internal validity because other variables, such as the helpfulness of volunteers (rather than availability of others to help), could be the real cause of the changes in the dependent variable. The experimenter could have avoided this confounding if he had randomly assigned to the two treatment groups participants who signed up at different times, as in the first experiment described.

Practice Thinking 4.2: Identifying Variables in Experiments

For each research example below, write the independent (or manipulated) variable and the dependent (or measured) variable. Think of an extraneous variable that is not controlled and that might confound the results.

1. An experimenter wanted to find out if a study strategy involving putting list items into categories was more effective for learning a list of words than a strategy involving rote rehearsal. One group of 30 randomly assigned participants studied words such as *chair, dog, rose, table, rabbit,* and *lily* by putting them into categories, such as "furniture," "flowers," and "pets." The rote rehearsal group of 30 participants simply repeated the list of words over and over to themselves. Then both groups recalled the words one week later.

   Independent variable: _____

   Dependent variable: _____

   Extraneous variable: _____

2. An experiment by Darley and Latané (1968) found that a person is more likely to help if alone than if part of a group. To replicate this study in a natural setting, Angie tested students at her university student center. An assistant would drop a stack of books in the presence of individual students walking alone or in front of groups of students walking together. Then Angie kept track of whether or not a subject (or subjects) helped in each case.

Independent variable: _____

Dependent variable: _____

Extraneous variable: _____

Quasi-experiments resemble true experiments in that they often involve the comparison of groups that undergo different treatment conditions; but unlike with true experiments, there is no true manipulation of an independent variable in quasi-experiments. Participants are not randomly assigned to treatment groups the way they are in true experiments. Instead, they are selected, often on the basis of some preexisting characteristic. For example, we might compare a group of college students with a group of high school students on their dating behaviors. Or we might compare men and women on their willingness to help. The comparison of college to high school students and of men to women does not entail true manipulation of the variables, even though they form different groups. We have simply selected people of different ages and sexes to be in our groups.

The problem is that, for instance, males and females might already differ from each other at the beginning of our study on a number of variables related to their willingness to help. Because we have merely selected males and females and cannot randomly assign participants to be male and female in a quasi-experiment, we are unable to control differences in our subjects that could be controlled through random assignment in a true experiment. Moreover, without truly manipulating an independent variable, we cannot establish time order; so we are not able to draw causal inferences from quasi-experiments, as we can with true experiments. Like true experiments, quasi-experiments can sometimes allow for control of extraneous variables—as when we test our groups under similar conditions in the laboratory—but possible preexisting differences in participants related to the sex variable remain uncontrolled.

In summary, the manipulation of independent variables allows the experimenter to meet the criteria of covariation and time order, and the control of extraneous variables allows for meeting the criterion of the elimination of plausible alternatives. At least with regard to making a causal inference, therefore, the experimental method provides better-quality data than the case study, correlational study, or quasi-experimental study. Table 4.3 summarizes the strengths and weaknesses of the various research designs we have discussed, with implications for the quality of data and evidence each provides.

Nevertheless, the conclusions based on scientific research are only as good as the quality of the evidence they are based on. Therefore, if a scientist did a research study and was not really measuring what was intended or perhaps made errors in measurement, then conclusions based on that research data could be erroneous. Fortunately, science is self-correcting, and the erroneous conclusion of the first scientist could be discovered by other scientists seeking to replicate and make sense of the observations of the first research study.

Table 4.3 also implies that we should be particularly persuaded when high-quality scientific research studies are used as evidence. When using scientific research as evidence in arguments, authors often cite the source author(s) and year of publication and mention the kind of research study that was done. Table 4.3 makes it clear that results of certain types of studies, such as true experiments, generally provide stronger support for a claim than do other types, such as case studies or other nonexperimental study designs. Scientific research is also used to support claims when a scientific authority or expert is cited, often someone who has written a literature review, summarizing the results of several studies supporting some hypothesis or theory.

These two citation methods demonstrate good practices in using scientific research as evidence, but we often hear arguments in the media and everyday life that do not specifically cite the study or research being discussed. For example, news reports will say, "Research shows . . ." or "Studies show . . ." without documenting the scientific research evidence being referred to. Although they have made a basic argument, their failing to cite specific research has weakened the argument. It also discourages critical thinking (CT) because it is harder to examine the quality of the evidence when no source is cited.

TABLE 4.3 **Strengths and Weaknesses of Scientific Research Methods/Designs Used as Sources of Evidence**

Method/Design	Strengths	Weaknesses
Case study Detailed description of one or a few subjects	• Provides much information about one person • May inform about a person with special or rare abilities, knowledge, or characteristics	• May be unique and hard to replicate • May not generalize to other people • Cannot show cause and effect
Naturalistic observation Observations of behavior made in the field or natural environment	• Allows observations to be readily generalized to the real world • Can be a source of hypotheses	• Allows little control of extraneous variables • Cannot test treatments • Cannot show cause and effect
Survey research A method, often in the form of a questionnaire, that allows many questions to be asked	• Allows economical collection of much data • Allows for study of many different questions at once	• May have problems of self-reports, such as dishonesty, forgetting, and misrepresentation of self • May involve biased sampling
Correlational study A method for finding a quantitative relationship between variables	• Allows researcher to calculate the strength and direction of relation between variables • Can be used to make predictions	• Does not allow random assignment of participants or much control of subject variables • Cannot test treatments • Cannot show cause and effect
Quasi-experiment A method for comparing treatment conditions without random assignment	• Allows comparison of treatments • Allows some control of extraneous variables	• Does not allow random assignment of participants or much control of subject variables • Cannot show cause and effect
True experiment A method for comparing treatment conditions in which variables can be controlled through random assignment	• Allows true manipulation of treatment conditions • Allows random assignment and much control of extraneous variables • Can show cause and effect	• Cannot manipulate and test certain variables • May control variables and conditions so much that they become artificial and unlike the "real world"

Information from Bensley (2010) and Bensley (1998).

Practice Thinking 4.3: Recognizing Kinds of Scientific Evidence

In the space provided for each of the following examples, first identify the claim and the evidence supporting the argument being made. Then identify the kind of research study used as evidence. Finally, using Table 4.3, think of a possible limitation associated with that kind of evidence.

1. The primatologist Jane Goodall studied the interactions of chimpanzees from the same group with nongroup chimps. She observed that bands of male chimps of the same group would patrol the boundaries of their territories and sometimes gang up on and even kill other chimps that strayed into their territories. This research suggests that male chimpanzees engage in warlike behavior similar to that of human males.

   Claim/evidence: _____

   Kind of study: _____

   Limitation: _____

2. After observing Anna O., both interviewing her and describing her behaviors, Freud argued that her numbness and other symptoms were due to her repressing her sexual feelings and that the conversion of those feelings to physical symptoms was a sort of unconscious defense mechanism.

   Claim/evidence: _____

   Kind of study: _____

   Limitation: _____

3. Make your own argument about some hypothesis in psychology and support it with a type of evidence listed in Table 4.3.

   Claim/evidence: _____

   Kind of study: _____

   Limitation: _____

Practice Thinking 4.4: Analyzing Research for Causal Relations

Your task is to decide whether a conclusion based on the research results is warranted. Evaluate the quality of the evidence on the basis of the results presented and the research methods used. Only if all three criteria for causation are met should you conclude that a causal inference can be drawn from the study. To help you judge the quality of the evidence presented in each example, answer the questions that follow the study description.

An educational psychologist, investigating college students' use of study time, asked students to study the same material over a one-week period and measured the number of breaks each student took. At the end of the week, the students were tested on the material they learned. The psychologist found that the students who took more scheduled breaks also tended to score higher, whereas students who took fewer scheduled breaks tended to have lower test scores.

1. What kind of research method was used?

_____

_____

2. Which criterion/criteria for causation were met?

_____

_____

3. Can the psychologist accurately infer that study breaks cause better learning? Why or why not? (*Hint:* Only true experiments allow causal inferences.)

_____

_____

4. After hearing these results, Joe Student decided to take more study breaks the next time he studied. Is Joe's decision justified, given the evidence presented? Explain your answer.

_____

_____

5. If the psychologist in the study previously described could not accurately infer that study breaks result in better learning, which research method/ design _would_ put him in a better position to infer causation? Explain in detail.

_____

_____

True experiments put us in a better position to identify the causes of behaviors, but the debate does not end there. For instance, as discussed in previous chapters, many true experiments have supported social learning theories of aggression and the hypothesis that observing media violence leads to increases in aggression. Yet some researchers object that the true cause of aggression has not yet been identified because the true experiments conducted thus far do not yet have sufficiently high quality to draw this conclusion (Ferguson, 2015).

It is clear from the preceding discussion that drawing an appropriate conclusion from the research is complicated and that we must be careful not to make various thinking errors. It often requires identifying various types of nonscientific and scientific evidence and evaluating the quality and quantity of the evidence, as well as trying to identify relationships among variables. Only then can we finally draw a conclusion that is consistent with all the relevant evidence. Table 4.4 provides definitions and examples of thinking errors discussed in this chapter. Review these before applying your knowledge in Practice Thinking 4.5.

TABLE 4.4	Summary of Thinking Errors Highlighted	
Error Name	**Description**	**How to Fix or Avoid It**
Illusory correlation	Perceiving a correlation or association between two things when no correlation or association exists	Pay attention to cells B and C in a fourfold table, because people tend to focus mostly on cell A.
Confirmation bias	The tendency to attend to, seek, and give more weight to evidence that supports one's favored position rather than evidence that could disconfirm it	Consider the opposite or an alternate position—look for evidence that could disconfirm one's favored position.
Post hoc ("after this, therefore because of this") reasoning	Concluding after an event occurs that something that happened before it was the actual cause of the event	Don't assume that some action or situation that preceded another event was the actual cause of it; conduct a well-controlled experiment to see whether manipulating the first variable actually causes changes in the second.
Confusing correlation with causation	Believing that a variable that is simply covarying or correlated with another variable is its cause; or, less commonly, failing to infer causation from results of a well-controlled true experiment	Make sure the action or situation thought to be the cause of an event actually occurred first; look for other possible causes and see if they can be eliminated; conduct a true experiment and don't be fooled into thinking that correlations or quasi-experiments can show causation.

Practice Thinking 4.5: Identifying and Fixing Thinking Errors

Identify the kind of thinking errors in the following examples and explain how to fix them.

1. A psychologist found that people who had been physically or sexually abused as children often tended to later become abusers themselves. He concluded that early abuse of a person causes that person to become abusive later.

   a. Thinking error: _____

   b. How to fix it: _____

2. Niki's mother was given a preliminary diagnosis that she had developed cancer. Niki had heard that maintaining a positive attitude could stave off cancer. She encouraged her mother to think positively about beating her cancer. In the next two weeks, Niki's mother said she felt better; when she went back to the doctor, he said he could find no trace of the cancer. Niki was convinced that positive thinking had rid her mother of cancer.

   a. Thinking error: _____

   b. How to fix it: _____

3. As Kevin took his first exam, he looked over each true–false question and thought about how confusing it was for him. A pattern seemed to emerge. He noticed that every time a question confused him, the answer seemed to be false. He was surprised when he got his test back and found that about an equal number of the confusing items were true as were false.

   a. Thinking error: _____

   b. How to fix it: _____

4. Julie was quite sure that her roommate Sarah was depressed. She asked whether Sarah ever felt a lack of energy, and Sarah answered that yes, she did. Another time, Julie asked if Sarah was unhappy with her classes, to which Sarah replied, "Sometimes." At a party with people they did not know, Sarah seemed nervous and anxious. Julie thought to herself, "Well, she lacks energy, is unhappy with her classes, and seems anxious. People who are depressed are often anxious, too. Sarah's depressed for sure."

   a. Thinking error: _____

   b. How to fix it: _____

WHAT IS SCIENTIFIC THINKING?

As we have seen, scientific thinking is complex. We have discussed how scientists use inductive reasoning to generalize from research studies to justify theories, as when Pierre Paul Broca induced that a certain area of the brain regulated speech production from observations of people with brain damage in the left frontal area who had speech-production problems. From theories, scientists deduce hypotheses, such as the prediction that a group of people with damage to Broca's area would have speech-production problems. Then they conduct research to test these hypotheses. If a prediction is confirmed, it lends inductive support to the theory; if it is not confirmed, then support for the theory is weakened. Although this description captures some of the scientific method that scientists use to develop their ideas, it does not address how they come up with those ideas nor how they think about specific problems. The following discussion introduces some of these issues, but the online supplement to this chapter goes into greater detail.

Taking a different approach, researchers in cognitive psychology have studied scientific thinking as a kind of problem solving (Dunbar & Fugelsang, 2005; Klahr, Matlen, & Jirout, 2013; Newell & Simon, 1972). Suppose you are striving to reach some goal but do not know how to get from your current state to the goal state—here you have a **problem**. For example, you are interested in meeting someone in your class, but you don't know how to meet this person without being too obvious. This presents a problem because you lack the knowledge and strategy to progress from your initial state to the goal of being introduced.

Likewise, scientists are problem solvers who start out not knowing how to achieve the goal state of solving some scientific problem. For instance, they may want to test a new hypothesis but lack the right method, equipment, or other resources to test it effectively. To solve a problem, scientists go through several stages: First, they must identify or find the problem; next, they must represent or understand the problem in order to generate a strategy that might lead to a solution; then they can apply the strategy to the problem and monitor whether they have solved it. It should therefore seem clear to you that scientific problem solving is closely related to CT because scientists reason about the quality of the information they have and the problem-solving strategies they use. They select and apply the best strategy that is practically available to them and then engage in metacognitive monitoring to evaluate their progress toward a solution (Willingham, 2007).

Often, scientific problem solving also involves **creative thinking**, which requires a scientist to think about the problem in new and useful ways. To solve difficult problems and questions, scientists must propose new hypotheses, invent new tools, and develop new ways to conduct their research. For example, the discovery of the double-stranded structure of DNA by James Watson and Francis Crick in 1953 required the development of new X-ray crystallography equipment; subsequent experiments by Maurice Wilkins and Rosalind Franklin made use of that new equipment. It involved evaluating and interpreting the data to decide whether they best fit a two-stranded or three-stranded DNA molecule. This, in turn, required Wilkins and Franklin to represent the possibilities using different models, to weigh the evidence for each, and then to evaluate all the information to draw the best conclusion (Weisberg, 2006). Thus, creative scientific thinking is like problem solving, but it also resembles CT in a general way (Willingham, 2007).

SUMMARY

In their study of the natural world, psychologists and other scientists seek to identify relationships between variables. These relationships are either associations or causal relationships. In associations (correlations), two variables simply change together in a consistent way. People seem to have a natural tendency to seek and find relationships. Unfortunately, they often find relationships that aren't really there, demonstrating the thinking error of illusory correlation.

This occurs because they pay attention to the co-occurrences of two variables, such as observing when the moon is full and people behave abnormally but not systematically observing when the moon is full and people are *not* behaving abnormally—or, conversely, disregarding abnormal behavior when the moon is *not* full. Once someone accepts this illusory correlation, he or she may only look for evidence to support his or her belief or to minimize the evidence that does not support it, demonstrating the thinking error of confirmation bias. In contrast, scientists who calculate correlations, conduct experiments, and review other people's research take into account negative evidence that does not support a relationship. In this way, science becomes self-correcting, allowing researchers to discover which relationships do *not* exist—a valuable and informative practice that allows them to correct misconceptions.

A causal relationship is harder to show than an association. In causal relationships, one variable—the cause—must occur before a second variable—the effect—and must lead to consistent changes in that second variable. Showing causation also requires eliminating any third or other variable that could account for the resulting changes. Only one research design, the true experiment, puts the researcher in a position to show cause and effect. To produce time order, the experimenter manipulates an independent variable (the cause) so that it precedes a dependent variable (the effect). She uses probability and statistics to determine whether the values of the two variables are co-varying, that is, if they change together consistently. To eliminate plausible alternative explanations (third or extraneous variables that could affect the dependent variable), she uses control procedures, such as random assignment of participants to treatment groups.

The degree to which different research methods can show causation is important to the quality of the evidence each can provide. For example, case studies, survey research, correlational studies, and field studies simply measure variables without any manipulation of them and so cannot show time order. Although quasi-experiments resemble true experiments, they—like the other nonexperimental methods—do not use random assignment to treatment groups and show less control over extraneous variables. Because only the true experiment meets the criteria for showing causation, it provides the strongest evidence. Failing to realize this, people often mistakenly infer causation when only a correlation exists, or they mistakenly assume that a variable (action or situation) that simply occurs prior to a second variable (event) actually caused the change in the second event (the post hoc fallacy).

In addition to the quality of evidence provided, the quantity of evidence affects the strength of an inductive argument. For instance, a case study is conducted on only one or a few people and so provides little in the way of quantitative support. In general, the larger the sample, the stronger the support a study can offer. Likewise, a theory is more strongly supported when many studies support it rather than fewer; however, quality trumps quantity. A poorly executed study with a large sample offers weak support.

Scientific thinking involves the use of inductive reasoning to generalize from research evidence to justify hypotheses and theories, and then deducing predictions from those theories to test. But it involves other kinds of thinking, too—such as problem solving and creative thinking, both of which resemble CT in important ways.

 Practice Thinking 4.6: WHAT DO YOU THINK **NOW**?
Please explain how you know.

1. When people join a cult, do they accept all the cult's beliefs and lose their ability to think critically? How could you find out?

2. Does observing aggressive behaviors in movies, TV, or video games cause a person to behave aggressively? How could you find out?

3. Does having been sexually abused as a child lead to personality problems as an adult and cause the victim to later become a sexual abuser?

4. Can science answer all questions? Why or why not?

REVIEW QUESTIONS

1. What are some differences between scientific and nonscientific sources of evidence?

2. What is science? What are its advantages as an approach to knowledge?

3. What are the three criteria for causation?
   - Why does the example of Lee Fried's presumed precognition not demonstrate causation?
   - How is the quality of scientific evidence related to causality?

4. Compare and contrast common research methods with respect to their strengths and weaknesses, especially with regard to showing causation.
   - What is survey research? What are its strengths and weaknesses?
   - What is a field study? What are its strengths and weaknesses?
   - What is correlation? What are its strengths and weaknesses?
   - What is a true experiment? What are its strengths and weaknesses?
   - What is a quasi-experiment? What are its strengths and weaknesses?
   - Can you identify independent, dependent, and extraneous variables?
   - What are confounding variables and how do they relate to internal validity?
   - Can you evaluate a research study to determine whether it allows for a causal inference?

5. What thinking errors are featured in this chapter?
   - What is an example of each?
   - How do you correct or counter each one?

6. What is scientific thinking? Is it just induction and deduction?
   - How does scientific thinking involve problem solving and creative thinking?
   - How is CT related to scientific thinking? To scientific problem solving? To scientific creativity?

7. What psychological misconceptions are featured in this chapter? Explain why each is a misconception.

5

PSEUDOSCIENCE, SCIENCE, AND EVIDENCE-BASED PRACTICE

LEARNING OUTCOMES

After studying this chapter, you should be able to:

1. Explain why it is important to recognize examples of pseudoscience.

2. Distinguish examples of pseudoscience from true science.

3. Distinguish poorly supported psychological treatments and practices from evidence-based ones.

WHAT DO YOU THINK?

Each year, millions of people with psychological problems seek professional help. Some want to improve themselves, others want to be happier, or still others just want to be better adjusted. In an attempt to achieve these goals, they read self-help books, undergo psychotherapy, or try chemical treatments.

People have spent millions of dollars on magnets that are advertised to reduce pain, restore balance, and enhance performance. They buy nutritional supplements to improve memory. Many take massive amounts of vitamin C to prevent colds and even cure cancer.

Do these treatments work? Are some of them pseudoscience? Could some treatments actually harm a person? How do you know?

Practice Thinking 5.1: What Do You Think?

Please explain how you know.

1. What is pseudoscience, and why study it?

   _____

2. Are some psychotherapies dangerous?

   _____

3. Are some therapies more effective than others? If so, which ones? How do you know?

   _____

4. Do self-help books and programs really help?

   _____

5. Can nutritional supplements improve your memory or cure psychological problems?

   _____

In 2000, 10-year-old Candace Newmaker was having trouble adjusting to her new life with her adoptive mother, Jeanne Newmaker. Nothing seemed to help the mother and daughter bond. Upon referral from a psychologist, Jeanne took Candace to Colorado for a $7,000, 2-week intensive program of attachment therapy. Candace's problem had been diagnosed as a failure to attach to her adoptive mother. Candace was referred to two other therapists (see Figure 5.1), who treated her with a rebirthing procedure that was supposed to help her become more closely attached to Jeanne. The girl was wrapped tightly in a blanket while four adults held her as she tried to wriggle her way through a crude model of the birth canal. She could not get through. Although Candace vomited, urinated, and cried out that she could not breathe, the therapists told her she was simply being weak and should try harder. After more than an hour of this "treatment," Candace suffocated from the ordeal (Lilienfeld, Fowler, Lohr, & Lynn, 2005).

AP Photo/Ed Andrieski

FIGURE 5.1 Unlicensed social workers Julie Ponder and Connell Watkins (center), who treated Candace Newmaker with a dangerous "rebirthing" therapy. They were convicted of reckless child abuse that resulted in Candace's death.

WHY LEARNING ABOUT PSEUDOSCIENCE IS IMPORTANT

It seems implausible that having Candace go through a simulation of the birthing process would help her bond more closely with her new mother. The assumption behind this program was that going through something that *looks like* the birthing process actually helps the person become properly attached, much as a child becomes normally attached to a parent following birth. This turns out to be an unwarranted assumption. It also illustrates inappropriate reasoning by the **representativeness heuristic**, a thinking error in which people assume that "like goes with like"—that is, a person will be cured by a treatment that looks like the problem (Gilovich & Savitsky, 1996; Kahneman & Tversky, 1972).

Clearly, Candace's therapists made thinking errors that had dire consequences for everyone involved in the process. Furthermore, the therapy they used seems to be pseudoscientific. **Pseudoscience** has been defined as "claims presented so that they appear scientific even though they lack support or plausibility" (Shermer, 1997, p. 33). Attachment therapy fits this definition because it is implausible that a 10-year-old child going through a superficial simulation of the birthing process would experience what a newborn experiences. Nothing in science would lead us to believe that this procedure would promote a new attachment. More importantly, it is pseudoscientific because therapists maintain that it works, despite the fact that no high-quality research has shown attachment therapy to be effective (Mercer, 2014).

The unfortunate case of Candace Newmaker raises serious ethical issues about pseudoscientific practices. One concern is that Candace's therapists used a treatment that was not likely to be effective. An even greater ethical concern is that such practices may cause harm or even death (Lilienfeld, 2007). The ethical guidelines developed by the American Psychological Association (2002) make it clear that psychologists should both do no harm and use effective treatments. Candace's therapists followed neither of these guidelines. Indeed, the emergence of several types of new therapies in recent years has raised ethical concerns among psychological scientists and practitioners that some of these new therapies may be ineffective or even pseudoscientific (Lilienfeld, 1998; Lilienfeld et al., 2005).

The definition of pseudoscience seems straightforward enough, but finding criteria that infallibly distinguish pseudoscientific theories and practices from scientific ones has proved difficult (Bensley, 2002; Pigliucci & Boudry, 2013). Often, the boundaries between science and pseudoscience are fuzzy (Shermer, 2001) and their differences are simply a matter of degree (Lilienfeld, 2007). Accordingly, we should proceed with caution, keep an open mind, and reason carefully when deciding whether the current status of a field indicates it is a pseudoscience.

Other good reasons exist to study the differences between pseudoscience and science. First, attempting to make such distinctions can be useful in learning to think about science in general and psychological practices in particular (Herbert, 2003). In many ways, pseudoscience results from *not* following the rules, methods, and practices that science and critical thinking (CT) prescribe (Kalal, 1999). Consequently, studying pseudoscience should help you better understand the advantages of taking a scientific and CT approach to the study and practice of psychology.

Second, studying pseudoscience in relation to science and evidence-based practices should help you protect yourself and others from potentially dangerous practices, guiding you toward more effective, safer ones. This guidance is needed because a study by Bensley, Lilienfeld, and Powell (2014) found that psychology students' stronger endorsement of a more intuitive thinking style (Type 1 thinking) and their weaker endorsement of CT dispositions (Type 2 thinking) was linked to endorsement of more psychological misconceptions and less ability to distinguish poorly supported and pseudoscientific practices from more scientifically supported ones.

Third, pseudoscience is found all over the world (Sagan, 1996) and popular interest in pseudoscience and poorly supported practices remains strong (Lilienfeld, Lynn, & Lohr, 2015). Using the number of Internet sites as an indicator of attention paid to a therapy, Olatunji, Parker, and Lohr (2005) found that the number of web hits for rebirthing/attachment therapy was 4,900 times the number of citations for it on PsycINFO, the major database indexing psychological research articles. The fact that the general public seems to pay much more attention to this pseudoscience than do those working in psychology raises questions about the scientific and psychological literacy of the general public.

Perhaps more or better science education is needed to address this discrepancy—yet belief in pseudoscientific ideas does not seem to decrease much as a result of students' taking ordinary psychology and science courses (e.g., Johnson & Pigiliucci, 2004; Walker, Hoekstra, & Vogl, 2002). One national study conducted in the United States found that although adults with more science education tend to accept astrology less, those adults also tend to accept UFOology more (Losh, Tavani, Njoroge, Wilke, & McAuley, 2003). UFOology is a pseudoscience maintaining the scientifically implausible claim that aliens travel many light years in spacecraft to visit Earth. Ideally, a critical examination of where pseudoscientific ideas came from and how to think about them would reduce belief in those ideas.

A BRIEF HISTORY OF PSEUDOSCIENCE AND SCIENCE

Astrology is the oldest example of a pseudoscience that is still practiced today. Originating in Babylonia at least 3,000 years ago, it appeared in similar forms among the ancient Greeks, Romans, and Egyptians. As people looked up in the night sky, they found patterns in the positions of the stars and planets—patterns that they associated with the myths of their culture. Do you see a pattern in the dots depicting stars in Figure 5.2 (on the next page)?

People are good at finding patterns in ambiguous and random displays, even when those patterns do not really exist—a phenomenon termed *visual pareidolia*. If you found a pattern in Figure 5.2, for example, it was probably different from the pattern found by the ancient Romans and Greeks. They saw Libra, the constellation corresponding to the scales of justice (see Figure 5.3), which was part of their mythology.

FIGURE 5.2 A star map containing a constellation in the dots. Do you see a pattern? Use your imagination.

FIGURE 5.3 Libra, the scales of justice, a pattern that many Romans saw in the stars depicted in Figure 5.2.

Astrologers use the zodiac, a system in which sets of traits correspond to patterns of stars. The zodiac includes 12 different "signs" (i.e., group of traits linked to a particular constellation), each one exemplified by an object, person, or story from traditional myths. For example, a person born between September 23 and October 22 has the sign of Libra, with traits corresponding to the pattern of stars found in the constellation Libra, represented by the scales of justice held by Themis. In Greek mythology, Themis was a Titaness who helped establish the laws of proper conduct and was a counselor to Zeus. Consistent with this idea, Libras are often said to be balanced, intelligent, diplomatic, and polite but also gullible and indecisive (i.e., not good critical thinkers).

The astrologer's use of precise and complicated calculations based on observation of the stars and planets, and the fact that the word *astrology* ends in *-ology,* may make astrology appear to be a true science. Yet it is not. The astrologer's complex calculations are useless because they are based on the incorrect assumption that patterns in the stars and planets at the time of someone's birth determine that person's traits and future. *Astronomy,* a true science, tells us that the constellations are simply random groups of stars, regardless of the fact that 2,000 to 3,000 years ago (many centuries before modern science developed), ancient Greeks and Romans, steeped in the mythology of their cultures, saw what appeared to be animals, people, and objects in those stars. In 1975, 192 of the world's leading astronomers and other scientists, including 19 Nobel laureates, signed a proclamation stating that the claims of astrology have no scientific basis (Bok, 1975). Although the collective opinion of many notable scientists is certainly persuasive, we should make our own decision as to the scientific status of astrology.

TABLE 5.1	**Distinguishing Pseudoscience From Science**

In contrast to scientists, those who practice pseudoscience tend to:

1. Make predictions that are vague, untestable, and not falsifiable.

2. Not systematically check outcomes of predictions, paying more attention to evidence that supports predictions and ignoring negative evidence (confirmation bias). As a result, pseudoscientific theory changes little, and pseudoscience is not self-correcting.

3. Incorrectly use general rules of reasoning to evaluate claims and hypotheses. For example:

   a. Reverse the burden of proof and argue from possibility.

   b. Ignore the rule that theories and hypotheses must be consistent with data.

4. Not use accepted standards of evidence, methods, techniques, and terminology from related scientific fields (i.e., they lack connectedness with other scientific fields):

   a. Make implausible claims (not likely to be true, given what is known in science).

   b. Use low-quality evidence (e.g., anecdotes, testimonials, and statements of authority), rather than high-quality evidence (e.g., true experiments).

   c. Use obscure terminology (not conventionally used in science).

Table 5.1 shows a set of guidelines that can help us distinguish a pseudoscience, such as astrology, from a true science, such as astronomy. Table 5.1 lists a set of characteristics that pseudosciences tend to have. When a field shows more of the characteristics in Table 5.1, it is more likely to be pseudoscientific than truly scientific.

Practice Thinking 5.2: Using Criteria to Decide Whether Astrology Is a Pseudoscience

In the space provided, write the characteristic of pseudoscience from Table 5.1 that goes with each of the following statements about astrology.

1. The traits that astrologers describe seem unreasonable given what is known about personality traits identified by psychological research.

2. Astrologers use tables of the positions of the stars and planets at the time of a person's birth, rather than valid and reliable personality inventories, to make predictions about a person's traits and behaviors.

_____

3. The predictions and trait descriptions used in astrology horoscopes are very general, so people find that the horoscopes seem to describe them well, especially when stated in positive terms (Glick, Gottesman, & Jolton, 1989).

_____

4. Astrology has not changed its fundamental ideas in thousands of years, despite the fact that many studies have failed to support it, such as studies showing that astrological signs and readings do not predict the occupation that a person with a particular sign will have (Tyson, 2001).

_____

Unlike scientists who make specific predictions, astrologers make general predictions and identify traits that people are likely to endorse—for example, "Being a Libra, you are usually diplomatic but sometimes appear to be indecisive in your efforts to maintain harmony." Although scientists, like astrologers, do sometimes make predictions from incorrect premises, scientists systematically check the outcomes of their predictions, whereas astrologers do not. If scientists find their predictions are in error, they will eventually reject the theory or change it to be consistent with their observations. Thus, science is a dynamic approach to knowledge that is self-correcting through continuous updating of its theories.

In contrast, astrology has remained mostly unchanged for centuries despite evidence that its predictions are usually wrong. Although no good scientific evidence supports astrology (Kelly, 1997), astrologers ignore these findings and tolerate inconsistencies between observation and theory. Instead of citing evidence obtained through the scientific process, they find support from personal experiences, the authority of astrologers, and other low-quality evidence. Astrology lacks connectedness with related fields owing to its failure to use successful measures and theories of personality and the instruments and theories of modern astronomy; instead, astrologers make scientifically implausible claims and do not link those claims to established science.

Despite their weaknesses, pseudosciences have sometimes contributed to the development of true sciences. For example, over the centuries, astrologers made careful observations of the stars and planets, providing reliable data that astronomers later used to predict planetary movement. As the scientific approach developed, some scientists actually practiced astrology; even the astronomer Johannes Kepler (1571–1630), who discovered the laws of planetary motion, was forced to cast horoscopes for the wealthy and powerful to support his family, even though he doubted the validity of astrology.

Although the scientific revolution was well underway in the seventeenth century, superstition and pseudoscience lingered on (Wootton, 2016). Even the great physicist Sir Isaac Newton (1643–1727), despite his fundamental scientific discoveries about gravity and other forms of energy, was a serious student of alchemy. The alchemists tried to produce a mythical substance called the *philosopher's stone* that they thought could transmute substances into gold, prolong life, and heal the body. Although alchemy now seems implausible and pseudoscientific, the alchemists contributed to the development of chemistry, a true science, through their careful study of chemicals and substances. Because astrology and alchemy existed long before the development of astronomy and chemistry, they might be better viewed as "proto-sciences," or prescientific fields that contributed to the development of true science.

The eighteenth century spawned another pseudoscience called mesmerism, named after its developer, Franz Anton Mesmer (1743–1850), a Viennese physician and student of astrology. Mesmer's technique for influencing people's behaviors and experiences resembles the modern technique of hypnosis. After a slow start in Vienna, Mesmer moved to Paris, where his technique became popular among the French aristocracy. Dressed in flowing purple robes, Mesmer would ask people to place parts of their bodies, such as their legs, in a large bath as he swirled the water around and gave them suggestions such as "Your leg is relaxed or numb." Sometimes people experienced strange feelings, felt relief from pains, or fainted. Mesmer explained this outcome as being due to his magnetizing the water and changing the flow of animal magnetism in a person.

Marie Antoinette, the wife of King Louis XVI, and many other Parisian aristocrats went to see Mesmer. To investigate mesmerism, the king commissioned a committee of esteemed scientists led by the great scientist and inventor Benjamin Franklin, who was serving as ambassador to France at the time (Leahey & Leahey, 1983). The committee also included Dr. Joseph Guillotin, inventor of the guillotine, and the great chemist Antoine Lavoisier, who was later beheaded by Guillotin's machine—as were the king and queen during the French Revolution.

In the best traditions of science, the committee conducted a systematic study of mesmerism. They tried it themselves and experienced no effects. They tested the water for the flow of electricity and found none. They also conducted several experiments on animal magnetism—medical experiments that are thought to have employed the first placebo controls (Best, Neuhauser, & Slavin, 2003). A **placebo** control involves administering a fake treatment, such as a sugar pill, to create the expectation that the person is receiving an active treatment. People who receive placebos often show improvement and relief of their symptoms even though they did not receive the active treatment that was expected to produce these effects (Beecher, 1955; Brown, 2013). A placebo serves as a control that allows the experimenter to test the effects of expectation. The mesmerism committee's placebo treatment involved telling one subject that she was to drink water that had been magnetized by the mesmerist when, in fact, the water had not been magnetized. She immediately fainted in response to drinking the water. Upon recovery, she was given water that *had* been magnetized, but the committee did not tell her so. When she drank it, she did not faint.

The committee also tested other subjects who were blind to their testing condition—that is, they were not told which treatment they had received. As a consequence, subjects were unable to detect which objects had been magnetized. Consistent with current research on hypnosis, the committee concluded that the effects of mesmerism were due to a combination of the expectations created by suggestions of the mesmerist and the imagination of the "mesmerized" subject. As we now know, hypnosis is not a trance or special state of consciousness distinct from ordinary consciousness, contrary to the popular psychological misconception (Lilienfeld et al., 2010).

By the nineteenth century, science had become firmly established as a useful approach to study the natural world, with its contributions including the discovery of the atom, the development of the periodic table of elements, and Darwin's theory of evolution. At the same time, new pseudosciences continued to develop as well. In the early 1800s, as the new science of psychology was developing, the anatomists Franz Joseph Gall (1758–1828) and Johann Spurzheim (1776–1832) developed the pseudoscience of phrenology. **Phrenology** posited that bumps and indentations on a person's skull indicate the specific characteristics and abilities of the person.

Gall developed the idea for phrenology when he reflected on his observation of a childhood schoolmate who had both a good verbal memory and protruding eyes (Leahey & Leahey, 1983). Gall began his exploration of phrenology with the working assumption that the structures in the brain underlying its faculties could be revealed in the surface features of the skull. Phrenology evolved into a pseudoscientific movement after Spurzheim and other phrenologists began taking a philosophical approach to the brain's faculties. Specifically, they added and subdivided faculties based on few or no actual observations. Figure 5.4 shows a

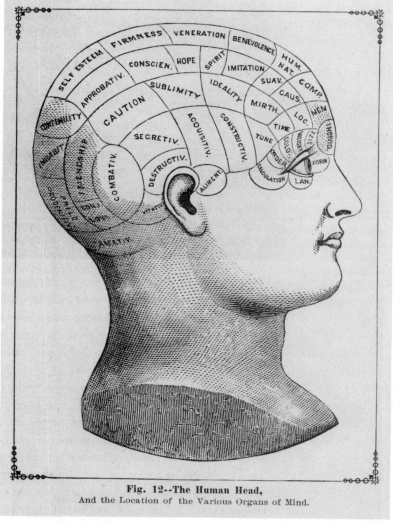

Fig. 12--The Human Head,
And the Location of the Various Organs of Mind.

FIGURE 5.4 A phrenological diagram illustrating many unsubstantiated characteristics.

phrenological map of the skull divided into many areas, each associated with a specific characteristic.

Phrenologists used the sophisticated-looking equipment shown in Figure 5.5 to measure the bumps and indentations on a person's skull, which made phrenology appear to be scientific. From the observations and information they collected about a person, they associated specific bumps and indentations with traits, such as

Topical Press Agency/Hulton Archive/Getty Images

FIGURE 5.5 This phrenological apparatus looks scientific—but is it?

benevolence and self-esteem. Although the equipment in Figure 5.5 looks sophisticated, the idea that relatively small bumps and indentations on the surface of the skull have anything to do with the contour of the brain underneath is implausible.

The brain is a gelatinous mass, and the skull need not have bumps or indentations to accommodate the rather small and specific brain areas that the phrenologists assumed corresponded to particular traits. In fact, the inside surface of the skull is relatively smooth and rounded. These facts were known, but apparently ignored, when phrenology began. From the perspective of current psychological science, phrenology was a complex theory with many untested assumptions. Psychology was in its preliminary stages as a scientific discipline in the nineteenth century and had no comprehensive, scientifically based theory of personality. Nevertheless, phrenologists proposed many traits, such as cautiousness and secretiveness, without scientifically establishing the existence of those traits.

Another reason phrenology was a pseudoscience is that phrenologists did not make systematic observations to develop a theory that could reliably predict a person's characteristics. Rather, they often found bumps and indentations *after* they thought they knew the traits of a person. In other cases, Spurzheim proposed many different traits corresponding to bumps and indentations without making any observations at all. Because the phrenologists did not test the predictions of their theory, they did not discover that it had no predictive power.

A story is told of how the great nineteenth-century physiologist François Magendie tested Spurzheim's use of phrenological theory to make predictions (Kolb & Whishaw, 1990). Magendie invited Spurzheim to his home to examine the preserved brain of the brilliant French philosopher and mathematician Pierre Laplace. Unbeknownst to Spurzheim, Magendie had replaced Laplace's brain with that of an intellectually challenged man. Spurzheim admired the substituted brain as if it had belonged to the brilliant Laplace. The fact that the leading phrenologist of the time could not use phrenology to accurately predict the traits of such a person raises serious doubts about phrenology's status as a scientific theory. Despite lacking a good scientific basis, phrenology became immensely popular in the United States, where post–Civil War Americans were attracted to moral and personal improvement techniques and had little knowledge of true science (Thurs, 2007).

Interest in the paranormal also increased in the latter part of the nineteenth century, leading to the development of *parapsychology* in the twentieth century, a new field with the stated goal of scientifically studying paranormal phenomena. The **paranormal** is often defined as any phenomenon that is beyond ordinary experience and cannot be explained by conventional science. For example, extrasensory perception (ESP), or the transmission of information without any use of the senses, is a paranormal event. But is parapsychology scientific?

Science is a very careful, deliberate, and conservative approach to knowledge. As such, it does not propose complex, untested ideas to explain phenomena that may have simpler and more empirically justified explanations. In contrast, practitioners of pseudoscience often propose ideas when simpler explanations are available that are based on what is already known. For instance, parapsychologists use psychic ability to explain incidents in which a person seems to know something that he or she would not ordinarily be expected to know. In many cases, the simpler, more plausible explanation of psychic feats is that the person is secretly receiving information from someone else or just making a lucky guess. These explanations are well documented, whereas nonphysical psychic abilities such as ESP have not been clearly demonstrated.

DISTINGUISHING MODERN EXAMPLES OF PSEUDOSCIENCE FROM SCIENCE

Pseudoscience merely appears to be a science; it lacks the characteristics that make a field or approach truly scientific. People who practice pseudoscience seem to just go through the motions of scientific practice. To illustrate this imitation of real science, the Nobel prize–winning physicist Richard Feynman compared pseudoscience with the beliefs and practices of islanders in the South Seas. During World War II, the scientifically uneducated natives saw wonderful goods arriving from the sky and assumed their technologically advanced visitors (i.e., supply planes) were benevolent gods. The natives thus engaged in rituals to recreate the situation: They imitated construction of runways, complete with setting fires alongside the simulated runways. They also built huts in which a man would sit while wearing two wooden pieces on his head to imitate radio headphones; they even stuck bamboo poles out of the hut to imitate radio antennae. The natives then waited for the next delivery of the gods' wonderful cargo—but, unsurprisingly, the planes never came. Although the natives went through the motions of the air delivery of cargo, their rituals did not capture the real practice of science and technology. In the same way, people who practice pseudoscience mimic the conduct of science, engaging in "cargo cult science" (Feynman, 1985).

We can apply the concepts outlined in Table 5.1 to analyze parapsychology and psychic predictions to determine whether parapsychology is a pseudoscience that merely goes through the motions of practicing real science. This analysis suggests that parapsychology meets several of the criteria for classification as a pseudoscience. Psychics who supposedly have precognition and the parapsychologists who study them often do not make specific, testable, and falsifiable predictions. Rather, psychics often make very general predictions about the future that are difficult to refute. If a parapsychologist can interpret a variety of outcomes as supporting a psychic's prediction, then the predictions are not falsifiable.

A good example of how parapsychologists are reluctant to develop hypotheses that can be tested and potentially shown to be false can be found in a book by Rogo and Bayless (1979), in which they claim to have discovered that many people receive phone calls from the dead. It is extremely difficult to determine whether such calls really came from spirits, however, because the calls are unpredictable and brief. When observations cannot be made that address a question, it is not a testable, scientific hypothesis. The implausible claim that spirits can make phone calls (when they do not have physical hands to dial) is not testable. More "earthly" alternative explanations should be considered, such as that some confused person mistakenly made the call and then hung up.

Another reason why parapsychology seems to be pseudoscientific is the tendency of parapsychologists to make excuses for negative findings. For instance, some parapsychologists have argued that certain ESP experiments have failed to produce evidence for the existence of ESP because the skeptical scientists running the experiments created "negative vibrations" as they made their observations. This phenomenon purportedly disturbs the subtle and fragile effects of ESP, preventing the observation of ESP as long as the skeptical observer is present. This special pleading makes the ESP hypothesis unfalsifiable because a failure to find evidence for ESP is interpreted not as disconfirming evidence for ESP, but as interference from the act of scientifically studying it. In explaining away unwanted results, parapsychologists demonstrate the thinking error of inappropriate post hoc reasoning (see Chapter 4), making their hypotheses impossible to test and, therefore, impossible to prove false.

Like astrologers, psychics who predict the future often do not keep track of all the times their predictions do not come true. Rather, they tend to emphasize successful predictions and ignore unsuccessful ones, showing a strong bias toward confirmation of their predictions. Similarly, parapsychologists sometimes interpret their data using a confirmatory strategy called *psi missing,* in which a long string of incorrect (random) guesses is interpreted as too improbable to be anything but evidence that psi (the ability underlying ESP) is operating. In contrast, scientists take seriously the results of experiments that do not turn out as predicted.

After decades of research, ESP has still not been reliably demonstrated. A meta-analysis by Milton and Wiseman (1999) of 30 well-conducted studies found that participants performed at approximately chance levels on ESP tasks. ESP seems to be unreliable and has, at best, a very minimal effect if it exists at all. Despite the many anecdotes and personal experiences offered to support it, well-controlled scientific experiments do not support psychic prediction. In this regard, comedian Jay Leno has asked, "How come you never see the headline, 'Psychic Wins Lottery'?" Nevertheless, believers in parapsychology continue to maintain that ESP and psi exist even though hard evidence to support them is lacking—a hallmark of pseudoscience (Bunge, 1984).

Practice Thinking 5.3: Providing Reasons Why a Field Is a Pseudoscience

For each of the following, list two reasons why the example may be classified as a pseudoscience.

Mesmerism

Reason 1: _____

Reason 2: _____

Phrenology

Reason 1: _____

Reason 2: _____

Parapsychology

Reason 1: _____

Reason 2: _____

THE DEVELOPMENT OF EVIDENCE-BASED TREATMENTS

The history of the treatment of mental disorders has been a mixture of prescientific, pseudoscientific, and even scary practices that have sometimes led to the more recent development of treatments that really work. For centuries, and in some places even today, people have used various techniques to cast out evil spirits believed to cause strange and unacceptable behaviors in "possessed" people. Psychologists would now regard many of these unfortunate people as having suffered from mental disorders. Sometimes an effective technique, such as electroconvulsive shock therapy (ECT), may have developed from earlier efforts to shock some evil entity out of a person. ECT, which to some might seem barbaric, has been refined so that nowadays the patient is unconscious during treatment to minimize the distress. Clinical researchers have found ECT to be an effective treatment for depression that is resistant to other therapies (Pagnin, de Queroz, Pini, & Cassano, 2004). In contrast, other treatments—such as the psychosurgery practiced in the 1940s, in which an ice pick was inserted through the nose to destroy frontal areas of the brain in an effort to control aggression—have been discarded because they were found to be ineffective.

These examples raise the important question of how we find out which treatments really help people with psychological problems and which treatments are ineffective or might even be harmful. This concern reflects an increasing commitment among many psychologists to **evidence-based treatments (EBTs)**—that is, treatments for psychological problems whose effectiveness is validated through high-quality scientific research. Paralleling this emphasis on EBTs is the concern that some psychotherapists use treatments that have no scientifically demonstrated effectiveness and that might be pseudoscientific. To better understand the development of this emphasis, it is useful to briefly review the history of the movement toward EBTs in psychology and psychiatry.

In a review tracing the evolution of EBTs, Gordon Paul (2007) began with what he called the "prescientific era" in psychology, which lasted until the 1920s. During this time, different schools of psychology had their own approaches and made little effort to empirically examine the effectiveness of the treatments they advocated. The movement toward EBTs partly coincides with the development of **behavior therapy** and its many spinoffs, which borrowed heavily from learning theory and the behaviorist approach while testing treatments scientifically.

In 1924, Mary Cover Jones, a student of J. B. Watson, applied the behaviorist learning theory approach to help Peter, a young boy with a phobia (irrational fear) of rabbits. She first allowed Peter to observe other children playing with a rabbit without any negative effects. Then she exposed Peter to the rabbit when he was not showing fear. Over time, Peter was able to move closer and closer to the rabbit without showing fear. Later, Joseph Wolpe (1958) developed a behavior therapy called *systematic desensitization,* combining elements of Jones's treatment with a relaxation technique that Edmond Jacobsen (1935) had shown to be effective in reducing anxiety. In systematic desensitization, a phobic person learns to move closer to a feared object or engage in a feared activity while being helped to relax. The behaviorists' early attempts to test the outcomes of treatments based on learning-theory principles were important to the scientific study of psychotherapy, but those early studies were often case studies and simple demonstrations.

After World War II, many clinicians, who had previously been trained in research but got involved in clinical and applied work during the war, became increasingly concerned about the best way to train their new students for clinical practice (Paul, 2007). This concern eventually led to an important conference in Boulder, Colorado, in 1950 that addressed graduate education in clinical psychology (Raimy, 1950). Out of this conference came the "Boulder Model," also known as the *scientist–practitioner model,* which proposes that graduate programs in clinical psychology should train psychotherapists to become both research scientists and practitioners.

Increasing attention to the scientific study of psychotherapy was followed by yet more conferences focused on the scientific basis of psychotherapy, but some clinicians continued to resist the idea that psychotherapy could be studied scientifically. Much debate centered on the "criterion problem," or how to determine what makes one outcome of psychotherapy better than another. Recall that critical thinkers seek to carefully define their terms and are often concerned with the criteria, standards, and conditions that must be met for a statement to be considered true. Increasingly, psychologists came to agree that demonstrating the effectiveness of psychotherapy would require careful use of scientific research methods like those applied in other parts of psychological science. In turn, clinical researchers needed to carefully design experiments that would allow them to unambiguously interpret the results of manipulating independent variables, such as the comparison of various treatments.

An important push in this direction came in the 1960s and 1970s, from clinical research that focused on behavior therapies. After conducting many studies, researchers discovered that cognitive versions of some therapies were effective as well. For example, covert desensitization, in which a phobic person simply imagines moving closer to the feared object, also helped some patients overcome their phobias. Recall from Chapter 1 that Bandura's social learning theory assumes that observing someone engaging in a behavior makes it more likely the observer will also engage in the behavior (especially if doing so was reinforced). This is likely a reason why Mary Cover Jones was successful in treating Peter— because Peter saw the other children playing with a rabbit without suffering any dire consequences and was subsequently able to imitate their behavior.

Still other types of cognitive behavior therapies were developed that could effectively treat depression. This led to refinements of the original behavioral learning theory, called *cognitive theories* of depression, and more generally to treatments called *cognitive behavior therapy* (Beck, 1963). Although the theory of how cognitive behavior therapy works still lags behind the therapeutic technology, scientific research has made some progress in this area, improving the theory's predictive and explanatory power (Beck, 2005). This lag of theory behind practice is common in the history of science. Researchers have discovered many effective treatments before formulating a theory as to *why* a particular treatment was effective. For instance, certain presurgical sedatives were observed to also help reduce psychosis in patients with schizophrenia—that is, to ease these patients' severe symptoms that reveal a disconnection from conventional reality. Subsequently, scientists began the careful, systematic study of the biochemical causes of schizophrenia that would explain *why* these drugs worked. This line of research ultimately led to the hypothesis that antipsychotic drugs block high levels of the neurotransmitter dopamine at certain receptor sites in the brain.

For many clinical researchers, the **efficacy** of a specific treatment came to mean how well people functioned after receiving that treatment when compared with other treatments for the same problem under well-controlled testing conditions. Specifically, the gold standard of efficacy research has become the **randomized-trial experiment** (Gaudiano, Dalrymple, Weinstock, & Lohr, 2015). In such studies, experimenters randomly assign clients with a certain psychological disorder to one of two groups: One group undergoes a specific treatment, while the other serves as a control group whose members either wait for treatment or receive some mock or alternative treatment. In this way, the effectiveness of treatments can be compared under controlled conditions, thereby reducing the chance that some extraneous variable might confound the results (see Chapter 4).

Clinical researchers use several strategies to control expectations and other potentially confounding variables to determine how effective a treatment actually is. For example, placebo groups are used to control for expectations created by the appearance of getting an effective treatment. In such a study, the experimental group receives the real treatment or therapy, and the placebo control group, which does not receive the treatment, is given a fake or treatment that looks like the active treatment but actually has no effect. By comparing the two groups, experimenters can be fairly sure that any observed effect was due to the treatment and not the expectations associated with receiving a treatment.

Another potential confounding variable, called **spontaneous remission**, can mask the true effectiveness of a treatment. In spontaneous remission, a person recovers from a problem spontaneously over time without the aid of a treatment. You have probably observed yourself recover from a condition on your own (spontaneously) without taking any kind of remedy. If a person gets better during the same time that treatment is given, it is difficult to determine whether that improvement was due to the treatment or to spontaneous improvement; alternatively, *both* factors might contribute to the improvement. Once again, the best way to determine the true relationship is to randomly assign participants to a control group that does not get the treatment, in which some participants are expected to improve spontaneously. When the control group's outcomes are compared with those of the group whose members actually received the active treatment, any observed effects can be shown to be over and above the usual rate of spontaneous remission.

Efficacy of a therapy can be demonstrated by results from an internally valid, true experiment. Nevertheless, these results do not allow us to conclude that the therapy will work in real-world clinical settings. Thus, after efficacy is shown, the therapy should be tested in actual clinical settings with real people in studies of its effectiveness.

By the end of the 1970s, many studies had been done on the effectiveness of various psychotherapies, but new tools were needed to determine the relative effectiveness of specific treatments or kinds of psychotherapy. In 1980, Smith, Glass, and Miller reported results from a new type of study called a *meta-analysis* that allowed for the quantitative comparison of different treatments. As discussed in Chapter 1, a meta-analytic study is a kind of statistical analysis, usually reported in a review of the research that allows researchers to statistically compare the effect sizes of treatments.

For instance, in a simple meta-analysis, the effect size or the size of a treatment effect in a study can be calculated by dividing the difference between the means of two treatment conditions by a measure of the variability for the comparison. After calculating the individual effect sizes for various comparisons of interest, all of the relevant effect sizes can be averaged to find the overall effect size for a treatment. Because all the treatments have been converted to the same metric or measurement units, the average effect sizes for different kinds of treatments can be compared to see whether they are small, medium, or large.

Many meta-analyses have been conducted to compare the effectiveness of psychotherapies as treatments for specific disorders since the study by Smith and colleagues (1980), with much controversy swirling around the various results. One of the main controversies has been whether any psychotherapy can be shown to be more effective than others. Recent commentaries and meta-analytic studies have tended to show that some treatments are more effective for specific problems and disorders than other treatments (e.g., Hunsley & Di Giulio, 2002). Although some EBTs have been found to be more effective for certain disorders, more research is needed on other therapies whose effectiveness remains less clear (Baker, McFall, & Shoham, 2009). In recent years, several books and articles have been published that make large-scale comparisons of psychotherapies for a range of disorders based on high-quality research (e.g., Chambless & Ollendick, 2001; Nathan & Gorman, 2007).

In contrast, when a pseudoscientific practice has been developed, its proponents fail to follow up with research that uses adequate controls to ensure the validity of their findings. As a result, they mistakenly conclude that the pseudoscientific theory presumed to underlie the effect has been supported when a placebo effect or other confounding variable might, in fact, have caused the improvement. In such cases, a person getting an ineffective treatment may report that the treatment was effective when it was actually the expectation, rather than the treatment itself, that led to the reported improvement.

This criticism applies to the use of many new therapies developed in recent years. Some of these treatments and practices have not yet been adequately tested, whereas others have been evaluated but failed to show effectiveness. In either case, the treatment is not well supported. Treatments that have been tested and shown to be ineffective may be considered pseudoscientific if they are still promoted as effective. A key concern about these new treatments is related to the profession's widespread acceptance of the idea that clinical practitioners should be trained to be scientists and be expected to behave as good scientists behave. Unfortunately, many clinicians continue to use poorly supported, pseudoscientific treatments, which contributes to what is perceived as a growing scientist–practitioner gap (Lilienfeld et al., 2015; Tavris, 2003).

EXAMPLES OF PSEUDOSCIENTIFIC AND POORLY SUPPORTED PRACTICES

The practices discussed in this section have several of the "marks" of pseudoscience or have not been adequately studied to determine their effectiveness. Some meet many of the criteria outlined in Table 5.1, indicating that a field or practice is pseudoscientific. At the very least, both professionals and clients should be skeptical about using such practices and treatments. Even if the treatment is harmless, a client who receives such a treatment may be less likely to get help than the same client would receive from a therapist who employs a more effective, evidence-based approach. Devoting resources to pseudoscientific therapies certainly wastes time and money that could have been better spent on more effective treatment.

Freudian psychoanalysis, developed by Sigmund Freud, was perhaps the first psychotherapy to be underpinned by an elaborate theory of how it worked. It may surprise you to learn that some who have examined psychoanalysis have persuasively argued that Freud's famous therapeutic approach is pseudoscientific (e.g., Blitz, 1991; Popper, 1959; Van Rillaers, 1991). The philosopher of science Karl Popper found in discussions with Alfred Adler, one of Freud's students, that Adler could use psychoanalytic theory to account for observations from any case, even when data contradicted the original prediction. Recall that true scientists make specific predictions that are testable and falsifiable. In contrast, Adler and other psychoanalysts sometimes expanded the meaning of predictions or hypotheses to account for data that did not fit their predictions.

Adler considered the ability of psychoanalysts to explain any observation to be a strength of the theory, but Popper argued that it was just the opposite. According to Popper, this sort of "after-the-fact" explanation made psychoanalysis incapable of being falsified or refuted. By shielding itself from falsification, he claimed, psychoanalysis was a pseudoscience.

Closer examination of psychoanalytic theory shows that it is the theory itself that tends to make it hard to test and falsify. One key assumption is that psychological problems are due to unconscious motives resulting from traumas, conflicts, and other problems that may have occurred in a person's childhood. The psychoanalyst is charged with helping the patient become aware of these unconscious motives so that the patient can gain insight and overcome the obstacles they impose. This process is difficult because the therapist knows about the unconscious motives and conflicts only through interpretation of the statements and actions of the patient, who is not consciously aware of them.

Freud also interpreted dreams that patients reported as a way to uncover unconscious material, applying a psychoanalytic interpretation of what he thought were symbolic elements of the dream. Subsequent research on dreams has shown that they are often about mundane, everyday events that lack any particular symbolic meaning. Sometimes patients would object to Freud's interpretations, but Freud argued that a patient's resistance to his interpretation indicated that he was getting closer to uncovering the unconscious origin of the problem. Of course, an alternative explanation is that Freud was showing confirmation bias and using the rather general ideas of psychoanalytic theory to impose his own symbolic interpretations of the statements and dreams that he assumed reflected unconscious motives of which neither he nor his client was aware.

Another problem with psychoanalysis is that it has been mostly supported by case study data, a relatively low-quality kind of evidence—and sometimes not even by *good* case study data. For example, one of Freud's important cases was that of Dora; by his own admission, this case was based largely on his memory of their exchanges (Eisner, 2000). Moreover, Freud was not particularly interested in verifying the history of his patients; this failure to confirm the facts of a case further weakened his claims that some unconscious event from his patient's past was causing the problem. It is not even clear whether Freud accurately diagnosed Dora, given modern ideas about psychological disorders (Eisner, 2000). Despite the fact that psychoanalysis has been supported primarily by case study data and almost no higher-quality data from experiments, followers of Freud continue to maintain that psychoanalytic theory is correct and that psychoanalysis is effective.

 Practice Thinking 5.4: Is It a Pseudoscience?

Use Table 5.1 to decide whether the approach in the following example is pseudoscientific. Write down reasons for your decision.

Developed by a science-fiction writer, this approach to therapy is based on the writer's observations of people and his philosophizing about the human condition of suffering. He reported his early findings and a description of successes with the approach in a science-fiction magazine. None of these case studies or any other research on the approach has been published in a peer-reviewed psychology or psychiatric journal, but testimonials from many of its adherents claim that the approach is effective.

The organization trains its counselors, called *auditors,* to interview and guide people who pay for these sessions as part of joining the organization. The auditing session involves use of an electropsychometer (e-meter) that works much like a galvanic skin-response device used to detect anxiety and stress. The auditor is said to help the person remove implants or problematic memory traces that lead to stress, anxiety, and other problems of the human condition. The approach claims that memory traces underlying human problems originated from "thetans" (extraterrestrial spirits) who were left here 75 million years ago by a galactic tyrant named Xenu. Thetans later entered the bodies of the humans populating Earth at the time. When these implants are removed, the person is said to be "clear."

In this respect, the approach resembles psychoanalysis, but its advocates have been critical of Freudian theory. Other published writings about the approach claim that Darwin's theory of evolution is misguided and that his theory originated in an ancient Egyptian myth about life originating from the primordial ocean.

Reason 1: _____

Reason 2: _____

Reason 3: _____

Reason 4: _____

Reason 5: _____

Conclusion: _____

Pseudoscientific Treatments for Autism

Autism is a serious condition usually associated with severe problems with language and communication, impaired intellectual development, and repetitive movements that sometimes become self-injurious behaviors. As you might expect, parents of autistic children are often desperate to find the cause of, as well as effective treatment for, this condition so that they can communicate better with their children. In recent years, the number of autism diagnoses has greatly increased, and the prevalence of the disorder is now about 1 in 100 children in the United States (Zaroff & Uhm, 2012).

It is not surprising, then, that many parents of autistic children were elated when in the early 1990s practitioners of **Facilitated Communication (FC)** claimed they could help autistic people learn to communicate as well as non-autistic people. According to FC theory, autism is not a language-ability problem, but rather a motor-control problem that is solved by having facilitators help autistic people steady their movements. In FC, a facilitator helps the autistic person communicate through a special keyboard. Amazingly, as soon as facilitators began to steady the hands of autistic people when typing on the keyboard, they observed that the autistic people could write articulate essays and even poems. Many cases were reported of autistic people showing normal and sometimes even gifted writing, suggesting their intellectual abilities had been greatly underestimated (Crossley, 1992).

When FC was tested in well-controlled experiments, however, it became clear that the facilitators—not the autistic children—were unconsciously authoring the communications (Mostert, 2001). Researchers experimentally manipulated the stimuli so that in some trials, trained facilitators were blind to (i.e., did not know) the target stimulus for the autistic participants; in other trials, they did know what the target stimulus was. Researchers consistently found that in trials in which facilitators knew what target their partners received, the facilitators typed that message; in contrast, in trials in which facilitators did not know the target, they did not type that message. When confronted with the evidence that they had authored the messages, facilitators claimed to be unaware of their actions.

Despite numerous studies that have failed to support claims of the effectiveness of FC, practitioners persist in using it, even though more effective treatments are available (Herbert, Sharp, & Gaudiano, 2002; Romanczyk, Arnstein, Soorya, & Gillis, 2003). In fact, upon further analysis, FC was shown not only to be ineffective but also to have done damage. Some facilitated messages had falsely claimed that the parents of autistic children had abused them, embroiling the parents in legal cases (Green, 2002). FC had also raised false hopes among parents of being able to at long last communicate with their children. Finally, FC had deprived autistic people of more effective treatment that was available, such as behavior therapy.

In the mid-1990s, new concerns about increases in autism cases led to other speculation about the source of autism. Some parents claimed that soon after getting the measles, mumps, and rubella (MMR) vaccine, their children had developed autism. In 1998, Dr. Andrew Wakefield published an article in the prestigious medical journal *The Lancet,* claiming that eight children who had received the MMR vaccine had developed autism. Wakefield and others initiated a campaign, conducted through the media, that urged people not to vaccinate their children. Despite a public outcry against vaccines, epidemiological studies reviewed by Offit (2008) clearly showed that greater use of vaccines was not related to the increased incidence of autism. Moreover, Wakefield's 1998 research was severely attacked for its low quality, and *The Lancet* eventually retracted the article. Unfortunately, the damage had been done: Many unvaccinated children developed measles and other potentially deadly diseases—and a few children even died from them.

Thought Field Therapy (TFT) is one of a number of recent therapies referred to as *power therapies* because they are said to produce fast-acting and strong results (Swenson, 1999). TFT and other power therapies, such as Ear Tapping Desensitization and Emotional Freedom Technique, assume that tapping certain acupressure points or meridians will help a person rapidly overcome even severe psychological problems. TFT is based on ideas that Roger Callahan (1997) adapted from Chinese traditional medicine, which claim that energy in the body becomes blocked or unbalanced at certain points called meridians. Tapping these points can restore the balance of energy. Callahan (1997) reported that he discovered TFT when working with a client named Mary, who suffered from a phobia of water that left her sick to her stomach. After trying other techniques without success, he tried tapping the acupressure points under the eye that correlate to the stomach. Mary immediately reported that she no longer feared water.

TFT is implausible, given what is known about psychology and therapy. Proponents of this therapy claim that it can cure almost everyone, almost immediately, of fairly severe psychological disorders. This prospect is particularly attractive to insurance companies, which would much rather reimburse patients for mental health care that is completed in one or two TFT sessions, as opposed to a year's worth of psychoanalyst visits.

TFT is perhaps most implausible in its claims about the energy fields involved. The therapy's effects have been explained in quantum physics terminology, which is not usually applied to explain psychological processes. It has been said that TFT acts by subsumption of the micro state of energy perturbations and active information to eliminate negative emotion at the macro state level. This explanation may "sound" scientific, but it does not directly follow from quantum theory in physics, especially at the level of the emotions. Besides quantum theory, TFT has been explained in terms of energy moving through channels in the body like the *chi* of ancient Chinese medicine—a view of energy that has been supported neither by physics nor by scientific study of the body's functioning. TFT has not received empirical support from well-controlled studies.

Practice Thinking 5.5: Reasons Why a Therapy May Be Pseudoscientific

For each of the following treatment examples, list two reasons why it may be classified as a pseudoscience.

Psychoanalysis

Reason 1: _____

Reason 2: _____

Facilitated Communication

Reason 1: _____

Reason 2: _____

Thought Field Therapy

Reason 1: _____

Reason 2: _____

Self-Help Techniques

The self-help industry in the United States reportedly pulls in $8.5 billion per year in gross revenues (Salerno, 2005). Proponents of self-help treatments have made diverse claims about their effectiveness, such as that these techniques can cure autism, "turn back the clock," cure depression, or unlock the secret to living a fulfilling life. Self-help treatments often are presented in book form, although tapes, CDs, videos, and Internet sites have become increasingly popular formats. The origins of the self-help movement in the United States can be traced back to the 1600s, with the popularity and influence of these techniques greatly increasing in the later part of the twentieth century. In the United States, their appeal has been associated with the emphasis on positive thinking and an ethic of personal responsibility that are interwoven into American culture (Watkins, 2008).

Commercialization of self-help techniques has created media and financial empires like the one presided over by Oprah Winfrey. Although the self-help tips Oprah featured on her television program tended to be good (Kosova & Wingert, 2009), she also featured implausible approaches, such as *The Secret*. Proponents of *The Secret* claim that life is governed by the "law of attraction," maintaining that the universe vibrates with energy and that all the energy a person projects into life comes back to the individual in positive or negative form. This view is not just metaphorical to proponents of *The Secret*; that is, they believe that if people think positively, they will attract positive energy and cause positive things to happen. Proponents tell stories of how they used positive visualization to change physical reality, such as causing irreparably damaged tissue to heal.

Such stories often have other, more plausible and less miraculous explanations. A person may also have received medical treatment that turned out to be more effective than expected or the severity of a medical problem may have been grossly overestimated. In other cases, when use of *The Secret*'s positive thinking principles failed to cure a person, the case has not been treated as a failure of *The Secret* but rather attributed to "God having other plans" for the person. As with creationism/intelligent design, introducing supernatural entities or forces that are not directly observable to explain observable events is a maneuver that makes predictions untestable and ultimately not falsifiable.

Applications of *The Secret* turned deadly when James Arthur Ray, a self-help superstar, attracted more than 50 people to a $10,000, five-day seminar at his Arizona sweat lodge. During a ritual procedure to overcome their fear of death, in which the participants were deprived of water in the sweat lodge during a 2-hour ceremony, 3 people died and 18 people were hospitalized. Ray was subsequently convicted of three counts of homicide.

The Secret is a prime example of the emphasis on positive thinking in self-help programs, but it is just one of the many instances. One of the first such approaches to receive wide attention was outlined in *The Power of Positive Thinking*, a book by the minister Norman Vincent Peale (1952). A more recent, related development has been the emphasis on self-esteem, in which a person's problems are usually assumed to result from not thinking positively enough about oneself. For example, low self-esteem has been suggested as the cause of problems such as violent behavior and poor academic performance. Many educators in the 1980s concluded that low self-esteem was the cause of poor performance, both in math and in school in general. What ensued were concerted efforts to raise students' self-esteem concerning their ability to do math and other schoolwork. After years of attempting to improve performance by raising self-esteem, U.S. students began to report that they felt happy about their math performance, even though their performance continued to lag far behind that of students in other developed nations.

Self-help books and materials offer several potential benefits. In the face of today's emphasis on managed care and limitations on how much insurance pays for mental health care, they could be an economical way to provide mental health services. Self-help can also increase people's self-efficacy or their evaluation of how well they can do some task or cope in general. Therapists often use a kind of supervised self-help as an adjunct to therapy when they have clients engage in guided practice outside the clinician's office.

But does self-help work? Self-help techniques are not always based on scientific research, so their true efficacy may be unknown (Watkins & Clum, 2008). Indeed, most self-help treatments have not been studied to determine their effectiveness (Rosen, Glasgow, Moore, & Barrera, 2014). Steve Salerno, an investigative journalist, has uncovered some illuminating facts about self-help programs that have raised important questions about these approaches. Rodale Press, where Salerno served as a self-help editor, conducted a study of who bought self-help books and found that the same people tend to repeatedly use self-help programs, buying new books in 18-month cycles. This raises a troubling question: Why would the same people need to use a new book or technique if a previous self-help program was effective?

Unfortunately, although they seem like an economical way to extend therapy services, self-help techniques do not always work. In one study, therapists instructed clients to use a well-documented treatment procedure; 50% of the clients did not improve because they failed to carry out their instructional assignments, even though many of them could successfully carry out the treatment procedure (Rosen, Glasgow, & Barrera, 1976).

Another danger is that those individuals who use self-help materials are essentially diagnosing themselves. As will be discussed in Chapter 13, diagnosis is a difficult task that even clinicians sometimes do not perform well. It is doubtful that unsupervised laypersons would be able to accurately diagnose their own problems; they may, therefore, misidentify their problems and treat themselves for the wrong thing.

Alternative Medicine and Natural Cures

Recent years have brought a surge of interest in natural cures for physical and mental problems—a type of care sometimes called *alternative medicine,* to distinguish it from more conventional medicine, which is also known as *traditional medicine.* In reality, alternative medicine is sometimes more "traditional" than traditional medicine, in that alternative medicines are often based on treatments that have been passed along for centuries in mostly the same form.

Today, multibillion-dollar companies promote nutritional supplements as effective ways to improve mental functioning, mood, sleep, and memory, and even as cures for psychological disorders. Indeed, even the famed scientist Linus Pauling, a Nobel Prize winner in chemistry, recommended taking megadoses of vitamin C as a cure for the common cold, cancer, and psychological problems. The idea of taking megadoses of vitamins became known as *ortho-molecular medicine.* Despite efforts to show that megadoses of vitamins can reduce both physical and mental health problems, no reliable effects have been found from this practice.

Nevertheless, companies continue to try to cash in on the power of vitamins. A recent example is the vitamin supplement "Airborne"; its manufacturer advertised that the supplement could prevent and effectively treat colds—that is, until the company was forced to recant these claims and pay a $23.3 million penalty for false advertising. Ginkgo biloba, a popular supplement for improving memory and cognitive function, may increase brain circulation, but its effect on memory is similar to the slight benefit produced by eating a candy bar or drinking a cup of coffee (Gold, Cahill, & Wenk, 2002).

A major problem with natural cures and nutritional supplements is that they often go untested. Although advertisers often brag that they are "clinically proven" to work, this designation has no standard meaning or recognition by the U.S. Food and Drug Administration. It could simply mean a company has given it to some people who reported that it worked, perhaps just showing a placebo effect.

Magnet therapy, in which a magnet is typically placed on or near the body to promote health, is an alternative treatment that generates more than $1 billion in annual worldwide revenues (Flamm, 2006). Magnets are often worn as a ring or bracelet, but magnet therapy may employ magnetized water or creams, too. The most common uses are to reduce pain or restore general well-being, but some proponents have even claimed that magnets can prevent or cure cancer. The commonly made claim that magnets work by improving blood flow is implausible and has not been supported by research (Polk & Postow, 1996). If the static magnets worked to attract red blood cells, then the skin under a magnet would turn red as blood flows to the region, but no such effects are observed.

Scientific studies comparing magnets with placebo (sham) magnets have not revealed any clear benefits of magnets, but testing with placebo controls is challenging (Flamm, 2006). Participants wearing actual magnets probably notice that their magnets attract small metal objects, such as paper clips, and so learn that they are in a real treatment group—which defeats the purpose of the placebo control. Nevertheless, the fact that the user's expectations and the placebo effect can be a part of so many different kinds of treatments, such as medical treatments, psychotherapies, and magnet therapy, makes it essential that researchers use good placebo control groups.

SUMMARY

Pseudoscience only appears to be scientific and makes implausible claims that lack the support of good scientific evidence. Numerous types of pseudoscientific practitioners, such as astrologers, mesmerists, and phrenologists, have often made claims of psychological insights and benefits in the past. Practitioners of some new therapies, such as attachment therapy and Thought Field Therapy (TFT), continue to make pseudoscientific claims in the twenty-first century.

In general, those who practice pseudoscience make what they are doing look scientific, but they are not really engaging in science. They often make vague, untestable, unfalsifiable predictions and fail to systematically check the outcomes of their predictions, showing a confirmatory bias. They reason incorrectly when making their claims and hypotheses, and they do not use accepted standards of evidence, methods, techniques, and terminology from related scientific fields, making implausible claims and using low-quality evidence and obscure terminology.

Increasingly, psychology has emphasized the need for treatments that show efficacy—that is, treatments shown by high-quality, empirical research to be effective. Clinical researchers often consider randomized trials or true experiments to be the "gold standard" for determining the efficacy of treatments, especially when the treatments are methodically compared with sham treatments, placebos, and other appropriate control groups. Despite the greater attention paid by scientific psychology to the development of evidence-based treatments for psychological problems, the use of pseudoscientific treatments, such as Facilitated Communication (FC) and TFT, persists. Also, many people continue to use many pseudoscientific alternative treatments such as magnet therapy that lack support. Likewise, people often use self-help therapies that lack support, although some of the few that have been studied have been shown to be effective.

 Practice Thinking 5.6: WHAT DO YOU THINK **NOW**?
Please explain how you know.

1. What is pseudoscience, and why study it?

   _____

2. Are some psychotherapies dangerous?

   _____

3. Are some therapies more effective than others? If so, which ones? How do you know?

   _____

4. Do self-help books and programs really help?

_____

5. Can nutritional supplements improve your memory or cure psychological problems?

_____

REVIEW QUESTIONS

1. What is pseudoscience? How does it differ from true science? What is cargo cult science?

2. Why is it important to learn about pseudoscience?

3. Where have pseudosciences come from?

4. How is astrology related to astronomy? Alchemy to chemistry? Mesmerism to hypnosis?

5. Which criteria are used to distinguish pseudoscience from science? (See Table 5.1.)

6. What is an evidence-based treatment (EBT)? What are some examples of EBTs?

   • What is the "gold standard" for determining the efficacy of a treatment?

   • Why are placebo control groups needed?

   • What is spontaneous remission?

   • What is a blind control?

7. How do pseudoscientific practices differ from poorly supported practices?

8. Why do many psychologists believe that psychoanalysis is pseudoscientific?

9. Why might you think FC is pseudoscientific?

10. Why might you think TFT is pseudoscientific?

11. What are the advantages and disadvantages of self-help treatments and techniques?

12. What are examples of alternative medicine that are ineffective? Why are they ineffective?

13. Why might you think that magnet therapy is pseudoscientific?

14. What did this chapter discuss regarding psychological misconceptions?

6

ERRORS IN ATTENTION, PERCEPTION, AND MEMORY THAT AFFECT THINKING

LEARNING OUTCOMES

After studying this chapter, you should be able to:

1. Recognize a variety of cognitive errors associated with attention, perception, and memory.

2. Give examples of how cognitive errors may impair critical thinking.

3. Actively and critically read a discussion about whether eyewitness memory is accurate.

4. Apply your knowledge of attention, perception, and memory to help you reach a well-reasoned inductive conclusion about the accuracy of memory.

5. Apply your knowledge of cognitive errors to analyze an actual eyewitness memory case.

WHAT DO YOU THINK?

In 2010, a Metro train engineer from California was texting while driving his train. He apparently did not see the red light signaling his train to stop for an approaching freight train that was cleared to enter the tunnel first. Because the engineer failed to stop the Metro train, it crashed into the oncoming freight train with such force that it pressed the front cars together like an accordion, killing him and 24 other people. How, if at all, might the engineer's texting have contributed to this horrible crash?

In 1978, a rare red panda escaped from the Rotterdam Zoo. A rust-colored native of India, this animal looks like a cross between a raccoon and a panda. Zoo officials published articles in the local newspapers asking the Dutch citizens to help find the animal. In the days that followed, people reported hundreds of red panda sightings—although zoo officials learned even before the articles hit newsstands that the red panda had been killed near the zoo, shortly after its escape. What are some plausible explanations for what the witnesses claimed to see?

Psychologist Susan Clancy (2005) interviewed several seemingly normal people who recalled having been abducted by aliens from outer space. Many reported waking up in the middle of the night, being unable to move, feeling the presence of one or more intruders, and being hurled through space. Some concluded right away that they had been abducted. Others came to this conclusion only after a lengthy search for an explanation, sometimes involving psychotherapy and hypnosis. Yet many astronomers think it highly unlikely that aliens have visited Earth and abducted people, given the vast distances to other stars and the limits on the speed at which spacecraft can travel. Astronomers do agree, however, that intelligent life probably exists in other parts of the universe. What might plausibly account for "memories" of alien abduction?

Practice Thinking 6.1: What Do You Think?

Please explain how you know.

1. What do these three chapter-opening scenarios have in common?

   _____

2. If you look directly at something, will you always see it?

   _____

3. Is something wrong with a person who has a hallucination?

   _____

4. How do magicians accomplish their amazing feats?

   _____

5. Is your memory like a video recorder that stores an exact copy of whatever you observe?

   _____

6. Is eyewitness memory accurate? Should jurors trust it?

   _____

COGNITIVE ERRORS AND CRITICAL THINKING

The failure of the train engineer to see the red stop signal, the mistaken red panda sightings, and the false memories of alien abduction are all examples of **cognitive errors**, or errors the mind makes as it processes information. Cognitive errors can occur as we attend to a stimulus, perceive it, and store information about it in memory, as well as when we retrieve information for use in reasoning, solving problems, and making decisions. Because reasoning is a cognitive activity that depends on attention, perception, and memory, problems associated with each of these cognitive processes can contribute to thinking errors.

First, not paying enough attention to a stimulus, as when the train engineer was texting instead of attending to his driving, impedes our ability to sufficiently process or even see that stimulus. Missing the red light apparently led the engineer to the false conclusion that it was safe to enter the tunnel. Second, the red panda sightings demonstrate that background knowledge and expectation can affect both what we perceive and what we remember; thus, people who expected to see a red panda incorrectly interpreted the sighting of a cat or some other similar-looking animal as the red panda. Finally, the people who recalled alien abduction probably misinterpreted experiences associated with sleeping, such as sleep paralysis and dreaming. Exposure to stories of alien abduction and images of aliens in the media probably contributed to their memory of such unusual experiences.

To think critically, we must avoid making not only logical errors, but also cognitive errors that can derail the reasoning process. Serious consequences can occur when we reason with inaccurate information obtained from perception or memory, as when an eyewitness inaccurately recalls what she saw at the scene of a crime. These errors can lead to wrongful convictions because jurors often find eyewitness testimony and identifications highly persuasive. As of June 2016, the Innocence Project had helped overturn 342 wrongful convictions; approximately 70% of those convictions were at least in part due to incorrect eyewitness testimony and identifications that resulted in innocent people spending years in prison (Innocence Project, 2017). In this chapter, we will examine cognitive errors associated with attention, perception, and memory in depth and then discuss how each can affect eyewitness memory.

ERRORS OF ATTENTION

Attention refers to how we focus and divide our cognitive resources among different tasks and inputs. Cognitive psychologists commonly assume that our cognitive resources are limited. Focusing attention on one thing in a demanding task can leave too little cognitive resources left over to process other information. The limits on attention can greatly impair performance when we try to multi-task. Dividing attention among multiple tasks or sets of stimuli (e.g., texting and driving) can have disastrous consequences. Many studies have shown that when people divide their attention between driving and talking on a cell phone, they take longer to stop and make more driving errors than do those whose attention is not divided (e.g., Strayer & Johnston, 2001). One study found that talking on a cell phone while driving puts a person at 4 times greater risk of being in an accident than not talking on a cell phone—similar to the increased risk associated with drinking and driving (Redelmeier & Tibshrani, 1997). Texting while driving makes an accident 10 times more likely.

Directing attention to a stimulus often results in our perceiving it, but when attention is directed away from the stimulus, we may not even see it. Mack and Rock (1998) found that when people pay attention to one part of a display, they might not see another part that is clearly in view—an error called inattentional blindness. You have probably heard the expression "It's the 500-pound gorilla in the room," which implies one's failure to see some obvious thing. Simons and Chabris (1999) conducted a study in which participants watched a video of people passing a basketball back and forth and were asked to count the number of passes they saw. Later in the video, someone dressed as a gorilla walked across the middle of the room while beating her chest. Only about half of the participants noticed the gorilla. Their focus on counting the basketball passes left few cognitive resources for seeing the gorilla. (You can watch this video at www.youtube.com/watch?v=vJG698U2MVo.)

Stage magicians are adept at creating illusions and magical tricks by misdirecting attention and exploiting inattentional blindness (Kuhn, Amiani, & Rensink, 2008). To make an object seem to disappear, a magician may first distract an audience with a movement that captures their attention and directs it away from the object. The magician then hides the object or moves it out of sight. Because observers are attending elsewhere, they do not see this deception and the object seems to have just disappeared.

Change blindness, an effect related to inattentional blindness, occurs when a person misses a change from one scene to the next that is in clear view. Figure 6.1 shows the setup of a study conducted by Simons and Levin (1998), in which participants giving a man directions were suddenly interrupted by two other men carrying a panel that obscured the participant's view of the man receiving directions. During this brief interruption, the man receiving directions was replaced with a different man. Most of the participants failed to notice the change.

(a)

(b)

(c)

FIGURE 6.1 In this illustration of the Simons and Levin (1998) experiment, the white-haired subject giving directions to the man in part (a) is separated from the man briefly when a panel in part (b) is suddenly moved between them; the man receiving the directions in part (a) is then replaced with a different man in part (c). Most participants did not notice the change in person, even though the facial features and clothing of the two men differed.

Change blindness likely occurs due to limits on how much a person can attend to and perceive in a brief exposure.

Do you think you would notice if a person you were looking at unexpectedly changed? If so, you might be overconfident in your ability. In one study, participants were asked if they thought they would notice changes such as the one shown in Figure 6.1 (Levin, Momen, Drivdahl, & Simons, 2000). Participants greatly overestimated the likelihood that they would detect the changes. Levin and colleagues called this overconfidence effect **change blindness blindness**, a label that describes the metacognitive error in which a person is unaware of, or blind to, his or her inability to detect change. This may contribute to people's susceptibility to magic tricks because they wrongly believe they could perceive a deceptive move by the magician right in front of them—and are then amazed when the trick is complete and they did not perceive it (Ekroll, Sayim, & Wagemans, 2017).

ERRORS OF PERCEPTION

Perception involves the senses taking in sensory data about energy changes in the environment. We recognize patterns in these data, then organize and interpret this information, which often leads to awareness of objects. Although people often assume that they are fully aware of what is "out there," scientists have long known that our senses detect only a small fraction of the available energy. For example, our eyes are sensitive only to changes in visible light, which spans just a small part of the electromagnetic spectrum of radiant energy. We do not detect radio waves, ultraviolet light, or most other kinds of radiant energy. We hear frequencies only as low as 16 Hz (cycles per second), whereas elephants hear frequencies as low as 5 Hz—like the rumble of storms so far away that humans cannot detect them. Likewise, we hear high frequencies only up to about 20,000 Hz, whereas dogs hear frequencies as high as 25,000 Hz—like the blasts from a dog whistle, which to us makes no sound.

Fortunately, science and technology have helped us to greatly extend our basic sensory abilities and thinking. Electron microscopes can achieve magnifications of 10 million times the size of the original object, and the transmission electron microscope has imaged a single hydrogen atom, the smallest of all atoms. The extreme deep-field images captured by the Hubble Space Telescope have revealed galaxies billions of light years away (1 light year = 5.87 trillion miles).

You can easily demonstrate the limits of your own unaided senses by first looking at a patch of the night sky with your naked eyes, and then examining the same area through binoculars. With the binoculars, you will see many stars that you did not perceive with your unaided vision. Similarly, if we want to think critically about evidence based on observation, we should trust observations made with sensitive scientific instruments more than those made with our unaided senses. Clearly, knowledge and inference contribute to this improved perception. Seeing stars you did not see before in the same area means that you have accessed your prior knowledge of what stars look like and infer that these new points of light are stars, too.

Our background knowledge guides our perceptions at a fundamental level. What we perceive is constructed from many sources besides the energy changes that our senses pick up, such as our background knowledge and expectations about what we are likely to perceive (Peterson, 2007). To see how accessing our knowledge helps us construct what we perceive, look at Figure 6.2.

Figure 6.2a is interesting because we tend to read the /-\ pattern as an "A" in the words *CAN* and *READ*, but then read the very same pattern as an "H" in the last word *THIS*. Your cognitive system appropriately infers the letter, based on the context provided by the surrounding letters and your knowledge of words stored in memory. By the time you get to the third /-\ pattern, the meaning associated with the first three words in the sentence and the context of the letters *T* and *IS* lead you to expect an *H*. You access your knowledge that the word *THIS* is much more likely to follow *READ* than is the nonword *TAIS*, and this inference makes your reading more efficient.

(a) C /-\ N YOι_I RE/-\D T/-\I S?

(b) *You* proablby could. W y?

(c) Is it ahrdre nwo?

FIGURE 6.2 How do you recognize the patterns in part (a)? In part (b)? In part (c)?

Figure 6.2b shows that your pattern recognition is flexible because you are able to recognize patterns appearing in three different fonts. It also illustrates that your brain uses your knowledge of words to fill in missing information, such as the missing *h* in *Why*. Figure 6.2b further shows that you are fairly good at reading words when letters are jumbled in the middle, as in *proablby*; by comparison, it is more difficult to recognize words when letters are turned around at the beginnings or endings of words, as shown in Figure 6.2c (Rayner, White, Johnson, & Liversedge, 2006).

Many studies have shown that people use their knowledge to help them perceive objects. In a classic experiment, Palmer (1975) found that first providing the environmental context in which an object typically appears can help participants later identify the object. Specifically, Palmer first presented participants with a kitchen scene before rapidly exposing them to an image of a loaf of bread, a similarly shaped mailbox, or a drum, as shown in Figure 6.3. Participants were much more accurate in their reporting when the drawing was a loaf of bread than when the drawing was one of the other two objects, suggesting that their knowledge of kitchens helped them perceive the bread.

Other studies have shown that background knowledge and expectations can bias perception rather than improve it. An interesting experiment by Thorne and

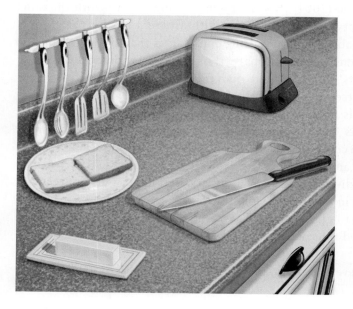

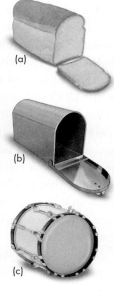

(a)

(b)

(c)

FIGURE 6.3 First briefly seeing a kitchen scene, similar to the one shown here, helped participants identify the briefly presented loaf of bread better than the other two objects in the Palmer (1975) experiment.

Himelstein (1984) tested whether expecting to hear satanic words in rock songs would make research participants more likely to report hearing such words in songs played backward than would those not expecting to hear satanic words. In the 1980s, some people believed that satanic messages were recorded in reverse on rock songs and that the backward messages were being subliminally broadcast to unsuspecting listeners. This claim seems implausible because music played backward sounds like a strange, garbled mess, and humans evolved to decode speech going in a forward direction.

What seems more plausible is that people expecting to hear words in backward speech would hear more of them, especially given the human tendency to find patterns in random noise. To test this, Thorne and Himelstein played a rock song in reverse and instructed three groups under three levels of expectation. One group was instructed to report whether they heard any satanic words, a second group was to report whether they heard any words, and a third (control) group was to report anything they heard without creating an expectation that they might hear any words. Consistent with the idea that expectation can bias perception, the group expecting to hear satanic words reported hearing the most satanic words; the group expecting to hear words reported hearing the second largest number of words; and the control group reported hearing the fewest satanic words.

Expectations about what will be perceived can fool even the experts. Morrot, Brochet, and Dubourdieu (2001) presented wine-tasting experts with the same average-priced wine in two different bottles with different labels. The experts judged the expensively labeled wine as tasting much better than the identical wine labeled as the less expensive wine. Apparently, the expectation created by the label affected the experts' judgment more than the actual taste of the wine.

Another type of perceptual error is the misidentification of objects. The history of UFO sightings is filled with cases of people misidentifying natural phenomena and aircraft as UFOs (Hines, 2003). On January 14, 2011, during a transatlantic flight, the copilot of an Air Canada jetliner woke up from a nap to see what he feared was another plane flying toward him. He immediately steered the plane into a steep dive when he saw another set of lights—an unnecessary maneuver that resulted in a near crash and the injury of 16 people. An investigation found that the first light the copilot saw was most likely the planet Venus, since it was determined that no other plane was close enough to be observed (Radford, 2012).

Figure 6.4 shows several aircraft and other objects originally thought by eyewitnesses to be UFOs. The sighting of UFOs that were called "flying saucers"

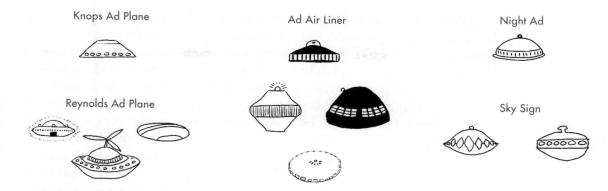

FIGURE 6.4 Airplanes and other objects originally identified as UFOs, based on Hendry (1979).

took off after a pilot named Kenneth Arnold reported on June 24, 1947, that he saw nine objects flying in formation near Mount Rainier, Washington. Arnold told a reporter the objects were crescent-shaped and described their movement as resembling a saucer skipping across the water. When the Associated Press picked up the story, headlines across the country dubbed the objects "flying saucers." In the years that followed, people reported thousands of sightings of flying saucers, creating a collective delusion (Bartholomew & Goode, 2000). Prior to this time, there were few UFO sightings—and very few were described as saucer-shaped.

HALLUCINATIONS: EXPERIENCING THINGS THAT AREN'T THERE

Have you ever heard someone call your name, only to discover no one was there? Although this is a mild form of hallucination, it is still a hallucination. Hallucinations are a kind of cognitive error in which a person experiences something so real, it is as if it were perceived—but that stimulus is not truly there. These are not simply perceptual errors, though: Unlike perception, hallucinations often do not correspond directly to anything in the environment at the time and are more like things imagined. Like imagined stimuli, they are internally generated because no external stimulation of a sensory organ corresponds to what has initiated the experience (Aleman & Laroi, 2008). Yet, unlike mental images that you can willfully change, hallucinations happen to you as if you are perceiving something. Although you could imagine a face and then change it in your mind, you could not willfully change your hallucination of a face.

Hearing voices that are not really there may seem particularly worrisome because people with serious mental disorders, such as schizophrenia, often experience auditory hallucinations and people who take hallucinogenic drugs tend to have visual hallucinations. But hallucinations occur in normal, nondrugged people, especially those who report experiencing stress and poor sleep quality. In one study, 71% of college students reported having had at least one such experience (Posey & Losch, 1983). In another study, almost half of the students who reported having a verbal hallucination said they experienced at least one per month (Barrett & Etheridge, 1992). Another normal condition in which hallucinations occur is when people begin to fall asleep. As they do this, they may enter a hypnagogic state, a state of reverie in which people sometimes experience wild imaginings that seem real.

Sometimes normal, nondrugged individuals hallucinate when faced with physically demanding conditions. Shermer (2011) reported accounts of competitors hallucinating during the grueling "Ride Across America" bicycle race. Competitors in this race ride as many as 350 miles per day, sometimes under extreme weather conditions and with little sleep. Some riders reported seeing hieroglyphics spread across the road and mythical creatures in splotches on the pavement.

Hallucinations are associated with a variety of medical and other conditions, too (Sacks, 2012). Some people who lose their hearing experience auditory hallucinations. Those who become blind often have visual hallucinations. Some people who are deprived of sensory stimulation also hallucinate. Temporal lobe epilepsy can produce hallucinations and religious visions (Aleman & Laroi, 2008). Migraines, too, can produce an aura—a kind of zigzag, wavy pattern in the visual field that usually lasts a few minutes and may signal the onset of a migraine headache. For example, I once had an "optical migraine" during class. As I went over a quiz with students, a wavy, kaleidoscopic pattern progressively filled my visual field until I could not see the quiz. I described the experience I was having to students, who were surprised when I discontinued class (I hardly ever call off class). Fortunately, the hallucination of light patterns subsided after a few minutes without the migraine headache.

Tracing the development of the idea of hallucinations can help explain why they are important to critical and scientific thinking. It was not until the eighteenth century that hallucinations became associated with errors of the senses or with disease. Before this time, they were usually referred to as "apparitions" (Aleman & Laroi, 2008). We know that the word *apparition* has long been associated with ghosts and the sensed presence of unseen beings. People who hallucinate unusual, but seemingly real, things may mistakenly interpret their experience as evidence for the existence of ghosts and strange beings. Like illusions, normal hallucinations raise doubts about the quality of personal experience as evidence.

Another normal hallucination that often occurs under stressful conditions is the "sensed presence" in which someone senses another person, either living or dead, who is present usually for a limited period of time. Sometimes a sensed presence has served as a "rational" voice to help mountain climbers overcome their fear and survive a catastrophe on the cliffs. Similarly, Charles Lindbergh, the first person to fly nonstop across the Atlantic, came to believe, after hours of sleep deprivation, that there was a presence in his plane guiding him to his destination. At other times, a sensed presence is not helpful. Under the extremely stressful conditions of the 1,000-mile Iditarod dogsled race in Alaska, a competitor named Joe Garnie believed he saw a man riding in his sled. After failing to persuade the presence to get out of the sled, Garnie reported that he swatted at it to get it to leave (Shermer, 2011).

Hallucinations, such as the appearance of the man in the dogsled, are internally generated experiences with little input from stimuli in the environment. This suggests that information stored in memory is likely being retrieved and somehow transformed and constructed into experiences that seem real. From this perspective, hallucinations seem like an extreme form of a memory error. As such, hallucinations can serve as the basis of strange experiences that people later remember. For example, a hypnotist may suggest to someone who is especially susceptible to hypnosis that she hears or sees something that is not there. Later, when no longer hypnotized, the person may recall the suggested experience of the hallucination as real. Even outside of hypnosis, a person's background knowledge and perceptual expectations may sometimes dominate mental processing and result in hallucination (Aleman & Vercammen, 2013).

Dreamlike states can also produce strange experiences that are later remembered as real. In the cases of recalling alien abduction, discussed earlier, those people likely remembered what was actually an experience of sleep paralysis and the contents of a dreamlike experience that occurs when sleeping and waking cycles fall out of sync (Clancy, 2005). Normally, sleep paralysis prevents us from moving so that we do not act out our irrational dream content, but occasionally people wake up before the sleep paralysis and dream have subsided. They fail to realize that they are still dreaming, which causes them to interpret the experience as actually being paralyzed when aliens draw them up off of their beds and abduct them. These examples suggest the need to examine the contribution of memory and memory errors to our experience and thinking.

KINDS OF MEMORY AND MEMORY ERRORS

Types of memory include both working memory and long-term memory. Long-term memory (LTM) functions like a vast storehouse that holds massive amounts of information for long periods of time. It stores all the words and facts we know, mental procedures for the things we know how to do, memories of our life experiences, and many other types of knowledge. In contrast, working memory (WM) is a form of short-term memory that temporarily activates very limited amounts of information from LTM and the environment as we do our mental work. Working memory is estimated to hold as few as 3 items (Cowan, 2000), but usually no more than between 5 and 9 items, at one time (Miller, 1956).

Working Memory

We use WM to temporarily hold information as we reason, solve problems, make decisions, and engage in other effortful cognitive tasks. Type 2 thinking makes severe demands on WM (Evans, 2008; Evans & Stanovich, 2013). For instance, as you read, your WM accesses information from your LTM so that you can understand the words you are reading. Your WM has to temporarily hold a representation of what you have just read so that you can integrate it with the new information you are reading. As you read more, your WM helps you update your understanding of what you have read with the new information. At the same time, much of the detailed information of what you have read falls out of WM as you continue reading, because WM and its components have very limited capacity, just as we saw with attention.

It is not surprising that WM sometimes fails to hold onto the information we need to execute a demanding cognitive task. For example, note-taking during a slide lecture places even greater demands on WM than reading, because to take good notes you often must read what is on a slide, summarize it while also integrating this information with a picture from the slide, and then write this combined information down in a short period of time. Research has shown that note-taking is a complex, effortful task (Piolat, Olive, & Kellogg, 2005). Perhaps not surprisingly given this complexity, you have probably experienced missing part of some new thing your instructor said because you were still trying to write what was said earlier.

Many cognitive errors associated with WM occur when information falls out of memory before it can be stored or used. This type of error may occur because the load on memory is too great. Cognitive load is the amount of information that is held or manipulated in WM as we do some task. If the load is too great on this limited capacity system, then performance will decline unless we can find a way to reduce or manage the load (Sweller, 2011). In a complex cognitive task, such as note-taking, cognitive load can increase when an instructor switches rapidly to another topic. One way to manage the load is to do relevant assigned reading before class. This practice helps with note-taking because already possessing knowledge makes it easier to acquire new, related knowledge. Also, increasing the speed with which you can write your notes may help because as note-writing becomes more automatic, it takes fewer cognitive resources. In turn, more resources are available to comprehend what is being said or written (Peverly & Sumowski, 2001).

Another problem occurs when competing information interferes with processing the contents of WM you are focusing on. For instance, listening to music with lyrics while reading or studying will likely interfere with holding verbal information in WM because we automatically process speech; this competing task reduces the amount of new information that is taken up by LTM (Salamé & Baddeley, 1989). If you begin to daydream during a lecture, you will replace the information about the lecture with the daydream. Likewise, texting during a lecture interferes with learning (Wood et al., 2012).

Some students do not even take notes, thinking that they will remember all the important information from class; unfortunately for them, most of what is presented is held only temporarily in WM and will be quickly forgotten. Such students will not have any notes that can serve as cues to help them later retrieve important ideas from the class to facilitate storing the information more permanently in LTM. Failing to store important information—or storing incorrect information—can lead to inaccuracies in LTM, which in turn can lead to errors in judgment and reasoning when we retrieve this faulty information from LTM.

How Accurate Is Long-Term Memory?

A common psychological misconception about LTM is that we store an exact copy of everything we have experienced, reproduced exactly from what we observe, as if memory were a video recorder that can play back exactly what happened. According to this flawed view, all of our experiences are "in there," and the problem is simply how to get them out. This view assumes that memory is reproductive, meaning that it reproduces a very accurate record of experience that corresponds in exact detail to the events in the world, similar to naive realism. Like perception, however, our memories are constructed and influenced by our prior knowledge and expectations.

When we try to recall something from our distant past, we use other things we know and details we remember to help us reconstruct our incomplete memories. This knowledge serves as a cue to help us fill in memory gaps. For example, I must reconstruct a memory from my college days as I try to recall my trip to Clinton, Iowa, to help its residents shore up their levee with sandbags to prevent the rising Mississippi River from flooding the town. To remember this event, I find myself searching my memory for information to fill in missing details. Thinking about how my friends and I filled sandbags and placed them on the levee brings to mind an image of us filling the sandbags and then putting them on the levee. Although I think I remember filling and lifting sandbags, I am not sure if I placed them on the levee. The people supervising us would probably not have trusted us to put them in the right places. When I try to recall who was there, I am certain my future girlfriend was there and another guy who was interested in her, but I do not recall exactly which other friends were there. I think I made sure I stood by her while we worked, because the other guy was the "competition." Clearly, part of my memory has been lost, and part of it has been updated by knowledge I acquired later as I reconstructed my memory of the event. Part of it may be in error—I don't know.

This view of memory as **reconstructive** assumes that we remember by using our prior knowledge and other available information in a situation to actively search for material that could help us fill in the gaps in our memories. Thus, memory is not an exact record that is passively retrieved in its entirety, but rather something that is reconstructed or "pieced together" from our knowledge, expectations, and perceptions and updated by later attempts to remember.

In pioneering research, British psychologist Frederick Bartlett (1932) showed that memory is often reconstructive and leads to selective recall. In one study, he gave his British participants short, unfamiliar passages and then had them repeatedly recall the stories days or even weeks later. What the study participants recalled, Bartlett discovered, was often consistent with their prior knowledge and attitudes. According to Bartlett, this prior knowledge is organized in a knowledge structure called a **schema**. In his study, participants used their schemas to try to make sense of the unfamiliar passages, filling in the gaps with schema-based information. Later, when they activated their schemas to recall the passage, their memories were reconstructed around the schema. The schemas helped them recall the main ideas of the passage fairly well, but also caused them to make errors in their recall that were consistent with their schemas.

To illustrate how you use schemas to make inferences and fill in the gaps, complete each of the following statements. Describe the schema you used in each case.

1. She began reading the fairy tale to her daughter. It began: Once _____

   _____ .

2. We sat down at the table in the restaurant, and the waitress brought us

   _____ .

The first example illustrates that you have a kind of schema for how stories proceed, called a *story grammar* (Mandler, 1987). You know that this kind of story often starts with "Once upon a time," based on your experience with many fairy tales. For the second sentence, you likely filled in the gap with "menus" or "glasses of water" based on your use of a *script*—a kind of schema for situation-action routines that specifies the usual order of events in familiar situations, such as going to a restaurant (Schank & Abelson, 1977). Importantly, these examples show that a schema could help you fill in missing information in a variety of new or unfamiliar situations.

At the same time, using a schema to fill in the gaps is a process that influences the selection of information from memory and can bias memory. This can further lead to incorrect inferences when we use our prior knowledge to answer questions posed to us. To demonstrate this relationship, fill in the gaps in order in the next three statements.

1. Marcie went to the bar and ordered a _____ .
2. She drank many _____ .
3. because _____ .
4. She talked loudly because _____ .

Using the schema for a bar, you probably filled in the first blank with "drink," implying an alcoholic beverage, or listed a specific drink such as "beer." Once activated, your schema for a bar and the related concept of alcoholic beverages made it more likely you would fill in the second blank with "drinks" or "beers." Subsequently, you would tend to fill the third blank with "she is an alcoholic" or "she has a drinking problem" or "she wanted to get drunk." Finally, you would be more likely to fill in the fourth blank with "she was drunk."

What if you had not made the initial schema-consistent assumption that Marcie went to the bar to drink alcoholic beverages? Suppose she went to socialize and did not want to drink alcohol. Before reading on, go back to the first of the three statements and fill in the blank with "a diet cola." Would this choice change your other responses? Now you are much more likely to fill in the other blanks with information that does not fit the bar schema as well, such as she drank many "colas" because "she was thirsty." She talked loudly because "the bar was noisy."

Many interpretations and answers are possible in this example, but once we begin constructing an interpretation, we are almost effortlessly guided to other responses consistent with it. In this way, the selectivity of a schema can make our thinking more efficient, but it may also lead to errors following from the schema and initial interpretation. Another danger of using a schema is that it can lead to stereotypical thinking. Drawing the conclusion that Marcie is an alcoholic when she is actually avoiding alcohol by drinking a soft drink would be seriously wrong. Unfortunately, people often draw conclusions based on minimal evidence and make hasty generalizations. This may remind you of how overreliance on Type 1 thinking and the use of knowledge acquired through everyday experience can lead to a quick, but incorrect answer (see Chapter 3). The solution is to use Type 2 thinking, to slow down thinking, and to rationally consider other information instead of automatically filling in missing information based on the expectations produced by your schema.

Clearly, a schema can guide our interpretation of new information, but it can also make us more likely to remember that interpretation and later reconstruct our memory in relation to the schema. Often we remember schema-consistent details (Brewer & Treyans, 1981), but at other times we recall details inconsistent with a schema (Pezdek, Whetstone, Reynolds, Askari, & Dougherty, 1989). In either case, the schema has a systematic effect on what we remember. Sometimes reliance on a schema may lead to inaccurate reconstruction, or even to a completely false memory. Also called a *memory illusion* (Roediger, 1996), a false memory is an error in which we mistakenly remember something we did not see, hear, or otherwise experience. Memory illusions often occur through some form of suggestion and are associated with activation of a schema.

To illustrate, get a piece of paper and a pen or pencil so you can write down some words. First, read the following list of words, about one word every 2 seconds. Then put the book aside and recall as many of the list words as you can in any order. After each word you recalled, rate your confidence that it was on the list using a 1–5 scale in which 1 = not at all confident, 3 = somewhat confident, and 5 = very confident. The list words are: *bed, rest, awake, tired, dream, wake, snooze, blanket, doze, slumber, snore, nap, peace, yawn, drowsy.*

This list was carefully designed to lure you into falsely recalling a word that was not on the list but was strongly associated with the other words on the list. Did you recall the lure word *sleep*? If so, how confident were you that it appeared on the list? Roediger and McDermott (1996) found that with college students, participants incorrectly recalled a lure word approximately 40% of the time. Moreover, the students were very confident that the lure word was on the list.

Researchers have used various techniques to produce false memories, including hypnotic suggestion (Laurence & Perry, 1983), false computer feedback, interview procedures (Loftus & Bernstein, 2005), feedback from psychologists interpreting participants' dreams, and suggestions from relatives to remember events. False memories can be successfully implanted when the suggested memory is plausible, that is, when it seems to fit within a person's life narrative and comes from a reliable, trusted source (Laney, 2013). For example, in the famous "lost in the mall" study, a graduate student, Jim, gave his younger brother, Chris, the false reminder, "Remember when you were lost in the mall?" (Loftus, Coan, & Pickrell, 1996). Chris initially said he could not recall the event, but after hearing this suggestion more times, he became convinced that he was recalling a real event—even though his caregivers said the event had never occurred.

People are susceptible to several other kinds of memory errors as well (Laney, 2013; Schacter, 2001). One common and important error is source forgetting or source confusion, in which a person attributes some memory or knowledge to the wrong source. You have probably had the experience of remembering that you heard something but were unable to recall from whom or where you heard it. Source forgetting can interfere with critical thinking (CT) when you cannot recall whether you heard something from a reputable news source or encountered it as a rumor on the Internet. Source confusion can also lead to plagiarism, as when a writer forgets the origin of some idea or information and fails to attribute it to the original source, implying that the idea is the writer's own.

Another memory error that threatens our ability to think critically and reject misconceptions is confusing familiarity with truth. Familiarity often helps us recognize objects and things we have experienced. Yet familiarity can lead us astray when later, after we have heard or read about some claim, we do not know whether it is true or false but just that it seems familiar. For example, shortly after a teaching a CT class in which we discussed the opposites-attract misconception and the correct notion that people are more attracted to others who are similar to them (see Chapter 1), one of my students said, "I remember talking about that topic, but which idea was it?" My student had forgotten the truth of the statement that people who are similar are more attracted to one another, and the two possibilities—opposites attract and similarity attracts—both seemed familiar. Skurnik Yoon, Park, and Schwartz (2005) showed that when participants were warned that the claims they were given were actually false, many of them, especially the older ones, misremembered the false claims as true only three days later. This tendency may create a problem when the goal is to dispel misconceptions, because many confidently held misconceptions may seem familiar (Bensley & Lilienfeld, 2015).

Based on this discussion of memory errors, you might jump to the conclusion that memory is invariably faulty, but this hasty generalization ignores other relevant evidence. For one thing, our cognitive system seems to be very good at taking in new information and updating our knowledge base (Laney, 2013; Schacter, 2001). We can use our vast knowledge of the world to help us further extend our knowledge. Even if we do not remember something exactly, we often remember the gist of a passage or situation quite well. However, the same cognitive system that allows us to update memory with new information and often integrate this information with fairly good comprehension and memory for gist can produce false memories, source confusions, distortions, forgetting of important details, and other memory errors.

Despite its flaws, human memory is quite remarkable and serves us well. Without special training, the average college student can recognize the meanings of approximately 40,000 different words (Pinker, 1994)—a phenomenon that underlies our amazing ability to understand language. In one study, students correctly recognized 93% of 2,560 photos of objects and scenes they had briefly viewed three days earlier (Standing, Conezio, & Haber, 1970). Often, through deliberate practice, people with ordinary memory abilities can achieve amazing feats of LTM, such as actors who learn to recall hundreds of lines, nearly word for word (Noice & Noice, 2006). Unfortunately, in many situations (e.g., eyewitness accounts of a crime), people cannot practice what they observe.

Practice Thinking 6.2: Identifying Cognitive Errors

As specifically as you can, first identify the cognitive error described in each of the following examples and then explain why it might have occurred.

1. Sara had been watching a horror movie about hauntings before going to bed. She woke up in the middle of the night and saw an entity materialize in front of her, hovering over the bed. Suppose that nothing was actually there.

   Cognitive error: _____ Explanation: _____

2. One night on the way back to his apartment, Gino looked up in the sky and saw a bright light that seemed to be pulsating. He squinted his eyes to get a better look and thought it looked saucer-shaped. He thought to himself, "Wow! I think it's a UFO or a flying saucer."

   Cognitive error: _____ Explanation: _____

   _____

3. Sienna was watching a movie she had seen two times before. In a big car-chase scene, one car made a right turn around a corner so fast that it tipped onto the edge of its tires on the right side of the car. As the car emerged from making the right turn, it was on the edge of its wheels on the left side of the car. Sienna thought, "That's strange—I never noticed that before."

   Cognitive error: _____ Explanation: _____

   _____

4. In a lecture on memory of traumatic events, Jay's instructor stated that despite the popular belief that people repress or are not able to access traumatic memories, no high-quality, scientific evidence has supported the claim that repressed memory occurs often, if at all. Later, when Jay was studying for an exam on the material, he found that he had not written down anything from that part of the lecture. Although he remembered his instructor talking about this topic, he could not remember if repressed memory was real. He decided that it was.

   Cognitive error: _____ Explanation: _____

   _____

Research on memory and other cognitive errors address the important question of whether eyewitness memory is accurate. To prepare you to critically read a literature review on the accuracy of eyewitness memory, we first apply what we have learned about cognition to better understand how to read effectively.

SUGGESTIONS FOR BECOMING AN ACTIVE READER

Reading is a complex cognitive skill for acquiring new information that involves attention, perception, WM, LTM, thinking, and metacognition. Recall that metacognition involves monitoring your own cognition so that you can regulate your mental processes and behaviors to reach your goals. Therefore, to get the most out of your reading, you should first set goals for your reading, then monitor your reading to ensure you are reaching your goals, and correct your approach if it is not working (Baker, 1989).

The approach you take depends on the goals you want to attain for a specific reading task. For example, you would approach reading a college textbook differently from reading a romantic novel. In this chapter, your task is to critically read a literature review that addresses the specific question, "Is eyewitness memory accurate?" Because your goal is to draw a well-reasoned inductive conclusion from the evidence presented, you should carefully read and seek to understand each bit of evidence presented so you can evaluate the support it provides.

Unfortunately, people often fail to attend sufficiently to their reading and just automatically say the words to themselves, without comprehending them. This kind of reading is passive and may leave you perplexed: "I just finished reading this, but I don't know what it said!" Adequately monitoring your comprehension is the best way to know whether you need to approach a task differently to improve your learning (Dunlosky & Lipko, 2007).

To avoid passive reading and inadequate monitoring of your comprehension, you should read the passage carefully and check your comprehension as you go along. Ask yourself frequently, "Do I understand what I just read? Am I following the major points being made?" If you do not understand a word, you may need to look it up. If you do not understand a sentence, it often helps to go back and reread it rather than just pushing on without comprehending. It may also help to try to make sense of the confusing sentence in the context of the surrounding sentences.

Active reading involves continuously accessing relevant background knowledge from LTM. To do so most effectively, it helps to know what you are looking for. Before you dig into the body of the article, a good way to prepare to access the needed knowledge is to preview the headings in the passage to see how the discussion is organized. For example, if you skip ahead into the critical reading passage in Practice Thinking 6.3, you will see that it has headings for "Eyewitness Testimony" and "Eyewitness Identification"; thus, the discussion of eyewitness memory can be envisioned as being divided into these two subtopics. Previewing the headings may help activate your prior knowledge and improve both your comprehension and memory of the passage (Bransford & Johnson, 1972; Klingner, Morrison, & Eppolito, 2011).

Questions to Prepare You for Critical Reading

Both active reading and critical reading demand a lot of cognitive resources, placing a very big load on WM. Fortunately, you can apply a variety of strategies to help you manage the demands of critical reading and improve your comprehension. For example, Table 6.1 provides a selected set of critical reading questions to guide you through analysis of the critical reading passage in Practice Thinking 6.3. These questions ask you to identify claims, specific pieces of evidence, and the kind and quality of each piece of evidence for both sides of the argument; they prompt you to evaluate the evidence thoroughly and draw a well-reasoned inductive conclusion from it.

TABLE 6.1 Questions for Completing the Critical Reading Task

1. What is the central question? Which claims are being made overall and within each section?

2. Which evidence has been presented that is relevant to evaluating each side of the question? To answer this question, first organize the relevant evidence into two categories: one category containing evidence that supports the claim and a second category containing evidence that does not support the claim. Next, label each piece of evidence as to its kind—that is, whether it is nonscientific (e.g., anecdotal) or scientific (e.g., comes from an authority on the subject—see Tables 3.1 and 4.3 for help). Repeat these steps for the evidence presented in each section (i.e., under each heading of the passage).

3. Evaluate the quality and quantity of the evidence both in each section of the passage and overall so that you can draw a well-reasoned conclusion based on all the evidence presented. How much good evidence supports one side versus the other? Can a clear conclusion be drawn, or is the evidence mixed? Does the conclusion need to be qualified because it seems to be true only under certain conditions? (Do not make a sweeping generalization.)

4. Evaluate the reasoning about this question.

   a. Were any assumptions made that could create problems for the conclusion you drew?

   b. Was the question addressed effectively? Were any thinking or logical errors made?

In a detailed literature review, such as the one that follows, you may encounter 10 to 20 pieces of evidence supporting each side of an argument. If you tried to hold all of that information in LTM, your memory would soon be seriously overloaded. To reduce this load, the form in Table 6.1 encourages you to externalize your thinking—that is, to make your internal thoughts explicit and visible. Writing a short summary of each piece of evidence provides you with an external record of your thinking that you can inspect later. Also, writing a brief summary that contains the most important words to describe the evidence may promote metacognitive reflection and reading comprehension (Dunlosky & Lipko, 2007; Fukaya, 2013). The questions in the critical reading form also serve as prompts to remind you of the basic components of the task: organizing, identifying, and evaluating the evidence and then drawing a well-reasoned inductive conclusion.

 Practice Thinking 6.3: Critical Reading: Is Eyewitness Memory Accurate?

Answer the questions from Table 6.1 to analyze the critical reading that follows.

CRITICAL READING: IS EYEWITNESS MEMORY ACCURATE?

Eyewitness Testimony

Jurors tend to trust the testimony of eyewitnesses, according to Semmler, Brewer, and Douglass (2012), who conducted an extensive literature review of many studies performed over the last three decades. The fact that many people believe they can trust eyewitness memory to be accurate might lead us to conclude that it is generally accurate. Should jurors indeed trust such testimony? When Wise and Safer (2004) surveyed 160 U.S. judges to assess their knowledge of eyewitness memory, they found that the judges did not consider many of the worrisome factors thought to influence the accuracy of eyewitness memory to be a problem. Can eyewitness memory be trusted to accurately reflect the details of a crime, or does it often lead to wrongful convictions?

On the one hand, some studies have shown that eyewitness memory can be quite accurate. Yuille and Cutshall (1986) tested the memories of

13 eyewitnesses to a fatal shooting that had occurred 5 months earlier. Although the eyewitnesses had been asked many misleading questions during this time, they were able to recall the original events quite accurately. Likewise, in a case study of 13 eyewitnesses to a robbery, Odinot, Wolters, and van Koppen (2009) found that witnesses accurately recalled 84% of the information 3 months after the crime, despite their exposure to a TV broadcast that could have provided misinformation.

On the other hand, examples abound of how testimony based on faulty eyewitness memory has sent innocent people to prison. As of February 2017, the Innocence Project had used DNA evidence to exonerate 349 people serving time in prison (Innocence Project, 2017). Of 250 wrongful convictions that have been examined, approximately 75% of them were convicted based on eyewitness testimony.

Many other studies have demonstrated that eyewitness memory errors are common and can easily be produced in response to other information provided after an event has been observed (Loftus, 1992). For instance, in a classic experiment, Loftus and Palmer (1974) found that asking different leading questions after participants observed an event affected how the participants recalled the event. First, the researchers showed participants a film of an automobile accident. They then asked one group, "About how fast were the cars going when they *smashed* into each other?" Other groups were asked the same question but using the word *hit* or *contacted* instead of *smashed*. The participants' estimated speed depended on the word used in the leading question. The group who heard the word *smashed,* which suggested a serious accident, estimated the car's speed to be 40.8 miles per hour; the group who heard the word *contacted,* which suggests a much less serious accident, estimated the speed at 31.8 miles per hour. This is an example of the **misinformation effect**, in which hearing misleading information after viewing an event produces biased or inaccurate memory of the event.

Loftus and Palmer (1974) argued that participants reconstructed their memories of the accident after they received the misleading post-event information. A second experiment with the same car-accident film further supported the contention that reconstruction had occurred, not just the biasing effects of words in the questions. This time, the researchers used only the words *smashed* or *hit* when asking participants a week later whether they had seen any broken glass from the accident in the film. Those who heard the word *smashed* were more likely to report having seen broken glass than those who heard the word *hit*. There was no broken glass shown in the film, so the fact that the participants "remembered" broken glass when its presence was merely implied by the post-event question supports the claim that their memory was reconstructed around the word *smashed*.

Loftus and Zanni (1975) provided further evidence for reconstruction of memory around a single word when they showed participants a film of a car accident in which no headlights were broken. On a questionnaire about the event, they asked one group an unbiased question, "Did you see *a* broken headlight?" and another group the leading question, "Did you see *the* broken headlight?" Approximately 17% of the group who read *the* in their question reported having seen broken glass, whereas only 7% of the group who read *a* reported having seen it. One plausible interpretation of the reconstruction that occurs in memories of car accidents and other events is that misleading or biasing post-event information activates different schemas for different kinds of accidents, such that the witness recalls the event consistent with the schema.

Many experiments have replicated the misinformation effect in both children and adults (e.g., Bonto & Payne, 1991; Loftus, Donders, & Hoffman, 1989; Sutherland & Hayne, 2001; Wilford, Chan, & Tuhn, 2014). Moreover, witnesses showing this effect are often very confident of their inaccurate memories (Loftus et al., 1989). In addition, repeated questioning of both children and adults may increase their confidence in their faulty memories (Shaw, 1996).

Interviewers can use leading questions and misinformation to produce inaccuracies in what eyewitnesses remember, but can they induce an innocent person to remember having committed a crime? In a recent experiment, Shaw and Porter (2015) interviewed 60 college students whose guardians had reported that the students had never committed crimes including assault, assault with a weapon, or theft. In an initial interview, none of the students reported having committed a crime. Over the course of three interviews, students were told that their guardians had verified that the youths had committed one of the crimes and that police contact had been involved; other false details about the fictitious event were also provided. If the students responded that they could not recall any details of the event, the experimenter told them to try harder, explaining that most people could remember such events if they tried hard enough. The students were also told to visualize the event at home each night. After three interviews, Shaw and Porter found that 70% of the students ultimately recalled the event as having happened and reported a number of details about their false memory.

Other evidence for schema effects in eyewitness memory comes from a study by Tuckey and Brewer (2003). First, participants were asked to describe a bank robbery. They consistently reported that bank robbers were male; wore sunglasses, dark clothes, and disguises; and demanded money and had getaway cars with drivers—all details that suggested the existence of a schema for a bank robbery. In a second experiment, different participants watched a simulation of a bank robbery. Consistent with schema theory, Tuckey and Brewer (2003) found that participants remembered more details relevant to the schema than irrelevant ones.

In another experiment, participants recalled details of a simulated bank robbery, but this time some information was ambiguous or open to different interpretations. Schema theory predicts that people will use their prior knowledge to interpret new and ambiguous information in ways consistent with a schema. Participants in Tuckey and Brewer's experiment, for example, recalled that one of the bank robbers, whose head was covered with a balaclava to hide the person's identity, was a male, consistent with the bank robber schema.

Eyewitness Identification

To correctly identify a suspect, an eyewitness must recollect a perpetrator's physical features, especially facial features. Facial recognition is very important to human social and emotional communication. The human brain includes an area called the fusiform facial gyrus that is specialized for processing the information necessary for face recognition and becomes active after learning of new face-like features (Gauthier, Tarr, Anderson, Skudlarski, & Gore, 1999). Experiments in various countries around the world, in which people were presented with faces expressing emotion, have shown that participants can reliably identify the facial expressions for basic emotions of people from their own and other cultures (Ekman, 1994). Likewise, in our own everyday experience, we know that we seldom fail to recognize the faces of our relatives, friends, and many acquaintances. Even so, the fact that people are good at recognizing the faces of familiar people, as well as recognizing the emotions of people in general, does not imply that they will accurately recognize the face of a perpetrator they do not know—even if they have been able to adequately view the perpetrator's face.

Research suggests that people are not very good at recognizing unfamiliar faces. One experiment tested this ability by showing participants various images from closed-circuit TV cameras (CCTV). Bruce and colleagues (1999) presented a target face from a CCTV video clip, along with 10 high-quality photos of faces, and asked participants to match the CCTV target face with one of the photographed faces when they could. Participants matched the target face with the correct face only 65% of the time when the corresponding photo was present. In 35% of the trials, they incorrectly matched it to a face when the target was not actually present. Although many businesses have CCTV cameras to deter potential criminals, witnesses may often be unable to identify robbers from the CCTV images.

This finding is consistent with the many findings reviewed by Lampinem, Neuschatz, and Cling (2012), which revealed that eyewitnesses often make errors in identification of faces. Such errors in eyewitness identification are a primary factor in the wrongful conviction of accused persons (Innocence Project, 2017). Moreover, in most cases, eyewitnesses observe crimes committed by people they do not know.

Source confusion can be another reason for eyewitness identification errors, as demonstrated in the real-world example provided by memory researcher Daniel Schacter (2001). In Australia, a woman who was raped confused her assailant with memory expert Donald Thomson, who was appearing on a program on her television at the time of the rape. Ironically, he was talking about memory on the program. Of course, Thomson's iron-clad alibi showed her accusation was false and due to source forgetting.

The context or other information that makes up the environment in which an eyewitness identifies a person can also affect accuracy. For instance, the clothes a suspect is wearing can provide cues used in identification (Davies & Thomson, 1988). In general, people are better at recognizing faces when they try to recognize them in the same context and setting as when they first observed them. A lineup in which a witness is asked to identify a potential perpetrator from among several similar-looking people provides very different contextual cues from the original situation in which a crime was committed. Lineups that contain individuals who are similar in appearance can lead to more misidentifications. Generally, smaller lineups lead to more accurate identification. Also, witnesses are more likely to misidentify an innocent suspect if the lineup is composed completely of suspects than when lineups are composed of only one suspect and the rest are known innocents (Wells, 1993).

Limitations in our perceptual and attentional abilities can lead to eyewitness memory errors. In one study, Davies and Hine (2007) showed participants a video of a burglary in which the actor portraying the burglar was replaced with a different-looking actor in the middle of the crime. The experimenters found that 61% of participants showed change blindness for the replacement. In another experiment, Davis, Loftus, Vanous, and Cucciare (2008) found that distracting participants with the task of memorizing items in a grocery aisle made those participants less likely than participants not given the distracting task to detect the replacement of a person committing a crime in front of them.

Much of the research reviewed so far has been based on studies of eyewitness memory conducted in the laboratory. But are the same findings obtained when memory of eyewitnesses to actual crimes is studied? A large study of 314 actual lineups from London police records revealed low levels of identification accuracy (Valentine, Pickering, & Darling, 2003). Of 640 eyewitnesses, only 40% were able to identify the actual suspect. Also troubling was the finding that 20% identified people who were not suspects.

The case of Jennifer Thompson illustrates some of the many different factors that contribute to eyewitness identification errors. One summer night in 1984, a man with a knife accosted the 22-year-old White college student and raped her. As the attack was taking place, Thompson told herself she would carefully study the features of her assailant so she could later identify him. She identified Ronald Cotton as her rapist in a photo lineup. At his trial, she again identified Cotton, testifying that she was certain he was her assailant, resulting in Cotton's conviction. After Cotton had spent 10 years in prison for the crime, DNA evidence was used to exonerate him and identify Bobby Poole as Thompson's rapist. Compare the faces of the two men in Figure 6.5.

The presence of a lethal weapon, such as a gun, can be an overwhelming factor in the ability of eyewitnesses to process the context. It can increase the stress and arousal of witnesses, riveting their attention to the weapon—an effect called **weapon focus**.

Burlington N.C. Police Department

FIGURE 6.5 Jennifer Thompson mistakenly identified Ronald Cotton (*left*) as her rapist. He was convicted and imprisoned until a DNA match with Bobby Poole (*right*) exonerated him. How could this mistake have happened?

When a gun or other weapon is involved, victims tend to narrow their focus and devote most of their attention to the weapon, paying less attention to the face of the offender and other details of the crime. This, in turn, reduces their ability to remember other features of the event (Loftus, Loftus, & Messo, 1987).

A meta-analysis of studies on the effects of stress on eyewitness identification and another meta-analysis on recall of details of crimes both offered considerable support for the hypothesis that stress impairs memory (Deffenbacher, Bornstein, Penrod, & McGorty, 2004). Although a study of the accuracy of eyewitness identification in actual lineups found no reliable effect in witnesses of crimes where a weapon was present (Valentine et al., 2003), a panel of psychologists who serve as expert witnesses on eyewitness memory agreed that weapon focus is a sufficiently reliable theory to present in a court as evidence (Kassin, Tubb, Hosch, & Memon, 2001). In Jennifer Thompson's case, the fact that she had a knife held to her throat during her attack probably made it difficult to focus her attention on anything other than that detail, even though she said she deliberately tried to study her assailant's face.

Another important factor in Thompson's misidentification may have been own-race bias, or what is now more commonly called the cross-race effect. Research has repeatedly shown that people are better at identifying the face of someone of their own race than the face of a person of a different race (Shriver, Young, Hugenberg, Bernstein, & Lanter, 2008). In Thompson's case, Poole and Cotton may have looked more similar to her than they would have appeared to an African American person.

Overconfidence in memory is another factor in eyewitness misidentification that likely contributed to the wrongful conviction of Ronald Cotton. Although jurors find confident identifications highly persuasive, eyewitness confidence often does not predict identification accuracy. Jennifer Thompson testified two times that she was certain Ronald Cotton was her assailant, yet she was wrong both times. A meta-analysis of many studies in which eyewitnesses reported their level of confidence after making an identification from a lineup found that the correlation between confidence and accuracy was $r = 0.41$ when eyewitnesses made a positive identification, but it was nearly $r = 0.00$ when eyewitnesses did not identify a suspect (Sporer, Penrod, Read, & Cutler, 1995).

A recent review of studies of confidence in eyewitness identifications revealed that confidence is more predictive of accuracy at the time of the initial identification (Wixted, Mickes, Clark, Gronlund, & Roedifer, 2015). In fact, Jennifer Thompson's initial identification of Cotton in a photo lineup showed more than 5 minutes of hesitation and culminated in her statement, "I think this is the guy"

(Thompson-Cannino, Cotton, & Torneo, 2009, p. 33). Somehow, Thompson's confidence in her misidentification greatly increased over time.

If confidence can be increased by factors that do not increase the accuracy of memory, then increases in confidence will not reflect memory accuracy. To test this idea, Bradfield, Wells, and Olson (2002) asked two groups of participants to watch a video of a young man committing a crime. Each group was asked to try to identify the young man in a six-person lineup and to rate their confidence in the identification. Following the confidence rating, Bradfield and colleagues gave confirmatory feedback to one group: "Good, you identified the actual suspect" (whether or not the participant correctly identified the young man). The second group received no such feedback. Both groups then rated their confidence again. The confidence ratings of participants who were both incorrect and received confirmatory feedback greatly increased after the reinforcement.

This study's findings clearly demonstrate that police officers who use confirmatory feedback after a lineup could unknowingly—and erroneously—inflate eyewitness confidence. Police gave Jennifer Thompson confirmatory feedback after she identified Ronald Cotton, which she has said made her more confident of her memory (Innocence Project, 2017) and may have made her a more convincing witness. Overconfidence can also be inflated when prosecutors coach witnesses to be confident in their testimony (Baddeley, Eysenck, & Anderson, 2015).

SUMMARY

Cognitive errors of attention, perception, and memory can lead to errors in thinking. Many errors originate from the fact that we have limited cognitive resources. We can attend to only so much information at once. Our inability to handle an overwhelming set of stimuli can produce errors when we try to do too many things simultaneously (e.g., driving while talking on a cell phone), when we focus on one thing and fail to see something else in clear view (e.g., inattentional blindness), and when we fail to perceive a change across scenes (e.g., change blindness).

Perception involves organizing, interpreting, and recognizing patterns in the data coming from the senses. Human perception is limited in how much our unaided senses allow us to take in; but fortunately, scientific and technological aids, such as the Hubble telescope and brain scanning devices, have greatly extended our ability to perceive the world. Our knowledge of the world also helps us perceive more accurately and efficiently, yet it can also lead to perceptual errors—as when expert wine-tasters judge an expensively labeled wine as tasting better than the same wine labeled as less expensive. Other perceptual errors occur when we misidentify a familiar object, such as mistaking a conventional aircraft for a UFO.

In contrast to perceptual errors, hallucinations occur when an individual believes he or she has perceived something that is not really there. Although people with certain serious mental disorders tend to hallucinate, people *without* disorders hallucinate more often than is commonly assumed, especially as a potential consequence of stress or poor sleep quality.

Working memory—a kind of short-term memory we use to do our cognitive work—also limits the amount of information we can retain for a brief period of time. If the cognitive load on memory is too great, we will forget or be unable to successfully complete a task. Interference from distracting stimuli can interfere with efficient attention and processing of information in WM as well.

Based on your prior knowledge and schemas, you form expectations that often aid perception and memory—but those same expectations can also lead you to perceive and remember incorrectly. Schemas can help fill in the gaps in information we encounter, thereby helping us make sense of this new information; at other times, however, schemas can bias and distort our memory. False memories occur when our established associations and prior knowledge induce us to recall something similar in meaning that is not really there or has not actually occurred.

Errors of LTM can lead to errors in eyewitness memory. The misinformation effect in eyewitness memory is an example of how misleading information that is presented after an event can produce memory errors, as when a leading question activates a schema that causes us to reconstruct a memory inaccurately. Source confusion can also produce errors in eyewitness identification, as when a witness confuses a perpetrator with an innocent person. Eyewitness identification errors are also more likely to occur when lineups or photo spreads are biased, when a witness views a weapon, and when witnesses are identifying someone of a different race. Unfortunately, witnesses are often very confident of their inaccurate memories. Because high-quality research has demonstrated that people may commit many different eyewitness memory errors, we must conclude that eyewitness testimony and identification are often, but not necessarily always, inaccurate.

Practice Thinking 6.4: WHAT DO YOU THINK **NOW?**
Please explain how you know.

1. What do the three chapter-opening scenarios have in common?

   _____

2. If you look directly at something, will you always see it?

   _____

3. Is something wrong with a person who has a hallucination?

   _____

4. How do magicians accomplish their amazing feats?

   _____

5. Is your memory like a video recorder that stores an exact copy of whatever you observe?

   _____

6. Is eyewitness memory accurate? Should jurors trust it?

   _____

REVIEW QUESTIONS

1. What is cognition? What are cognitive errors?
2. What are errors in attention?
   - What is inattentional blindness?
   - What is change blindness?
   - Describe some problems with dividing attention.

3. What are errors in perception?
   - Explain pareidolia (finding patterns that are not there).
   - Describe expectancy and errors in pattern recognition.
   - What are illusions?
4. What are hallucinations, and do "normal" people have them?
5. How can errors of perception and attention contribute to inaccurate memory?
6. How does working memory work? Which types of errors are associated with it?
7. What is working memory load? What can you do to reduce it?
8. How is the accuracy of memory important to good reasoning and critical thinking?
9. What is the evidence that memory can be very accurate?
10. What is a schema? How does it affect comprehension and memory?
11. What are memory errors?
    - What are false memories, or memory illusions? How are they produced?
    - What is source forgetting?
    - What is the misinformation effect? How is it related to leading questions?
12. How good is confidence in predicting how well an eyewitness will remember something?
13. How might a schema affect eyewitness memory?
14. What factors can affect the accuracy of eyewitness identification?
    - What is weapon focus? How is it explained?
    - What is own-race bias?
    - How can lineup procedures affect the accuracy of eyewitness identification?
15. What misconceptions do people have about perception? Attention? Memory?

7

CAN THE MIND LEAVE THE BODY?
THE MIND–BRAIN QUESTION

LEARNING OUTCOMES

After studying this chapter, you should be able to:

1. Explain your own philosophical position on the mind–brain question.

2. Explain how assumptions affect the way you approach a psychological question.

3. Explain how various methods for studying the brain provide different information.

4. Critically analyze and evaluate the information in a discussion about how the mind and the brain are related.

WHAT DO YOU THINK?

Certain television programs claim to provide images of ghostly figures and show what they say are houses haunted by ghosts. In a 2013 online Harris poll of 2,250 American adults, 42% of the respondents said they believed in ghosts and 24% believed in reincarnation. Many people who believe in ghosts think the mind or spirit is a nonphysical entity that leaves the physical body at death. What do you think?

Practice Thinking 7.1: What Do You Think?

Please explain how you know.

1. Do ghosts really exist? Can a soul or spirit be reincarnated in another person?

   _____

2. How can an amputee experience pain in a foot or hand that is not there?

   _____

3. Imagine a purple strawberry with yellow spots. How can your mind think of something that does not physically exist?

   _____

4. In an out-of-body experience, does the person's mind really leave the body?

   _____

If you believe that ghosts exist, then you likely believe that a nonphysical entity, such as a soul or spirit, can exist in a physical body and then leave it at death. Likewise, those who think that the mind or soul actually leaves a person's body during an out-of-body experience (OBE) view the mind as separable from the brain. In these two examples, mental experience seems distinct and separable from the physical dimension. The other two examples listed previously—feeling pain in an amputated appendage and imagining a purple strawberry with yellow spots—imply that a person can experience something that does not physically exist. These examples raise questions about the relationship between brain activity and mental experience. Can the brain somehow go beyond physical reality to produce the experience of something that does not physically exist? Each of these examples concerns the **mind–brain (M–B) question** (also called the *mind–body question* or *mind–body problem*), the perplexing question of how the mind is related to the brain.

PHILOSOPHICAL POSITIONS ON THE MIND–BRAIN QUESTION

To understand how various thinkers have approached the M–B problem, we focus on four common positions. Probably the most prevalent is **M–B dualism**, a position which assumes that the mind and body are two different entities—exactly as the term *dual* implies (Hergenhahn, 1992). Some dualists believe that the mind and the body are two different substances or have completely different properties (Brook & Stainton, 2000).

The French philosopher René Descartes contributed much to this dualistic view. His famous saying, "I think, therefore I am," shows that Descartes did not doubt the reality of his mind doing the doubting, even though he could doubt the reality of the physical world. Although the soul or mind seems to lack physical substance, his scientific observations told him that the body was a physical entity. To resolve this conflict, Descartes proposed that the nonphysical mind and the physical body are two separate entities that interact by means of a small gland near the center of the brain called the *pineal gland*.

Many dualists believe that although our bodies are limited by time and space, our minds or souls can go beyond these limitations, even surviving physical death. For example, many Christians believe that the body is material, or physical, and that the soul is immaterial, or nonphysical (Robinson, 1981). The nonphysical soul resides in a person's body during life, but it leaves the physical form that contains it at the time of death. It is not surprising, then, that M–B dualists also tend to believe that when people have an OBE, the mind actually leaves the body (Blanchfield, Bensley, Hierstetter, Mahdavi, & Rowan, 2007).

In contrast to dualism, many other philosophers, psychologists, and scientists endorse **monism**, the position that the world is really all *one* thing, exactly as the term implies. According to monists, the mind and the body simply *appear* to be different—but they are actually one entity. The most common form of monism, called **materialism** (or physicalism), assumes the world is physical and governed by the influence of the environment on the physical body. Mental experience, therefore, is just an aspect of the physical operation of the brain. Still other monists believe that the mind and the brain are really identical and that every mental state has a corresponding brain state.

Some materialists believe that if we knew enough, we would see that all behavior and mental processes could be reduced to the brain processes operating in the physical world. These so-called **reductionists** assume that scientific research will ultimately be able to explain mental states when we understand the relevant biochemical and other physical changes that occur in the nervous system.

Accordingly, reductionists focus on research investigating how the nervous system provides the basis for behavior and mental processes.

Still other scientists, known as **functionalists**, regard mental states and processes as something to be explained in their own right and assume that mental processes serve certain functions. Although many functionalists are sympathetic to materialism and would likely agree that the mind is what the brain does, they do not assume that all behavior and mental processes can be reduced to physical events. They might agree that the function of the brain is to produce mental processes and experience, but they are less concerned with *how* the brain accomplishes this amazing feat.

Practice Thinking 7.2: Identifying Positions on the M–B Question

In the examples that follow, which philosophical position on the M–B question does each person hold?

Example 1

Marla is a neuroscientist working on a project involving the search for hormones that, when present in the fetal brain, may determine before birth the sexual preferences of individuals later in life. She thinks these hormones largely determine a person's sexuality and that later learning has little influence on sexual preference. She further believes that research on these biochemical mechanisms will ultimately explain the origins of sexual identity. Marla is a _____.

Example 2

Larry is a psychology major who has been attending a Christian church all his life. He is not sure what happens to the mind when someone dies, but he firmly believes that his soul will survive death even though his body will not. Larry is a _____.

Example 3

A cognitive psychologist conducted experiments to find out how the manner in which students attend to material they are studying is related to their subsequent memory of the material. She concluded that students who focus their attention more on the material can recall more of what they studied.

She intends to further study the relationship between these cognitive processes without concern for how the brain processes the information. This cognitive psychologist is a _____.

Example 4

Which M–B position is closest to your own? Explain. _____

_____.

HOW ASSUMPTIONS AFFECT EXPLANATIONS OF MIND AND BEHAVIOR

An individual's position on the M–B question can greatly affect his or her approach to understanding the world. M–B dualism can even be a dangerous position, as evidenced by the mass suicide of 39 members of the Heaven's Gate cult who, as they put it, "exited the vehicle" (i.e., killed the body) so that their spirits could be free to rendezvous with aliens in a spaceship approaching Earth (see Chapter 4). In this extreme dualistic view, the body is merely a conveyance for carrying the spirit around. If the spirit is assumed to be separable and the most important part of a person, then sacrificing the body does not seem to be much of a sacrifice at all.

Your own stance on the M–B question can influence which theory you endorse and which approach you take to psychological questions. For example, many scientists studying the brain who are physicalists may be less inclined to examine subjective experience and more inclined to focus on the brain. If they neglect subjective mental states, their explanation of the mind and brain may be incomplete.

Sometimes lawyers take extreme materialistic positions in defense of their clients, arguing as an excuse for a criminal's behavior that "his brain made him do it." As evidence, they may present images of damage in the client's brain or show a scan of abnormal activity in a brain area, comparing it with the scan of a normal brain (Thornton, 2011). This extreme materialistic approach is wrong-headed, in that it assumes that we are only our brains. The mind and the brain are closely related—they are part of the same person. Saying that a person's "brain made him do it" ignores the interconnected nature of the brain and mental processes that emerge as the brain operates in a complex environment—one in which some environmental events are simply random. Locating a brain area that becomes activated when a person behaves a certain way may *seem* to demonstrate the cause of the behavior, but this assumption is unwarranted. Brain-scanning technology is not yet able to predict who will commit a crime, and events often have multiple causes.

In contrast, radical behaviorism is a materialistic approach assuming that mental processes are unimportant. John Watson, the founder of behaviorism, argued that psychologists should not study mental processes because the mind is not directly observable. Instead, psychologists should study the relationships between stimuli and responses, which are observable. One consequence of the dominance of behaviorism in U.S. psychology was that many psychologists were discouraged for decades from studying memories, mental imagery, emotion, consciousness, and other mental events.

Finally, the assumptions that some M–B dualists make can prevent the scientific study of the relationship between mind and brain. Suppose someone believes that the mind is nonphysical and the brain is physical; then what kind of observation could show the action of the mind? In psychology, we make observations of external, physical events as indicators of the action of the mind. How can we do this if the mind is nonphysical?

SCIENTIFIC TECHNIQUES FOR STUDYING THE BRAIN

Scientists have developed powerful new observational tools to study how the brain functions both during ordinary conscious states and during more unusual states, such as an OBE. **Consciousness** refers to a person's current, subjective state of awareness. An important part of your consciousness of yourself is awareness of your own body—what it looks like, where it is positioned, how it feels. To perceive your body, your brain integrates information from various senses, including vision, touch, and body sense, and associates these with a conscious, experiencing self. For example, the vestibular system helps you sense the position of your body and maintain your balance by registering the orientation of receptors in your inner ear and sending this information to specific areas of the brain.

To understand how specific parts of the brain contribute to our conscious mental experience, scientists have tried to **localize function** in the brain—that is, to locate specific areas of the brain that become activated during particular behaviors and mental states. As part of this line of investigation, scientists have used case studies to understand how damage to specific brain areas is associated with specific changes in function. For instance, Broca used the case studies of Tan and others to localize the production of speech to (what later became known as) Broca's area. Although case studies are still used today, they are limited in terms of the quality of information they provide, as described in Chapter 3. Additionally, case studies of brain damage often involve people who have had strokes, diseases, or accidents—circumstances that tend to result in damage that is "messy" and not clearly localized to one brain area. Until recently, verifying the damaged area was possible only after the case study patient had died and an autopsy was performed.

Fortunately, newer techniques for imaging and activating the living brain have advanced our ability to more precisely study specific brain areas. **Electrostimulation of the brain (ESB)** can provide fairly precise information about localized function. ESB involves sending minute amounts of electricity to specific cells or small groups of cells, usually stimulating cells in the cortex, the neurons in the outer layers of the brain.

The Canadian neurosurgeon Wilder Penfield used ESB to distinguish healthy cortical areas from damaged areas in patients with epilepsy who were undergoing surgery. Epilepsy is a brain disorder in which electrical activity from a damaged area spreads to other areas in an out-of-control fashion, causing seizures. Penfield used ESB, systematically stimulating cells in the cortex, to identify not only the damaged brain tissue that needed to be removed but also the healthy tissue to be preserved. Patients were conscious during surgery, which enabled Penfield to record their responses after applying a microcurrent through a tiny electrode. Penfield used only a local anesthetic during this procedure because the brain has no pain receptors. In response to the ESB, patients reported sensations in parts of the body, moved a body part, described a memory, or reported nothing. Based on results from ESB in many patients, Penfield constructed a map of the cortical areas of the brain that were associated with sensation in specific parts of the body, as shown in Figure 7.1. If Penfield stimulated the area mapped to a sensation in a certain part of the body, the patient would have a sensation in that part of the body.

An obvious limitation of ESB is that it can be ethically used only with people who have severe problems requiring brain surgery. Fortunately, a new technique called **transcranial magnetic stimulation (TMS)** is available that can increase or decrease activity in very specific brain areas by stimulating the brain from outside the skull. In TMS, a magnetic pulse is applied to the scalp over the region to be stimulated, setting up tiny electric currents in that region. For example,

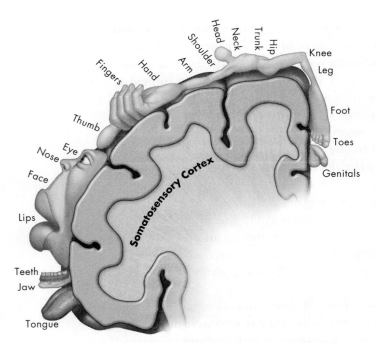

FIGURE 7.1 The drawing of the body part and its size indicate the place and relative size of the cortical area in the somatosensory cortex, based on Penfield's mapping from ESB responses. Notice that the area corresponding to sensation in the face is much larger than the area of some other parts of the body, such as the knee.

if the TMS wand were placed over the area mapping the hand in the somatosensory cortex shown in Figure 7.1, the subject might experience a tingling in the hand. Applying TMS at specific voltages and in certain sequences can even cause a person to be unaware of a visual stimulus that is in the field of view (Overgaard, Nielsen, & Fuglsang-Frederiksen, 2004). TMS is very useful for experimentally producing temporary changes in relatively small areas of the brains of healthy people.

Another technique, called electroencephalography (EEG), has been used for decades to record activity in large areas of the brain as a subject is presented with a stimulus or task. Although the EEG device is not sensitive to activity in small areas of the brain, it can show the waves of electrical activity that arise very rapidly in large groups of nerve cells. This technology can be used to monitor changes in consciousness, such as periods of alert concentration and the stages of sleep.

A more recent technique that is especially useful for studying localization of function in the living, working brain is functional magnetic resonance imaging (fMRI). In fMRI studies, a magnetic resonance imaging (MRI) machine monitors a person's brain activity as he or she does some task or engages in some mental activity. This activity is observable because during mental processing, glucose and oxygenated blood go to the brain area doing the work. Powerful magnets that encircle the head in the fMRI machine disturb the oxygen particles in the blood and give off radio frequencies. Sensors detect changes in these signals as oxygen in the blood is used by a specific brain area. Using these data, computers construct an image of this activity in relation to a standard reference brain map. In this way, neuroscientists can isolate the most active brain area(s) in a person having an OBE, for example.

Practice Thinking 7.3: Critical Reading of a Literature Review

Use what you have learned about the M–B question and OBE, as well as what you have learned from Tables 3.1 and 4.3, to answer the following questions. Evaluate the quality and quantity of evidence supporting each side of the argument and draw a well-reasoned conclusion.

1. What is the central question, and how is it being approached or defined? Which claim or claims are being made? How is each side of the argument related to major positions on the M–B question (e.g., M–B dualism versus physicalism)?

2. What is the evidence supporting each side of the argument? Which kind of evidence is it, and how good is that evidence? Organize each bit of evidence under the side it supports, beneath the appropriate heading from the passage. (Preview the headings in the passage to see where evidence will fit in the discussion.)

   a. Write a brief summary of each piece of evidence you encounter under the heading and the side of the argument it supports. For example, the common idea that the soul can leave the body is evidence supporting the claim that the soul is separate from the body; this information therefore belongs under "Origins in Philosophy and Religion." Evidence that does not support the claim should be written separately under that heading.

   b. Label each type of evidence and comment on its quality, using Tables 3.1 and 4.3. For example, the evidence mentioned above should be labeled as a commonsense belief documented by the anthropologist Frazer (1996), who is a scientific authority.

   c. Review each bit of evidence you described, labeled, and evaluated for both sides of the argument under their respective headings. Summarize the evidence on each side under the appropriate headings and generalize about which side is better supported by more high-quality evidence.

   d. Repeat steps (a) through (c) for the evidence presented under the next heading, "Dualistic Philosophy and Beliefs." Organize it into two categories: evidence that supports the claim and evidence that does not support the claim. Do this for the evidence under the remaining headings until you have analyzed all of the information.

3. Evaluate the quality and quantity of the evidence in each section of the passage so that you can draw a well-reasoned general conclusion based on *all* the evidence presented. How much good evidence supports one side versus the other? Can a clear conclusion be drawn from the evidence, or is the evidence mixed? Does the conclusion need to be qualified because it seems to be true only under certain conditions?

CRITICAL READING: CAN THE MIND ACTUALLY LEAVE THE BODY?

Origins in Philosophy and Religion

The idea that the soul can leave the body is a very old one, found in many cultures and religions, according to a pioneering study by the anthropologist Sir James Frazer (1996) that explored religious rites and beliefs from around the world. For example, in some cultures, people believe that when someone dreams of traveling somewhere, the dreamer's soul actually leaves the body and journeys to that place. The ancient Egyptians viewed the soul as a part of a person that could leave the body at death. In their burial ceremonies, the Ba, a human-headed bird representing the soul or breath of life, was breathed back into the mummified body to ensure life after death. In the book of Genesis, God breathed the spirit of life into Adam's body, formed from the dust of the Earth, to give man a living soul.

In many traditions, the soul or spirit has been associated with air and breath. Like the air that is breathed, the spirit is ephemeral, is essential to life, and can leave the body. Frazer (1996) reported that the Itonamas of South America close a dying person's mouth and nose to prevent the soul from departing and taking other souls with it. In some cultures, people have used traps in an attempt to recapture souls that have escaped. Figure 7.2 shows one such spirit trap used by shamans to keep the soul from leaving the body. Comparing the beliefs of 67 non-Western cultures from archived anthropological records, Shiels (1978) found evidence that almost 95% of them believed that a soul or spiritual entity could leave the body in some form. The occasion on which these OBEs most commonly

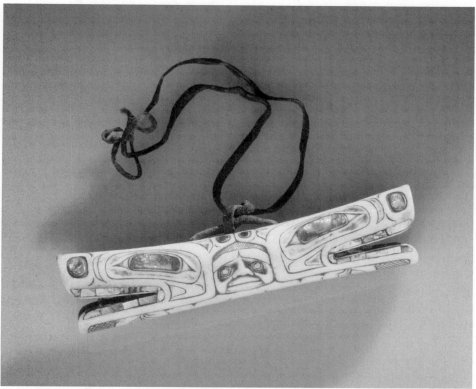

FIGURE 7.2 Shaman's spirit trap from Laos—Thai border.

Werner Forman/Art Resource, NY

occurred was during sleep, but such experiences were also reported to occur from illness, drug use, and trance states.

Much of modern dualistic belief in the ability to separate the soul and the body had its origins in Greek and Christian thought. Plato, a highly influential Greek philosopher who lived during the fifth century BCE, believed that the body is a vessel that contains the soul, whereas the mind is the immortal part of the soul that leaves the body at death and can be reincarnated in the body of another person (Plato, 1956). Many Christians over the centuries have believed that the soul is an entity that lives on after physical death and that it retains the powers of perception and feeling despite being separated from the body.

Dualistic Philosophy and Beliefs

Famous and influential philosophers and scientists have lent their support to M–B dualism. René Descartes, the brilliant French philosopher–mathematician of the seventeenth century, believed that the mind and the body are fundamentally different. He believed the body is made of physical substance extended in space, while the mind or soul is nonphysical and not extended in space (Descartes, 1999). Likewise, the influential philosopher of science, Karl Popper, and the Nobel prize–winning neuroscientist, Sir John Eccles, both endorsed a modern form of M–B dualism (Popper & Eccles, 1980).

More support for M–B dualism comes from the personal belief systems of many people, as revealed in national polls focused on paranormal beliefs. For example, a recent poll of 2,250 Americans revealed that 42% believed in ghosts (Harris Polls, 2013). A 2001 Gallup poll on paranormal beliefs in the United States indicated that dualistic, paranormal beliefs are widespread: 42% of respondents believed in hauntings, 28% believed that people can communicate mentally with the dead, 15% believed that dead people's spirits can be channeled through a living person, and 25% believed in reincarnation (Newport & Strausberg, 2001).

In surveys of U.S. college students, the cognitive psychologist Keith Stanovich (1989) found that not only did many students have high scores on a dualistic belief scale, but those students with stronger dualistic belief tended to report stronger belief in extrasensory perception (ESP; see Chapters 3 and 5), except for Baptists. Similarly, Thalbourne (1999) found that dualism in Australian students was significantly correlated with belief in life after death and in the possibility of contact with spirits of the dead. Not surprisingly, many famous parapsychologists, such as J. B. Rhine (1947), John Beloff (1989), and Loyd Auerbach (1986), have made statements supporting dualism, including claims of the separation of mind and body. James Alcock (1987), a noted scientific critic of parapsychology, has contended that M–B dualism is a basic assumption made by parapsychologists.

The paranormal belief most directly related to our discussion is the belief in astral projection, or soul travel. According to this view, the soul can leave the body and move to a higher spiritual plane of existence. As shown in Figure 7.3, believers in astral projection suggest that the soul or spiritual body is connected to the physical body by a silver strand.

As the preceding discussion indicated, several studies have demonstrated that belief in M–B dualism is very prevalent. Many people from different cultures, including many college students, have dualistic beliefs about the mind and body. Many experts on parapsychology and even some noted philosophers and scientists are M–B dualists, but most neuroscientists and cognitive psychologists reject it.

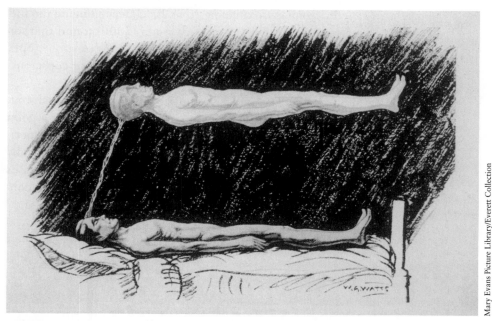

Mary Evans Picture Library/Everett Collection

FIGURE 7.3 Astral projection is the paranormal belief, which originated in the early twentieth century, that a person's soul can leave the body and travel to another, nonphysical spiritual plane.

Considering that so many individuals take this position, perhaps the dualist view is correct. People seem to find it natural and intuitively appealing. In his book, Yale psychologist Paul Bloom (2004) pointed out that considerable research on child development suggests that even young children hold dualistic ideas. It is not surprising, then, that so many people from so many different cultures hold dualistic beliefs. Does the popularity of this notion lead to the conclusion that the mind and the brain are ultimately separable, as some people claim?

The Out-of-Body Experience

At least initially, the OBE would seem to provide good evidence that the mind can separate from the body. We should note, however, that the term *out-of-body experience* is neutral (i.e., not definitive) with respect to whether the experiencing self *actually* leaves the body. This term simply asserts that a person has had the experience or impression of being outside of the body. OBEs do not seem to be associated with any psychological disorder (Tabacyk & Mitchell, 1987), although those who have OBEs tend to experience hallucinations more (Parra, 2009). In fact, OBEs are fairly common in the general population, with estimates of their reported incidence ranging from approximately 10 to 20%, depending on the survey (Rogo, 1984). In a review of the literature, Alvarado (2000) found that, on average, 25% of college students reported having experienced at least one OBE. Thus, the issue is not whether OBEs occur, but whether the mind or consciousness actually leaves the body as it appears to do.

The standard, waking OBE occurs as a spontaneous experience in which consciousness or the experiencing part of a person is perceived as located at a point outside of the physical body. OBEs may also occur as a part of other experiences, such as religious, drug-induced, near-death, meditational, or hypnotically induced experiences, as well as during dreams (Grosso, 1976). The fact that OBEs occur relatively often, to so many different people and under such different conditions, could suggest that they are due to an unusual type of brain functioning.

A famous incident of OBE was reported in 1903 by Mr. S. R. Wilmot, a British man taking an ocean voyage (Blackmore, 1992a). In the cabin of their ship en route to New York, Wilmot and his roommate observed Wilmot's wife, who had stayed behind in Liverpool. Later, when reunited with her husband and apparently without prompting, Mrs. Wilmot asked him if he had received a "visit" from her. Mrs. Wilmot was reported to have accurately described the appearance of his cabin, even though she had not actually seen it—that is, unless she had gone on an out-of-body excursion.

OBEs often occur as part of near-death experiences, such as when a person undergoing surgery "flatlines" briefly; people have offered these reports as evidence that the mind actually leaves the body. Dr. Raymond Moody, a physician, conducted interviews with numerous people who described observing their body from above when medical personnel were working on them as they lay unconscious and near death. In many cases, the patients reported entering a dark tunnel as they moved toward death (Moody, 1976). The following example of a near-death experience involving OBE illustrates some common features of such events:

> I was awake and aware of my surroundings. A nurse came in to take my blood pressure every half hour. On one occasion, I remember her taking my blood pressure and then running out of the room, which I thought was unusual. I don't remember anything more after that consciously, but I was then aware of being above my body as if I was floating on the ceiling and looking down at myself in the hospital bed with a crowd of doctors and nurses around me.

(Parnia, 2006, p. 54)

Research on Individuals Who Have OBEs

To obtain scientific evidence, researchers have tested subjects on the accuracy of their perceptions during an OBE by looking for some physical sign in the environment that the OBE subject has left the body. For example, Karlis Osis and Donna McCormick (1980) tested Alex Tanous, an experienced subject who claimed to be able to leave his body. To test the accuracy of his out-of-body perception, they instructed him to "project" himself to another room, where an optical projection device would display a picture stimulus that could be identified only if he looked directly into it. Without telling Tanous, the researchers also placed strain gauges outside the visual projection device to measure possible psychokinetic or other mechanical disturbances in the area.

Osis and McCormick (1980) found that Tanous was able to correctly report at least part of the display in 114 of 197 trials (58%)—but it is not clear that his performance was significantly better than the probability of correctly reporting the display by chance alone. They did, however, find that the strain gauge activity from trials with hits was significantly higher than the strain gauge activity during trials without hits. These results are consistent with the idea that Tanous was able to position his perceiving self in front of the device to see the display and that this somehow had a physical effect on his surroundings. Nevertheless, because his performance was not significantly better than chance, he may have been guessing on the trials on which he had hits, and only coincidentally did those trials happen to show higher strain gauge activity than occurred on misses. Unfortunately, no attempt to replicate this result has been published since the initial experiment.

Charles Tart (1968) conducted a study in which he asked another subject, Miss Z, who reportedly had many spontaneous OBEs, to identify a specific hidden target on her next out-of-body excursion. Tart also monitored her brain-wave activity on an EEG device that was connected to Miss Z while she reclined in his lab. One night, she was able to exactly identify the target—a five-digit number that could supposedly be viewed only when she left her body (Tart, 1968). Unfortunately, Tart had placed the target on a shelf in the same room where Miss Z was being tested. Although he slept during some of the experiment, Tart argued that he would have noticed if Miss Z had gotten up to look at the target because she would have disturbed the EEG wires, leading to noise in the recordings. In fact, the 60-cycle EEG noise that Tart reported could indeed have been Miss Z moving to see the target.

Although both Tart (1968) and Osis and Mitchell (1977) found electrical brain-wave changes on the EEG that they associated with reported out-of-body experiences, OBEs were generally found during stage 1 sleep. It is well known that hypnagogic hallucinations—that is, dreamlike imagery and illusory perceptions—can occur as a person begins to fall asleep (Cheyne, Rueffer, & Newby-Clark, 1999).

Questions also arise about why the OBE subjects' demonstrations have not been replicated. Other studies investigating the accuracy of perception during OBEs have shown subjects to be inaccurate (Tart, 1968) and sometimes accurate (Rogo, 1978; Tart, 1998).

Psychological and Neuroscientific Research on OBE

Psychologists and brain scientists look for natural, alternative explanations of the experience of being outside the body that are more plausible than the claim that the spirit is actually leaving the body. For instance, they explain the OBE as the "mind" experiencing itself as outside the body while not really leaving it. They argue that the OBE may be the result of an illusion or hallucination stemming from a mistake the mind/brain makes in constructing its usual representation of the experiencing self as in the body.

Following this line of thinking, Susan Blackmore (1982) applied the cognitive psychological approach to try to explain OBEs. Cognitive scientists view the brain as a kind of complex information-processing system somewhat like a computer. The human information-processing system inputs data through the senses, holds the information in memory, and transforms it into various intermediate states before outputting it in the form of behavior. Information processing occurs in the brain as nerve cells send and receive messages using special chemical substances called *neurotransmitters*.

Many of these nerve cells are organized into processing units and circuits dedicated to processing specific kinds of information. Research with brain scanning has found specific areas of the brain that "light up," or become active, when individuals engage in specific mental processes, such as perceiving, attending, remembering, forming mental images, and using language (Posner & Raichle, 1994). The brain uses the activity of these specific neural processors to form mental representations—representations that construct an elaborate and usually accurate model of the physical world. This sort of running simulation of parts of the world faithfully captures some, but certainly not all, aspects in its model.

As discussed earlier, the brain has map-like representations of various parts of the body such as the face, arm, and hand. These maps in the brain represent the body in visual and somatic form; that is, they carry detailed information of both how the body looks and how it feels (Ladavas, Zelon, & Farne, 1998).

Sometimes, however, the brain makes a mistake in constructing its model, and we misperceive part or all of the body.

Perhaps the brain constructs a representation of a missing part of the body when an amputee experiences phantom limb, the perception of a limb that is not physically there. People who have lost a limb, such as a hand, often report that they feel the sensation of pain or cramping in the missing hand. This, of course, is physically impossible if we assume the pain is originating from the missing hand. In contrast, if we assume that the brain still has a representation of the missing limb, then the experience of pain depends on brain activity corresponding to the representation of the hand (Ramachandran & Hirstein, 1998). Could the explanation of phantom limb provide a useful analogy for how OBE occurs? Could the brain's representation of the body be activated in some unusual way, leading to the misperception of the entire body as separate from the perceiving self?

Individual differences in cognition could also contribute to the tendency to misperceive the body and have unusual experiences. Susan Blackmore (1987) found that people who have OBEs (known as "OBErs") used mental imagery differently from non-OBErs. The OBErs were more likely to use an observer or bird's-eye-view perspective in describing their dreams, were better able to switch their viewpoint in a mental image, and had clearer and more vivid imagery of their dreams than did non-OBErs. Blackmore argued that this bird's-eye-view perspective is analogous to the OBErs viewing their body from above. When a person begins to lose normal sensory contact, such as when falling asleep or during sensory deprivation, the normal flow of sensory data is disrupted and the system seeks to reestablish sensory contact. It mistakenly picks the wrong model from memory, such as the over-the-head perspective, and treats it as real. OBErs' greater vividness and clarity of imagery may contribute to the sense of reality they experience during OBEs.

In addition, studies have found that people who have OBEs exhibit other individual differences that predispose them to having such experiences. Several studies have shown that having an OBE is positively correlated with the tendency to become absorbed in fantasy (Gow, Lang, & Chant, 2004); in fact, OBErs often score higher on the Absorption Scale developed by Tellegen and Atkinson (1974). For example, OBErs are more fantasy prone, reporting that they are more likely to become absorbed in a movie's story (i.e., they forget they are watching a movie). They also tend to have lucid dreams (i.e., they become aware that they are dreaming while dreaming) (Irwin, 1985). Other research reviewed by Parra (2009) has shown that OBErs tend to experience more hallucinations, which is also correlated with the tendency to become absorbed.

Blackmore's research suggests that disturbances in the brain could produce OBEs. Canadian neurosurgeon Wilder Penfield (1955) found that temporal lobe epilepsy may produce OBEs. Damage to the temporal lobe is a common cause of epileptic seizures. On one occasion, when Penfield applied ESB (discussed on page 173) to the right temporal lobe of a patient who had previously had an OBE, the patient exclaimed, "I am leaving my body!" and then showed a strong fear reaction (p. 458).

Drug effects on the brain can also produce OBEs. Ketamine, called "Special K" on the street and used as an anesthetic before surgery, is one example of a drug that can induce these experiences. Karl Jansen (1997) has argued that the experience produced by ketamine is very much like the near-death experience in which users often report floating above their body, traveling through a dark tunnel into the light, seeing God, and being convinced that they actually died briefly. Moreover, Jansen has proposed that nerve cells in the temporal lobe can respond to ketamine instead of to their usual neurotransmitter, with ketamine producing an artificial version of a non-drug-induced OBE.

How could physical events in the natural environment produce electrochemical changes in the brain that lead to OBEs? One possibility proposed by Michael Persinger (1995) is that variations in the earth's magnetic field produced by movement of the planet's tectonic plates could lead to OBEs under the right conditions. Persinger obtained data on the changes in the earth's geomagnetic activity from the National Geophysical Data Center so that he could keep track of the particular activity level that each subject experienced during testing. He also asked subjects to rate on a questionnaire the degree to which they felt detached from their bodies. At a separate session, subjects answered questions from which Persinger could infer each subject's history of complex, partial epileptic-like experiences. The subjects who had the most epileptic-like experiences also tended to report the most detachment from their bodies on days when geomagnetic activity was at a medium level. The magnetic disturbance may have destabilized activity in their temporal lobes.

Another group of researchers used ESB to produce a more convincing OBE in a 43-year-old epileptic woman (Blanke, Ortigue, Landis, & Seeck, 2002). While trying to find the focus of her brain damage, they stimulated points in the right angular gyrus within the temporal parietal junction (TPJ), shown in Figure 7.4. This stimulation produced various disturbances in the perception of her body. When stimulated at different intensities, the woman reported feeling that she was "sinking into the bed," "falling from a height," and seeing parts of her body shorten (p. 269). At one point, she had an OBE in which she

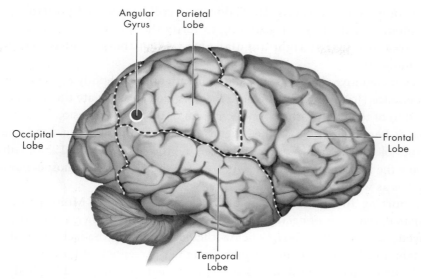

FIGURE 7.4 The right-hemisphere view of the angular gyrus in the temporal parietal junction stimulated by Blanke and his colleagues that produced an OBE.

saw her trunk and legs from above—the same portion of her body she had felt when stimulated before. However, when they stimulated the epileptic focus in her temporal lobe more than 5 cm away from the angular gyrus in the TPJ, she did not have an OBE.

Blanke and his colleagues proposed that stimulating this woman's TPJ produced the OBE by disrupting the integration of somatosensory and vestibular information—that is, information about the feel and position of her body. These findings further support the idea that the brain produces the conscious perception of an embodied self from the coordinated activity of various brain regions. Stimulating the TPJ can disrupt the brain's ability to integrate visual and tactile information, as well as information about feedback from muscle movements, balance, and body position.

Other studies have since supported Blanke's hypothesis (Cheyne & Girard, 2009). For instance, one group of researchers electrostimulated the right angular gyrus of a 63-year-old man who had brain implants as a means of treating his tinnitus (ringing of the ears) (De Ridder, Van Laere, Dupont, Menovsky, & Van De Heyning, 2007). They alternated actual stimulation with placebo stimulation in which no electrical stimulation was delivered. In the trials involving actual stimulation, the man reported a feeling of disembodiment without other changes in his consciousness. De Ridder and colleagues used positron emission tomography (PET) brain scanning to verify that greater activity occurred in the area around the right angular gyrus when the patient experienced disembodiment.

Recent cognitive theories have paid more attention to bodily aspects of mental experience (Johnson, 1995). These theories closely associate the brain's representation of the body with its representation of the self (Domasio, 1999; Eilan, Mareel, & Bermudez, 1995). Other scientists, such as James Gibson, have emphasized the role of the environment in perceiving the self (Neisser, 1993). Gibson has made the important point that when we see the world, we almost always see our bodies as well.

Supporting an embodied view of conscious experience, Monica Meijsing (2000) analyzed cases of nervous system damage in which patients had little sensory feedback from their bodies below the neck. Despite the lack of feedback, they maintained their body image, including their perception of how they looked and how much space their bodies occupied. One patient compared her body to a machine, saying she felt as if she were a pilot lodged in a ship that was difficult to steer.

If an OBE is viewed as analogous to an illusion or hallucination in which the brain constructs a mistaken model or representation of the location of self with respect to the body, it should be possible to trick a person into experiencing such an illusion. In two laboratories, researchers have done just that. In one study conducted by Ehrsson (2007), participants wore goggles that allowed them to see their body in a video display projected from a camera behind them. The display also provided a second view of their body as though in front of them. When Ehrsson touched participants in the chest, they saw their body being touched in the display at the same time. This information disrupted their usual integration of their experience of the body and induced the impression that their projected image was being touched and that they were at a location outside of the body. In a comparable study, Lenggenhager, Tadi, Metzinger, and Blanke (2007) used a virtual reality setup to produce a similar illusion for participants.

Although these kinds of studies have produced the feeling of an observing self, located outside the body, it is important to recognize that the experiments have not produced a full-blown OBE in which participants also see their physical body from a location outside the body, a phenomenon called *autoscopy*. Likewise, by stimulating the TPJ area, Blanke and his colleagues (2002) produced visual distortions in the patient's body but not the observation of the body from a vantage point outside the body as if separate. Notably, however, one ESB study has induced a full-blown OBE and another produced a feeling of separation from the body with verification from brain scanning that the TPJ area was indeed activated during the OBEs (De Ridder et al., 2007). A review of several case studies also found that when the same areas in the region of the TPJ were damaged, it produced the experience of bodily distortions and OBE just as stimulation of the area did (Blanke & Thut, 2007).

Blanke and his colleagues (2005) conducted an experiment that helped explain how stimulation of the TPJ could affect manipulation of an image of the entire body. These researchers hypothesized that the TPJ is involved in the manipulation of a person's body image, while another area is involved in the ability to manipulate images of non-body objects in a control site. Participants in their experiment were healthy volunteers who had never had an OBE. Each participant performed one task that was thought to require manipulation of the body image and another task that was thought to require manipulation of a non-body image. Blanke and colleagues used TMS (discussed on page 173) to stimulate the TPJ and the other control site during performance of each task. They found that TPJ stimulation disrupted the processing on the task involving manipulation of their body image but not processing of the task involving manipulation of the image of a non-body object.

Smith and Messier (2014) obtained more evidence in support of the hypothesis that having an OBE involves manipulation of the image of the body and processing in the TPJ. They used fMRI to examine the brain activity of a young college student who claimed she had been able to voluntarily have an OBE since she was young. They signaled her when to begin and end her OBE, while simultaneously monitoring her brain activity at various sites. They found increased activity not just in two sites in the TPJ but also in motor control areas known to involve imagining and controlling movement. The subject also reported that she had learned how to have an OBE as an aid to falling asleep. Perhaps this ability was related to the fact that an OBE sometimes occurs as part of hypnogogia, a state in which some people hallucinate as they enter sleep (Cheyne et al., 1999; Terhune, 2009). Taken together, these findings further support the hypothesis that activity in that TPJ area is involved in having an OBE, but they also underscore the contribution of individual differences to having an OBE.

SUMMARY

This chapter described three positions on the M–B question. The most common view held by the general public is M–B dualism. It assumes that the mind and the brain are two separate entities. Monism, especially physicalism or materialism, assumes that the mind and brain are one thing and that both are part of the physical world. Many psychologists and brain scientists are physicalists, while some are reductionists who believe that we should seek to reduce or explain all mental phenomena in terms of physical events. Functionalism, another position also popular among scientists, focuses on how the mind works without much concern for connecting this process to nervous system function. The assumptions people make about the relationship between mind and brain can greatly affect their outlook on life.

The critical reading passage examined the M–B question in the context of whether the mind could leave the body. It reviewed evidence showing that many people from around the world are M–B dualists and that many religious and paranormal beliefs assume that the mind or at least the spirit can separate from the body. Scientific studies attempting to clearly demonstrate that the mind can leave the body have had limited success and have been difficult to replicate.

In contrast, the efforts of psychologists and neuroscientists to explain OBEs in natural terms have been more successful. Research has shown that people who have OBEs tend to become more absorbed in their experience, have more unusual experiences, and have more lucid dreams and sleep-related hallucinations. Efforts to find a brain area have repeatedly shown involvement of the TPJ in OBE. Other studies have shown that OBE-like experiences can be induced in people who have not previously had an OBE. Taken together, this research suggests that OBEs are natural events in which the OBEr experiences an illusion or hallucination of the mind leaving the body.

 Practice Thinking 7.4: WHAT DO YOU THINK **NOW**?
Please explain how you know.

1. Do ghosts really exist? Can a soul or spirit be reincarnated in another person?

2. How can an amputee experience pain in a foot or hand that is not there?

3. Imagine a purple strawberry with yellow spots. How can your mind think of something that does not physically exist?

4. In an OBE, does the person's mind really leave the body?

REVIEW QUESTIONS

1. What is the M–B problem? What are basic positions on it?
   - Who tends to believe in M–B dualism?
   - Who tends to believe in physicalism (a kind of monism)? Reductionism?
   - Who tends to believe in functionalism?
2. How can your position on the M–B problem lead to difficulties?
3. How does one's position on the M–B problem affect the study of the mind and the brain?
4. What is localization of function? How is it a strategy for studying the brain?
5. Describe some techniques for studying the brain.
   - How have cases been used to study the OBE? What are the limitations in using such cases?
   - What are the advantages and disadvantages of using ESB to study OBE?
   - What is an advantage of using TMS to study the OBE?
   - What is an advantage of using fMRI to study the TPJ?
6. What is the basic cross-cultural view that the soul/spirit actually leaves the body? Which kinds of evidence support this view?

7. How does Susan Blackmore's cognitive theory explain OBEs? How are individual differences (e.g., in imagery, lucid dreaming, proneness to fantasy) related to having an OBE?

8. Can phantom limb help us understand how the brain might produce an OBE?

9. Which evidence (e.g., from research by Penfield and Blanke) supports the notion that stimulating the brain can induce an OBE?

10. What should we conclude from the fact that OBEs can be experimentally induced?

11. Does scientific research support the dualistic view that the mind can leave the body?

12. Can a person believe that the soul/spirit can leave the body at death but that the mind does not actually leave the body during an OBE? What is the distinction here?

13. What does the critical reading discussion imply about the ability of scientists to explain in natural terms a phenomenon such as OBE, which has previously been referred to as a paranormal phenomenon?

14. Could M–B dualism be an unwarranted assumption that many people make in explaining their personal experience? How?

15. Could naive realism help explain why an OBEr may be convinced that the experience was real and that the mind really left the body?

16. What psychological misconceptions were discussed in this chapter?

CRITICAL THINKING AND THE INTERNET

8

LEARNING OUTCOMES

After studying this chapter, you should be able to:

1. Identify potential problems and benefits of using information from the Internet.

2. Critically evaluate Internet sources for credibility, accuracy, reasonableness, and evidence.

3. Decide whether Internet claims about a therapy should be believed.

WHAT DO YOU THINK?

Suppose it is your final year in college and you receive the email notification shown in Figure 8.1. What do you think about this message, and how would you respond to it?

Dear Promising College Student:

You have been selected to be featured in the upcoming edition of *Who's Outstanding among Undergraduates*. You are receiving this singular honor because you have already provided a valuable contribution to your college or university. Every year, our team of experts searches for and recognizes those college students whose academic achievement, extracurricular activity, or service to their institution is outstanding. Many college students who are selected consider this to be one of the highest accolades they receive in their college career.

   Publishing your achievement is our way of honoring you, and so your inclusion in the book is absolutely free. To help us complete your entry in this year's registry, please click on the following link to complete the **brief biographical questionnaire**. Once again, congratulations on your achievement.

Sincerely,

Mr. David Gormich, Senior Editor

Who's Who in Undergraduates, Inc.

FIGURE 8.1 A simulation of an email promotion for college students. What would you think if you received this?

Practice Thinking 8.1: What Do You Think?

Please explain how you know.

1. How do you know if you can trust information you find on the web?

   _____

2. Which questions should you ask to critically evaluate information you find on the Internet?

   _____

3. How would you know if a therapy described on the web is a good one?

   _____

4. What are some advantages and disadvantages of using the Internet?

   _____

I received an email like the one shown in Figure 8.1, but the subject was honoring academic professionals and the message was addressed to "Dear Academic Professional." It struck me as odd that the organization had selected me to be in its "Who's Who" book for my professional achievements—yet the sender of the email did not know my name. The sender also asked me to provide background information on my achievements. Why do this if the organization had already selected me based on my achievements? I also wondered, "How is the company making money if it is offering to put my information in its publication for free?" I didn't fall for this scheme, but what about others who have?

When people fail to see the deception inherent in such an offer, their problem is likely to be gullibility. In other words, they lack a skeptical attitude, the critical thinking (CT) disposition that would dispose them to question information they encounter, in this case the motives behind the "Who's Who" book email. It is not enough to have the CT skill of being able to ask good questions—you have to be willing to actually pose those queries and follow up on them, too. In this chapter, we discuss the questions a skeptical inquirer should ask to evaluate information on the Internet and thereby avoid being taken in by false claims, but you must be willing to vigorously question the information you encounter. At the same time, you must recognize that the Internet is a powerful tool that can provide much valuable information when used properly.

THE INTERNET: INFLUENCE AND BENEFITS

The Internet (worldwide web) is an international network of computers that are linked together for the purpose of sharing email and many other kinds of communication among any users who can log onto it. Originally developed for the exchange of information among scientists and the military, its popularity grew to more than 3 billion users worldwide in 2015, with innumerable other applications. Amazon.com, the giant Internet retail outlet, is now the ninth largest retail company in the United States—its Internet sales for the third quarter of 2015 were $87.5 billion in the United States alone (U.S. Census Bureau, 2016).

The Internet greatly affects our social lives as well. For example, at least 5% of all current U.S. marriages started with introductions made on online dating services (Pew Research Center, 2013). Facebook, the social media titan, now has more than 1.5 billion active users worldwide. Furthermore, people now look predominantly to the web for all types of entertainment, from downloading movies, television shows, and music to playing electronic games. The Internet is the most far-reaching and influential communication tool in history. In the 1400s, the printing press greatly increased the availability of books, but the Internet has made even more massive amounts of information rapidly available to billions more people, and its reach continues to expand exponentially.

The Internet is a library for the world. With just a few keystrokes, you can access information from any region—whether housed in an actual library or a virtual one. In 2010, the Internet giant Google began scanning all of the out-of-print books ever published, with the goal of making them available to people around the world. Each day, professional Internet listservs notify their subscribers about new scientific research studies, sometimes even before the journal article is available in print form. Often, users can obtain a copy of a scientific article by simply "Googling" the title (i.e., using a search engine) because so many scientists have now posted their articles on the web or via web services such as Researchgate.

As online publication of news has exploded, with countless sites posting up-to-the-minute reports, the more costly and slower print newspapers and magazines have found that their circulations are shrinking. Many other kinds of information are almost instantly available from sources such as the "popular" online encyclopedia Wikipedia, providing users with information about the myriad topics they encounter in their daily lives. But, like me, they often wonder whether they can trust this information to be accurate and reliable.

The scope of this ocean of information is truly mind-boggling. IBM has estimated that 2.5 *quintillion* bytes of information is added each day. A byte is roughly equivalent to one word in digital form; 1 quintillion is equivalent to 10^{18} (about 2.5 million) trillion bytes every day. Is there too much information? How can we sort through so much data? Certainly, a large portion of this material is not relevant to us, but what about the vast amount that is?

THE INTERNET: PSYCHOLOGICAL PROBLEMS AND THINKING ERRORS

The web is a powerful tool that also poses dangers, however. People may actually become addicted to the Internet and to using digital resources (Han, Hwang, & Renshaw, 2011). Some studies have shown dramatic changes in the brain function of Internet users (Carr, 2010; Small, Moody, Siddarth, & Brookheimer, 2009). Other researchers have argued that use of the Internet across multiple web-dependent, simultaneously running communication devices is creating a host of attentional problems in users. As described in Chapter 6, people often have trouble multitasking or dividing their attention efficiently. The demands of these new technologies may overwhelm the capacities of our cognitive systems, thereby creating information overload (Klingberg, 2009).

Another disadvantage of the Internet—though it might initially seem like an advantage—is that we can be more selective and efficient in obtaining information. The problem is that, although the Internet enables us to easily access more information than ever before, it also makes it easier to find information that is consistent with our existing beliefs and to avoid information that might contradict or weaken those beliefs. Recall from Chapter 4 that such a tendency to choose information that reinforces (rather than calls into question) our currently held beliefs is how we defined the thinking error of confirmation bias.

Confirmation bias can be found in multiple arenas on the Internet. For example, communications researchers found that when political partisans in both the United States and Germany searched for information online, they preferred information to be consistent with their attitudes; it is worth noting, however, that encountering opposing information did weaken their beliefs (Knoblich-Westerwick, Mothes, Johnson, Westerwick, & Donsbach, 2015). The researchers observed confirmation bias in both countries, but it was stronger in the

United States than in Germany. People seem especially prone to selectively search for information that reinforces their political beliefs (Garrett, 2009). Moreover, if the news sources found during such searches favor one side versus another and people tend to select one side over another, then news sources will become increasingly one-sided, which can reduce the opportunity for people to change their minds or even compromise (Garrett & Stroud, 2015).

Of particular interest to us in this chapter is how people use information on the Internet, because it turns out that it could have implications for what we think we know. Fisher, Goddhu, and Keil (2015) found that when people use the Internet to look up information, they tend to inflate how much they think they know, misattributing their ease of access to how much knowledge is actually stored in their memories. This overestimation is a metacognitive error, and while it is certainly problematic, it does not take into account the important fact that not all information on the Internet is equally accurate and useful. Some of it is simply misinformation. What is important is the ability to distinguish what you know from what you don't know, as well as good information from bad information.

THE INTERNET, MISINFORMATION, AND CONSPIRACY THEORIES

Many Internet users self-publish misinformation out of ignorance and sometimes even deliberately. They create and pass along misconceptions and rumors that may go viral on social media. For instance, a false Internet news story recently stated that James Hughston, one of the three winners of the record $1.5 billion Powerball lottery, had died of a cocaine overdose shortly after winning. The story falsely claimed that Hughston could not wait to get his share of the winnings, so he took out a loan and bought a huge house, purchased a kilo of cocaine, employed 10 prostitutes, and promptly died of a cocaine overdose. Snopes.com, a website dedicated to dispelling misconceptions and falsehoods, quickly put this rumor to rest, pointing out that the story appeared even before any winner was announced, so it was obviously false.

Misinformation is rampant on the web because anyone can publish on this forum, including pseudoscientists, terrorists, hoaxsters, charlatans, and conspiracy theorists. Fortunately, sites like Snopes.com are dedicated to eliminating misconceptions and pseudoscientific ideas. Quackwatch.org is especially good at debunking ineffective and pseudoscientific treatments.

People who self-publish on the Internet typically are not required to meet standards for the quality of the information they publish. The many bloggers who freely offer their opinions on all manner of subjects usually do not run these ideas by an editor or a reviewer. They may not even fact-check their information. As a result, these outlets do not serve the gatekeeping function that newspapers and traditional news organizations are meant to perform. Information, regardless of its truthfulness, simply appears on the Internet when someone puts it there, and it becomes accessible to millions of people immediately (Mohammed, 2012).

In contrast, scientists and other scholars typically publish their ideas in professional outlets only after they have been peer reviewed and any errors are corrected. Some journals reject as many as 90% of the articles submitted to them because the articles do not meet their high standards for publication. In recent years, however, an increasing number of peer-reviewed psychology journals have begun to publish online; unfortunately, some of them do not maintain the high standards of the more well-established scientific print journals.

Fake news stories on the Internet are a particularly troublesome example of what can happen when information is published on the web without any type of peer review or editorial gatekeeping. The popularity of fake news stories has raised serious questions about the ability of citizens to critically evaluate claims on the web—an essential skill for participating in a democracy in the Information Age. In a recent study, Sam Wineburg and his colleagues at Stanford University recorded 7,800 middle school, high school, and college students' responses to various news stories; results showed that students at all three levels often could not tell real news from fake news (Domonoske, 2016). This is troubling because political partisans and others who are simply motivated to profit from false news stories have spread fake claims widely through social media and fake news sites.

This proliferation of false news can have dangerous consequences because nowadays people often get their information from such online sources and can be misled by outrageous stories. For instance, during the 2016 U.S. presidential election, one of the most disturbing of the many fake stories circulating around the web claimed that presidential candidate Hillary Clinton and her campaign adviser John Podesta were leading a child sex–trafficking ring. This was revealed, according to believers, in Hillary Clinton's emails. The alleged ring became associated with a Washington, DC, pizzeria called "Comet Ping Pong," so the conspiracy came to be called "Pizzagate." The Comet Ping Pong sex ring story is a classic example of a **conspiracy theory**, which is an alternative explanation offered in place of a conventional understanding of events (McCaffrey, 2012).

This conspiracy theory seemed to take hold when a Reddit user summarized the story and sent it to *r/The Donald,* a group of Donald Trump supporters on Reddit. The *New York Times* and the fact-checking site Snopes.com soon disproved the stories (LaCapria, 2016), but this did not discourage believers from embellishing and passing along the many versions of this conspiracy theory on Facebook, Twitter, and fake news sites. Readers were encouraged to find new "evidence" in the emails by looking for so-called code words, such as references to "pizza" that conspiracy theorists said referred to illegal sex trafficking.

The unquestioning acceptance of outrageously implausible stories such as this one can affect voters' decisions and may harm innocent persons. Believers in this conspiracy theory threatened people at the pizzeria and neighboring businesses. On December 4, 2016, Edgar M. Welch, a 28-year-old North Carolina man, believed in it enough to travel to Comet Ping Pong to investigate for himself. He fired his assault rifle inside the building and found no children held in the pizzeria (Kang & Goldman, 2016). Welch surrendered peacefully without any loss of life. In an interview from his jail, Welch told a *New York Times* reporter (Goldman, 2016) that he regretted how he handled the situation but continued to maintain that the Internet stories could be true, demonstrating the thinking error of belief perseverance (see Chapter 1).

Conspiracy theories are enacted using three classic roles: conspirators, saviors, and dupes (Ruscio, 2006). In the Pizzagate example, the conspirators who supposedly engaged in the nefarious activities were Hillary Clinton, John Podesto, and Comet Ping Pong. The saviors were those who called attention to the conspiracy online and who recruited other saviors to find evidence of the conspiracy in the emails. The dupes were all the mainstream people being fooled by the conspiracy, who accepted the conventional explanation that Comet Ping Pong was just a pizzeria and that pizza was just pizza.

Many conspiracy theories, such as Pizzagate, are political in nature. Two other good examples are the theory that President George W. Bush and government officials knew about the 9/11 attacks on the World Trade Center and the Pentagon beforehand, and the theory that Lee Harvey Oswald was not the lone gunman who assassinated President John F. Kennedy, as the official Warren Commission had concluded, but was rather part of a conspiracy organized by the CIA, the Mafia, or both. Conspiracy theories like these often arise in response to national catastrophes that leave people feeling powerless and vulnerable in the face of situations that are beyond their control. Likewise, believers in conspiracy theories are often marginalized members of a group who lack power and seek a scapegoat or someone to blame for their disadvantaged situation. Conspiracy theorists believe that they are "in the know," so their special knowledge of the conspiracy may empower them, raise their self-esteem, and make them feel morally superior to those who do not know the hidden truth (Byford, 2011).

People who disseminate fake news and false conspiracy theories to individuals in their social media network and to other web-based outlets are likely sending this information to people who are receptive to it. This trend suggests that people who accept fake news and false conspiracy theories are motivated to draw a conclusion that they likely already favor, as discussed more fully in the next chapter. Indeed, the tendency for people to seek out partisan news outlets that are in agreement with their own views makes the web function like an echo chamber in which people hear what they want to hear. This propensity seems to support the idea that conspiracy theorists are irrational and not inclined to critically examine all sides of an argument.

Ironically, Harambam and Aupers (2017) have recently found that conspiracy theorists tend to view themselves as critical freethinkers, distinguishing themselves from the "sheepish" people in the mainstream who fail to question conventional explanations. Are they right? Sometimes conspiracy theorists are correct, as happened when an international conspiracy of organized crime groups was suspected of colluding to plan and coordinate criminal activities—a theory that was verified when a meeting of these crime groups was discovered in upstate New York. Yet, as we have seen, many conspiracy theories are implausible and do not seem to be well-reasoned.

At this point, it is instructive to examine other conspiracy theories that make claims related to *science*. For instance, climate change deniers maintain that the notion that human activity causes global warming (anthropogenic global warming) is a hoax perpetrated by scientists and politicians. A second science-related conspiracy theory asserts that NASA's landing of astronauts on the moon was a hoax staged by NASA and shot in the desert to make it appear as though the United States beat the Soviet Union in the space race to the moon.

Another popular conspiracy theory that is partly science fiction claims that the U.S. military and government have engaged in a massive cover-up of the 1947 crash of an alien spacecraft in Roswell, New Mexico. Despite convincing scientific evidence to the contrary, many people still maintain that this conspiracy theory is true, which suggests that the theory has met important criteria for determining that it is pseudoscientific (see Table 5.1). Thus, it is useful to compare false, science-related, conspiracy theories to pseudoscience.

Like pseudoscience, science-related conspiracy theories take on the appearance of real science, but they do not develop the way scientific theories do. Good scientific theories are largely consistent with high-quality research evidence, but conspiracy theorists seldom test their hypotheses in any rigorous fashion. When a scientific test is conducted and does not support their predictions, conspiracy theorists often add assumptions to create excuses for their failed predictions, making the theories ever more complex and ultimately unfalsifiable. In contrast, true scientists value **parsimony**, or keeping their theories as simple as possible while still accounting for the data.

Rather than testing their hypotheses, conspiracy theorists often focus on unresolved questions and minor inconsistencies in the evidence supporting established scientific theories (Prothero, 2013). For instance, moon-landing deniers have objected that the photograph of the flag that astronaut Buzz Aldrin planted on the moon showed the flag waving in the wind—yet there is no wind on the moon. NASA explained that Aldrin had to twist the flagpole to get it into the lunar soil, thus causing the ripples seen in the photo. After raising doubts, conspiracy theorists often argue that scientists have not proven that their theory is true. This response shows a fundamental misunderstanding of science because scientists cannot *prove* anything, due to the inductive nature of the scientific method. Moreover, scientists try to connect their research to other scientific theories and research, whereas conspiracy theorists show little interest in established research and instead rail against mainstream science.

Like proponents of pseudoscience, conspiracy theorists also commit errors in reasoning, such as arguing that if 100% of all scientists do not accept the theory of anthropogenic global warming, then it may not be true, raising further doubts about the theory. But considering that 97% of climate scientists agree that, based on scientific research, human activities are indeed contributing to global warming (Cook et al., 2016), it seems that the conspiracy theorists are trying to shift the burden of proof *away* from their side to escape disconfirmation (see Chapter 2). This example also shows how conspiracy theorists commit another thinking error known as **black-and-white thinking**, also called *either-or thinking*, when they propose that there are only two extreme positions or options to be considered. Climate change deniers do this when they encourage people to incorrectly conclude that if there are any doubts about a scientific theory, then the theory must be false (Prothero, 2013). But acceptance of a scientific theory is not all or none and depends on the strength of the evidence overall.

These examples suggest that to avoid drawing incorrect conclusions from misinformation on the Internet, we must use good scientific reasoning and be alert to potential thinking errors. Studies suggest that people who take a more analytic approach to conspiracy theories endorse them less (Van Prooijen, 2017) and that exposing conspiracy theory believers to rational counterarguments can reduce their belief in that theory (Orosz et al., 2016). Nevertheless, convincing believers to reject false conspiracy theories is challenging, especially when the believers' worldview conflicts with scientifically accepted theories (Lewandowsky & Oberauer, 2016) and when believers are prone to a more intuitive thinking style (Swami, Voracek, Stieger, Tran, & Furnham, 2014).

Specifically, Lewandowsky, Gignac, and Oberauer (2013) found that people with a free-market worldview were more likely to reject climate science, which implies the need for regulation—a view that opposes their core belief. As we examine how to critically evaluate information on the Internet, it is important to recognize that having the know-how is not enough—we must be disposed to using our CT knowledge and skills, too.

Other guidelines for evaluating information discussed in earlier chapters can also be applied to the critical evaluation of information on the web, including conspiracy theories. For instance, we want to check the source of information to see whether it is reliable and credible to verify that it can be trusted. Assessing the authority and expertise of the source is also helpful. Another good guideline is to ask yourself whether the claims are plausible or reasonable, given what you know. Examining the method in which the evidence was acquired is vital to evaluating the quality of claims both on the Internet and elsewhere. Detecting bias and an unbalanced presentation of evidence can help, too. In this chapter, we examine many of these strategies in detail.

The variability in the sources of information on the web raises important questions about how you can assess the quality of any particular material. Fortunately, you can apply many of the same principles of CT, science, and standards of evidence discussed thus far to evaluate this information. These principles are often similar to guidelines for critically evaluating information on the web offered by experts (e.g., Harris, 1997; Kapoun, 1998; Linn, Bell, & Hsi, 1999).

To help clarify issues related to quality of information, it is useful to distinguish *web-based* from *web-placed* Internet resources. **Web-based** resources that are delivered via the Internet tend to be of higher quality, more reliable, and easier to use because they are maintained by professional scholars and library services (Arnold & Jayne, 2003). For example, academic databases such as PsycINFO and PsycArticles are high-quality, reliable databases that index journal articles and books that, for the most part, have been peer reviewed by scientific experts prior to publication. Likewise, listservs for psychology professionals are web-based resources because psychologists and authorities in related fields commonly use the Internet as a platform to communicate with scholars about new research. They moderate discussions of psychological questions in these Internet groups and provide links to other published research and discussions, but the discussion is typically monitored for quality only informally by the listserv users themselves.

Other web resources are **web-placed**—that is, individuals and groups place information at various websites for differing purposes. These resources are maintained by companies, social organizations, individuals, academic institutions, and other parties, who often post the information to promote their own ideas, products, and services. Because web-placed sites tend to vary more in quality and reliability than academic databases, they place greater demands on users' CT skills.

Using a web-based site like PsycINFO does not eliminate the need to use CT to assess the studies found at that site. In fact, even some indexed research is of lower quality than other research. However, accessing web-placed information requires particular care in your analysis because the source may not even use scientific research evidence to support its claims. Specifically, the source may rely on lower-quality evidence such as commonsense belief, statements of authority, anecdotes, and testimonials. How should you evaluate the information found at websites that vary so broadly in terms of their quality and accuracy?

USING CARE TO EVALUATE INTERNET INFORMATION

Our discussion implies that navigating the sea of web-placed information on the Internet requires extreme C-A-R-E to avoid drawing the wrong conclusion. CARE is a first-letter mnemonic that will help you remember how best to approach information found on the web. As outlined in Table 8.1, each letter stands for an important issue related to the quality of web information. By going through each letter of the acronym, you can remember to ask specific questions about the information you encounter regarding its credibility, accuracy, reasonableness, and

TABLE 8.1 Use CARE to Evaluate Information on the Internet	
Credibility	Are sources believable, authentic, and trustworthy?
Accuracy	Is the information true, factual, and correct?
Reasonableness	How plausible and consistent are the claims? Are sources objective?
Evidence	How much good evidence supports and does not support the claims being made?

Information from Harris (1997, 2000).

the evidence supporting it. The CARE questions are based on the discussion of CT presented earlier in this book, as well as suggestions made by experts such as Kapoun (1998) and especially the work of Robert Harris (1997, 2000) from which CARE was adapted.

We elaborate on the general questions listed in Table 8.1 in the discussion that follows. First, we examine more specific questions for analyzing and evaluating the credibility of a website. Then, we apply the credibility questions to analyze and evaluate information from a fictitious website shown in Figures 8.2–8.5.

Credibility Questions

Just as a credible witness in a trial is one whose testimony you tend to believe and trust, a source of information on a website is credible to the extent that the source is believable, authentic, and trustworthy. Knowing whom and what to believe is a central problem in the evaluation of sources in our everyday lives (Carlsen, 1995). This challenge is similar to the problem of evaluating statements of authority and deciding who is likely to be in a position to know something relevant to a claim. For scientific claims, the credentials and affiliation of sources suggest the credibility of the information they provide. For example, someone with a PhD or MD who is associated with a reputable university or research institute would tend to be more credible as a source. In particular, a scientific expert with special knowledge of the claim, such as a scientist who knows which research is relevant or has studied it extensively, should be judged as more credible. By comparison, a supposedly authoritative source or so-called scientific expert who bases his or her statements on low-quality research should be considered less credible.

Often, authorities and experts do not author the websites where their work or statements are cited. For instance, websites often quote famous scientists or mention their ideas to support claims the sites are making. Unless the famous scientist's statements, ideas, or findings are directly relevant to the claims being made, that work should not be viewed as offering credible support. Being an expert in physics or chemistry does not make someone an expert in psychology. Likewise, being an expert in cognitive psychology does not make someone an expert in another subfield, such as clinical psychology.

If the source or author of the website is not identified, it is very difficult to assess the credibility of the site, which in turn makes the credibility of the unidentified authors and sources suspect. The specific questions that follow identify other markers that should lower our estimate of the credibility of a site, such as spelling, typographical, and grammatical errors. It is difficult to take a source seriously when simple errors escape its scrutiny.

Specific Credibility Questions

1. Is the author listed, or did a webmaster write the material on the site?

2. What are the credentials of the author (e.g., PhD, MD)? Is special training or some other qualification listed? Is other relevant biographical information provided? In particular, does the person/authority/expert have *relevant* knowledge?

3. Is the author's affiliation provided? An educational institution? A company? Is a government agency being sourced?

4. Do other markers suggest the source/author is not credible or lacks expertise, such as spelling or grammatical errors or misuse of technical terminology?

5. How good is the quality control of information provided? Is it based on peer-reviewed research? Have any independent experts commented on its quality?

Now, before reading on, answer these questions to evaluate the credibility of the information provided in the mock website shown in Figures 8.2–8.5.

Regarding the first credibility question, neither the name nor the affiliation of the author or source of the Telepatherapy site is provided, making it difficult to evaluate the site author's relevant expertise. We should not assume expertise of a source if no indicators are provided to document it. The author invokes the names of psychologists and psychotherapists who have argued for a connection between telepathy (ESP) and therapy. This appeal to the authority of others may be intended to make Telepatherapy sound legitimate, but it should not automatically be assumed that these authorities are actually experts or endorse Telepatherapy.

Furthermore, the only connection to an association mentioned is the International Telepatherapy Association's certification of therapists (see Figure 8.5). But what is this organization? Is it a name only, such that it does not actually provide any rigorous oversight of what telepatherapists do? Is it recognized by other major associations such as the American Psychological Association? Moreover, the website's content includes a typographical mistake in "peoples' problems," misspells the words *connect* and *Privacy* (see Figure 8.2), and omits the word *have* from "depression shown that" (see Figure 8.4). Taken together, all of these errors and tactics raise serious concerns about the website's credibility.

FIGURE 8.2 Mock-up of an "About" page for a fictitious website describing Telepatherapy, a new psychotherapy. (Graphic design by Kaitlin Bensley)

FIGURE 8.3 Mock-up of a testimonials page for a fictitious website on Telepatherapy. (Graphic design by Kaitlin Bensley)

Scientists have shown that telepathy and ESP exist. Now, many psychoanalysts and psychotherapists believe that telepathy between therapist and patient exists, too. In 1996, Dr. Reed reported the results of an experiment in the Journal of Analytical Psychology that proved ESP occurs. He had pairs of workshop participants imagine a psychic connection between them and then verbalize their thoughts. The pairs showed striking similarities in their thoughts and reported they felt a connection that went beyond ordinary communication. We can only conclude that this was a telepathic connection.

In 1976, Dr. David Shainberg, then dean of a program in psychoanalytic medicine in New York, reported a telepathic dream of one of his patients. The patient dreamed he was traveling with his brother or someone who needed an operation to be performed by Dr. Shainberg in a dentist's chair. In fact, Shainberg had planned to travel to be with his sick father who needed an operation, but he had not told his patient about his travel plans or his father's illness. The striking resemblance between the client's dream and Shainberg's situation could only be explained as a telepathic connection established in therapy.

Case studies of people treated with Telepatherapy for anxiety and depression shown that it was effective in treating nearly all of these cases.

Terms of Use | Privicy Policy | Admin

FIGURE 8.4 Mock-up of a research page for a fictitious website on Telepatherapy. (Graphic design by Kaitlin Bensley)

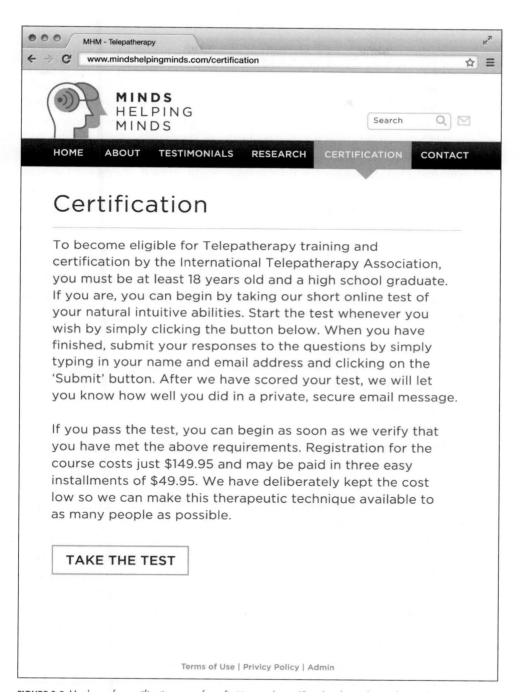

● ● ●   MHM - Telepatherapy

www.mindshelpingminds.com/certification

MINDS HELPING MINDS

Search

HOME   ABOUT   TESTIMONIALS   RESEARCH   CERTIFICATION   CONTACT

Certification

To become eligible for Telepatherapy training and certification by the International Telepatherapy Association, you must be at least 18 years old and a high school graduate. If you are, you can begin by taking our short online test of your natural intuitive abilities. Start the test whenever you wish by simply clicking the button below. When you have finished, submit your responses to the questions by simply typing in your name and email address and clicking on the 'Submit' button. After we have scored your test, we will let you know how well you did in a private, secure email message.

If you pass the test, you can begin as soon as we verify that you have met the above requirements. Registration for the course costs just $149.95 and may be paid in three easy installments of $49.95. We have deliberately kept the cost low so we can make this therapeutic technique available to as many people as possible.

TAKE THE TEST

Terms of Use | Privicy Policy | Admin

FIGURE 8.5 Mock-up of a certification page for a fictitious website. (Graphic design by Kaitlin Bensley)

Accuracy Questions

Accuracy concerns the correctness, factual basis, and truthfulness of information provided and claims made. To be accurate, information must be timely, comprehensive, and complete (Harris, 1997). *Inaccurate* information makes it difficult, if not impossible, to draw a good conclusion from it. The presence of *outdated* information indicates that the website may be disregarding, ignoring, or unaware of new and relevant information that might change our judgments about the site.

Another red flag is raised when a website makes vague, sweeping generalizations. For example, a site discussing scientific matters might claim that a theory has been proven or is always true in all cases. This kind of claim is an overgeneralization and misrepresents what science can tell us. Technically, because scientific knowledge is at least partly based on induction, it cannot logically prove that a theory or hypothesis is *always* true. Some as-yet-uncollected data could always disconfirm a theory.

Lastly, information tends to be more accurate when it is independently corroborated—that is, when it has been verified by other sources or research not conducted by the source of the website. The following questions should help you assess the accuracy of information found on the web.

Specific Accuracy Questions

1. How recent is the information provided? When was the research performed? When was the site last updated?

2. How complete is the information? Are facts omitted? Are all sides of an argument represented by evidence?

3. Does more than one authority, researcher, or independent person corroborate factual and other claims being made?

Before reading on, answer these questions to evaluate the accuracy of the information provided in the mock website shown in Figures 8.2–8.6.

Regarding the first accuracy question, the research cited is not very recent—one study is dated 1976 and another is dated 1996 (see Figure 8.4). This raises the question about whether newer, more relevant research has been conducted, because neither of these older studies examined Telepatherapy directly. As for the second accuracy question, no evidence *opposing* the telepathy argument has been included, despite the considerable scientific research that calls into question the very existence of ESP. Thus, the website makes an unwarranted assumption, and it is not accurate to imply that there is a scientific consensus in favor of ESP's existence. Regarding the third question, the website relates Einstein's ideas about energy to how Telepatherapy helps people tap into a "reservoir of psychic energy" (see Figure 8.2). This discussion may be an effort to corroborate the theory behind Telepatherapy, but it inaccurately represents Einstein's ideas, which have to do with *physical* energy, not psychic energy.

Reasonableness Questions

Reasonableness refers to how plausible, consistent, and objective a source seems. A claim that seems scientifically plausible gives us the sense that it is reasonable, considering other things we know from science. When you visit a website, you will form a general impression of how reasonable the information seems even before you thoroughly check the claims being made. A website may appear less reasonable and more biased when it appeals to emotion or offers a slanted presentation. Sometimes bias enters the picture when the site's author is motivated to show only one side of an argument because of a conflict of interest, as when a dot-com (.com) or commercial site seeks to persuade users to buy some product. At other times, a claim may seem unreasonable if it is extreme, as when a website claims much more than what conventional science would predict. Finally, a site that makes logically inconsistent claims or provides conflicting information would be judged as unreasonable. Answer the following questions about Figures 8.2–8.5.

Specific Reasonableness Questions

1. Is the information in the website plausible? Does it seem reasonable, given what else is known in science and from other authoritative sources?

2. Is the presentation of information objective, or is it slanted, biased, or designed to arouse your emotions?

3. Is there a conflict of interest?

4. Are the claims moderate or are they extreme and inconsistent with what is known from psychological science and science in general?

5. Are the claims consistent or do they contradict each other?

Returning to our fictitious website in Figures 8.2–8.5, the reasonableness of information seems to be in doubt almost immediately, given the scientific implausibility of many of the claims being made. As discussed in other chapters, the existence of ESP is implausible given what is known in physics. For many scientists, the idea that a therapy could work based on telepathy or the non-physical transfer of thought would seem implausible. Mind-reading and communication without the involvement of the senses in some capacity has not been demonstrated scientifically. Likewise, it seems implausible, given what is known about the effectiveness of therapies, that taking a primarily intuitive (rather than scientific) approach to psychotherapy would be effective. Becoming an expert therapist takes years of scientific training and deliberate, intelligent practice in interacting with clients; it is not something a person automatically knows how to do (Gambrill, 2010; Garb, 1989).

Regarding the third reasonableness question, the website shows a possible conflict of interest. It is a dot-com site that, as evidenced by the navigation bar atop each web page and the information about payment at the end, seems to be trying to recruit new customers for its educational business. Telepatherapy might well be a company designed more to make money than to serve the needs of people.

As for the fourth question, the website makes extreme claims. In Figure 8.4, the claim that case studies show Telepatherapy to be effective in virtually all cases of anxiety and depression is probably extreme and implausible, given the typical results found in evidence-based research. The claim that traditional psychotherapy takes too much time is a sweeping generalization that applies more to psychoanalysis than to behavior therapy. Furthermore, stating that "a telepathic connection" is the *only* explanation for the Reed and Shainberg findings is an extreme conclusion that disregards other, more plausible explanations, such as the idea that participants simply made lucky guesses. This extreme claim is an example of the thinking error of black-and-white thinking and further suggests a lack of objectivity in the source.

Regarding the fifth question, thinking about psychoanalytic assumptions can alert you to an inconsistency in the claim that Telepatherapy can achieve rapid results without conventional communication. It is doubtful that proponents of psychoanalysis, also called *talk therapy,* would argue for using telepathy as the main means of communication and for diagnosing mental disorders. Put simply, eliminating the verbal communication from psychoanalysis and psychotherapy would take the *talk* out of talk therapy.

Evidence Questions

We must critically evaluate both the quality of the evidence that supports a website's claims and the quality of the evidence that does not support those claims. Websites that provide little evidence to support their arguments offer little reason to accept their claims. Moreover, any evidence that is provided must be assessed carefully in terms of the strength of support offered by different types of evidence.

This kind of judgment is difficult when a website does not explicitly identify the evidence it marshals in support of its views. For example, saying that "research" has found or shown some therapy to be effective, without citing any specific studies supporting the claim, is a weak argument because the specific research studies have not been provided as evidence, only a vague reference to "research." Clear citations of specific research studies listed in a reference or bibliography section can strengthen the evidentiary support of a website.

For websites that make scientific claims, scientific research should undoubtedly be valued more highly than nonscientific information. For instance, evidence from experiments, correlational studies, and even lower-quality evidence from actual case studies and naturalistic observations provides stronger support for a claim than does nonscientific evidence such as commonsense belief, anecdotes, testimonials, and nonscientific authority. All scientific evidence should be based on carefully and systematically made observations that can be repeated; nonscientific evidence, however, is typically based on informal observations that are often unique and unrepeatable.

As discussed in Chapter 4, even though case studies may resemble anecdotes and testimonials in that they are often based on information about a single, unique individual, they provide stronger support than these nonscientific kinds of evidence. The reason is that they are based on the objective descriptions of a clinical scientist or researcher making systematic observations. In contrast, the observations described in anecdotes are secondhand and informal. Likewise, while the personal experiences described in testimonials are firsthand accounts, they are also informal and not made systematically. Of course, true experiments provide the strongest support for scientific claims because they are performed under better-controlled conditions and may allow for causal inferences to be made. Now, use the following questions to analyze Figures 8.2–8.5.

Specific Evidence Questions

1. Are sources, references, or bibliographic citations listed? Was research published in a reputable, peer-reviewed scientific journal?

2. Which type of evidence, if any, is offered in support of a claim? Statements of authority? Anecdotes? Scientific research, such as case studies, correlation studies, quasi-experiments, or true experiments? (See Tables 3.1 and 4.3 for information on evaluating the relative quality of evidence typically afforded by each type of research.)

3. How good is the evidence provided? Was it based on carefully and systematically made observations under controlled conditions? Was it done by independent scientists at, say, a university or was it funded by a company or other interested party?

Regarding the first evidence question, minimal information is offered about the research cited in Figure 8.4, and no references or bibliography section is provided, which makes it difficult to evaluate the research. In its defense, the website did provide the author, year of publication, and journal name for the Reed study. In contrast, the claim that case studies show Telepatherapy to be effective in virtually all cases of anxiety and depression is not supported by research evidence cited anywhere in the website, so no argument was actually offered.

As to the second question, the Telepatherapy site uses five main kinds of evidence: commonsense belief, statements of authority, personal experience, anecdotes, and scientific research evidence. It begins by appealing to people's commonsense belief that we can often know something about other individuals without them telling us about it. As we have seen before, though, our intuitions about our own and other people's behavior and mental processes are often in error. Likewise, the testimonials in Figure 8.3 provide weak support for Telepatherapy because they are merely accounts of personal experiences that could be biased and incorrect interpretations that are unique to the three testimonials provided.

Regarding the third question, the research supporting Telepatherapy seems to be of low quality and its relevance is often not stated. For example, the Shainberg study (Figure 8.4) is more like an anecdote than a true case study. Although the website appeals to scientific authority based on statements from psychoanalysts, no well-controlled outcome research studies are cited in which Telepatherapy was compared with other appropriate therapies or any control group on standard measures of therapeutic effectiveness. This stance is at odds with the position taken by many professionals in psychology and the American Psychological Association—namely, that treatments should be based on solid, high-quality evidence.

The Reed study is the only actual study cited—yet it was performed not to test Telepatherapy, but rather to support claims of possible ESP communication abilities among workshop attendees. Also, although it is described as an experiment, there was no control group. Thus, the "similarities" and "connection" felt between pairs of people could have easily resulted from mere similarities in vague descriptions of those individuals' thoughts, rather than representing real evidence of ESP.

Practice Thinking 8.2: Critical Evaluation of the Deep Mind Therapy (Mock) Website

Reference Table 8.1 on page 201, which outlines the CARE approach to evaluating information, to critically analyze the "Deep Mind Therapy" mock website shown in Figures 8.6–8.9.

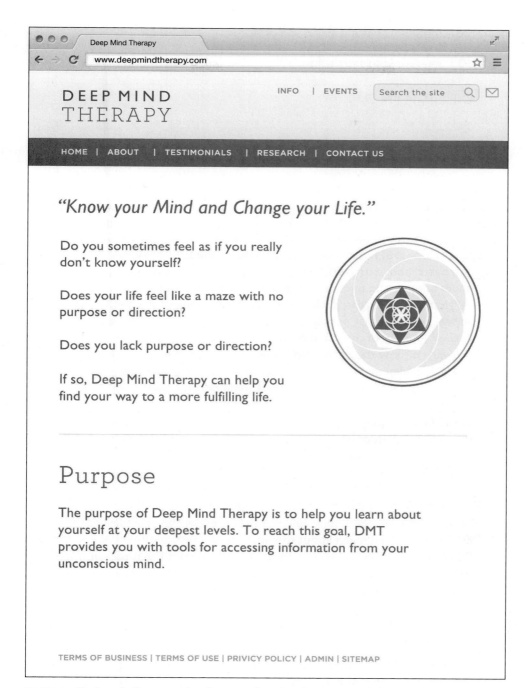

FIGURE 8.6 Mock-up of a Home page for a fictitious website describing Deep Mind Therapy. (Graphic design by Kaitlin Bensley)

← → C | www.deepmindtherapy.com/about

DEEP MIND
THERAPY

INFO | EVENTS | Search the site

HOME | ABOUT | TESTIMONIALS | RESEARCH | CONTACT US

About Deep Mind Therapy

DMT is based on the work of the brilliant Swiss psychologist, C. G. Jung (1875-1961). Although Jung originated the familiar terms, 'introvert' and 'extrovert,' his greatest contribution was in understanding the unconscious mind. Through his study of dreams, religion, and mandalas, such as the circular drawing of the Self shown above, he found that people from all cultures show the same themes in their journey of psychic development. Yet, most people are unaware of how the unconscious mind can guide them on their path toward fulfillment. Using Jung's theory and powerful spiritual techniques, DMT helps the conscious mind become aware of unconscious forces that can guide a person on their path to self-fulfillment. Jung found that when his patients drew mandelas and then contemplated them they became more centered. He discovered that people could also get more connected with their unconscious minds through spiritualism. Jung wrote his MD dissertation on research he did on his cousin Helly who was a gifted spiritualist medium. While in a trance state, she communicated with the spirits of their dead relatives. Jung believed that study of this spiritualistic contact could tell much about the unconscious part of the mind. DMT works by helping your conscious mind contact the forces in your unconscious mind, employing two main tools: mandela work and channeling or mediumistic contact with the spirit world.

TERMS OF BUSINESS | TERMS OF USE | PRIVICY POLICY | ADMIN | SITEMAP

FIGURE 8.7 Mock-up of an "About" page for a fictitious website describing Deep Mind Therapy. (Graphic design by Kaitlin Bensley)

FIGURE 8.8 Mock-up of a testimonials page for a fictitious website describing Deep Mind Therapy. (Graphic design by Kaitlin Bensley)

www.deepmindtherapy.com/research

DEEP MIND
THERAPY

INFO | EVENTS

Search the site

HOME | ABOUT | TESTIMONIALS | RESEARCH | CONTACT US

Research

In his book, Mandala Symbolism, Jung (1972) described his research on using mandalas in therapy. He found that many patients drew mandalas that revealed their inner conflicts and their striving to become more integrated persons. Jung reported that patients often found drawing mandala figures to have a soothing effect on them. He also observed that the mandalas drawn by his patients had common themes with mandelas drawn by people from various cultures and different times in history. This allowed Jung to uncover the universal unconscious striving toward integration of the self. For example, he described the case of an American woman who was a scholar, had read all the major psychological works of the time, and wanted to study with him. Although she had never painted before, she did paintings of mandelas that contained similar themes in the form of lightening and a snake found in the work of the Greek alchemists from hundreds of years ago. These were evidence of unconscious themes of striving to become an individual. Recently, DMT researchers interviewed patients who had used channeling in therapy. The researchers found that 100% of those interviewed reported that contact with the spirits of their departed relatives was useful in their self-development.

Find a Therapist Near You

Schedule an Appointment

TERMS OF BUSINESS | TERMS OF USE | PRIVICY POLICY | ADMIN | SITEMAP

FIGURE 8.9 Mock-up of a research page for a fictitious website describing Deep Mind Therapy. (Graphic design by Kaitlin Bensley)

SUMMARY

The Internet is the most widely used, broadest-scope communication tool in the world, but its use carries both costs and benefits. This worldwide network allows people to communicate almost instantaneously, to conduct their business and finances online, to access the information found in major libraries, to find a mate, and to entertain themselves endlessly. Unfortunately, those advantages are also matched by some notable disadvantages—particularly, the proliferation of vast amounts of data that may potentially produce cognitive overload and confusion about which information is relevant and trustworthy. The Internet can be especially problematic as a vehicle for spreading misinformation, fake news, and false conspiracy theories.

Fortunately, good strategies exist for analyzing and evaluating information on the Internet. One guideline is that web-based information found on large and more public, professionally maintained databases, such as PsycINFO, tend to provide higher-quality information than web-placed information. Web-placed sources often demonstrate little quality control and involve self-publication in the form of blogs, personal websites, and some business websites.

Another helpful strategy is to use the CARE mnemonic and associated questions to analyze and evaluate information on the web. CARE stands for credibility, accuracy, reasonableness, and evidence for a claim. Specifically, credibility refers to how believable, authentic, and trustworthy a source might be. Accuracy concerns whether the information is true, factual, and correct. Reasonableness applies to how plausible and consistent the claims might be. Finally, evidence concerns the extent to which good evidence supports and does not support a claim.

 Practice Thinking 8.3: What Do You Think NOW?
Please explain how you know.

1. How do you know if you can trust information you find on the web?

   _____

2. Which questions should you ask to critically evaluate information you find on the Internet? _____

   _____

3. How would you know if a therapy described on the web was a good one?

_____

4. What are some advantages and disadvantages of using the Internet?

_____

REVIEW QUESTIONS

1. What is the Internet?
2. Why is skepticism needed to evaluate information on the Internet?
3. Describe some benefits of using the Internet.
4. Describe some dangers and problems in using the Internet (e.g., fake news).
5. What is a conspiracy theory? Why do people endorse false conspiracy theories?
   - How do those who endorse science-related conspiracy theories and pseudoscientific theories fail to engage in good scientific reasoning?
   - What thinking errors do they commit?
6. What is the difference between web-based and web-placed resources in psychology?
7. Compare the peer-review process for print journals with how information is often published on the Internet.
8. What does the first-letter mnemonic CARE stand for?
9. Can you distinguish between credibility, accuracy, reasonableness, and evidence as criteria for evaluating information on Internet sites?
   - Which questions and markers are used to assess credibility?
   - Which questions and markers are used to assess accuracy?
   - Which questions and markers are used to assess reasonableness?
   - Which questions and markers are used to assess evidence?
10. What is black-and-white thinking? How is this thinking error problematic in the Telepatherapy mock website?
11. How do you distinguish evidence-based treatments and practices from pseudoscientific ones on the Internet? See the two mock websites.
12. What are some examples of psychological misconceptions and misinformation found on the Internet?

9

EMOTION, MOTIVATED REASONING, AND CRITICAL THINKING

LEARNING OUTCOMES

After studying this chapter, you should be able to:

1. Explain the roles of motivation and emotion in thinking.

2. Critically analyze situations in which motivation and emotion may lead to thinking errors.

3. Apply what is known about the influences of motivation and emotion on thinking to improve thinking.

4. Apply what you know about motivation and emotion to draw a well-reasoned conclusion from a discussion about whether emotions make us irrational.

WHAT DO YOU THINK?

Example 1: One time when I was taking a statistics exam, I got so anxious that I could not concentrate. Although I was motivated to do well, I sat there watching the time tick-tick-ticking away. My mind was racing, but it was going in circles. I fretted about not knowing how to do the problems and what would happen if I did not do them. Needless to say, I did poorly on the exam. It seemed as if this strong, negative emotion was at odds with my motivation to do well.

Has a strong emotion ever impaired your ability to think clearly? What is going on in this situation?

Example 2: "Julie and Mark are brother and sister. They are traveling together in France on summer vacation from college. One night they are staying alone in a cabin near the beach. They decide that it would be interesting and fun if they tried making love. At the very least it would be an interesting experience for them. Julie was already taking birth control pills, but Mark uses a condom too, just to be safe. They both enjoy making love, but they decide not to do it again. They keep that night a special secret, which makes them feel even closer to each other. Was it OK for them to make love?" (Haidt, 2001, p. 814). *Give two reasons to support your opinion.*

These examples raise questions about how motivation and emotion are related to thinking.

Practice Thinking 9.1: What Do You Think?

Please explain how you know.

1. How do our motives and emotions affect our thinking?

   _____

2. How do lie detectors work? Do they accurately identify when people are lying?

   _____

3. Is good reasoning "cool" or rational and unaffected by the "heat" of passion or emotion? Do strong emotions make us irrational?

   _____

When people are asked what they think about the incest between Mark and Julie, they almost always say it is wrong. When pressed to give reasons for their objection, some say it is wrong because Julie might get pregnant, but the passage makes it clear that the siblings have taken adequate precautions to prevent this outcome. Other people object because they think Julie and Mark may be harmed emotionally, but the passage says the siblings enjoy the experience and feel closer afterward.

Once their initial objections are countered with the preceding explanations, people often respond that they do not know why they object—they just know it is wrong for Julie and Mark to make love (Haidt, 2001). Their vague response suggests that they are basing their moral judgment on intuition, a feeling of repulsion at the thought of incest, and the strong conviction that it is wrong (Type 1 thinking); their efforts to give reasons for their belief are just rationalizations offered after the fact to justify their beliefs (Type 2 thinking). To better understand how motivation and emotion can affect our thinking and beliefs, we need to examine each of these more carefully.

GOALS AND MOTIVATION

Motivation involves arousing and directing behavior toward a goal. Taking good notes during class helps you reach the immediate goal of learning the new material presented that day, which can help you reach the longer-term goals of doing well on tests in a course. This, in turn, can help you reach the long-term achievement goals of passing the course and eventually graduating from college. Besides achievement motivation, motives take the form of desires, wishes, and preferences (Kunda, 1990). The most basic motives are the drives for thirst, hunger, and sex that help us reach the goals of self-preservation and species-preservation. Related to emotions, we want certain things to happen and others not to happen. Positive emotions, such as interest and joy, help sustain our motivation so we can reach our goals. Negative emotions, such as anger and frustration, occur when we interpret some event as keeping us from reaching our goals.

The relationships among motivation, emotion, and cognition can be clearly seen in mass contagions, in which a fear reaction rapidly spreads through a group of people. For instance, in 1938, a radio broadcast dramatizing H. G. Wells's science fiction novel, *The War of the Worlds,* described an invasion by Martians—and thousands of listeners panicked upon learning of this "news." Prior to the broadcast, the famous actor Orson Welles, who narrated the program, had been concerned that the radio adaptation would not seem realistic, so he and the radio producers decided to add the names of real places and other factual references to make the story more convincing. At one point, Welles broke into the broadcast with a fake announcement that the Martians had reached Grover's Mill, New Jersey, just 60 miles from New York City.

Even though Welles had mentioned a few times during the broadcast that they were performing a radio play, many listeners who had not been paying close attention or who had tuned in late believed the invasion was real. Some residents of Grover's Mill even became convinced that the town's long-time water tower (shown in Figure 9.1) was actually a Martian spaceship. This example demonstrates how interpretation of an event (cognition) that poses a threat to survival (motivation) can lead to fear (an emotion) and sometimes a perceptual error.

(a)

(b)

FIGURE 9.1 (a) A *War of the Worlds* adaptation in comic book form. (b) The water tower in Grover's Mill, New Jersey, which some residents mistakenly perceived to be a Martian ship in the panic following the 1938 broadcast of the *War of the Worlds* radio play.

Likewise, motivation can affect another aspect of cognition: what we believe. The concept of **motivated reasoning**, or how people's reasoning is motivated to reach specific goals, can help us understand how people form and maintain beliefs. Ziva Kunda (1990) described motivated reasoning as being organized into two categories: (1) the motive to arrive at a particular, often favored conclusion and (2) the motive to arrive at an accurate conclusion. Generally speaking, Type 1 thinking corresponds to the motivation to arrive at a favored conclusion, whereas Type 2 thinking corresponds to the motive to arrive at an accurate conclusion—the kind we associate with critical thinking (CT).

Fortunately, research shows that getting people to attend to the motive of arriving at an accurate conclusion can help them improve their thinking. Tetlock and Kim (1987) expected that making participants in a study more accountable for their judgments about others would cause them to process information about other people in "more complex, self-critical, and effort-demanding ways" (p. 700). To test this hypothesis, Tetlock and Kim varied the accountability levels of three randomly assigned groups who were asked to write predictions about how other people responded on a personality test. A no-accountability control group was told that their written responses would be anonymous. The two other accountability groups were told that they would have to justify their responses: One was a pre-reading accountability group whose members were told *before* they read the other people's personality test responses that they would have to justify their predictions; the other was a post-reading accountability group whose members were told they would have to justify their predictions only *after* they had already read the test responses. Tetlock and Kim found that the pre-reading accountability group wrote descriptions that were more cognitively complex, considered more alternative interpretations, and drew more connections than did the no-accountability and post-reading accountability groups.

Unfortunately, when people are not given instructions that motivate them to be more accurate, they are likely to make judgments that are consistent with their prior beliefs and go in the direction of their expectations. As a result, they may show bias in favor of those prior beliefs and thereby commit various thinking errors. In the next section, we discuss some examples of motivated reasoning and consider how they are related to the thinking errors previously discussed.

Humans show a very pervasive bias called the self-serving bias, a tendency to evaluate oneself favorably, which contributes to multiple thinking errors (Myers, 2013). Also called *positivity bias,* this tendency to view oneself positively is found in people from many different cultures but is more prominent in Western than Asian peoples (Mezulis, Abramson, Hide, & Hankin, 2004) and may function to maintain self-esteem (Alicke & Govorun, 2005).

A common thinking error based on the self-serving bias is the fundamental attribution error, in which people attribute their success to their possession of positive traits and skills but blame their failures on situational factors. For example, a student who does well on an exam might think, "I got an A because I am smart and a hard worker." But if that student does poorly, he is more likely to think, "I got a D because I did not have time to study" or "My instructor is a tough grader." Conversely, when someone *else* does well, this same student is more likely to attribute that success to situational factors: "She did well because she studied with some smart students who helped her prepare for the test." If the other student fails, however, he may attribute that outcome to her disposition: "She is lazy."

Another form of the self-serving bias is the better than average effect, which is the tendency for individuals to judge themselves as better than the average person in their peer group on positive and socially valued traits. For instance, studies show that individuals judge themselves to be more tolerant than the average person (Gallup Poll, 1997) and more intelligent (Wylie, 1979). Myers

(2013) reviews studies showing that, among many other examples, business people judge themselves to be more ethical than the average business person, and that both business managers and workers judge their performance to be superior to that of their peers. As discussed in Chapter 11, "average" is what most people are. If most people judge themselves to be above average, this thinking clearly shows a bias, because in reality most will be average and some will even be below average.

Critical thinkers should be able to accurately assess their own traits and biases, such as how fair-minded they are. Unfortunately, the better than average effect extends to people's judgments of their own biases. Studies have repeatedly shown that people judge themselves to be less biased than the average person. Apparently unaware of their own biases, they display a **bias blind spot** (Pronin, Gilovich, & Ross, 2004). For example, in a study performed by Pronin, Lin, and Ross (2002), participants reported they would be more likely to provide unbiased self-assessments than would other people. The bias blind spot also extends to people's self-perceptions of their fairness and may interfere with their ability to see both sides of an issue (Franz, 2006).

Psychology students display the better than average effect in the evaluation of their own CT dispositions, too. Recently, my colleagues and I found that psychology students judged themselves to be significantly more open-minded, more flexible in their thinking, and more intellectually engaged than the average student (Bensley, Rainey, Bernhardt, Grain, & Rowan, 2017). Because the many students who rate themselves as better than the average student on these dispositions could not all really be better than the average, this finding suggests that many students are overconfident of their own CT dispositions. Judging yourself to be less biased and more open-minded than you actually are could obstruct your perception of the need for change in these dispositions and hinder your development as a critical thinker.

The failure to recognize your own confirmation bias could be especially problematic. Recall from Chapter 4 that confirmation bias is the tendency for people to search for and find evidence that confirms their favored beliefs, existing ideas, and expectations (Nickerson, 1998). Failing to recognize your own inclination to show confirmation bias makes it less likely that you will see the need to think about evidence on the other side. Confirmation bias is an instance of motivated reasoning; the conclusions and inferences you draw are motivated by the goal of maintaining your existing beliefs. Countering this natural tendency takes a conscious decision and a deliberate effort.

People who show confirmation bias may not be consciously trying to screen out evidence and information that contradicts their favored beliefs. Instead, they may be engaged in a biased search that leads them to access positive instances from memory, supporting their beliefs. For example, when I was interviewed for my position at Frostburg State University, I was very interested in learning about one of the university's benefits—namely, tuition remission for family members of faculty. My wife wanted to take graduate courses, so I hoped they would be free of charge. When I asked about this benefit, a psychology faculty member told me she thought the university did offer this perk, but she also indicated that I should inquire further. After I was hired, I learned that the wife of my wife's graduate adviser took courses for free. I followed up with personnel in the financial aid office, who confirmed that the university offered tuition remission for faculty members' spouses.

When I applied for the benefit, however, I was surprised to learn that we were not eligible for it. The university had discontinued this practice a few years before I was hired, but had maintained it for faculty hired prior to that time. This example illustrates how wishful thinking led to my biased search and confirmation bias. I was not trying to ignore evidence that would disconfirm my existing idea, but I did not seek evidence to disconfirm it either. If I had thought to ask whether the university had graduate tuition remission for family members of *newly* hired faculty, I could have easily disconfirmed my mistaken idea.

Partisan politics is plagued with instances of confirmation bias where strong feelings and rigid beliefs often motivate reasoning. For instance, the partisan divide between Democrats and Republicans in the U.S. Congress shows the unwillingness of these groups to fairly examine ideas presented by members of the "other side." It can also explain why people who take extreme ideological positions are so certain they are right and their opponents are wrong (Lilienfeld, Ammirati, & Landfield, 2009). Because Democrats tend to listen to more liberal news outlets, and Republicans to more conservative outlets, each side insulates itself from differing views. Garrett (2009) found that people selectively search online for information that reinforces their political beliefs. This makes it easy to identify a person's political party affiliation from his or her preferred news outlet (Shermer, 2011).

Motivated reasoning, confirmation bias, and belief perseverance help explain why people continue to believe things that have been disconfirmed by good evidence. For example, creationists continue to argue that the earth is less than 10,000 years old and deny the truth of evolutionary theory even though mountains of scientific evidence from biology and geology have confirmed its predictions (Coyne, 2009; Dawkins, 2009; Palmer, 2009). Parapsychologists and believers in the paranormal persist in believing that psychic predictions are accurate, even though no good, replicable research exists to support this claim.

Why might a group continue believing a prediction it had made when that prediction did not turn out to be accurate? To answer this question, Festinger, Riecken, and Schacter (1956) studied members of a UFO cult who believed that a massive flood was going to destroy the world but that the cult members themselves would be saved from this deluge by alien beings from the planet Clarion. Festinger and his colleagues infiltrated the group after learning about it from a local newspaper article in which the group warned of the coming flood. Dorothy Martin, the group leader, had learned about the flood through her automatic writing of messages from the Guardians, the beings who were trying to protect the chosen people who would be saved from the devastating flood. Automatic writing is a technique in which a person, often in a trance, writes messages channeled from a spirit or received telepathically. Cult members believed that Martin received many messages this way from Sananda, the name for Jesus Christ on the other planet.

One message instructed Martin to go to a specific airfield where a flying saucer would land on August 1, 1954. When no saucer landed, she and other members of the group were disappointed—yet she did meet a mysterious stranger there. Later, she interpreted the stranger to be Sananda. This seemed to reassure her and some of the group's members despite the failed prophesy, but a few members left the group anyway. Martin soon received another message that a spaceship would land at midnight on December 20, 1954, in time for her and the chosen group to be escorted to the ship on December 21, thereby saving them from the coming flood. She and members of the group stayed up late into the morning of December 21, only to be disappointed yet again when no ship arrived. This time, many members wept and questioned whether they had been right. Finally, through automatic writing, another message informed Martin that the God of Earth had decided to spare the planet because the little group had waited dutifully all night for the ship.

Festinger and his colleagues used cognitive dissonance theory to explain the group's reaction to the disconfirmed prediction. When a prophesy fails, a believer will experience dissonance, an intense state of discomfort, until the discrepancy with the belief is resolved. Dissonance is especially strong when believers have invested in or publicly supported a belief. Many group members had sold their property and had distanced themselves from the world they believed they would be leaving behind. The new message they received through Martin helped reduce their dissonance by explaining that their belief had served a good purpose and that there was a good reason why the spaceship had not come.

According to Festinger and his colleagues, another strategy that groups use to reduce their dissonance following a failed prophesy is to proselytize about their belief system in an effort to gain new converts. Spreading their beliefs to potential new members reduces dissonance because the believers infer that if other people join the group, then their beliefs must be right. In support of this idea, Festinger and colleagues observed that members began to spread the group's ideas at an increased rate, recruiting more members in the months following the failed prophesy.

Boudry and Braekman (2012) proposed that strategies for reducing dissonance in the face of a failed prophesy can serve as "escape clauses" that allow a group to survive such inaccurate predictions. We have already seen that people rationalize and make excuses to explain away failed predictions. For example, when scientific evidence fails to support psychic predictions, parapsychologists may say that the experimenter's observations disturbed the subtle psychic energy needed for the predictions to succeed (see Chapter 5). Another strategy is to shift the meaning of a specific prediction to have a metaphorical meaning. Martin did this when she moved away from a very specific date on which the world would end and toward a metaphorical cancellation of the prediction by saying that the God of Earth had decided to spare the planet. These strategies help avoid the cognitive dissonance that comes with failed predictions.

Research shows, however, that as dissonance and anxiety continue to increase, people cannot forever explain away their failed predictions and the evidence accumulating against their strongly held beliefs, so they ultimately abandon their position (Redlawsk, Civettini, & Emmerson, 2010).

Practice Thinking 9.2: Recognizing Thinking Errors From Motivated Reasoning

In each of the following examples, first identify the specific thinking error/ bias associated with motivated reasoning. List all thinking errors that seem to apply, and then suggest how one might correct the error(s) and reduce the bias in each.

1. On the question of abortion, Emily, who prides herself on being fair and open-minded, is pro-choice. Jacob is pro-life. Jacob says to Emily, "You must agree that the fetus is alive when the heart starts to beat?" Emily replies, "I'm not going to respond to that because the fetal brain is not yet developed enough to support life." Jacob answers, "Why not respond?

That doesn't seem open-minded." Emily says, "You're wrong—I am much more open-minded than the average pro-lifer."

Thinking error(s): _____

_____

How to fix it: _____

_____

2. Jenna joined a group whose members believed the world was coming to an end, but that the group would be saved by aliens from another world. When the supposed doomsday came and went without the world ending, Jenna and other group members wondered why the prophesy had failed and worried that their beliefs were wrong. The group leader reassured them, "You should feel proud that you did all you could to prepare for the next world. The Beings appreciated your efforts and decided to postpone the end, but we must be ever vigilant that we follow our chosen path." Jenna and the others became even more convinced that they had been right all along.

Thinking error(s): _____

_____

How to fix it: _____

_____

3. Dani was writing an essay about why people are unemployed. She concluded that people like her who lost their jobs after working at the same company for at least two years were victims of the recession, and that people who could not get a job in the last two years were lazy.

Thinking error(s): _____

_____

How to fix it: _____

_____

4. Lee and Waite (2005) studied the perceptions of 265 U.S. married couples about how much responsibility each partner assumed for doing household chores. They found that husbands estimated they did 42% of the work but actually did 39% of it, while the wives estimated that their husbands did only 33% of the work.

   Thinking error(s): _____

   _____

   How to fix it: _____

   _____

5. Mario was very jealous of his girlfriend, Tina, because he feared she was interested in one of his good friends, James. The more he worried about this possible attraction, the more evidence he found to make him suspicious. When all three were together, Mario looked for ways to interpret things Tina and James said or did that suggested they were more than just friends. When he confided his suspicions to Jen, a mutual friend of all three people, she said there were other interpretations for what James and Tina said or did besides their wanting to become a couple.

   Thinking error(s): _____

   _____

   How to fix it: _____

   _____

WHAT IS EMOTION?

An **emotion** is a mental state elicited by an event that a person has appraised as relevant to fulfilling his or her needs, and that motivates behavior to fulfill those needs and reach the individual's goals (Schirmer, 2015). To illustrate, suppose you have been dating someone for two years and learn that your partner, with whom you have shared personal information, has divulged some of that information to someone else. Your goal is to maintain trust and closeness with your partner, yet he or she has betrayed your trust. In such a case, you are likely to experience the emotion of anger.

Emotions are often marked by expressive behaviors, subjective experience, motivated dispositions to behave a certain way, and changes in physiological arousal—that is, changes in bodily functions (Buck, 1988). For example, if you responded to this situation with anger, your lips might be compressed together tightly, or your mouth might be set in a square pattern showing your teeth (a common facial expression of anger). Your muscles and entire body may feel tense, and a hot feeling may pour over your body (subjective experience). You may want to yell at or hit the person who betrayed you (behavioral disposition), and your heart may beat faster (a physiological change, showing increased arousal).

If you interpreted the situation another way, however, you might experience a different emotion. What if you thought about how this betrayal could end your relationship? Now, you might feel sad at your anticipated loss. Again, your goal of maintaining a close relationship is thwarted, but now, focusing on the imminent loss of love and affection, you feel sad. How you interpret or appraise a situation is an important factor contributing to which emotion you experience, but it does not necessarily cause or determine that emotion.

Although the process of experiencing an emotion often begins with an appraisal, it almost simultaneously involves other components, such as physiological, motor, and psychological changes (Ellsworth, 2013). Appraisal theories generally assume that emotional experience has many variations that differ by degree. Thus, a person who is betrayed might feel sadness, anger, or something in between. The many different shades of mood, feeling, and evaluative experience related to emotion are generally referred to as affect.

In contrast to supporters of appraisal theory, proponents of basic or discrete emotions theories assume that we have a small set of basic emotions that fall into distinct categories. One commonly defined set of discrete emotions includes happiness, interest, anger, sadness, disgust, and fear (Izard, 2007). These discrete emotions are natural kinds, in that they have a biological or evolutionary basis. As such, each emotion is thought to have its own form of facial and bodily expression, its own pattern of physiological response, and its own action tendency.

One type of evidence for discrete emotions comes from research suggesting that people from different cultures share the same discrete, facial expressions for the six basic emotions shown in Figure 9.2. Can you recognize the emotion displayed in each? Not only can people from one culture typically recognize the facial expressions of people from other cultures but each discrete emotion is also associated with a specific pattern of facial expression (Ekman, 1994).

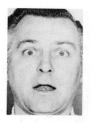     

Paul Ekman, Ph.D. / Paul Ekman Group, LLC

FIGURE 9.2 Which emotion is associated with each expression?

Other evidence supporting discrete emotions comes from research on the action tendencies that people report as part of specific emotions (Roseman, Wiest, & Swartz, 1994). If emotions evolved through natural selection, then we would expect them to serve adaptive functions. Roseman and colleagues found that the dominant action tendency for fear was the urge to run away and that the motivational goal was to get to a safe place. The distinction between positive and negative emotions also helps us understand their adaptive functions. For example, the two positive emotions of interest and joy function early in life to help the infant learn and explore the environment (Izard, 2007). In contrast, negative emotions such as fear, anger, disgust, and sadness, which occur less frequently, function to interrupt some behavior or to signal that action is needed in response to an aversive or threatening event.

Attempts to differentiate emotions using physiological changes have met with limited success. Lench, Flores, and Bench (2011) conducted a meta-analysis of 687 studies in which the discrete emotions of happiness, sadness, anger, and anxiety were thought to have been elicited. Although Lench and colleagues did find some evidence that behavioral changes, experiences, and physiological responses were correlated within emotions and that patterns of discrete emotions differed, their results did not convince all researchers (Lindquist, Siegel, Quigley, & Barrett, 2013). In another study, Fernandez and colleagues (2012) found that a fearful mood was induced after participants viewed either a fear-inducing film or an anger-inducing film, and both film types significantly increased heart rate compared with viewing a neutral film. By comparison, only skin conductance level increased after watching the fear film.

Given the difficulties in distinguishing one emotion from another based on physiological measures, it is not surprising that polygraphs (lie detector machines) that use physiological responses to distinguish liars from truth-tellers do not produce very good results. Figure 9.3a shows a man hooked up to a polygraph that measures physiological changes. You can see in the graph shown in Figure 9.3b

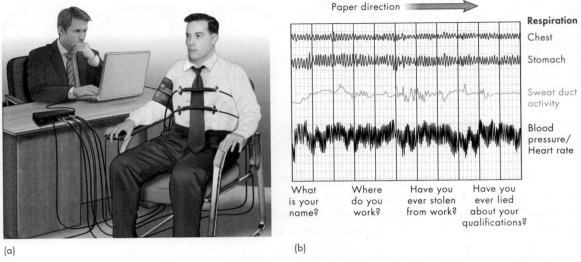

FIGURE 9.3 The polygraph (*poly* = many; *graph* = write) records physiological changes on multiple channels, such as breathing (respiration), skin conductance (GSR), and blood pressure, to detect stress and anxiety. Stress and anxiety levels supposedly increase when someone lies while answering a question.

that the man's galvanic skin response (GSR) rose sharply from baseline control types of questions after being asked, "Have you ever taken money from the bank?" The elevation in this physiological marker suggests that the man is sweating more—a sign of stress and anxiety, which indicates that the man is lying. Increased blood pressure, skin conductance, and more irregularities in breathing from baseline measures are also thought to indicate lying.

Movies and television programs often suggest that the polygraph is infallible in its ability to detect lying. The lie detector machines certainly look scientific, and the name implies that such a device detects lies, but is it really infallible?

To date, research has shown that there is no particular pattern of physiological response that corresponds to lying (Vrij, 2008). Thus, even a skilled polygraph operator cannot know exactly what to look for as a sign of deception. In addition, people show large individual differences in their physiological responses to various questions or situations. An honest person who tends to be very reactive could easily be misidentified as someone who is lying.

I once failed a lie detector test. A girl I knew was caught stealing from the store where I worked, and employees were subjected to polygraph examinations. I knew just enough psychology to get myself into trouble when taking the polygraph test: I knew that if I showed anxiety on certain questions, I would be identified as lying. When asked, "Have you stolen from this store?" my anxiety shot up—even though I had not stolen a thing. The polygraph operator mistakenly concluded from this reaction that I was lying, resulting in a *false positive* error. False positives can also occur when someone who is angry at being falsely accused experiences increased arousal (Lilienfeld, Lynn, Ruscio, & Beyerstein, 2010). The polygraph does not take into account a person's appraisal, only his arousal. Therefore, the machine is more of an "arousal detector" than a "lie detector" (Saxe, Dougherty, & Cross, 1985).

Yet another problem is that sometimes people can beat the polygraph. One strategy to do so is to artificially elevate one's baseline arousal. That way, when lying on later questions, little difference in physiological arousal is registered. Taking into consideration how these factors can affect a polygraph reading, it seems clear that not properly detecting a liar could release a criminal into society; by the same token, a false positive result could unfairly cause a person to be imprisoned, lose his or her job, or be stigmatized. Fortunately, most courts now recognize that the idea of the lie detector as infallible is a misconception and, therefore, do not admit as evidence any information obtained through polygraph testing.

From this discussion of the polygraph, we can see how misconceptions about the nature of emotion can lead to incorrect judgments about a person and misinterpretations of a person's mental processes. When I took the lie detector test, the polygraph operator mistakenly concluded that I was lying based on the faulty theory that changes in certain physiological responses would accurately identify a liar. At the same time, my belief that the polygraph operator would judge me to be a liar based on his perception of my increased anxiety level was an appraisal that indeed led me to react anxiously. In doing so, I failed to regulate my negative emotion, which in turn caused me to think and behave irrationally, in the sense that my self-induced anxiety caused me to go against my goal of not being identified as a liar. After developing a better understanding of how brain activity contributes to emotion, we will directly examine this question of whether emotion makes us irrational, as well as how to regulate negative emotion.

BRAIN AND EMOTION

You may have heard of the case of Phineas Gage, the railroad foreman who survived a horrific injury in 1848—an iron tamping rod accidentally shot through his head while he and an assistant prepared to blast rock to lay new track. Before the accident, Gage had been a trusted and respected employee. After the accident, his personality changed dramatically. His judgment was severely impaired, and he was given to fits of anger, extreme emotion, and profanity. Despite the fact that his language, perception, memory, and intellectual abilities remained intact, he ultimately lost his job with the railroad.

What did the tamping rod do to Gage's brain to so disrupt his ability to regulate his emotions, control his behavior, and make good decisions? To find out, Hannah Damasio and her colleagues measured the damage to his skull using modern brain-imaging techniques to precisely estimate the angle and position of the rod's trajectory, as shown in Figure 9.4 (Damasio, Grabowski, Frank, Galaburda, & Damasio, 1994). The researchers learned that the tamping rod had damaged the ventromedial, prefrontal cortex (lower part at the midline of the prefrontal cortex), an area known to be associated with normal decision making (Damasio, 1994). The case record shows it was Gage's decision making and control of his emotions that were disrupted, not his perception, language, or other cognitive functions.

Damasio also studied the case of a man called Elliot, who had an orange-sized tumor surgically removed from his ventromedial, prefrontal cortex, along with tissue from the neighboring orbitofrontal area. Before the surgery, Elliot had been a successful businessman and happily married. After his surgery, he lost his job and could not keep any subsequent jobs; a number of his later business

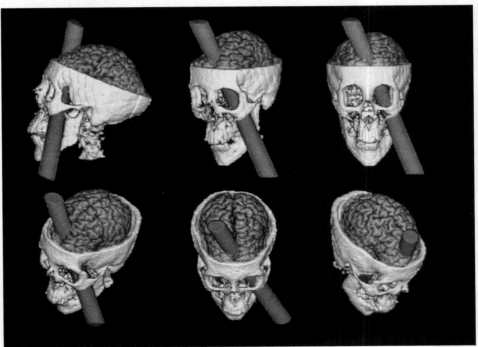

FIGURE 9.4 The path of the rod through Phineas Gage's head shows damage to the ventromedial, prefrontal cortex.

Patrick Landmann/Science Source

ventures failed as well, one of which led to bankruptcy. He and his first wife ultimately divorced, and he was later briefly married to a prostitute.

Damasio interviewed Elliot and administered numerous cognitive tests, which showed that Elliot's language, perception, movement, knowledge base, and intelligence all seemed normal—thus making Elliot's bad decisions seem all the more baffling. At the same time, Elliot lacked emotional expressiveness and was unperturbed by things that should have upset him. Unlike Gage, who displayed impulsive outbursts of anger and profanity, Elliot was not profane and showed little emotion. Yet both of these men had lost the ability to make sound decisions.

The two cases make more sense when we consider that the prefrontal region exerts control on other areas of the brain partly through inhibition and partly through communicating with brain areas that process emotion-related information. The medial prefrontal cortex acts to inhibit fear responses that are set up in the amygdala, an almond-shaped part of the brain's limbic system (illustrated in Figure 9.5) that is involved in processing information related to fear and anxiety (e.g., threatening stimuli and fearful facial expressions). When confronted with an important environmental challenge, the amygdala and the cortex work together to help the brain organize a fine-tuned, adaptive response (Baars & Gage, 2010). When the medial prefrontal cortex inhibits the amygdala, the amygdala reduces activation of areas in the brainstem and hypothalamus associated with fear responses (Quirk, Likhtik, Pelletier, & Pare, 2003).

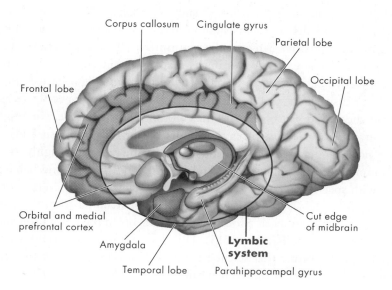

FIGURE 9.5 The limbic system contains the amygdala, hippocampus, and other structures connected to the medial prefrontal cortex, the orbitofrontal cortex, and the cingulate cortex.

The amygdala and brainstem are also involved in processing information related to anger and other emotions. It seems plausible that damage to the medial prefrontal cortex could have reduced inhibition of Gage's amygdala and other parts of the limbic system, leading to outbursts of emotion. In contrast, the damage to Elliot's brain was more concentrated in the orbitofrontal region, an area needed for perceiving the consequences of one's decisions, including emotional consequences. Damasio (1994) concluded that the cases of Gage and Elliot imply that emotional processing is essential to rational decision making—which challenges the idea that reasoning is a cool or unemotional process.

To study the brain areas that contribute to emotional responses and motivated reasoning, Drew Westen and his colleagues used functional magnetic resonance imaging (fMRI) to scan the brains of committed Democrats and Republicans prior to the 2004 U.S. presidential election (Westen, Blagov, Harenski, Kilts, & Hamaan, 2006). They confronted participants with statements made by the participants' favored candidates that were inconsistent with the positions the candidates would be expected to take. Westen and colleagues predicted this would create dissonance in participants, arousing emotion and activating brain areas known to be involved in emotion processing.

Activation in the amygdala was evident in the first half of the experiment, perhaps from participants' anxiety about being confronted with the contradictory information. In connection with motivated reasoning, the researchers also found activation of the ventromedial prefrontal cortex, cingulate cortex, insular cortex, and lateral orbital cortex. (The cingulate cortex is an area known to be involved when conflicting information is presented; the insular cortex is an area involved in experiencing "gut feelings" such as disgust.) Westen and colleagues argued that these results were consistent with the longstanding theory that people seek to maximize positive affect and to minimize negative affect. Viewed from this perspective, motivated reasoning is a strategy the brain uses to regulate emotion, thereby maximizing positive affect and minimizing negative affect.

From our discussion, you might mistakenly assume that specific areas of the brain are dedicated to processing specific emotions—for example, you might infer that the amygdala is the brain area that underlies the fear response. This simplistic view ignores the fact that the various areas of the brain are highly interactive and communicate in complex ways to produce the experiences and behaviors we associate with specific emotions. Recent research suggests it would be more accurate to say that what we label as an emotion is constructed from the combined activation of a number of basic processing components in the brain (Tourouteglou, Lindquist, Dickerson, & Barrett, 2015). This does not mean emotions are not real (Barrett, 2015), but rather that science has once again revealed that the mind and the brain are more complex than our intuitions would lead us to believe.

Practice Thinking 9.3: Critical Reading: Do Emotions Make Thinking Irrational?

Use what you have learned about motivation and emotion, as well as the information in Tables 3.1 and 4.3, to answer the following questions. Evaluate the quality and quantity of evidence supporting each side of the argument and draw a well-reasoned conclusion.

1. What is the central question, and how is it being approached or defined? Which claim or claims are being made? _____

   _____

2. What is the evidence supporting each side of the argument? Which kind of evidence is it, and how good is that evidence? Organize each bit of evidence under the side it supports, beneath the appropriate heading from the passage.

   a. Write a brief summary of each piece of evidence you encounter under the heading and the side of the argument it supports. For example, evidence supporting the claim that emotion impairs reasoning belongs under "Emotion and Rationality"; evidence that does not support the claim should be written separately under that heading.

   b. Label each type of evidence and comment on its quality, using Tables 3.1 and 4.3.

   c. Review each bit of evidence you described, labeled, and evaluated for both sides of the argument under their respective headings. Summarize the evidence on each side under the appropriate headings, and generalize about which side is better supported by more high-quality evidence.

   d. Repeat steps (a) through (c) for the evidence presented under the next heading, "Negative Affect and Rationality." Organize it into two categories: evidence that supports the claim and evidence that does not support the claim. Do this for the evidence under the remaining headings until you have analyzed all of the information.

3. Evaluate the quality and quantity of the evidence in each section of the passage so that you can draw a well-reasoned general conclusion based on *all* the evidence presented. How much good evidence supports one side

versus the other? Can a clear conclusion be drawn from the evidence, or is the evidence mixed? Does the conclusion need to be qualified because it seems to be true only under certain conditions? _____

CRITICAL READING: DO EMOTIONS MAKE THINKING IRRATIONAL?

Emotion and Rationality

The idea that our emotions make us think and behave irrationally is an old one in Western thought that remains popular today. You have no doubt heard someone say, "Don't get emotional," during a heated discussion, which assumes that people experiencing emotion cannot "think straight."

People often view emotion as an involuntary state that cannot be controlled, whereas reason is viewed as voluntary and deliberate. Penalties for crimes in the U.S. justice system reflect this distinction. For example, the punishment for premeditated murder committed "in cold blood" is stiffer than that for murder committed in a fit of passion (Oatley, 1990). In particular, people often assume that negative emotions (e.g., anger and anxiety), rather than positive emotions (e.g., joy and interest), make us irrational. But is this view correct? To find out, we examine the evidence on both sides of the question for negative emotions as well as for positive emotions. First, however, we will define rationality and identify how emotion might interfere with being rational.

One sense of the word *rational* is that a person is following the norms and rules for good reasoning (Stanovich, 2011). A rational person thinks logically and clearly. *Irrationality,* in this sense, means that a person is thinking in a way that violates the norms for rationality. If emotion impairs a person's rationality, then a person who becomes emotional may make worse decisions, draw less reasonable conclusions, or be more susceptible to thinking errors and biases than a person who is less emotional. Conversely, if emotion (perhaps positive emotion) is thought to *improve* a person's ability to think or behave rationally, the opposite outcomes are expected to occur.

Another sense of the word *rational* defines this term as thinking that helps a person achieve his or her goals (Baron, 2008). Conversely, if emotion induces individuals to act or think in ways that go against their goals, then they are thinking or behaving irrationally. A good example is an excellent wrestler I knew in college, who, after losing a tournament match, got so angry he punched a glass door, severely injuring his hand. His decision to respond this way was irrational because the damage he incurred could have seriously impaired his ability to ever compete again or to reach many other goals that required use of his hand.

Negative Affect and Rationality

The tension between the passions (emotion) and reason was an important theme in early Greek philosophy, culminating in the writings of the philosopher Plato in the fourth century BCE. Plato wrote that reason must subdue and master emotion to reach an ideal state of being (Russell, 1972). The notion that reason is in conflict with emotion has persisted into our own time. It is not surprising that an informal survey of Georgetown University students showed that most of them associated emotion with a disruption in thinking (Parrott, 1995).

Several lines of evidence suggest that emotional states, especially negative ones, impair the ability to think rationally. Many studies have shown that negative, irrational thinking is related to depression (Ellis, 1977b). According to Albert Ellis (1977a), people become depressed because they hold irrational beliefs about themselves and the world. Depressed people who do not believe they can succeed in life look for evidence that success is not possible. In so doing, they create a situation that makes it unlikely they will succeed, thereby confirming their irrational belief. This serves to maintain their depression, which in turn makes negative thoughts and beliefs more accessible (Auerbach, Webb, Gardiner, & Pechtel, 2013).

However, it is difficult to show cause and effect when studying clinical depression because it is unethical to cause a person to become clinically depressed. A major advance in the scientific study of emotion was the development of mood induction procedures to experimentally manipulate emotions and moods. In one such procedure, a participant is made to feel depressed after reading negative, self-devaluing statements; made to feel happy after reading positive statements; or put in a neutral state after reading factual statements not expected to induce a particular mood (Velten, 1968).

Using the experimental induction of depressed mood, happy mood, and neutral mood, Palfai and Salovey (1993) found that depression does not always impair performance on reasoning tasks. Depressed participants demonstrated significantly slower performance on an inductive reasoning task than participants in a neutral mood, but happy participants performed significantly more slowly than depressed and neutral mood participants on a deductive reasoning task.

Other research has shown that fear and anxiety can interfere with rational thinking, too. Fear often involves an emotional reaction to an imminent threat, whereas with anxiety the threat may be something that could happen farther into the future (Schirmer, 2015). Keinan (1987) found that participants in whom fear was induced by the threat of an electric shock were less likely to examine alternatives on an anagram problem-solving task than were participants who were not made to feel such fear. Leon and Revelle (1985) found that more anxious and stressed participants made more errors on an analogical reasoning task than did less anxious participants.

As for research in student testing, Zeidner (2007) reviewed many studies in which test anxiety negatively impacted cognitive performance. Test anxiety can impair performance by distracting the test taker from thinking about the task at hand and instead focusing attention on self-doubt, a counterproductive, test-taking strategy. Moreover, test-anxious students may avoid studying for a test because this focuses their attention on the anxiety-inducing event, an irrational strategy for preparing to take a test.

Anxiety can also impact the perspective a person takes when evaluating information. A group of researchers found that participants who were made to feel anxious tended to be more self-centered in the perspective they took when reasoning about other people's mental states compared with participants in an angry, disgusted, or neutral emotional state (Todd, Forstmann, Burgmer, Brooks, & Galinsky, 2015). Likewise, participants who were induced to feel surprise—a positive emotion related to experiencing uncertainty—took a more self-centered perspective; this finding suggests that uncertainty in these emotional states makes people more reliant on self-centered perspectives than they would be in other emotional states.

Still other research indicates that emotions and moods can affect the judgment of risk. Johnson and Tversky (1983) found that participants whose mood changed after reading a tragic newspaper story increased their frequency estimates of the risk posed by various events, whereas those participants who read a positive story decreased their estimates of potential risk. In another study, participants who were induced to feel happy were willing to bet more on a "long shot" than were participants who were not made to feel happy, which suggests that sometimes happiness can lead to greater risk taking (Isen & Patrick, 1983).

In a review of research on anger, Litvak, Lerner, Tiedens, and Shonk (2010) found many studies showing that people who were feeling angry were led to make more optimistic estimates of various kinds of risks than were people experiencing other emotions or neutral emotion. Specifically, Baumann and DeSteno (2012) found that participants who were made to feel angry were willing to take greater risks than were neutral-mood participants when tested under conditions that encouraged the use of affective information.

Nevertheless, negative emotion can sometimes *improve* reasoning. Moons and Mackie (2007) found that participants who were induced to feel a little angry were better able to distinguish weak from strong arguments than were participants in a neutral mood. In another study on anger, Young, Tiedens, Jung, and Tsai (2011) found that participants who were made to feel angry were more likely to seek disconfirming information (i.e., they showed less confirmation bias) in a debate than were sad participants. In a follow-up study, angry participants again showed less confirmation bias, as they reported being more likely to oppose a person in the 2008 election than did sad participants. Moving against an object or person is thought to be an action tendency associated with anger.

Positive Affect and Rationality

If strong, negative emotions often impair thinking, then one might expect that positive affect and emotions could, in turn, facilitate reasoning and decision making. Some emotion experts have argued that positive affect can improve cognitive processing. For example, Scherer (1984) has suggested that low levels of a positive emotion, such as happiness, may help maintain behavior. According to Thorndike's law of effect, a person is more likely to engage in a behavior when it leads to a pleasant outcome. In this way, positive affect can aid learning. Moreover, the urge to minimize negative emotion can encourage belief formation (Berenbaum & Boden, 2014).

More to the point, Carnevale and Isen (1986) found that positive mood can improve the efficiency and thoroughness of thinking, especially when people are engaged in complex tasks. Additionally, Djamasbi (2007) found that people induced to be in a positive mood after receiving a small gift used more cues in a decision support system than did participants who did not receive the small gift. Their judgments were also more accurate.

Other research has shown that positive mood can bias thinking and judgment. For instance, Isen and Daubman (1984) found that positive mood causes people to be more inclusive when grouping things into categories. For example, people in a positive mood would be more likely than participants not in a positive mood to say that the object *ring* belongs in the category "clothing." Similarly, participants in a positive mood would rate poorer instances of the category "vehicle"—such as *elevator, camel,* and *feet*—higher than participants who were not in a positive mood. Schwartz and Bless (1991) have argued that people in a positive mood are likely to use a processing strategy that lacks logical consistency and attention to detail.

Although positive mood may impair performance on tasks requiring logical, detail-oriented strategies, it may actually help us when we undertake more creative tasks (Isen, Johnson, Mertz, & Robinson, 1985). Creative thinking often requires that we see remote connections between stimuli, so positive mood might help in solving problems that require more unusual associations. In another study, Isen and Means (1983) found that participants who were put into a positive mood were more efficient in their decision making compared with participants who were not in a positive mood.

In their review of research from an edited book and other studies on emotion and decision making, Roy Baumeister, DeWall, and Zhang (2007) argued that emotion can both improve and hinder decision making. Emotion is most likely to hinder decision making when we experience a current, full-blown emotion. In contrast, milder emotion often operates unconsciously to guide us toward effective judgments and choices. The anticipation of which emotion we will experience if we pursue a particular course of action can also help us respond more adaptively as we seek to achieve certain goals. Moreover, emotions provide feedback that helps us learn how to deal with future events and how to distinguish right from wrong in moral decision making.

In another review of the research presented in her edited book on emotion and reasoning, Isabelle Blanchette (2014) argued that emotion affects reasoning in multiple ways. Although it may sometimes impair reasoning, emotion can have an adaptive effect and lead to correct responses on tasks with logically correct answers. The effect of emotion depends on the particular emotion aroused in relation to the task performed. Blanchette also reviewed several studies showing that the emotional content of the material with which we reason can affect that reasoning, sometimes hindering it and sometimes facilitating it. For instance, in an early study, Lefford (1946) found that participants made more logical errors in a deductive reasoning task when the syllogisms contained emotional content than when the syllogisms did not contain emotional content. In more recent studies, Blanchette, Gavigan, and Johnston (2014) have observed that if what we are reasoning about has emotional meaning or relevance to us, then we sometimes reason more effectively than when the content is not relevant to us.

DEALING WITH THINKING ERRORS ASSOCIATED WITH EMOTION

If we conclude that emotions can sometimes get in the way of reasoning effectively, while at other times they help us respond adaptively, then we need to understand how to regulate our emotions to reach our goals. Fortunately, people can learn how to regulate their emotions by increasing, decreasing, or maintaining their emotions (Koole, 2009). Part of regulation entails first becoming aware of thinking errors and problems related to emotion so that you can respond more adaptively and rationally. In this section, we consider different ways that emotion can contribute to thinking errors and strategies for dealing with these problems.

Countering Appeals to Emotion

Appealing to emotion is a strategy used in argumentation in which a person tries to elicit fear, anger, pity, or another emotion to support a claim or persuade another person. This approach may be intended to deflect attention away from relevant evidence. For example, a defense lawyer may appeal to pity to persuade a jury that his client's criminal actions are understandable given the abusive conditions that characterized the client's childhood. Pity for a defendant's unfortunate childhood is not relevant in deciding a person's guilt, but it might be relevant when considering leniency in the sentencing phase of a trial (Neimark, 1987).

Politicians often appeal to fear to persuade citizens to support a war. For instance, in the run-up to the Iraq War in 2003, President George W. Bush and his administration often warned that Iraq had weapons of mass destruction (WMDs) and was developing nuclear weapons that it might use against the United States (Isikoff & Corn, 2006). This appeal to fear was successful and resulted in Congress authorizing a war that cost thousands of lives and $1 trillion—even though no WMDs were ever found.

To counter an appeal to emotion, it helps to separate the claim from the emotion being appealed to. If lawmakers had realized that the Bush administration's appeal to fear was related to its claim that the problem was urgent and needed a quick solution, then they might have refocused the argument on the quality of evidence for WMDs. Instead, they rapidly agreed to invade Iraq based on the hasty generalization that Iraq was threatening us with WMDs.

Modifying Strong Negative Emotion

Because strong negative emotions often impair a person's ability to think rationally, it can help to reduce or change the emotion so that rational thinking can proceed. For example, anger can provoke us to draw a rapid conclusion or respond aggressively to an insult or attack without much thought. This response demonstrates how a strong emotion may lead us to rely more on fast Type 1 thinking than on slower Type 2 thinking.

A good strategy to reduce anger is to slow down your response to the elicitor of anger, such as by counting to 10 before responding. This delay can de-escalate an attack and give you time to construct an effective response, rather than launching into a thoughtless reaction. Another strategy for reducing emotional response is to try to relax the mind and body. It is very difficult to experience strong emotion when a person is relaxed (Benson, 1975; Jacobsen, 1929).

A third strategy is to shift attention away from the negative situation, such as thinking about positive events and happy memories. A good example of this approach is seen in how Dounia Bouzar's French de-indoctrination team handled a potentially volatile situation: They prevented a young Muslim man who had kidnapped his daughter from sacrificing their lives in jihad in Syria (Bouzar, 2016). The team urged the man's wife, Meriam, to remind him of positive events when they communicated—such as when they had met, the birth of their child, and places they had visited—and not to try to reason with him about his beliefs or plans.

After 10 months, the young man returned his daughter to his wife. According to Bouzar (2016), in this and 500 other cases, researchers found that changing emotion—not reasoning—returned the person to a more rational outlook. This tactic is similar to Haidt's suggestion that when trying to persuade individuals to change their thinking about a moral or political question that goes against their intuition, you should first appeal to their Type 1 thinking (Haidt, 2012).

Reappraising a Situation

An incorrect interpretation or appraisal of a situation can lead to an inappropriate or immoderate emotional response to the situation. For instance, when people who are quick to anger look for signs of an attack and provocation in ambiguous situations, they may incorrectly interpret more neutral signals as an attack, which could lead them to retaliate for no good reason. Likewise, people who are anxious or fearful may be quick to interpret harmless signals as posing a threat, prompting them to cower in fear when they should be actively pursuing their goals.

In these situations, it often helps to reappraise the situation so that a more adaptive response can be made. **Reappraisal** involves reevaluating a situation to look for other possible interpretations of an event. Reinterpreting a situation in which strong emotion may interfere with reasoning can lead to a more moderate emotional response or even a different emotion altogether. Notice that reappraisal might be part of an adaptive response, along with the other strategies described. For example, a reappraisal of the evidence for WMDs and other information would have helped Congress make a more rational decision about invading Iraq. Similarly, a reduction in negative emotion is often necessary before a reappraisal can be done.

Practice Thinking 9.4: Identifying and Dealing With Emotional Effects on Thinking

For each of the following examples, identify the effect(s) of emotion on thinking and describe a strategy or strategies for solving the problem(s) related to the emotion.

1. For two years, Tim has been dreading the thought of taking a statistics class. Although his previous math course performance has been average, Tim has convinced himself that he is not good at math. When he finally takes his first statistics exam for class, he reads the first question and does not know how to answer it. Tim's mouth is dry, and he feels tense and jittery. From that point on, he cannot concentrate on any other questions, and he runs out of time. As a result, he fails the exam. _____

   _____

2. Lee and Selena had been dating for two years and were discussing their plans after graduation. Lee was about to accept a job in forestry at a national park, but Selena wanted to get an advertising job in a big city. Lee said, "I think we should move near the park." With a tear in her voice, Selena said, "How can I get a job out in the woods?" Lee replied, "I already have a job—isn't it more reasonable to move to where I have a job?" Selena began to sob and said that Lee didn't care enough to try to work things out. _____

   _____

3. In a speech to his followers, a political leader warns of the danger that a foreign country poses. He describes the foreigners as savages who have invaded their land and committed terrorist acts. He argues that their country should engage in a military attack before its people are further harmed by this treacherous foreign country. _____

   _____

SUMMARY

Motives arouse and direct behavior toward a goal. Reasoning is often motivated to help a person achieve specific goals. Sometimes reasoning is motivated to arrive at an accurate conclusion, but at other times it is motivated to arrive at a favored conclusion. Prime examples of this second kind of motivated reasoning are belief perseverance, in which people are motivated to maintain a belief in the face of negative evidence, and confirmation bias, in which people seek evidence to support their favored view and ignore or weigh less heavily any evidence for the opposite view. People also show a strong self-serving bias, in which they tend to rate themselves favorably, blaming their own failures on outside circumstances and evaluating themselves as better than the average person.

Emotions are motivated mental states; as such, they direct and arouse behavior. Proponents of the existence of a small set of basic or discrete emotions argue that emotions can be differentiated by changes in subjective experience (e.g., feeling state), by expressive behaviors (e.g., frowning), by physiological changes (e.g., changes in heart rate), and by action tendencies (e.g., the tendency to recoil in fear). Although researchers agree that appraisal or interpretation of a situation is an important factor in arousing emotion, they disagree about whether discrete emotions have been demonstrated. In particular, differentiating emotions by patterns of physiological arousal has not been clearly demonstrated. Nor can a polygraph test reliably distinguish an individual who is lying from one who is telling the truth based on the person's pattern of physiological arousal—which shows that the claim that the lie detector test is an accurate way to detect dishonesty is a psychological misconception.

Strong negative emotions may interfere with a person's ability to reason or use evidence to draw sound conclusions. They may also direct or change a person's behavior in a way that hinders the person in achieving his or her goals. Nevertheless, the review of the literature on the effects of emotion on thinking reveals mixed effects and a more complicated picture. Some evidence indicates that strong negative emotions, such as depression and anxiety, may interrupt and interfere with organized behaviors and thinking. In fact, evidence shows that irrational thinking may help to *maintain* depression. Conversely, other research suggests that depression may lead to better deductive reasoning than does happiness.

Still other research has demonstrated that happiness may lead to both positive and negative effects on thinking. Positive mood may make a person more creative, but also more inclusive in the use of categories. Moreover, while emotions appear to interrupt and disrupt thinking, they may also serve useful functions, such as regulating behavior and orienting people to important events. Therefore, the conclusion that emotion and affect always impair rational thinking is a sweeping generalization, and believing this, as many people do, is a psychological misconception.

In cases where emotion may interfere with the ability to reason well, certain strategies for regulating emotion may be useful. For example, separating the argument from an appeal to emotion can serve to focus a discussion on the relevant evidence. To modify a strong emotion and reduce its effects, it may help to slow down responses to emotions such as anger. Strong negative emotion can be countered through relaxation and shifting attention to positive affect and memories. Reappraising or reinterpreting a situation can help modify an emotional response.

Practice Thinking 9.5: What Do You Think **NOW**?
Please provide reasons for your answers.

1. How do our motives and emotions affect our thinking? _____

   _____

2. How do lie detectors work? Do they accurately identify when people are lying? _____

   _____

3. Is good reasoning "cool" or rational and unaffected by the "heat" of passion or emotion? Do strong emotions make us irrational? _____

   _____

REVIEW QUESTIONS

1. What is motivation? How is it related to goals?

2. What is motivated reasoning?

   - How are belief perseverance and confirmation bias related to motivated reasoning?

   - Why do people hold on to discredited beliefs? Belief perseverance?

   - What is cognitive dissonance?

   - What are "escape clauses" that people use to rescue beliefs from disconfirmation?

   - What is self-serving bias? The fundamental attribution error? The better than average effect?

3. What is an emotion? What is affect?

4. How does appraisal relate to the emotion one experiences?

5. What does discrete emotions theory propose?

   - Can emotions be distinguished by physiological response?

   - Do lie detectors reliably identify liars?

6. Which parts of the brain are involved in emotion?

7. What do the cases of Phineas Gage and Elliot suggest about the role of emotion in decision making?

8. Define *rational* in two different ways.

9. In what ways might emotions make us irrational?

10. What effects have emotions been shown to have on thinking?

    - In what ways have emotions impaired reasoning, decision making, and judgment?

    - In what ways have emotions and affect facilitated thinking?

11. Name some strategies that can be used to regulate emotion and reduce its negative effects on thinking.

12. What psychological misconceptions are related to emotion?

CRITICALLY ANALYZING A PSYCHOLOGICAL QUESTION: ARE PEOPLE BASICALLY SELFISH?

LEARNING OUTCOMES

After studying this chapter, you should be able to:

1. Take different perspectives to understand and think about a question.

2. Critically read and analyze a literature review on helping behavior.

3. Avoid thinking errors such as myside bias, circular reasoning, sweeping generalization, and black-and-white thinking (either-or thinking).

4. Recognize and avoid misconceptions about heredity, the nature-versus-nurture debate, and the conditions under which a person is likely to receive help.

WHAT DO YOU THINK?

During World War II, a factory owner and member of the Nazi Party named Oscar Schindler helped his Jewish factory employees hide from the Nazis who were determined to relocate them to concentration camps so they could be executed. The Nazis considered anyone who helped the Jews to have committed a serious crime against the state, punishable by death. Schindler recognized the danger, yet he still protected these Jews, lying to the German government and putting himself at great risk. But apart from protecting the Jews, Schindler was no paragon of virtue. He gambled, drank too much, and regularly cheated on his wife (Baumeister & Bushman, 2008). Why did he help his Jewish employees?

Each day we have the opportunity to help others, sometimes in small ways and sometimes in important ways. Social psychologists are interested in why people help or do not help. Suppose you were confronted with the situation depicted in Figure 10.1. Would you help? How would you act—or not act?

FIGURE 10.1 Would you help the man lying on the sidewalk? Why or why not?

Practice Thinking 10.1: What Do You Think?

Please explain how you know.

1. Are people basically selfish?

   _____

2. In which ways is selfishness beneficial? In which ways is it harmful? Are you always helpful?

   _____

3. Do infants and young children start out being selfish and learn to be more helpful?

   _____

4. Is there a biological basis to helping—that is, did we evolve to be helpful or selfish?

_____

5. What should you do if you need help in a group of people?

_____

Sometimes people have helped you when you needed it. Why do you think that is? Were they unselfish and not really concerned about getting something in return? Or did they hope to get noticed for their good deeds? Maybe they were just trying to avoid the guilt or shame that comes from not helping someone in need. Or maybe they helped you so that they could feel good about themselves. Perhaps people are basically selfish and are simply watching out for themselves.

We consider these important questions in this chapter. Answering them is important because humans are social animals, and helpfulness is the "social glue" that holds communities together. Of course, answering any complex question, including whether people are basically selfish, is not easy. A systematic approach must be taken to analyze and evaluate what is known about the question, which requires a familiarity with the important terms and approaches to the question. Consequently, we will begin by reviewing some of these terms and then discuss possible approaches and perspectives to understanding the question, which should help prepare you to critically analyze the discussion of the question later in the chapter.

The question of whether people are basically selfish is so fundamental to our view of what it means to be human that it has long intrigued philosophers, psychologists, biologists, sociologists, and other thinkers. In psychology, research on helping is part of the larger investigation of **prosocial behavior**, which is defined as any behavior that is focused on benefiting others or society at large. In many discussions of whether people are selfish, the question is phrased in terms or whether people are _altruistic_. Altruism refers to helping or aiding another person without the expectation of receiving any benefit in return (Schroeder, Penner, Dovidio, & Piliavin, 1995). Many people view altruism as essentially the opposite of selfishness, or egoism. Selfish persons are assumed to help others less because helping others does not benefit them and might take up some of their time and resources. In this chapter, we examine whether people are altruistic or egoistic to illustrate how to critically read and analyze a discussion of this complex psychological question.

APPROACHING THE QUESTION FROM DIFFERENT PERSPECTIVES

If your response to the first "What Do You Think?" question was "Yes, people are basically selfish," many people would disagree with you. How do you know you are right? Although we may not want to admit it, we are all sometimes wrong. People often have differing views on fundamental questions about human nature and behavior. These differences often depend on a person's perspective in examining the question, which involves making assumptions that guide the approach taken. To understand or see an issue from someone else's vantage point, we must engage in **perspective taking,** an active process of trying to look at a question from another person's viewpoint, making the same assumptions he or she has made. This practice can help us avoid the problem of missing important information in an argument and can help clarify our own assumptions and perspective.

Perspective taking is important when we are seeking and evaluating evidence because critical thinking (CT) involves evaluating evidence from *all* sides of an argument—not just the evidence that favors our own view. Unfortunately, people often show **myside bias,** a thinking error similar to confirmation bias in which thinking is one-sided, thereby neglecting the information and evidence that support the other side of a question (Baron, 1995; Stanovich, West, & Toplak, 2013). Confirmation bias often goes one step further, however, in that information for the other side may be disparaged or given less weight, in which case the information is considered, but inadequately. Nevertheless, both myside bias and confirmation bias involve a failure or at least a reluctance to adopt the perspective of another person and consider other views. To avoid myside bias, we must examine the evidence on all sides of the question, including both the evidence that supports altruism and the evidence that supports egoism.

A useful strategy for broadening one's understanding and perspective on a complex question is to consider what fields other than one's own might have to offer. The differing perspectives and approaches used in these fields provide information about the various aspects of a complex question and about systems that operate at different levels. For example, the field of philosophy has a lot to say about the second "What Do You Think?" question: "In which ways is self-ishness beneficial? In which ways is it harmful? Are you always helpful?" This is a "value" question, posed from an ethical perspective. The usual position on this question is that helping is the right thing to do, and a person has an ethical obligation to help others in need. Many philosophers and supporters of religion have extolled the virtues of altruism, epitomized in the Christian story of the good Samaritan who stops on the road to selflessly help the victim of a robbery—one who is not even from his own group.

Other philosophers have argued that enlightened self-interest is the best approach. For instance, Ayn Rand, the Russian-born philosopher and author of the novels *The Fountainhead* and *Atlas Shrugged,* argued that selfishness is a virtue. According to Rand, when people are altruistic, they sacrifice their own individuality and achieve less than when they promote their own self-interest. Rand further argued that society's emphasis on altruism saps the initiative of individuals, reduces their self-esteem, and generally works against their welfare. She proposed that people should pursue their own interests and goals while not obstructing the interests of others (Rand & Branden, 1964).

Philosophers propose ethical principles about how people "should" behave and make arguments about what they "should" value. In contrast, although many psychologists assume that helping is a good thing, they are more concerned with how people *actually* behave (Batson, 2011). Psychologists are more likely to observe the extent to which people are influenced by and follow normative rules for helping. Indeed, research shows that people are influenced by the social norm that one should help someone in need, regardless of whether one will receive something in return (Berkowitz, 1972). From a psychological perspective, then, the question becomes "What are the conditions that produce or motivate helping behavior or the lack of it?"

The field of psychology has developed into specialized subfields, often influenced by and borrowing from biology and other fields. Each subfield—such as social psychology, biopsychology, and developmental psychology—offers a different perspective and approach to the complex question of whether people are basically selfish. For example, social psychologists might investigate whether the man lying on the ground in Figure 10.1 would be more likely to be helped if several people saw him, as opposed to if just one person encountered the man. Social psychologists often seek to understand the motives and personality traits of individuals who help others. Taking a different perspective, developmental psychologists might examine whether people of different ages would be more likely to help, such as very young children versus adults.

Psychologists in each of these subfields seek to find the causes and mechanisms that underlie altruism, egoism, and helping behavior. It is not enough to say that altruistic people tend to help other people whereas selfish people do not. To see why this kind of blanket statement is not sufficient, analyze the following argument. What is wrong with it?

Allison donates blood every time there is a blood drive at her college because she is altruistic. How do we know Allison is altruistic? Because she donates blood every time.

Psychologists would avoid this kind of circular reasoning, in which the conclusion simply renames what is claimed in the premise and does not use reasoning to build new knowledge. Instead, they would closely examine the conditions triggering the altruistic motive that produce the helping behavior. They might try to eliminate other, more selfish motives as explanations for helping, such as avoiding the guilt or shame associated with not helping or getting positive attention for helping, to ensure that genuine altruism led to the helping.

Approaching questions from the perspective of one's own scientific area has both advantages and disadvantages. On the plus side, by using the tools of inquiry and ideas from their own area, scientists can advance discussion of a question based on existing knowledge. On the minus side, they may miss the opportunity to inform the discussion with material and evidence presented by scientists in other areas that offer a different perspective. Creative answers to complex questions often result from the integration of information from different fields, as in the case of Darwin's development of the theory of natural selection. From natural history, Darwin borrowed the idea of the diversity of species and combined it with the idea from geology of the great age of the earth; he then integrated this understanding with an idea from economics, dealing with competition for scarce resources. His integrative theory proposed that organisms with traits that helped them to better compete for scarce resources would be better able to pass along those adaptive traits to their offspring.

Efforts to integrate knowledge from biology and related fields led to the development of "biopsychology," a broad subfield of psychology that has borrowed heavily from Darwin's evolutionary theory and from genetics to study the evolution and inheritance of behavioral tendencies in humans and other animals. From neuroscience and physiology, biopsychology has borrowed ideas about how the brain functions to support behaviors like helping. The development of biopsychology and other subfields is an acknowledgment that the mind/brain is a complex system that operates at multiple levels and should be studied from multiple perspectives.

Approaching the complex question of whether people are basically selfish or unselfish from the different perspectives offered by the subfields of psychology should yield a more complete understanding and lead to a better conclusion. To help you prepare to think critically about this question, let's examine what the approaches of these subfields offer in greater detail.

Practice Thinking 10.2: Which Perspectives Do Different Subfields of Psychology Offer?

How might people in the subfields of psychology offer different perspectives on the question of whether people are basically selfish? How might they approach the study of this question?

1. How might biopsychologists study the brain in relation to helping?

   _____

   _____

2. How might biopsychologists use evolutionary theory to study helping behavior? _____

   _____

3. How might developmental psychologists study helping behavior in relation to age? _____

   _____

4. How might social psychologists study helping behavior? (*Hint:* Apply social learning theory.) _____

   _____

5. How might ideas from these different subfields of psychology be combined to help answer the question of whether people are basically selfish or altruistic? _____

   _____

The following critical reading exercise offers the chance to apply your knowledge of how different perspectives can inform a discussion of a literature review on the question of whether people are basically selfish or unselfish. The questions are designed to help you critically analyze the passage. If you are not sure how to do this, review the discussion on critical reading in Chapter 6.

Practice Thinking 10.3: Critical Reading: Are People Basically Selfish or Unselfish?

1. What is the central question, and how is it being approached or defined? Which claim or claims are being made?

2. What is the evidence supporting each side of the argument? Which kind of evidence is it, and how good is that evidence? Organize each bit of evidence under the side it supports, beneath the appropriate heading from the passage. More specifically, answer each of the following questions.

   a. Write a brief summary of each piece of evidence you encounter under the heading and the side of the argument it supports. For example, evidence supporting the claim that people are selfish belongs under "Biological Basis of Altruism"; evidence that does not support the claim should be written separately under that heading.

   b. Label each type of evidence and comment on its quality, using Tables 3.1 and 4.3.

   c. Review each bit of evidence you described, labeled, and evaluated for both sides of the argument under their respective headings. Summarize the evidence on each side under the appropriate headings, and generalize about which side is better supported by more high-quality evidence.

   d. Repeat steps (a) through (c) for the evidence presented under the next heading, "Social Psychological Research on Empathy and Altruism." Organize it into two categories: evidence that supports the claim and evidence that does not support the claim. Do this for the evidence under the remaining headings until you have analyzed all of the information.

3. Evaluate the quality and quantity of the evidence in each section of the passage so that you can draw a well-reasoned general conclusion based on *all* the evidence presented. How much good evidence supports one side versus the other? Can a clear conclusion be drawn from the evidence, or is the evidence mixed? Does the conclusion need to be qualified because it seems to be true only under certain conditions?

CRITICAL READING: ARE PEOPLE BASICALLY SELFISH OR UNSELFISH?

To say that an individual is basically selfish is to assert that he or she has a fundamental trait or tendency to behave in his or her own self-interest without regard for the welfare of others. We would expect a selfish individual to show very little helping behavior. In contrast, someone who typically helps other people without regard for personal benefit shows selflessness or altruism. Being basically selfish or basically altruistic could also mean that a person's biological makeup predisposes that person to be selfish versus altruistic, respectively. According to this view, altruistic people have innate tendencies or traits "hardwired" into their nervous system that motivate them to help without concern for receiving rewards. This extreme position on the nature-versus-nurture debate maintains that it is in their *nature* to demonstrate unselfishness.

On the *nurture* side of the question, it is assumed that people are not basically altruistic because they must acquire these traits through learning, experience, or the influence of their culture. The following review begins with a discussion of altruism and selfishness from a biological perspective and then examines various psychological aspects of altruism and egoism, such as motivation for helping, learning, development, and other factors that contribute to helping behavior.

The Biological Basis of Altruism

Scientists have used Darwin's evolutionary theory to argue both for and against the idea that people are, by nature, altruistic (Rapoport, 1991). According to evolutionary theory, a trait such as altruism could be preserved in a species if it helped members of the group survive. Evolutionary biologist Robert Trivers (1971) argued that an important way that altruism could be preserved in a species is along kinship lines. An individual will be more likely to sacrifice resources—even his or her life—for a close relative than for an unrelated person because close kin, such as a brother or offspring, share 50% of the individual's genes. Individuals with genes that produce a tendency to help close blood relatives would be inclined to preserve their own genes by helping kin, including the genes for helping. In contrast, helping unrelated individuals would put the helper at greater risk and, if that increased risk led to the helper's demise, would tend to reduce the chance that the helper's offspring would inherit the genes for altruism.

Many studies have shown that people are more inclined to help blood relatives compared with unrelated persons (e.g., Burnstein, Crandall, & Kitayama, 1994; Maner & Gailliot, 2007). In one experiment, Maner and Gailliot randomly assigned people to read the same scenarios under two conditions, involving either a relative who needed help or a stranger who needed help. Those who read the scenarios of a relative needing help indicated a greater willingness to help than did those who read the scenarios involving a stranger.

The evolution of helping along kinship lines makes sense according to British biologist Richard Dawkins. In his book *The Selfish Gene,* Dawkins argues that natural selection of traits such as altruism actually occurs at the individual level (Dawkins, 1989). There is no selective advantage for altruistic individuals who sacrifice their own resources or threaten their own lives to help an unrelated individual. In such a case, the genes for altruism might not be passed along to the young if the individual died before reproducing or if the individual's offspring died because the individual was not around to care for its young. Even if the unrelated individual receiving help survived, it might not have the genes for altruism, so the genes for altruism would not get passed on.

Why, then, do individuals help unrelated individuals? Robert Trivers proposed the idea of *reciprocal altruism,* a kind of motivational mechanism that could be passed along to unrelated individuals and enables them to play "tit-for-tat" with helping (Trivers, 1971). A good example is how vampire bats in South America regurgitate blood to help unrelated (and hungry) bats avoid starvation; later, those same bats receive regurgitated blood from other bats in the group when needed (Wilkinson, cited in Boysen, 2012). This give-and-take arrangement—that is, the bat with the gene for reciprocal altruism feeding the hungry unrelated bat, and the unrelated bat later reciprocating by providing blood to the first bat—can help both bats survive and preserve the genes for reciprocal altruism in their offspring.

Support for reciprocal altruism in humans was found in a large cross-cultural survey of people in six different countries from around the world (Johnson et al., 1989). The researchers found consistent correlations among the surveys that measured the participants' tendencies to give help and to receive help, which supports reciprocal altruism. Reciprocal altruism can work as long as the first helper is likely to receive help later, and if cheaters who do not help are penalized for not returning the favor. In a review of the research on reciprocal altruism, Abigail Marsh (2016) has argued that neuroimaging studies have shown that reciprocal altruism involves the expectancy of receiving a reward; specifically, the brain areas for reward are most active when a person behaves in a cooperative way that will lead not to immediate, but to later reward.

To explain how altruistic behavior could be motivated, Hoffman (1981) proposed that brain mechanisms have evolved for empathy, or a feeling of sympathy, compassion, or tenderness in response to the suffering of others. To have empathy, one must be able to take the perspective of those in distress so as to understand their feelings and need for help. Because the great apes are closely related to humans and have complex social lives, we would expect them to have evolved the capacity for empathy as well. Preston and de Waal (2002) cited several studies providing evidence that empathy occurs in monkeys and apes, not just in humans. For example, when a 3-year-old boy fell 18 feet into the ape enclosure at Chicago's Brookfield Zoo, Binti Jua, a female gorilla gently cradled him in her powerful arms until zoo workers could rescue him (DeWaal, 2005). Preston (2013) argued that altruism evolved from the same mechanisms that underlie the caring of helpless offspring based on an analysis of brain systems and similarities across mammalian species in maternal caregiving, further supporting an evolutionary basis to empathy.

To help sort out the contribution of genes versus environment to empathy in humans, scientists calculate the heritability index, a measure of the amount of variability attributed to inheritance. The heritability of empathy is calculated by comparing the similarity of self-reported endorsement of trait labels for empathy (e.g., generous, helpful, self-centered) in monozygotic twins (identical twins from one fertilized egg), who share 100% of the same genes, with that of dizygotic twins (fraternal twins from two fertilized eggs), who share 50% of the same genes. Researchers typically assume that the two kinds of twins live in the same home situation, which tends to control for environmental variables. If the monozygotic twins show greater similarity in their endorsement of empathy trait words than do dizygotic twins, then this greater similarity is attributed to a greater genetic influence. The heritability index for empathy in such circumstances, therefore, is higher compared with when dizygotic twins show relatively less similarity.

One study that used these methods obtained a heritability index of .72, suggesting "a genetic influence on individual differences in empathic concern for others" (Matthews, Batson, Horn, & Rosenan, 1981, p. 237). Another study examined ratings of trait words corresponding to three aspects of empathy—empathic concern, personal distress, and perspective taking—and found heritability index values of .32 for personal distress and .28 for empathic concern, but a low value for perspective taking (Davis, Luce, & Kraus, 1994).

Although the results of both of these studies suggest a genetic influence of empathy on individual differences measured in a population, these findings should not be interpreted to imply that empathy is a trait that causes or otherwise determines behavior. For instance, the heritability of .72 in the study by Matthews and colleagues (1981) is high, but it does not mean that 72% of an individual's empathy is genetic or that a person's behavior is mostly controlled by his or her genes and cannot be changed. This attribution is a common misconception (Lilienfeld, Lynn, Ruscio, & Beyerstein, 2010). Rather, people can choose to help based on a number of factors and can learn to be more helpful, as discussed later.

If empathy is an innate motive, then people may inherit genes controlling brain development such that specific brain areas support an empathic response. Studies of brain-damaged people suggest that the prefrontal region, parts of the temporal lobe, and the amygdala in the limbic system are involved in emotional regulation and empathy (Leigh et al., 2013). An experimental study of brain activity in healthy volunteers also showed that the amygdala and some other prefrontal regions were active in empathetic responses (Lamm, Batson, & Decety, 2007). Taken together, these results suggest that empathy involves a network of brain structures.

Developmental studies have provided further support for the presence of an innate empathic response in infants only 1 to 2 days old. Sagi and Hoffman (1976) randomly assigned the infants to one of three groups: One group heard other babies cry; the second group heard a synthetic, nonhuman cry; and the third group heard no cry. Infants in the group who heard the recording of another infant crying cried significantly more than infants in the other two groups. However, Batson (2011), a leading expert on altruism, argued that factors other than empathy could account for the infants' responses. They may have been showing a fear response, in which the crying served as an alarm signal for help, or they may have been competing with other infants for food or attention.

The idea that humans have an innate empathic response is further supported by the example of the apparently automatic, altruistic response of a bystander named Lenny Skutnik, who was willing to risk his life for unrelated strangers. When an airliner crashed in the icy Potomac River outside Washington, DC, one winter several years ago, Skutnik risked his own life by repeatedly diving into the frigid waters to save passengers. Skutnik eventually had to be dragged out of the water himself because he was in danger of drowning. When people like Skutnik are asked why they risked their own lives to help, they often say that they helped without even stopping to think about it. These comments are consistent with studies suggesting that prosocial responses are automatic—that is, they occur rapidly without thought—and as such are part of Type 1 thinking (Zaki & Mitchell, 2013).

Social Psychological Research on Empathy and Altruism

Other evidence suggests that people help to potentially relieve their own negative feelings that arise in response to a person in need rather than out of genuine empathy. A story about Abraham Lincoln illustrates this motive. While riding in his carriage, Lincoln saw some drowning pigs out the window and is said to have ordered the carriage to stop so that the pigs could be saved. Lincoln reported that he did so, not out of an altruistic motive, but rather to avoid having a guilty conscience had he not told the driver to stop (Batson, Bolen, Cross, & Neuringer-Benefiel, 1986).

A group of researchers has proposed that the reason empathic people help is to relieve their sadness from observing a sufferer in need (Cialdini et al., 1987). In a study in which Cialdini and colleagues separated sadness and empathy as experimental conditions, they found that sadness predicted subjects' levels of helping, whereas the subjects' level of empathy did not. In a second experiment, the researchers found that empathic subjects did not help much when they were led to believe that their moods would not be changed if they helped another person.

Further support for the claim that helping may occur for selfish reasons was found in a study carried out by Batson and colleagues (1986). They found that helping occurred more often when the failure to help was likely to be detected by someone else than when it was unlikely to be detected, suggesting that avoidance of guilt or shame may have motivated the subjects to help. Correlations with empathy scores in this study also supported the idea that people help others to avoid feeling distress, as opposed to being motivated by feelings of unselfish, empathic concern for the person in need.

In contrast, other studies have found that people may experience real empathy, rather than the need to escape personal distress, which may indeed induce them to help. In one study testing this, Carrera and his colleagues (2012) asked participants to read a scenario of a person needing help that could elicit both empathy and personal distress. They found that the participants who reported more empathy and less distress tended to help more when they were unexpectedly given the opportunity to help, whereas those who reported more distress and less empathy helped less.

In another study that yielded similar results, Coke, Batson, and McDavis (1978) had participants listen to a radio broadcast that requested volunteers to help a graduate student complete a study. They found that respondents' feelings of personal distress expressed on a questionnaire were only modestly related to their willingness to volunteer for the study, whereas feelings of empathy were strongly related to willingness to help. This outcome suggests that people may be altruistic primarily for unselfish, empathic reasons; however, research reviewed by Eisenberg and Fabes (1990) suggests that empathy can result in either sympathy for a person or personal distress in response to another's distress.

Better support for the hypothesis that empathy produces genuine altruism comes from a study by Fultz, Batson, Fortenbach, McCarthy, and Varney (1986). These researchers found that participants who felt more empathy offered to help even when they did not think they were going to be evaluated for helping. This result suggests that the empathy the participants felt did not lead them to help for the egoistic or selfish reason of avoiding social disapproval. In another study, Sibicky, Schroeder, and Dovidio (1995) randomly assigned their subjects to groups that were induced to feel either high or low empathy, depending on certain statements they read. Consistent with Fultz et al.'s results, Sibicky and colleagues found that empathic subjects gave fewer hints to help other subjects when told that the hints could hurt the subjects later in the experiment. This outcome suggests that empathy increases sensitivity to the needs of others.

Some of the most convincing support for the existence of genuine empathy and altruism was provided by an experiment conducted by Dovidio, Allen, and Schroeder (1990). These researchers found that a group of participants induced to feel empathy helped more when they perceived that what they were doing aided the person in solving his main problem as compared with helping him on an unrelated problem. These results suggest that people who feel empathy can be sensitive to those needing help and are not just motivated to do something to achieve the selfish goal of reducing their own distress.

Investigators of this question continue to disagree about whether people can show empathy and helping behavior in a manner completely devoid of self-interest. On the one hand, Dennis Krebs (1991), a social psychologist who has studied helping for many years, and Douglas Mook (1991), an expert on motivation, have both argued that genuine altruism has not been demonstrated. On the other hand, Jane Piliavin (2008) concluded that findings from her own and others' research support the conclusion that at least some people, some of the time, show true altruism and genuine empathy and are not simply motivated by the desire to relieve their negative state. Likewise, in his more recent book-length review of research on altruism, Daniel Batson (2011) has argued that genuine empathy and altruism do sometimes occur.

Social Psychological Research on the Bystander Effect

Many cases exist of bystanders who apparently lacked sufficient empathy to help a suffering person, which raises questions about why the bystanders did not help. For example, in 1964 in New York City, a 28-year-old woman named Kitty Genovese was assaulted three different times over a 30-minute period. Many people apparently observed the assaults but failed to come to her aid, and Genovese ultimately died as a result of the attack. According to a *New York Times* article about the case, 38 different people in Genovese's neighborhood were aware of her plight but did nothing to intervene or to help her, not even call the police. This goes against a common belief that there is "safety in numbers," a view that assumes a person is more likely to be helped if there are many people around to help rather than just one.

The *New York Times* story drew considerable national attention, alarming the nation, and the incident became an example often cited in psychology textbook discussions of helping behavior. Later, investigators studying court records discovered that the story exaggerated both the number of people who knew about the attack and the lack of help from bystanders (Manning, Levine, & Collins, 2007). Even so, many other cases have documented the *bystander effect,* whereby multiple bystanders in emergency situations could have helped someone in need but did not (see Lilienfeld et al., 2010).

The Kitty Genovese tragedy inspired John Darley and Bibb Latané to investigate why a bystander would (or would not) help another person in an emergency. Darley and Latané (1968) staged a situation in which college students were randomly assigned to two groups who heard over an intercom what sounded like a person having an epileptic seizure. Participants in one condition thought that other people were aware of the problem; those in a second condition thought they alone had overheard the seizure. Of the participants who thought they alone knew about it, 85% tried to get help for the victim, but only 30% sought help when they thought others knew about it. Darley and Latané attributed this greater reluctance of bystanders to help when they thought more people were available to help to *diffusion of responsibility.*

In a review of 10 years of research, Latané and Nida (1981) showed that many studies testing the effect under very different conditions had replicated the initial finding that a bystander was less likely to help when other people were present. Their review also showed that bystanders were less likely to help when the situation was ambiguous and not clearly an emergency. Bystanders were much more likely to help if cues signaled that it was an actual emergency and no one else in a group was providing help. These findings suggest that people are not simply altruistic and willing to help in every situation; rather, their willingness to help depends on other factors such as how many people are available to help.

Other Psychological Factors That Influence Helping

Some people's willingness to consistently help others without concern for getting something in return may indicate a stable individual difference in personality in those who tend to behave altruistically, compared with those who tend to behave more selfishly. To test this hypothesis, Romer, Gruder, and Lizardo (1986) conducted a study in which they first asked subjects to complete a personality test that classified them as *altruistic, receptive–giving,* or *selfish.* Altruistic subjects indicated that typically they were helpful to others with no expectation of something in return; receptive–giving subjects would help others when they got something in

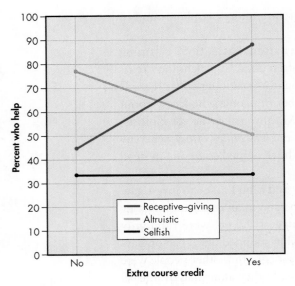

FIGURE 10.2 The extent to which receptive–giving and altruistic groups helped depended not only on their trait (personality type) but also on the situation (reward versus no reward).

return; and selfish subjects wanted help from others but were not interested in giving any help. This initial testing suggested that some people tend to be basically selfish, others are receptive–giving, and still others are altruistic.

In a second experimental phase of the same study, Romer and colleagues asked participants if they would be willing to help a graduate student experimenter complete her research project before the end of the semester. Participants in the three personality classifications were randomly assigned to one of two conditions—half of the participants in each group were promised course credit for further participation, while the other half were not promised any reward. Do you think getting a reward affected the groups differently in terms of how much they helped? Figure 10.2 shows the results in what is called a *person-by-situation interaction*. As shown in the figure, whether subjects volunteered depended on both the trait of the person (altruistic, selfish, or receptive–giving) *and* on details of the situation (whether they were offered a reward).

The graph also shows—just as we might expect from the personality traits—that selfish people did not want to help even if they were offered a reward, whereas the receptive–giving participants would help if promised a reward. The surprising finding was that altruistic subjects volunteered more when they were *not* offered course credit than when they were. We might expect that the altruistic subjects would help no matter what, but their helpfulness actually depended on whether they were promised a reward. The unexpected tendency of the altruistic subjects to volunteer more when *not* promised a reward suggests the possibility that they may have been less likely to help for other, perhaps selfish reasons.

What if the motive for altruistic people to help is that they get the internal reward of feeling good for helping "out of the goodness of their own heart"? Receiving an external reward for helping may make them feel less entitled to the intrinsic reward of feeling good about themselves for helping. This line of thinking is supported by research showing that people often feel good after helping another person. If a good feeling about themselves is the reward that altruistic people seek when they help, then they may be less inclined to help if they will not receive it. It should be noted that reward may be a basic mechanism for motivating many evolved behaviors, not just altruism (Marsh, 2016).

Several other studies have shown that mood can influence whether a person helps. For example, Isen and Levin (1972) found that subjects who were first given a cookie were more likely to volunteer to help than were those who were not given a cookie. In a second experiment, Isen and Levin found that subjects who found a dime in a phone booth were more likely to help someone pick up some dropped papers than were subjects who did not find a dime. Both experiments show that helping depends on a situational determinant (i.e., receiving a gift) and perhaps on the positive mood induced by the free gift. Consistent with the idea that mood influences helping, Batson (1990) reviewed several studies showing that positive mood can make people more likely to help.

Another factor—whether one has observed a model helping—can affect later helping behavior. In one study, Bryan and Test (1967) created a situation in which drivers were randomly assigned to two groups. One group of driver participants observed someone stop to help another person with a flat tire (both the helpful driver and the driver in need worked for the experimenter to stage the incident). A second group of driver participants did not observe a person help the driver with a flat tire. Farther down the road, both groups saw a second person by the side of the road in need of help. The drivers who first observed the helping model were more likely to stop and help the second motorist than were those who did not observe the helping model.

These results suggest the influence of social learning on helping behavior. They might further lead us to expect that people from different cultures, which have different norms and rewards for helping and which provide different examples of helping, might vary in terms of how much they help. Indeed, in large studies of helping behavior in different countries, Levine, Reysen, and Ganz (2008) found that people in economically advanced countries helped less than did people in less developed countries; also, the more densely populated an urban area was, the less frequently people helped (Levine, 2003). Results of three large field studies of 24 U.S. cities showed that people tended to help less in larger and more densely populated cities and in those where citizens have more purchasing power (Levine et al., 2008).

Development and Learning of Helping Behavior

In addition to the research on the empathic crying of very young infants in response to the cries of other infants, more recent studies have shown that older infants may show signs of empathy and genuine concern for others needing help. During the second year of life, children begin to show helping behavior in the form of sharing even when this action costs them (Brownell, Svetlova, & Nichols,

2009). By the age of 18 months, they will help someone grasp an object that is out of reach (Warneken & Tomasello, 2006).

Developmental research suggests that a young person's reasons for helping may be complex. For example, Kenrick (1989) found that by the age of approximately 6 years, children will engage in helping behavior as punishment to make up for a bad deed they have done. In a review of the literature, Cialdini, Baumann, and Kenrick (1981) reported that by the time people reach their late teens, they will help others when no one is watching or even though no one will know they have helped.

Other studies have shown that children can learn to be more altruistic through reinforcement of such behavior with praise (Grusec & Redler, 1980) and when they observe the generous behavior of a model experiencing positive feelings after making a donation (Midlarsky & Bryan, 1972). Grusec and Redler found that 10-year-olds tended to donate more than 5-year-olds either after being praised for an earlier donation or after being told they must have donated because they were helpful persons; by comparison, 5-year-olds did not increase their donation levels in response to either of these reinforcements.

Likewise, research shows that as people acquire characteristics and values through their social groups, they become more altruistic through considerable practice, rewards, observation of altruistic models, and the internalization of altruistic values (Grusec, 1991). Based on their own review of the research on the socialization of prosocial behavior, Kim and Stevens (1987) argued that parents exert considerable influence on the development of altruism and other prosocial characteristics when they communicate their expectations for prosocial behavior, reward young children for showing it, punish them for failing to show it, and model prosocial behavior for their children to observe in various situations. These researchers also suggested that parents who use inductive reasoning with their children to justify the need for prosocial behavior will likely be more effective in helping their children develop the disposition to behave prosocially than will parents who simply request such behavior.

Research on college students learning about the bystander effect has shown that this newfound knowledge could increase the students' own propensity to intervene as bystanders. For example, Beamon, Barnes, Klentz, and McQuirk (1978) found that students in a class that described research on the bystander effect more often helped a man slumped over on a bench than did students in a class that did not receive this instruction when tested two weeks after the class.

EVALUATING THE PROCESS OF REASONING ABOUT THIS QUESTION

One useful way to evaluate the reasoning about the selfishness/altruism question is to examine the assumptions made in the discussion. You may have noted that the discussion assumed that helping behavior indicates altruism, whereas not helping indicates selfishness. The discussion did not consider other ways of being unselfish, such as being friendly or looking out for another's welfare. Nor did it consider other ways of being selfish, such as being self-absorbed, conceited, or hypercompetitive. Considering these traits might lead to a different conclusion.

A more fundamental problem in the way that the reasoning proceeded in the passage is that the question may have been posed improperly, due to a conceptual thinking error. Dennis Krebs (1991), an expert on the selfishness/altruism question, has argued that defining altruism and egoism as qualitatively distinct motives creates a *false dichotomy,* a thinking error sometimes also referred to as *either-or thinking* or *black-and-white thinking.* As discussed in Chapter 8, in a false dichotomy, people treat two concepts or extreme positions as the only alternatives to be considered, when in reality at least one other position exists. False dichotomies treat their extreme alternatives as mutually exclusive, which means that if one is true, the other must be false; however, perhaps a third, intermediate alternative is true. In actuality, there are often shades of gray in between the extreme positions. For instance, someone who says, "You are either for us or against us," when other positions are actually possible—such as that you agree with the position in some ways but disagree in others—is demonstrating either-or thinking.

The false dichotomy in the current discussion is that if the argument for altruism is true, then the argument for egoism must be false, and vice versa. Instead, the research reviewed suggests that sometimes an individual may show true empathy and genuine altruism (although this is still debated), but many times that individual's helping behavior depends on one or more other factors—such as the person's mood, the number of other people who know about the need for help, individual differences in the trait for altruism, the possibility of a reward, who needs help, and people's development/learning. The complexity of factors that might affect helping behavior raises doubts about the simple conclusion that people are basically altruistic, and it suggests that people may never help without some other, more selfish motive; but it also suggests that another approach to the question is needed.

Whenever numerous high-quality research studies provide support for both sides of a scientific question, as is the case here, it is a good idea to examine how the question is conceived and to suspect a false dichotomy might be present. Perhaps both sides are at least partly right and a third position is more consistent with the evidence. In the case of the selfishness/altruism question, perhaps people can have more than one motive operating at once (Marsh, 2016). It may be that someone who feels genuine empathy for another person would also like to help in an effort to feel good about himself or herself or would like to help in a way that avoids conflict with another person. From this perspective, helping behavior depends on a cost–benefit analysis (Piliavin, 2008) as a person seeks to reach multiple goals. To do so, a person may decide to help after considering multiple factors, depending on the situation.

What about the nature-versus-nurture controversy—could it be a false dichotomy, too? Plenty of evidence in the discussion is consistent with a third position on the question, which claims that both nature and nurture interact to affect helping behavior. For example, although infants may show early empathic responses to the distress of others, empathy and helping tendencies might develop further through social learning and life experience. Empathic responses seem to take different forms, depending on experience and details of the situation. In general, the nature-versus-nurture distinction is a false one because the environment in which genes are expressed has a large influence on how those genes are ultimately expressed (Marcus, 2004). Moreover, from this revised perspective, it is more accurate to view a trait such as empathy not as hardwired in the brain, but rather as prewired such that we are not born with fully developed empathy but rather with the *capacity* to develop it.

SUMMARY

This chapter addressed an important question in the study of prosocial behavior, or behavior (e.g., helping) that is focused on benefiting others. Analysis of complex questions, such as whether people are basically selfish, can benefit from taking multiple perspectives, thereby enabling us to understand more aspects of the question and to avoid myside bias.

The question of whether people are basically selfish is one aspect of the nature-versus-nurture debate. Some biologists have questioned whether the genes for helping anyone except close relatives could be passed on to others through natural selection. Reciprocal altruism suggests an explanation for why unrelated individuals might help each other. One motivation for helping another person might be the feeling of empathy for others. Research on empathy in other primates suggests that humans may have evolved empathy. The heritability of empathy further suggests a substantial genetic contribution to empathy, but we must be careful not to interpret this high heritability index as meaning that empathy is determined by our genes and is unchangeable—a common psychological misconception.

Many cases can be cited in which people have helped others, sometimes risking their own lives, yet other cases demonstrate that people may help for selfish reasons. Of course, all of these cases are anecdotal. In contrast, much research has focused on whether people help out of unselfish empathic concern or sympathy or because they want to avoid feeling the personal distress that their failure to help might bring. Developmental research suggests that empathy may be innate, but helping behavior must be learned or socialized. Other research suggests that there are individual differences in the tendency to help; some people are classified as selfish, others as receptive–giving, and still others as altruistic. Even so, helping behavior often depends on situational variables, such as the helper's mood, the availability of a reward, and whether the helper recently observed someone else engage in helping behavior.

Evaluating the evidence on this question does not lead to a clear conclusion. Instead, some research suggests that even altruistic people do not help others for totally unselfish reasons, such as the reward of feeling good about oneself for helping. Whether someone helps or not turns out to be a complex matter in which an individual must weigh the costs and benefits of numerous factors.

Practice Thinking 10.4: WHAT DO YOU THINK **NOW**?
Please explain how you know.

1. Are people basically selfish? _____

   _____

2. In which ways is selfishness beneficial? In which ways is it harmful? Are you always helpful? _____

   _____

3. Do infants and young children start out being selfish and learn to be more helpful? _____

   _____

4. Is there a biological basis to helping—that is, did we evolve to be helpful or selfish? _____

_____

5. What should you do if you need help in a group of people? _____

_____

REVIEW QUESTIONS

1. Why is it useful to take different perspectives on complex, fundamental questions?

2. Compare and contrast the perspectives discussed in this chapter regarding how each approaches the study of prosocial behavior.

3. What is altruism? How does it relate to selfishness or egoism?

4. What are values questions? Is this the kind of question psychologists focus on?

5. Is there an evolutionary basis for altruism?
   - How does kinship selection account for altruistic behavior?
   - How does reciprocal altruism account for altruistic behavior?

6. What is empathy?
   - How does empathy relate to altruism?
   - Which evidence shows that empathy has an evolutionary basis?

7. What is heritability? How should we interpret it?

8. How should we think about the nature-versus-nurture question?

9. What psychological factors contribute to helping behaviors?
   - What is the bystander effect?
   - What is a trait-by-situation interaction?
   - What is the contribution of development? Of learning?
   - How do rewards and the modeling of helping affect helping behavior?
   - What is the role of positive mood?

10. Explain how thinking errors, such as black-and-white thinking, myside bias, and circular reasoning, can get in the way of thinking effectively about the ideas in this chapter.

11. What psychological misconceptions did you encounter in this chapter?

JUDGMENT, DECISION MAKING, AND TYPES OF THINKING

LEARNING OUTCOMES

After studying this chapter, you should be able to:

1. Explain how good judgment and decision making are related to critical thinking.

2. Distinguish intuitive from rational approaches to judgment and decision making.

3. Make good judgments based on probability.

4. Identify judgment and decision errors and understand how best to deal with them.

WHAT DO YOU THINK?

Suppose you interviewed with the manager of a small company for your dream job. You thought the interview went well, and the manager seemed impressed with your qualifications. Later, you received a letter from the company, thanking you for applying but informing you that the company has hired someone else. This decision disappoints and puzzles you, so you ask a friend who works for the company if he knows anything about it. He says, "It may have been your handwriting. Before hiring anyone, the manager has a graphologist or handwriting expert look at each applicant's handwriting. Maybe the graphologist thought you had a personality defect based on your handwriting."

Practice Thinking 11.1: What Do You Think?

Please explain how you know.

1. Can a graphologist accurately judge someone's character or personality based on analysis of the person's handwriting?

   _____

2. Suppose a basketball player has a "hot hand" and makes four baskets in a row. Should a coach tell the other team members to pass the ball to him or her? Why or why not?

   _____

3. Is someone who has already played a slot machine 30 times without winning more likely to win the next time he puts in a quarter than someone who put in just a single quarter and did not win—in other words, is the 30-time loser "due" compared to the one-time loser?

   _____

4. Describe a judgment error or bad decision that caused a problem for you. Why did it occur?

   _____

5. What could you do to improve your judgment and decision making?

   _____

IMPROVING JUDGMENT AND DECISION MAKING

We make numerous judgments throughout each day, evaluating various aspects of our lives. Often these judgments provide the basis for our decisions. **Decision making** involves evaluating options and then selecting a course of action. In the hiring decision scenario that opened the chapter, the manager compared the job applicant options and then used the judgment of a graphologist to finally select the applicant with the better handwriting. But is using graphology and handwriting likely to lead to a good hiring decision? Scientific research says no, because handwriting is not a valid cue for making a hiring decision. A **valid cue** provides information that is predictive of good judgments and decisions. For decades, research has shown that graphology does not provide a sound basis for judging personality and character (Klimoski, 1992). Instead, the relevance of an applicant's experience, level of motivation, and fit with the job are valid cues for good hiring decisions.

The valid cues for a decision are akin to good reasons for supporting a conclusion. Critical thinkers make judgments and decisions that are supported by good reasons (Lipman, 1991). As in the hiring example, judgments and decisions are often made under conditions of uncertainty, involving risk. To accurately assess risk, the critical thinker must be able to accurately estimate probability (Halpern, 1998). Making good judgments and decisions requires appropriate use of probability, logic, and the rules of reasoning, while avoiding the thinking errors and biases that lead to poor judgments and decisions. To illustrate, choose one of the following two options adapted from a study by Tversky and Kahneman (1981):

Which treatment for a serious disease would you favor?
(a) A treatment that was 75% effective and would save 750 out of 1,000 people with the disease
(b) A treatment that would result in the death of 250 out of 1,000 people with the disease who have received a treatment that is 75% effective

More people choose option (a), which promises to *save* 750 lives, over option (b), which would cause 250 *deaths*. Looking carefully at these two options, however, you can see that each one results in the same exact probabilities of survival and loss of life. Therefore, from a rational perspective, *neither* should be favored over the other if only the probabilities mattered. Yet, when an option is framed or expressed in a positive, emotionally desirable way (i.e., lives saved), more people tend to choose it than when the same option is framed in negative terms (i.e., 250 deaths). This pattern suggests that people do not always use probability correctly in their judgments and are not purely rational in their thinking. Their judgments are also influenced by psychological factors, such as how the question is framed. Because people tend to be averse to loss in general, they are more likely to select option (a) when option (b) is framed as a loss.

We could further explain the **framing effect** in relation to a reliance on Type 1 thinking. Framing the question as a loss of life automatically activates our intuitive aversion to death, and we fail to use probability and Type 2 thinking to make our judgment. A recent study showed that framing effects are especially pronounced when participants are induced to engage in fast, Type 1 thinking (Guo, Trueblood, & Diederich, 2017). In this chapter, you will see that many judgment errors are due to an overreliance on Type 1 thinking instead of correct use of probability and proper reasoning to make judgments.

Sometimes people (and businesses) exploit our tendency to rely on Type 1 thinking to their own benefit. Have you ever wondered why stores display candy, magazines, and other impulse items near the checkout counters? This strategy takes advantage of our tendency to rely on Type 1 thinking. As we walk through the store, we tend to rely more on Type 2 thinking, comparing the prices and quality of products, deliberately making choices. At the checkout counter, however, we see these attractive items at eye level, presented in a way that captures our attention. With our attention subtly directed in this way, we are more likely to buy a readily available magazine than if we had to walk to the store's magazine section to get one.

As this example suggests, our tendency to engage in Type 1 thinking can be manipulated to affect our decision making (Kahneman, 2011)—but these tendencies can be manipulated to *improve* decision outcomes, too. Nudge theory proposes that we can prod people to improve their decisions without reducing their freedom of choice by manipulating the way in which options are framed and the context in which they are presented (Thaler & Sunstein, 2008). A nudge gently pushes decision makers toward an option they might prefer anyway, but that they often do not choose because of the tendency to make judgments automatically, without much effort. This is related to the *status quo bias,* or the tendency of people to not change their initial response (Kahneman, 2011). In many situations, people go with the default or normal response and do not expend the effort to change.

A nudge can be implemented by simply changing the decision environment so that the default option is the one that promotes the welfare of the individual decision maker—and, in many cases, the welfare of an entire group. For instance, although most people favor organ donation and say they are willing to donate their organs, a serious shortage of organs for transplants persists because a much smaller percentage of people actually consent to donate their organs when asked directly. In many locations, the default option is *not* to donate, so a person must actively opt into a program to be a donor. Changing the default option to *consenting* to donation results in only a small percentage of people failing to give consent. In this situation, people are still free to not donate, but they must *apply effort* to not donate, and because of their usual reliance on Type 1 thinking they are less likely to withhold their consent.

A classic example of how a nudge may work by directing attention to a neglected option or behavior is seen in the men's restrooms in Amsterdam's Schiphol Airport, where adding a simple design feature to the urinals improved men's aim. Men do not intend to make a mess when they urinate, but they ordinarily do not apply much effort or attention in aiming accurately. When economist Aad Kieboom instructed authorities to engrave the image of a housefly on each urinal, men improved their aim and reduced spillage by 80% (Thaler & Sunstein, 2008).

Nudging can improve decision making by taking advantage of the vulnerabilities of Type 1 thinking, but it certainly does not address all shortcomings of Type 1 thinking or problems with Type 2 thinking. For instance, nudging does not improve our ability to accurately estimate probabilities. Although many studies have shown that people are often not good at estimating probabilities, other studies indicate that the right kind of instruction and practice can improve the ability to think about probability and statistics (Lehman & Nisbett, 1990; Shaughnessy & Vander Stoep, 1997). To understand how probability estimation occurs, we next review some basic probability concepts.

PROBABILITY AND RATIONAL JUDGMENT

Let's first review how to calculate the probability of an event:

$$\text{Probability of an event} = \frac{\text{number of ways an event of interest could occur}}{\text{total number of outcomes that could occur in that situation}}$$

The event of interest could be almost anything, but let's say it is getting heads in the toss of a fair coin. The chance of getting heads on a particular fair coin toss is 1 out of 2, because there is only one way to get heads (the event of interest) in the two possible outcomes of a coin toss (heads or tails).

Probabilities can be expressed in various ways. We may express the chance of getting heads as 1 out of 2 or as the fraction, ½. In gambling, the probability of getting heads versus tails might be expressed as the odds being 50–50. We more often express probabilities as a decimal proportion—for example, the probability of getting heads is .50 or $p = .50$. The decimal scale used to express the probability of an outcome ranges from 0.00, interpreted as "The event will not occur," to 1.00, interpreted as "The event is certain to occur." Expressing the probability of getting heads as a percentage, we are 50% certain of getting heads or, stated another way, we expect to get heads 50% of the time. Necessarily, we are 100% − 50% = 50% uncertain that we will get heads.

The probability of getting heads, $p = .50$, states the overall outcome we expect to obtain over the long run when we repeatedly toss a coin an infinite number of times—that is, in the *population* of all possible coin tosses. A **population** is all the possible observations on some variable (e.g., coin tosses), or some behavior or characteristic, that could be made. In real-world situations, a variable in a population often has so many possible values that it is impractical to observe them all. Consequently, we can only estimate the population's characteristics. To infer what the population is like, we observe or test a smaller subset of the population, called a **sample**, and estimate the characteristics of the population based on the characteristics of the sample.

Complicating our estimation is the fact that the values obtained from samples may vary. Repeatedly tossing a fair coin with only six tosses per set or sample will likely yield results that vary from the 50% heads (H) and 50% tails (T) expected over the long run. We might get T-H-T-H-T-T, T-H-H-H-H-T, H-T-T-T-T-T, H-H-T-T-H-H, or even occasionally H-H-H-H-H-H. The values that the samples take on tend to vary from sample to sample, a phenomenon called *sampling variability*.

SAMPLING AND THE LAW OF LARGE NUMBERS

Increasing the sample size helps with the sampling variability problem. According to the law of large numbers, if we increase the sample size—say, to 100 coin tosses—and count the number of heads and tails, we are more likely to get a distribution that is closer to 50% heads and 50% tails. With even more coin tosses, there will be less variability around the 50–50 split. The **law of large numbers** states that the larger the size of a randomly selected sample, the more closely it will tend to approximate the actual percentage of some characteristic in the population. In this case, the more coin tosses that are made, the closer the overall outcome will be to 50% heads and 50% tails. Theoretically, sampling with an infinitely large sample or averaging the results over an infinite number of smaller samples would produce exactly 50% heads and 50% tails.

The law of large numbers also tells us that when a large sample is randomly selected from a population, it will tend to represent the population better than a smaller random sample does. A **representative** sample is one that tends to have the same characteristics, in the same proportion, as found in the population. For example, a large random sample of the U.S. population should have nearly 50.8%

females and 49.2% males, corresponding to the percentages found in the total U.S. population.

The implications of the law of large numbers are clear in terms of what scientists should do to generalize from the values obtained in samples to make valid estimates of the values in the larger population. Specifically, scientists should use a sample that is sufficiently large and randomly selected, making it more likely to be representative of the population. Scientists trust data from large random samples more than data from small samples because larger, randomly selected samples tend to produce more reliable (i.e., consistent and accurate) estimates than smaller samples. As discussed in Chapter 4, this is a "quantity of evidence" consideration, with larger amounts of data more strongly supporting an inductive conclusion than smaller amounts of data.

Unfortunately, people often behave as if the "law of *small* numbers" were true instead of the law of *large* numbers (Tversky & Kahneman, 1971). In other words, they mistakenly put greater trust in inferences from small samples than they should, failing to recognize that judgment errors can occur when sample size is not considered. Fong, Krantz, and Nisbett (1986) found that unless college students received special training, they had trouble explaining how the law of large numbers applies to everyday examples. Likewise, in response to scientific evidence based on a large randomly selected sample, you sometimes hear someone say, "That's not true—I know a man who shows just the opposite effect." Responding with a personal anecdote is really using a very small sample that was not randomly selected and acting as if it were as reliable as a large random sample.

THE NORMAL DISTRIBUTION AND PROBABILITY

Scientists use probability and the law of large numbers to make decisions about what a population is like and to decide whether an individual's score or a treatment group's mean differs from what is expected by chance. To do so, they often use a special probability distribution called the **normal distribution,** or normal curve, which serves as a model for how the values of different variables are expected to occur by chance.

Figure 11.1 is a graph of the normal distribution showing how scores from each of the SAT subscales are distributed. The horizontal axis represents the SAT subscale scores, which range from 200 to 800. As you can see, the normal distribution is bell-shaped. The left half is a mirror image of the right half, with a single high point in the middle where the mean or arithmetic average of all the scores is found. The curve drops lower and lower as one moves farther and

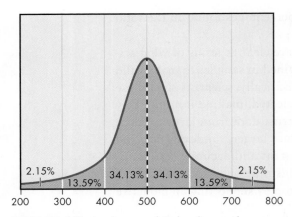

FIGURE 11.1 SAT subscale scores plotted on the normal curve.

farther into the "tails," or endpoints, of the curve. How high the curve is over the horizontal axis indicates how many scores of a particular value are expected to occur in that area. Thus, higher points on the curve indicate that more scores are expected to occur in that area. As you can see, the highest point and the largest area under the curve are found around the middle, where the mean lies. Most people are "average" (rather than high- or low-scorers), meaning that their SAT scores fall at or close to the mean. Extreme scores are much less frequent than the mean. Some people score very low, perhaps only 200, out in the left tail of the curve, while a correspondingly small number score very high, perhaps 800, in the right tail. In Figure 11.1, only 2.15% of the SAT scores are between 200 and 300 and 2.15% are between 700 and 800.

To simplify how sampling from different places in the normal distribution is related to probability, Figure 11.2 shows a distribution that resembles a normal distribution of SAT subscale scores. The chance of getting a very high score of 800 is $p = 1/50$ or .02; the chance of getting a very low score of 200 is also $p = 1/50$ or .02. We are much more likely to get the mean of 500, $p = 8/50$ or .16. Suppose a student named Mike took the SAT and you did not know his score. What would be your best guess of Mike's score? According to Figure 11.2 and given what we know about the normal distribution, your best guess would be "500." That is the mean and the value most likely to occur.

Now suppose that by chance, Mike made a very low score of 200 when, in fact, he is an average student. Scoring this low by chance is a relatively rare event, as illustrated in Figure 11.2. But suppose that Mike takes the test again. His score the second time would tend to be less extreme (closer to the mean). In this pattern of results called **regression toward the mean**, a person who initially has an extreme score tends to produce a score that is less extreme (moving closer to the mean) when measured again. If Mike takes the

				Mean						
				500						
				500						
			450	500	550					
		400	450	500	550	600				
	350	400	450	500	550	600	650			
300	350	400	450	500	550	600	650	700		
250	300	350	400	450	500	550	600	650	700	750
200	250	300	350	400	450	500	550	600	650	700	750	800

FIGURE 11.2 A distribution of 50 SAT math subscale scores organized around the mean of 500, approximating a normal distribution.

test several more times (without any change in his performance due to practice or fatigue) and we calculate the mean of all his scores, his *overall* score would likely regress even closer to his true mean.

According to the law of large numbers, the more times he takes the test, the closer the mean of those scores would be to Mike's true mean of 500. Therefore, when we observe that someone has performed extremely well or extremely poorly the first time around, we must be careful not to assume this extreme performance is typical or representative of the person's true performance or ability—such an assumption could lead to an incorrect assessment of the person's abilities.

 ## Practice Thinking 11.2: Use Your Knowledge of Probability

1. Suppose you toss a fair die (a six-sided cube with numbers 1–6 on the sides).

   a. What is the probability of getting a 6 when tossing one die?

   _____

   b. What is the probability of getting a 7 when tossing one die?

   _____

   c. What is the probability of getting a 1, 2, 3, 4, 5, or 6 when tossing one die?

   _____

2. A multiple-choice exam has four response options; the correct answer is randomized throughout the test questions, such that options (a), (b), (c), and (d) have an equal chance of being the correct answer.

   a. What is the probability of simply guessing the correct answer on the test?

   _____

   b. What is the probability of answering incorrectly on the test?

   _____

3. Thomas is an average writing student in high school. He took the SAT, an achievement test, and scored 700 on the writing portion of the test, significantly higher than the average of 500. Thomas said, "Wow, I'm a better writer than I thought!" Suppose Thomas did no special studying for the test before taking it again.

a. Would his score on the second test likely be higher, lower, or about the same? _____

_____

b. Explain your answer. _____

_____

HEURISTICS AND BIASES IN JUDGMENT

Using probability to make judgments can be demanding of our time and mental resources. But people have limited cognitive resources and display what Simon (1990) called *bounded rationality*. People have even been called "cognitive misers" because of their tendency to conserve these resources. Like the miser Ebenezer Scrooge, who spent little of his monetary resources, people typically spend little of their cognitive resources to make judgments. To make these rapid, intuitive judgments, they often use mental shortcuts called **heuristics**, or rules of thumb that can simplify and speed up the process. Relying on heuristics and intuition, they often engage in rapid, Type 1 thinking rather than on the slower and more effortful rational-analytic approach of Type 2 thinking. So although heuristics can indeed accelerate the judgment process, they do not necessarily lead to well-reasoned conclusions. They can even produce bias or a systematic distortion in judgment.

Avoiding bias is an important part of critical thinking (West, Toplak, & Stanovich, 2008). Type 2 thinking helps us reflect on the quality of our thinking and devise ways to correct and avoid bad judgments. In the next section, we examine some of the problems that can be introduced through the use of heuristics, and we suggest **debiasing** strategies or techniques that can be used to counteract or avoid the biasing effects of heuristic use.

Representativeness Heuristic

The representativeness heuristic assumes that "like goes with like"—that is, something that appears to be similar to something else has the properties of that other entity. As an example of this concept, some traditional medical treatments for health problems are based on representativeness. Historically, physicians have prescribed the yellow spice turmeric as a treatment for jaundice, a condition that turns the skin yellow, because natural healing substances were thought to show a sign of the disease they were expected to heal (Nisbett & Ross, 1980). The approach to healing called *homeopathy,* developed in the eighteenth century by Samuel Hahnemann, assumes that administering substances that produce symptoms that are like the symptoms of a disease is an effective way to treat the disease (Gilovich & Savitsky, 1996). By this logic, miniscule amounts of arsenic would be expected to effectively treat arsenic poisoning. (Don't try it—arsenic accumulates in the body.)

Another popular remedy that involves representativeness is the folk remedy for hangovers described in the expression "Hair of the dog that bit you." The idea is that a hangover is caused by drinking too many alcoholic beverages (metaphorically, "the dog that bit you") and can thus be cured by having another drink. This remedy seems implausible, given that alcohol is what created the problem in the first place. Although drinking more alcohol might reduce the sensation of the pain of a hangover, having another drink is certainly no cure. More effective treatments, such as drinking water or a sports drink to replenish lost fluids and electrolytes, take into account what actually causes the physiological effects of a hangover.

Sometimes, even physicians make unwarranted assumptions based on the representativeness heuristic. For decades, physicians believed that stomach ulcers were caused by stress that produced excess stomach acid. The perceived similarity between the burning irritation of an ulcerated stomach and the "gut-wrenching, stomach-churning feeling of extreme stress" is an example of representativeness operating to associate the two conditions (Gilovich & Savitsky, 1996, p. 36). The similarity seemed so convincing that many scientists and physicians resisted accepting the discovery by Marshall and Warren that bacteria actually caused stomach ulcers.

People favor the representativeness heuristic in making judgments because it often works. One example is thinking a sick person who is shivering from a fever should be treated in the same way as someone who is shivering from the cold—both situations are likely to elicit the adaptive response of giving the person a blanket to warm up. Yet, as we have seen, the representativeness heuristic can bias estimation of the probability of events. Does it bias your estimation?

Practice Thinking 11.3: Examining Randomness and Representativeness

1. Consider these two sequences of coin tosses (H = heads; T = tails):

    a.   H-T-H-H-H-T-T-T-T-H-T-H-H-T-T-T-H-H-H-T

    b.   H-T-H-T-H-T-T-T-H-H-T-H-T-H-T-T-H-H-T-H

    Does one of these sequences seem more random? Why? _____

    _____

2. Suppose you were betting on the sixth toss of a fair coin in the following
    sequence:

    Toss: 1   2   3   4   5   6

    Outcome: H   T   T   T   T   ?

    Should you bet on heads or tails for the sixth toss? Why? _____

    _____

3. Suppose a basketball player shows the following pattern of baskets (B)
    and misses (M):

    M   B   B   B   M   B   B   B   ?

    If the player's shooting average is 52% from the floor, is the chance of
    his making the next shot much greater than 52% because he has a "hot
    hand"? Explain. _____

    _____

Many people apply the representativeness heuristic and misunderstand the coin-toss probability when answering Practice Thinking 11.3, question 1—which leads them to incorrectly pick the second set of coin tosses (b) as appearing more random than the first (a). Sequence (b) looks more random because it switches more frequently between heads and tails; a streak of the same outcome seems less random because it repeats the same outcome (Kida, 2006). In fact, sequences (a) and (b) are both completely random strings and are equally likely to occur (Nickerson, 2002).

In Practice Thinking 11.3, question 2, people often mistakenly think that the sixth toss is more likely to be heads. This judgment error, called the **gambler's fallacy**, occurs when a person mistakenly expects the probability of one independent trial to affect the outcome of another independent trial. In a game of chance, a person might expect to win after incurring a string of losses. For example, after getting four tails in a row when betting heads on each toss, an individual might think it best to again bet on heads because heads is more likely or might be "due" to occur on the next toss. In actuality, the gambler may just be in the midst of a long random string of coin tosses in which there are five, six, or more tails in row. Of course, the gambler could not know this if the string is truly random.

The important thing to note is that every time a fair coin is tossed, the probability of getting tails remains the same (i.e., $p = .50$), regardless of how a previous toss turned out. In this situation, the trials are **independent**, meaning that the outcome of one trial does not affect the outcome of another trial. The gambler's fallacy, then, is partly due to a misunderstanding of randomness and relies on the application of the representativeness heuristic by which a random sequence of the same outcome does not look random. In fact, according to the American Psychiatric Association, one of the criteria for diagnosing a gambling disorder (a kind of addiction) is that after the gambler has lost money, he or she returns to gamble some more to "get even." Research has also shown that people with a gambling problem are more susceptible to the gambler's fallacy than are those without a gambling problem (Petry, 2005; Toplak, Liu, Macpherson, Toneatto, & Stanovich, 2007).

Individuals' misunderstanding of probability affects their everyday judgments, too. For example, a couple who thinks that, after having five daughters in a row, they are bound to have a boy and thus continue to try for a son is falling prey to the gambler's fallacy. They do not realize that the sex of a newborn baby is independent of the baby born before it, with the probability staying the same. The long string of girls does not look representative of how luck works, and people may mistakenly judge that the probability of having a boy will increase.

Incorrect answers to Practice Thinking 11.3, question 3, reveal another problem in perceiving random strings. If you are like 84% of people in a study by Gilovich, Vallone, and Tversky (1985), you answered the third question by saying a coach should advise the other players to pass the ball to another player who has made three shots in a row. This mistaken belief in the "hot hand" is also a mistaken perception of a set of random events that demonstrates what is called the **hot-hand illusion**. In this case, a random string is attributed to a player's good luck or a temporary display of exceptional performance. When Gilovich and colleagues examined the probability of professional basketball players from the

1980–1981 Philadelphia 76ers and the Boston Celtics teams making a third shot after making the two before it, they found no increase in the probability of making the earlier shots. The belief in streak shooting seems to be influenced by the representativeness heuristic that convinces people the result is not just a random string of successful shots.

Representativeness can also bias estimates of the probability that an individual is a member of a specific group. The simple probability that an individual randomly selected from a population is a member of a particular group is equal to the number of individuals in that group divided by the total number of individuals. For example, if 47% of all psychologists are clinical psychologists (the most common field of specialization for psychologists), then the probability that an individual drawn randomly from the population of all psychologists will be a clinical psychologist is .47 (American Psychological Association, 2004). This known probability is often referred to as the **base rate**. The base rate for experimental psychologists is just 1%. In making probability estimates, however, people often commit an error called **base rate neglect**. Instead of basing their judgments on a known probability, frequency, or average, they base their estimates on details of an example and the expectations they create.

To illustrate, read the following description of a psychologist. Assume that in any random sample of 100 psychologists, 47 are clinical psychologists and 1 is an experimental psychologist. On a probability scale from 0.00 to 1.00, what is the probability p that Bill is an experimental psychologist? What is the probability p that he is a clinical psychologist?

> Bill has always liked figuring out why people do the things they do. He has enjoyed doing research and is very exacting in his measurements and very careful in his observations of people. He likes to learn about new psychological studies and intellectual challenges.

If you estimated the probability that Bill is an experimental psychologist to be much higher than .01 and the probability that he is a clinical psychologist to be much less than .47, then you are failing to take into account the base rate. Although the description may seem to better fit your stereotype of a researcher than your stereotype of a clinician, your best guess of the probability that Bill is an experimental psychologist should be the base rate of .01, or 1%. Because many clinicians could also fit the description, and because it is not known how the characteristics mentioned relate to the clinical versus experimental categories, you should go with the base rate.

Another type of error associated with the representativeness heuristic is the **conjunction fallacy**. This error occurs when a person judges that someone or something is more likely to belong to a category that includes two or more features, rather than deciding that the person or item belongs to a category that includes only one of the same features. To illustrate, read the following description adapted from Tversky and Kahneman (1982).

Linda is 31 years old, single, outspoken, and very bright. She majored in philosophy. As a student, she was deeply concerned with issues of discrimination and social justice, and also participated in antinuclear demonstrations.

Check the most likely alternative.

—— Linda is a bank teller.

—— Linda is active in the feminist movement.

—— Linda is a bank teller and active in the feminist movement.

Tversky and Kahneman found that most people thought that Linda was more likely to be *both* a bank teller and a feminist. Although initially it might seem as though Linda has the stereotypical features of both of these, we should slow down thinking and use probability and logic to make this judgment. Instead of relying on representativeness and the appearance of the individual described, we should realize that logically the probability of two events occurring together cannot be greater than the probability of the two events occurring separately. To debias the conjunction fallacy, we must first recognize that the question involves the conjunction of two categories, signaled by the word *and*. Next, we must understand that the probability of the intersection of the two categories cannot be greater than the probability of the more general category that includes it as a subcategory or subset.

The Venn diagram in Figure 11.3 shows that "bank teller" is a larger category that includes the smaller subset of feminist bank tellers in the intersection (cross-hatched area). In other words, some bank tellers are feminists and some

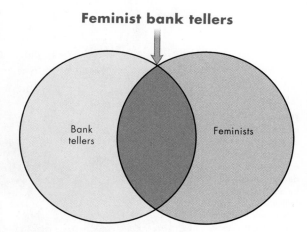

FIGURE 11.3 Feminist bank tellers are a subset of all bank tellers; this group is, therefore, less likely to include Linda than is the larger set of all bank tellers. (From Plous, 1993)

are not. Likewise, some feminists are bank tellers and some are not. The intersection of bank tellers who *are* feminists (the cross-hatched area) is smaller than the entire circle for bank tellers as well as the entire circle for feminists; therefore, this event has a lower probability.

Availability Heuristic

People who use the availability heuristic to estimate the frequency of events are basing their judgment on how easily they can bring related information to mind. Which do you think is the more likely cause of death, tornadoes or asthma? When Slovic, Fischoff, and Lichtenstein (1976) asked subjects this question, they found that 58% of the respondents thought that tornadoes were the more likely cause of death. In reality, nearly 45 times as many people die from asthma each year as die from tornadoes. If you answered tornadoes, then you may have been influenced by the availability heuristic.

How does availability lead people to overestimate tornadoes as a cause of death as compared with asthma? Memories of killer tornadoes may be vivid (Figure 11.4), and the media cover these events more extensively than they cover fatal cases of asthma. As a consequence, people can more easily access memories of deaths from tornadoes than deaths from asthma. When the actual frequencies

FIGURE 11.4 The media publish dramatic images of destruction from tornadoes, such as the devastation caused by a 2010 tornado in Millbury, Ohio, that killed several people. In contrast, the media seldom report on the many more deaths caused by asthma.

AP Photo/Paul Sancya

of events do not correspond to how readily we access these events from memory, then our estimates based on availability will be in error.

Would you feel safer traveling by car or by air? Once again, the greater media coverage of dramatic air crashes with many fatalities, compared with the sparser coverage of fatal automobile accidents that lead to fewer deaths per event, lead people to overestimate the number of deaths due to air travel. Dramatic depictions of horrific accidents may make the memories of them more available by increasing the vividness of those memories. Vividness refers to how concrete and imaginatively evocative a memory is. In an experiment conducted by Reyes, Thompson, and Bower (1980), subjects were asked to make judgments about a mock court case in which the evidence was described in either vivid or pallid (not vivid) form. The vividness of statements did not initially affect an average of these ratings, but when participants were tested two days later and were allowed to change their initial ratings of the accused person's guilt if they wished, significantly more subjects who had read the vivid prosecution statements judged the accused to be guilty than did those who had read the pallid prosecution statements.

Availability can also affect the evidence considered in drawing a conclusion. When making an argument, people tend to present the evidence that is available to them and can easily be brought to mind. Likewise, people arguing the other side of the question may think of the evidence that is most available and supportive of their own positions. If both groups enter into a dialogue in which they consider the evidence presented by the other side, they will become aware of less available information that is unfamiliar, neglected, or forgotten. This is why "consider the opposite" can be a good strategy for debiasing the effects of availability.

Like other heuristics, the availability heuristic often helps us make good judgments. For instance, if someone asked you how often people are killed in large terrorist attacks, and the recent attacks in Manchester, Paris, San Bernardino, and Orlando came readily to mind, you might answer, "Fairly often." Although availability might lead you to overestimate the actual number of incidents, you would be correct to assume that such attacks occur fairly often. In fact, according to statistics from the Global Terrorism Index, terrorist acts shot up 80% between 2013 and 2014 alone (Reicher & Haslam, 2016).

Anchoring and Adjustment Heuristic

What percentage of all United Nations (UN) countries are African countries? Is that proportion greater or smaller than 10%? Suppose instead you were asked, "Is it greater or smaller than 65%?" If you have little idea of the actual number, then you may be susceptible to using a number provided as an "anchor" to start your estimate. Tversky and Kahneman (1974) rigged a "wheel of fortune" so that it looked and spun like a roulette wheel, but always stopped at either the number 10 or 65. When one group of undergraduates spun it and it stopped at 10, they wrote down the number 10; a second group wrote down 65 after their spin stopped at that number. Tversky and Kahneman then asked the two groups, "Is the percentage of African nations among UN members larger or smaller than the number you just wrote?" Next, they asked, "What is your best guess as to the percentage of African nations in the UN?" Those students who initially wrote down the number 10 estimated the percentage of African nations in the UN as 25%, whereas those who initially wrote down 65 anchored from that higher number and estimated 45%—20% higher than the other group.

In another study, graduate students were asked to write down the last two digits of their Social Security number, ranging from 00 to 99 (Ariely, Loewenstein, & Prelec, 2003). The students were then asked whether they would be willing to pay more or less than the number they wrote down for a rare bottle of wine, and precisely how much they would pay for the wine. The students with higher Social Security numbers reported they would pay significantly more for the rare wine than did those with lower Social Security numbers. These results demonstrate the **anchoring effect**, or the tendency to be overly influenced by a starting value or information provided before making a judgment, even if that information is not useful for the judgment. The fact that the anchoring effect occurs with both relevant and irrelevant information suggests to some that people's judgments are irrational.

Everyday examples of the anchoring effect abound in sales, negotiations, and solicitation of contributions. Have you noticed that when charities ask for contributions, they often first suggest a large amount, such as "Consider giving at our platinum level of $1,000," but then go on to request $500, then $100, then perhaps $50? Even if they expect few contributions of $1,000, the high initial amount may anchor people to that value and increase the amount they ultimately donate.

Kahneman (2011) reported the results of a study in which charitable contributions to a fund for conservation of seabirds were greater when a higher amount was first mentioned than when a lower amount was first mentioned. More disturbing is the finding that German judges with an average of 15 years of experience on the bench also showed the anchoring effect in the length of sentence they said they would issue a female shoplifter whose description they read. After rolling dice, the judges were asked if they would give a sentence in months that was lesser or greater than the number rolled on the dice. Those who rolled a higher number said they would issue longer sentences than those who rolled a lower number (Englich, Mussweiler, & Strack, 2006).

According to Tversky and Kahneman (1974), people use the **anchoring and adjustment heuristic** to make such estimates. Starting with the anchor, individuals assess whether it is too high or too low, and then they mentally adjust away from the anchor until they are unsure whether further adjustments are appropriate. A common explanation of the error in using an anchor is that the person stops adjusting prematurely. Recent research suggests that dual process theory can help explain why such adjustments tend to be insufficient. Giving someone an anchor automatically activates Type 1 associations with the anchor, which in turn exert influence on judgment—unless Type 2 thinking intervenes. Adjustment is a deliberate Type 2 activity, which takes effort on the individual's part. Epley and Gilovich (2006) found that unless people are willing to search further for a value that is more accurate, adjustment from self-generated anchors remains insufficient because people stop when they reach what seems to be an adequate value.

Debiasing the effects of anchors is challenging. Even when people are forewarned that an anchor could bias thinking, they still tend to show an anchoring effect. Offering people monetary incentives to avoid the bias of anchors does not help, either (Simmons, LeBeouf, & Nelson, 2010). Even real estate agents can fall prey to the anchoring effects when estimating house values (Northcraft & Neale, 1987). Table 11.1 summarizes anchoring and adjustment and other heuristics.

TABLE 11.1 Summary of Heuristics and How to Debias Their Negative Effects		
Name	**Description**	**How to Fix or Avoid It**
Representativeness	Assuming something is a member of a category because it looks like the category; "like goes with like"; involved in the gambler's fallacy, the hot-hand illusion, and homeopathy	Know that events in random strings are independent and that treatments do not have to look like the problem.
Availability	Assuming that something that comes readily to mind is more frequent; affected by vividness and coverage in the media	Draw conclusions based on facts and knowledge, not on what is familiar, what is vivid in memory, or what readily comes to mind.
Anchoring and adjustment	Making a judgment by starting with some arbitrary value when lacking good information upon which to base a decision and then insufficiently adjusting from it; for example, people anchor from prices others supply and do not adjust enough	"Shop around" for information relevant to the decision—that is, valid facts and knowledge on which to base a decision. Adjust more from values that others provide.

Practice Thinking 11.4: Recognizing and Fixing Judgment Errors

For each of the following situations, find the heuristic and/or thinking error and bias in judgment that seems to account for the problem in thinking. Then suggest a way to avoid or fix the error or bias.

1. A clinical psychologist was discussing the problem of sexual abuse with a client. The therapist told her client that the sexual abuse of women was very prevalent. When her client asked her how often it occurred, the psychologist thought for a moment, recalling several clients she had seen recently whom she thought had been sexually abused. Based on the many cases that came to mind, the psychologist said that more than 70% of all women had been sexually abused (a much higher proportion than is usually the case).

   a. Thinking error: _____

   _____

   b. How to fix it: _____

   _____

2. Emily read the profile of a man on a dating site who described himself as 25 years old and looking for a serious relationship. The man said he liked to swim and was a serious runner who competed in local runs on weekends. He listed the college he attended and said that he liked a good conversation and reading. She told herself, "I bet he not only went to college but also competed on a college athletic team; he is not just someone who went to college."

   a. Thinking error: _____

   _____

   b. How to fix it: _____

   _____

3. Every week, Alex buys five lottery tickets. He has never won, but he knows two people who have won in the past year. Alex firmly believes that it's just a question of time before his luck changes and he wins, too.

    a. Thinking errors (list two): _____

_____

    b. How to fix them: _____

_____

4. Kiana likes to help people in struggling nations, so she is on the mailing lists for several charities. One recent advertisement said, "If you can't give $200, please give $100." The actual average donation for this charity was $50, but Kiana did not know that. She thought to herself, "I can't afford $200, but I think I could manage $100," which is more than she usually donates.

    a. Thinking error: _____

_____

    b. How to fix it: _____

_____

5. Describe a situation in which you inappropriately used or were adversely affected by one of the heuristics summarized in Table 11.1.

    a. Thinking error: _____

_____

    b. How to fix it: _____

_____

METACOGNITION AND OVERCONFIDENCE

To debias your own thinking, you must first reflect on its quality to recognize when judgment errors are likely to occur. This metacognitive monitoring is associated with Type 2 thinking. Many of the errors we have discussed result from automatic thinking and the use of mental shortcuts that we rapidly deploy without much thought—all indicative of Type 1 thinking (Kahneman, 2011). In contrast, monitoring the quality of our thinking can help us slow down our processing, allowing us to engage the conscious, deliberate, analytical thought processes of Type 2 thinking which, in turn, can help prevent judgment and decision errors.

One of the most fundamental problems in judgment and decision making is overconfidence, an error related to deficient self-monitoring. People often overestimate their own judgment abilities and are unaware of their errors. In 1988, the captain of a U.S. Navy ship mistakenly judged an Iranian commercial airplane to be a military aircraft flying toward his ship and decided that the commercial pilot intended to attack his ship. The captain's decision was based primarily on information from his radar; he did not seek to verify what the commercial plane was doing. As a result, he decided to launch two missiles at the plane—and all 290 passengers on board were killed when the plane exploded (Matlin, 1994). Had the captain checked his own judgment for errors and realized how easy it is to make such errors based on limited information, he might have been less confident of his judgment and the catastrophe might have been averted.

Overconfidence is pervasive in many types of social judgment. One study found that college students who were interviewing other students consistently overestimated the accuracy of their judgments about what those other students would do in various situations (Dunning, Griffin, Milojkovic, & Ross, 1990). In another study, college students were very overconfident in their predictions about both what they would do and what other students would do in various situations (Vallone, Griffin, Lin, & Ross, 1990). Overconfidence and bias may be partly due to a *bias blind spot* (Pronin, Lin, & Ross, 2002), wherein people are not aware of their own biases and may even insulate themselves from seeing those biases. Specifically, although individuals realize that people are frequently biased, they perceive that it is those *other* people who are biased, not *themselves*.

Often, the people who know the least and perform the worst are the most overconfident in their performance. For instance, on tests of vocabulary, grammar, reasoning, and knowledge of hunting, the individuals who performed the worst tended to overestimate their performance on those tests more than people who did the best on those tests (Dunning, Johnson, Ehrlinger, & Kruger, 2003). An explanation is that those who overestimate the most are "unskilled and unaware." These overconfident, poor performers may be unaware of their poor performance because they lack the knowledge and skills that would indicate to them that they are not doing well on the tests. Fortunately, other studies have shown that explicit instruction in reasoning can both improve the reasoning test performance of poor-performing students and reduce their overconfidence (Bensley & Spero, 2014; Kruger & Dunning, 1999).

Decision making in groups can lead to overconfidence in a bad decision, too. Irving Janis (1972) studied the decision making of President John F. Kennedy as he and his cabinet wrestled with the question of whether to invade Cuba in 1961 after the communist leader Fidel Castro took control of the island country. The group advised Kennedy to invade, but the troops they sent in the Bay of Pigs invasion were killed or captured soon after landing in Cuba—a humiliating failure for the U.S. government. Janis described this decision failure as an instance of **groupthink**, in which dissenting ideas are suppressed when a cohesive group isolated from outside input is aware of a strong leader's position on a course of action and conforms to the leader's position.

This chain of events occurred when Kennedy was presented with a plan by the Central Intelligence Agency (which had been supported by the preceding Eisenhower administration) to invade Cuba. Kennedy's advisers went along with the flawed plan and did not offer resistance to it, even when they had reservations about its wisdom. One adviser, James Schlesinger, sent a memo to Kennedy expressing his concerns, but he did not voice his qualms at meetings and was urged by the president's brother, Robert Kennedy, not to oppose the plan.

The lack of dissent probably increased President Kennedy's confidence that he was right, only to be surprised when his assumptions turned out to be wrong. After this faulty decision, Kennedy reviewed what went wrong and deliberately sought out dissenting views when making decisions in the future. In fact, Janis (1972) recommended that a group leader should do just that—encourage group members to voice their dissenting views, with the leader withholding information about his or her position on a question to avoid suppressing dissent.

Hindsight bias is another type of metacognitive error in which people are overconfident of what they knew before an event. After learning the outcome of an event, it may seem to us that we knew it would happen all along. Hindsight bias is sometimes called *Monday morning quarterbacking* because after the Sunday game, we know what the quarterback or team should have done to win (e.g., run the football instead of passing it on that last play to avoid the interception). In hindsight bias, the outcome seems more foreseeable than it actually was because we are looking back on it, safe in the knowledge of the actual outcome.

In an early experimental demonstration of hindsight bias by Fischhoff (1975), participants with knowledge of an event that had already taken place were asked to estimate the likelihood that that event would have occurred; their estimates were greater than those of other participants who had no knowledge of the outcome when they made their estimates. This "belief that an event is more pre-dictable after it becomes known than it was before it became known" is hindsight bias (Roese & Vohs, 2012, p. 411).

A good example is the conspiracy theory that the U.S. government must have known in advance about the September 11, 2001, terrorist attacks on the World Trade Center (WTC) and the Pentagon. To many people, it seemed that such a terrorist strike should have been expected. Al Qaeda had warned of an attack on the United States in the weeks leading to that fateful day. In fact, one of the hun-dreds of intercepted messages before September 11 even mentioned that Osama bin Laden wanted to strike the United States and suggested that an attack with planes on the WTC and Washington, DC, was possible.

In hindsight, this information does seem highly predictive of the terrorists' horrific plans, but the key to understanding how to assess the risk of such an attack is that the government intelligence had intercepted *hundreds* of memos discussing possible strikes by Al Qaeda. The U.S. government may have failed to "connect the dots," but the September 11 attack was only one of many possible scenarios. To keep this in perspective, we should think of how a future terrorist attack is highly likely even now, yet it remains extremely difficult to say where or when such an attack is likely to occur (Shermer, 2011).

Hindsight bias is both a common and a consequential thinking error demon-strated by people across the life span, but both the very young (3–4 years) and older adults (61–95 years) are especially susceptible to it (Bernstein, Erdfelder, Meltzoff, Peria, & Loftus, 2011). Other research suggests that such bias occurs in both Easterners and Westerners, yet Japanese and Korean participants in one study showed greater hindsight bias than did French and British participants (Yama & Adachi, 2011). As noted by Roese and Vohs (2012), hindsight bias has several applications in legal judgments, such as in liability cases that claim some third party should have anticipated problems with a certain product or treatment that, in hindsight, might seem to be obvious.

Debiasing hindsight can be tricky. The strategy of considering the opposite or thinking of alternative outcomes sometimes reduces hindsight bias (Arkes, 1991; Larrick, 2004). However, recent research suggests that the effectiveness of considering alternatives depends on how difficult it is to think of alterna-tives. For instance, Sanna, Schwartz, and Stocker (2002) asked participants to think of many different outcomes for an event. When the participants reported that this was difficult, the exercise actually *increased* their hindsight bias! Per-haps participants inferred that their original interpretation of the outcome that showed hindsight bias was correct and, therefore, that they should not revise their interpretation. The finding from this study suggests that thinking of alternatives to the actual event can backfire as a debiasing strategy and can actually increase hindsight bias when people engage in metacognitive monitoring of how easily they can think of alternative outcomes and encounter difficulty in doing so.

Practice Thinking 11.5: Recognizing and Fixing Metacognitive Errors

For each of the following situations, label and describe the kind of metacognitive error and then suggest a way to avoid or fix it.

1. Mariah was thinking about the events that led to the 2008 recession. She recalled how banks irresponsibly approved risky loans for potential home buyers who could not reasonably be expected to make their monthly house payments, and how big banks and investment firms were assigning to other investors the risk of people defaulting on their loans. She said to herself, "This was a recipe for disaster—how could people not have known what was going to happen?"

    a. Thinking error: _____

    _____

    b. How to fix it: _____

    _____

2. A student told his professor he could not understand how he did so poorly on the final exam. After the test, the student was sure he had gotten at least a B. The professor, however, was not so surprised because she knew the student had a D average going into the final.

    a. Thinking error: _____

    _____

    b. How to fix it: _____

    _____

3. The CEO of a company was discussing her plans for adding a new branch office with her staff and asked them what they thought. Her staff admired her, but they were also concerned about keeping their jobs. Although two staff members secretly wondered if there was enough business to support the new office, they did not voice their concerns. The company went ahead with opening the new branch, but soon the lack of business made the CEO ask herself, "I was sure that the new branch office would succeed. Why didn't any of my staff advise me against it?"

a. Thinking error: _____

_____

b. How to fix it: _____

_____

IS INTUITIVE, TYPE 1 THINKING BAD?

Despite the problems sometimes associated with their application, intuition and Type 1 thinking are not always bad. Being able to use two types of thinking can help us make the wide range of judgments and decisions we encounter throughout our lives. Often a task will require both types, and for some judgments, a rapid intuitive response (Type 1) is both better and faster than a rational, analytic response (Type 2). In many cases, the representativeness and availability heuristics can help us respond efficiently in time-sensitive situations. Likewise, intuition may lead to better judgments than a rational–analytic approach when an emotional judgment or personal preference is needed.

Wilson and Schooler (1991) tested this notion by asking participants to indicate which brands of strawberry jam they preferred in a taste test; one group wrote reasons for their ratings, while the control group did not provide reasons. The researchers found that the control group's ratings were more consistent with expert ratings of the jams, suggesting that taking a rational–analytic approach was not as effective as an intuitive approach. Another study showed that having to provide explicit justification for their decisions impaired participants' decision making compared with the control group, whose members did not have to justify their preferences (McMackin & Slovic, 2000).

Intuitive, Type 1 thinking is especially useful when it is based on genuine expertise. In his study of fire-ground commanders, Gary Klein has shown how these expert firefighters can make rapid, intuitive decisions that are quite accurate under conditions of uncertainty and without considering a number of options (Kahneman & Klein, 2009). For example, a fire-ground commander may simply know intuitively when the floor of a burning building is about to collapse and what the best course of action is to fight a fire, perhaps considering only one course of action rather than multiple options—a tactic used in the much slower mode of Type 2 thinking. The expertise that makes the fire commander's intuition possible comes from thousands of hours of firefighting experience. The expert learns to recognize the patterns that lead to identifying a problem and its solution.

Likewise, master chess players acquire 50,000 to 100,000 patterns for chess positions as a result of playing thousands of games and simply learn to recognize which next move is best. In the terms discussed earlier, the true expert develops valid cues for making decisions. Valid cues exist if regular patterns in the environment objectively correspond to the knowledge and skill needed to make a good decision or prediction.

In other environments, such as learning to be a good clinician, it is more difficult to acquire real expertise through practice and experience because few valid cues are available and insufficient feedback about performance is provided (Kahneman & Klein, 2009). Consequently, the idea that clinicians show expert (high levels of) performance when using their intuition to make judgments about clients is a misconception, as discussed further in Chapter 13.

SUMMARY

People show bounded rationality; that is, they are often limited in the cognitive resources they can use to estimate probabilities and make other challenging judgments and decisions. They often make errors in judgment because they do not understand probability and because they inappropriately use heuristics, or rules of thumb that act as cognitive shortcuts. For instance, they may not understand randomness and instead expect more switches in random strings, failing to understand that the probability of one independent trial does not affect the probability of another independent trial. These misunderstandings, along with the representativeness heuristic ("like goes with like"), may contribute to errors such as the gambler's fallacy and belief in streak shooting.

Other errors that occur from an overreliance on representativeness and a misunderstanding of probability estimation include base rate neglect and the conjunction fallacy. And although scientists recognize that the law of large numbers suggests that they should rely on large randomly selected samples, many people behave as if the law of small numbers were true—that is, they place greater trust in the evidence from anecdotes and fail to recognize regression to the mean.

Inappropriate application of other heuristics, such as availability and anchoring and adjustment, can also lead to errors in judgment and decision making. Availability, or the ease with which something comes to mind, can bias probability estimates when it does not correspond to an event's objective frequency. In the anchoring and adjustment heuristic, people anchor their estimates to values provided to them, such as prices, and then adjust those values higher or lower, but they often do not adjust enough.

Metacognitive errors, such as overconfidence, can also lead to judgment and decision errors. People often overestimate the quality of their judgments and decisions and are overconfident in their knowledge of themselves and others; people even overestimate their own lack of bias. Poorer performers on tests are especially prone to overestimating their performance, showing the unskilled and unaware effect. In addition, people may demonstrate hindsight bias by overestimating the predictability of an event after the outcome is known. Cohesive groups demonstrate groupthink when they know of the group leader's preference and conform to that view, even though they might have concerns about it; their failure to speak up may reflect the fact that they are overly confident in the quality of the group's decision.

Type 1 and Type 2 thinking can both contribute to good judgment and decision making. Although Type 2 thinking is most often called upon to debias the inappropriate use of heuristics, Type 1 thinking and heuristics can be quite effective when someone must make rapid, intuitive judgments. In some environments, people can find valid cues—the regular patterns that objectively correspond to the information needed to make a good decision or prediction. After much practice, people can learn to use these valid cues to rapidly make intuitive judgments and decisions and to become expert judges and decision makers, as in the case of expert firefighters and chess masters.

 ## Practice Thinking 11.6: WHAT DO YOU THINK **NOW**?
Please explain how you know.

1. Can a graphologist accurately judge someone's character or personality based on analysis of the person's handwriting? _____

_____

2. Suppose a basketball player has a "hot hand" and makes four baskets in a row. Should a coach tell the other team members to pass the ball to him or her? Why or why not? _____

_____

3. Is someone who has already played a slot machine 30 times without winning more likely to win the next time he puts in a quarter than someone who put in just a single quarter and did not win—in other words, is the 30-time loser "due" compared to the one-time loser? _____

_____

4. Describe a judgment error or bad decision that caused a problem for you. Why did it occur? _____

_____

5. What could you do to improve your judgment and decision making?

_____

REVIEW QUESTIONS

1. How are judgment and decision making related to critical thinking?

2. What is framing? How does it affect judgment?

3. What is simple probability? How do you calculate it?

4. What are errors in estimating probability?

- Describe errors in recognizing random strings.

- What is the gambler's fallacy?

- What is the hot-hand illusion?

5. What is the law of large numbers? How does it relate to random sampling?

6. What is regression to the mean?

7. What is bounded rationality? Are people cognitive misers?

8. What is a heuristic?
   - How are heuristics related to Type 1 thinking?
   - What is bias? Are there different types of bias?

9. What is the representativeness heuristic? How might it lead to faulty judgments?
   - Can representativeness explain homeopathy and certain natural cures?
   - What is base rate neglect?
   - What is the conjunction fallacy?

10. How does availability contribute to faulty judgments? How can we correct for it?

11. How does anchoring and adjustment contribute to faulty judgments? How do we correct for it?

12. How are Type 1 and Type 2 thinking related to judgment errors and debiasing?

13. How is metacognition related to the quality of judgments?
    - What is overconfidence, and why is it a problem? How do we correct for it?
    - How is groupthink related to overconfidence? How could we prevent groupthink?

14. What is hindsight bias? What causes it? How do we correct for it?

15. Does Type 1 thinking always lead to judgment errors and bias?

16. What psychological misconceptions are discussed in this chapter?

12

SUPERSTITION, MAGIC, SCIENCE, AND CRITICAL THINKING

LEARNING OUTCOMES

After studying this chapter, you should be able to:

1. Identify examples and sources of superstition in everyday life.

2. Identify examples and sources of magical thinking in everyday life.

3. Explain how thinking and judgment errors contribute to superstitions and magical thinking.

4. Deal effectively with superstition and magical thinking.

WHAT DO YOU THINK?

Let's begin with a riddle. Which specific belief did U.S. presidents Herbert Hoover and Franklin Delano Roosevelt have in common with Senator John McCain, who ran for president in 2008? No, it wasn't that they all believed in democracy—that is too general. Nor was it their political beliefs—Hoover and McCain were Republicans and Roosevelt was a Democrat.

The answer is that all three were superstitious about the number 13. Neither Hoover nor Roosevelt wished to dine at a table that seated 13 people. Senator John McCain is said to always keep 31 cents in his pocket because 31 is 13 backwards and helps ward off the bad luck of the number 13 (Wargo, 2008). When his campaign headquarters happened to be on the 13th floor, McCain renamed it the "M" floor for "McCain" to ward off possible bad luck.

Believing that the number 13 is unlucky is a superstition, an irrational belief. Do you think our political leaders should not be superstitious? Or are superstitions harmless quirks in human behavior? Would you vote for someone who is superstitious?

Practice Thinking 12.1: What Do You Think?

Please explain how you know.

1. How much would knowing that a politician was superstitious affect your vote? Why?

   _____

2. Do you have a lucky shirt or some other object that brings you luck? How does something become "lucky"?

   _____

3. When things are going right, are you careful of what you do next so you do not tempt fate or push your luck?

   _____

4. Is science education reducing belief in superstition, magic, and supernatural events?

   _____

5. Should we try to eliminate superstition and magical thinking? Why or why not?

   _____

SUPERSTITION, FALSE BELIEFS, AND POOR JUDGMENT

Believing in a superstition is a sign that a person is not thinking critically. Superstitions, like other false beliefs, can result from poor reasoning. Conversely, reasoning from a false belief, such as a superstition, can lead to a faulty judgment or conclusion. In contrast, critical thinking (CT) involves making judgments and forming beliefs that are supported by good reasons (Lipman, 1991) while discarding unsupported, irrational, false beliefs.

   People often use the term *superstition* to refer to beliefs that are incorrect or recognized as untrue from the perspective of some belief system they presume is true. From a scientific perspective, a **superstition** is a commonsense belief that is not plausible, given what we know from scientific research and rational principles. Superstitions are like pseudoscientific beliefs in this regard; but *unlike* pseudoscience, people do not claim that superstitious ideas are scientific. For example, many individuals—even U.S. presidents—behave as if they accept the superstition that the number 13 is unlucky, but they do not claim that this belief has a scientific basis. However, many proponents of the pseudoscience Scientology would maintain that Scientology is scientific, even though its tenets are not empirically supported.

Superstitions also resemble paranormal beliefs in that they often assume that people have supernatural and magical powers. For instance, the superstition that witches can cause misfortune simply by thinking a malevolent thought is a supernatural claim involving magical thinking. Superstitious people are often obliged to engage in repetitive behaviors and rituals to increase their chances of success or reduce the risk of negative outcomes; however, these actions have no rational basis in changing objective probabilities in the world.

In addition, superstitions resemble psychological misconceptions in that both are false commonsense beliefs; but unlike misconceptions, superstitions often make claims that sound unrelated to specific behaviors and mental processes. For example, the superstitious belief that a lucky charm will improve performance is nonspecific about how the mind works, whereas the psychological misconception that venting anger reduces aggression makes a specific psychological (albeit false) claim. Likewise, the misconception that hypnosis is a unique state of consciousness, in which people can be compelled to do things they would not ordinarily do, makes a specific psychological claim, although the claim has not been supported by psychological research.

In contrast to superstitions lacking connection to psychological theory and research, some psychological misconceptions are actually derived from incorrect interpretations of ideas that have been researched by psychologists. For instance, although studies on hemispheric differences have shown that the left hemisphere is dominant for language processing and the right hemisphere is dominant during spatial and nonverbal tasks, it is a psychological misconception (and a sweeping generalization) to claim that some people are left-brained and others are right-brained (Lilienfeld, Lynn, Ruscio, & Beyerstein, 2010). Moreover, the notion that people repress memories of traumatic events—a specific claim originated by Sigmund Freud and favored by some psychologists today—is a psychological misconception because research has not supported the claim. Thus, unlike misconceptions, superstitions have virtually nothing specific to say about brain function, memory, and other psychological processes.

THE HISTORY OF SUPERSTITION

The idea of superstition is very old and has been associated with religion in various ways. The word *superstition* comes from the Latin word *superstitio*, meaning to "stand over in amazement," as with religious awe. Some superstitions even have their origins in specific religious traditions. For example, some view the number 13 and the date Friday the 13th as unlucky because 13 people (Jesus and his 12 disciples) attended the "last supper" before the Friday of Jesus's crucifixion. Sometimes, religious believers have viewed the beliefs of other religious groups as superstitious. For instance, the Catholic Church has for many years objected to superstition as adhering to magical and other practices that deny God's divine providence. In the fifteenth century, when the Protestant reformer Martin Luther rejected certain Roman Catholic practices, he said the office of the pope was a source of superstition. Ironically, Luther also believed in witches who had supernatural powers—a belief that is now considered a superstition.

Individuals who believe in **magic** may assume that certain practices and rituals can harness supernatural forces to achieve seemingly impossible feats, even controlling the forces of nature. People may also view magic as a means to counteract evil forces and the magical powers of witches and others. The belief in witches is quite old. The Hebrew Bible and the New Testament both mention witches, for example. In the late Middle Ages in Europe, fears of their supernatural powers led to the execution of many people, often women, for witchcraft. Using magic, these so-called witches were said to fly through the air and cause harmful events, such as disease, pestilence, and storms. During the Inquisition in Europe, when religious and political institutions collaborated to prosecute and execute people accused of witchcraft, between 60,000 and 600,000 people were sentenced to death by hanging, being burned at the stake, or in some other way for this supposed crime.

With the dawn of the Scientific Revolution in the 1600s, science has increasingly been viewed as a way to harness the powers of nature without resorting to supernatural explanations such as witchcraft (Wootton, 2016). In fact, magic and superstition themselves became the subjects of scientific investigation. In the nineteenth century, scientists identified an important kind of magic, called *sympathetic magic*, found in many cultures (Frazer, 1996; Tylor, 1974). Two fundamental laws of sympathetic magic are the law of similarity and the law of contagion. According to the **law of similarity**, things that resemble each other share important properties, captured in the expression "like goes with like." An example is the Haitian ritual in which a practitioner of voodoo burns a doll that looks like the intended victim in an attempt to harm that person. According to the law of contagion, things that come into contact may change each other for a period of time, even after they are no longer in contact. For instance, a person might not want to handle an item that belonged to an evil individual, fearing that some evil essence may linger in the object and be transferred to the "uncontaminated" person.

Today, many scientific-minded people reject as superstition any magical and supernatural explanations of events in the natural world (Park, 2008). For example, most would reject the idea that witches fly through the air on broomsticks, despite the many images of these feats at Halloween and in Harry Potter movies. Although most people today accept scientific ideas, they may at the same time accept some superstitions and magical thinking. But how can an individual maintain such superstitions *and* believe in scientific thinking at the same time (Gelman, 2011)?

THE PSYCHOLOGY OF SUPERSTITION

Superstitious behavior and magical thinking are found in many developing countries, but we can easily observe them in athletes and college students in developed countries as well. For instance, the Hall of Fame baseball player Wade Boggs ate chicken before every game for 20 years. As part of his 5-hour, ritualized pregame preparation, he would finish a drill by stepping on third base, then second base, then first base, and would finally take two steps toward the coaching box and exactly four steps toward the dugout. Furthermore, when he first stepped into the batter's box, he would draw in the dirt the Hebrew word *chai* with the tip of his bat (Vyse, 2014). In a telling remark, Boggs reported that he made these elaborate preparations so as not to leave anything to chance.

This example illustrates how superstitious behavior is used to prepare a person for a high-stakes, risky activity. It is not surprising that athletes, fighter pilots, gamblers, and others who are confronted with risky choices tend to engage in superstitious behavior. John McCain probably acquired some of his superstitious habits when he was a fighter pilot (Wargo, 2008). Those individuals who engage in superstitious rituals often incorrectly believe they are increasing their chances of success by affecting some forces in the world related to luck. Of course, engaging in some superstitious ritual, such as drawing a symbol in the dirt with your bat, does nothing to objectively change the probability of success. So why do people perform these acts anyway?

Perhaps their tendency to make errors in estimating the likelihood of events leads superstitious people to misinterpret the effects of their actions on outcomes. For instance, what is the probability that any two people in a group of 30 share the same birthday? People often estimate this event as having a low probability, but it is actually more than .70. Individuals often underestimate the probabilities of coincidences, in general, and tend to consider a coincidence in their own lives as much more meaningful than when the same coincidence happens to someone else (Falk, 1989). Moreover, they may be especially likely to attribute a correct prediction to precognition rather than just to coincidence (Blackmore, 1992b). Likewise, failure to take coincidence into account might help explain how people come to believe that some random activity they have engaged in has led to a favorable outcome, rather than interpreting the result as a chance occurrence.

Engaging in superstitious rituals may also help people manage the stress and tension associated with unpredictable outcomes, especially when the stakes are high. In simulations of athletic competitions, athletes who reported higher levels of superstition also reported that athletics was more important to them and that their pregame tension was greater. Psychological tension was also greater when a game was more important and its outcome more uncertain (Brevers, Dan, Noel, & Nils, 2011). In other cases, such as gambling, in which stress reduction is not likely to affect the outcome, the illusion of control that a gambler experiences by engaging in the ritual may reduce his or her stress level.

Superstitious behavior may have a motivational effect, by increasing the hope for a positive outcome (Keinan, 2003). Experiencing a reduction of stress might bring a similar reward, thereby reinforcing the use of a superstitious ritual even when it has had no other effect on an outcome. More generally, superstitious rituals may offer compensatory control over the anxiety-provoking randomness of life by helping people believe that random, unconnected behaviors can exert causal control.

B. F. Skinner was the first psychologist to show that superstitious behavior might arise through random reinforcement of the performance of unusual behaviors. He based this claim on research in which pigeons were conditioned through reinforcement to engage in what he argued were superstitious behaviors (Skinner, 1948). When Skinner placed pigeons in operant chambers (cages designed to dispense a food reward when an animal made a desired response) but randomly dispensed food, the pigeons acquired some very unusual and distinctive behaviors. Before the food reinforcer arrived, pigeons engaged in behaviors such as bobbing their heads, poking their heads in one direction, and walking in circles. Whatever behavior the pigeon happened to be performing before the food reward was dispensed tended to get reinforced—eventually leading the pigeon to associate that behavior with the reward, strengthening the response through a kind of learning called *operant conditioning*. After this operant conditioning, the pigeon would engage in the "ritualistic" behavior unique to its own learning experience, behaving as if it believed the behavior had the power to cause food to be dispensed. Other psychologists have shown that superstitious behaviors can be operantly conditioned in children, using marbles as reinforcers (Wagner & Morris, 1987), and in college students, using points on a counter as reinforcers (Ono, 1987).

Sometimes, superstitious behavior involves treating an object as if it is imbued with a special power or the ability to bring good luck. Usually, such "lucky" objects are used to improve the chances of success in some important contest or challenge that poses significant risk of failure. For instance, approximately one-third of college students have lucky pens or special clothing they wear whenever they take a test (Albas & Albas, 1989). A famous example from the basketball world is Hall-of-Famer Michael Jordan, who, throughout his long NBA career with the Chicago Bulls, continued to wear his University of North Carolina shorts under his regular Bulls uniform because he believed they brought him good luck (Wargo, 2008).

Such superstitious practices can be partly explained as the individuals learning (falsely) through operant conditioning that the ritual use of an object predicts success, but these practices also seem to involve thinking errors. In the cases just mentioned, the person seems to have fallen prey to *post hoc, ergo propter hoc* thinking—translated as "after this, therefore because of this" (introduced in Chapter 2). For example, a student might mistakenly conclude that after acing an exam using a particular blue pen, it was the pen that produced the positive outcome. This kind of thinking error may prove dangerous if the student assumes that the next time he or she brings the lucky pen, it will somehow affect what the student needs to know for the exam. A much better strategy to prepare for the exam would be to go through the textbook and class notes to identify the important information to study.

The law of similarity can operate through the use of the representativeness heuristic, too (see Chapter 11). The voodoo practice of sticking pins into a doll to harm the person it represents demonstrates the thinking that "like goes with like." Although movies and popular culture have associated harming someone with the voodoo practice of harming an effigy of that individual, this inappropriate use of the representativeness heuristic dates back to the magical practices

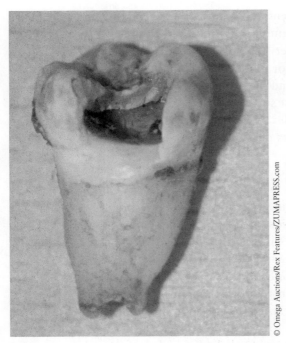

© Omega Auctions/Rex Features/ZUMAPRESS.com

FIGURE 12.1 John Lennon's decayed molar later became valuable because of its association with him.

of "the cunning folk," who were practitioners of white magic in Britain during the late Medieval period (Hutton, 1999). White magic was used for benevolent purposes to promote health and counteract malevolent witchcraft that sometimes involved sticking pins in the image of a malevolent witch.

The law of contagion can account for how objects take on special, even magical, powers through their positive association with people, objects, and events. Many of us have keepsakes or memorabilia—that is, objects that have special meaning for us because of the associations they evoke. Sometimes these associations can take a strange turn. Recently, a decayed molar from Beatle John Lennon (shown in Figure 12.1), extracted by his dentist in the 1960s, was auctioned off for $3,200! Although a Canadian dentist with an interest in celebrity teeth made the purchase, it was really just a rotten molar extracted in the 1960s. Its value was purely the result of its positive association with Lennon's celebrity status. Similarly, when psychologist Bruce Hood asked people at one of his lectures if they wanted to hold a pen owned by the great scientist Albert Einstein, they were eager to do so (Hood, 2009).

More often, the law of contagion is expressed as the desire to avoid contact with—and contamination from—an object that is negatively associated with someone or something viewed as harmful or damaged. People may avoid contact with the object even though there is no rational or scientific reason for the reaction beyond the psychological association with the thing or object. For instance, Rozin and Nemeroff (1990) found that participants who were asked if they would wear a sweater worn by someone who had lost a limb or worn by someone else who was a convicted killer were reluctant to do so.

Contagion effects have been found with several contaminating agents. For example, despite the fact that it is known that acquired immunodeficiency syndrome (AIDS) is not transmitted without the exchange of bodily fluids, people will avoid contact with clothing worn just once by an AIDS patient and then washed (Rozin, Markwith, & MacCauley, 1994).

Practice Thinking 12.2: Recognizing Magical Thinking Related to Real-World Examples

Identify whether the law of similarity or the law of contagion applies in each of the following examples. If prompted, fill in which heuristic may be associated with it as well.

1. Amee is a strict vegetarian who feels slightly nauseous at even the sight of meat. At her friend's party, she was hungry and wanted to eat some veggies, but the vegetable platter had been arranged to look just like a turkey. Amee suddenly felt queasy and lost her appetite. This scenario seems to involve the law of _____ of sympathetic magic and the _____ heuristic.

2. Daniel's friend Mindy gave him an unmarked textbook that still had the original bookstore receipt inside the cover. She had gotten the book from another student. Although Daniel was grateful that he would not have to buy a new textbook for the course, he later found out that the original owner of the textbook had been caught cheating on an exam in a previous class and was expelled from school. At that point, Daniel stopped using the book and bought himself a brand-new copy at the bookstore. This example involves the law of _____.

3. Frazer (1996) documented how an Indian wizard from British Columbia would put an image of a fish swimming in the water to ensure that fish would come to feed his people. This scenario seems to involve the law of _____ and the use of the _____ heuristic.

People's reluctance to tempt fate is another kind of superstitious thinking that involves difficulty with judging the probability of events. Many individuals behave as if they should not do anything to tempt fate so as to reduce their chance of a negative outcome. To examine this issue, Risen and Gilovich (2007) asked participants to read a scenario in which a young man named Jon, applying to Stanford, was sent a Stanford T-shirt by his optimistic mother. One group read a version of the scenario in which Jon stuffed the shirt in his drawer and did not wear it until he heard about Stanford's decision, so as not to tempt fate. A second group read a different version in which Jon began wearing the T-shirt the next day. All the participants then rated how likely it was that Stanford would accept Jon for admittance. The group who read the scenario in which Jon tempted fate by wearing the T-shirt immediately rated him as significantly less likely to be accepted, despite the fact that whether he wore the T-shirt would have no objective effect on his chances of acceptance.

In later experiments, Risen and Gilovich (2007) showed that negative outcomes were made more accessible after actions that tempted fate. In other words, actions that tempted fate brought negative outcomes more readily to mind than actions that did not. This influence of the availability heuristic tended to increase participants' judgments that a negative outcome would occur. In the context of superstitious thinking, this study provided another example of how Type 1 thinking is associated with acceptance of commonsense, unsubstantiated claims.

Superstition and magical thinking share the paranormal assumption that mental events can directly affect physical ones—that is, that simply having a thought can change an outcome or alter physical reality in some way. This idea might seem intuitively appealing. After all, we know we can affect physical reality by first having a thought or intention and then acting on that thought in the "external" world. We know, too, that stressful thoughts can affect our own physical well-being. It is another thing entirely, however, to make the claim that merely having a thought, without the intervention of some behavior or physical factor, could affect another person or cause an event. This kind of thinking error, which is grounded in a paranormal claim, is called **apparent mental causation.**

In an experimental test of belief in apparent mental causation, Emily Pronin and her colleagues instructed participants that they would act as a "witch doctor" in a voodoo-like ceremony, in the context of studying psychosomatic effects, by reading a scientific account of voodoo effects on people (Pronin, Wegner, McCarthy, & Rodriguez, 2006). This study involved both actual participants and a confederate (i.e., a person in cahoots with the experimenter posing as another participant). For one group, the confederate had been instructed to arrive late and behave and dress offensively in the presence of the actual subject, which was expected to induce evil thoughts about the confederate. For a second neutral-thoughts control group, the confederate arrived on time and was well mannered, so that the actual participants would be induced to have neutral thoughts about the confederate.

Before the evil-versus-neutral-thoughts manipulation, the actual and confederate participants completed a symptom questionnaire, and the experimenter verified aloud that the confederate participant had reported that he was feeling fine. Then the experimenter separated the actual participant and the confederate (who was to be the victim) and instructed the participant to form vivid and concrete thoughts of the confederate while sticking pins into a voodoo doll. When the confederate, posing as victim, again reported his symptoms, he indicated that he had developed a mild headache, and the experimenter confirmed this symptom out loud.

To test effects of the evil-thoughts manipulation, the experimenter asked participants to report whether they felt they had *caused* the headache in the victim participant and then to rate their levels of guilt, regret, and other emotions. The researchers found that, compared with the neutral-thoughts group, the evil-thoughts group reported significantly higher levels of negative thinking toward the victim and gave significantly higher ratings regarding their belief in having caused the headache. These results suggest that college students can be induced to show apparent mental causation using a superstitious ritual.

Consistent with this first demonstration of apparent mental causation, participants in a second study who were instructed to form positive visualizations of a peer's successful basketball shooting performance believed that they had influenced the peer to shoot better.

WHY DO SUPERSTITION AND MAGICAL THINKING PERSIST?

The examples of the influence of the law of contagion and other forms of magical thinking seem irrational, but closer inspection suggests that sometimes they may serve an adaptive function. For instance, people, influenced by the law of contagion, have avoided sick individuals for centuries, out of fear they could catch the victims' disease—long before they understood why this behavior was adaptive. We now know from germ theory that disease-causing microbes can be transmitted from person to person, often by contact with objects that have been touched by someone who is ill.

The principle underlying quarantines is that minimizing contact with a sick individual can reduce the risk of spreading disease. People who avoid contact with a sick individual or with the objects touched by that individual will be less likely to contract a disease and more likely to survive and pass along their genes for this behavioral tendency, regardless of whether they understand the scientific rationale for avoiding contact. Through natural selection, a general tendency to avoid contact with contaminated people and objects could have evolved in humans, with this genetic basis underlying the law of contagion in magical thinking.

Likewise, it could be that humans are biologically prepared to readily acquire certain kinds of associations that help them avoid foods that make them ill. Humans can acquire a classically conditioned taste aversion to a food that makes them sick in a single exposure (Garcia, Kimeldorf, & Koelling, 1955). Nemeroff and Rozin (2000) have further connected the emotion of disgust to operation of a food selection system. The mouth is the first "line of defense" against ingesting dangerous substances. Disgust is a core emotion that is conveyed with the same facial expression cross-culturally—an expression that is emblematic of the rejection of food. Perhaps innate tendencies related to disgust and food selection expanded into the interpersonal and moral domains as well (Nemeroff & Rozin, 2000). In this way, the emotion of disgust could have evolved to support a rejection of contaminated objects and people, consistent with the magical thinking that underlies the law of contagion.

Because associations based on contagion and other kinds of magical thinking are readily formed and may seem intuitive to people, superstition and magical thinking are likely to be both common and difficult to resist. This notion is supported by research showing that people who believe more in superstitions tend to adopt a more intuitive and less rational thinking style (Lindeman & Aarnio, 2006; Pacini & Epstein, 1999). Like the idea of "tempting fate," magical thinking tends to be more associated with Type 1 thinking. Changing a person's thinking is likely to be a difficult undertaking because the default mode of processing is Type 1 thinking. Another problem is that sometimes people know that a superstition is irrational, yet they do not reject it. We would expect that questioning a superstition and finding it to be irrational (a Type 2 activity) would be sufficient to reject it—but that is not always the case. Although psychologists like Jane Risen (2016) are working to answer the question of why superstitions persist in the face of hard evidence, it remains unresolved.

Further complicating the matter, there seem to be advantages and disadvantages, costs and benefits, to superstitions and magical thinking. On the positive side, they may help people to function adaptively by avoiding infection and dangerous substances without having to think much about reaching these important goals. Likewise, superstitious, ritualistic behaviors may serve the adaptive functions of reducing stress, enhancing control, and encouraging hope, thereby enhancing performance.

On the negative side, magical thinking, like the law of contagion, is a type of overgeneralization that can lead to biased evaluations of other people and situations. An individual who resists any kind of contact with a person with AIDS is mistakenly treating the development of AIDS as being akin to the usual transfer by infectious agents, rather than recognizing the narrow set of circumstances in which transfer of the human immunodeficiency virus (HIV) can occur. Similarly, treating the clothing of a person perceived to be immoral as "unclean" or repugnant is a type of overgeneralization in which the characteristic of a person is misattributed to an inanimate object. This makes the ethical question of how to deal with superstitious and magical thinking an important social problem.

DEALING WITH SUPERSTITION AND MAGICAL THINKING

Should we try to reduce or eliminate superstition and magical thinking? It is clear that these types of beliefs can create a variety of problems, but they sometimes serve adaptive functions, too. What if engaging in superstitious rituals actually improves performance? Damisch, Stroberock, and Mussweiler (2010) conducted a series of experiments in which the task performance of university students engaging in activities said to promote good luck was better than the performance of other students in control groups who were given instructions that omitted the variable of good luck.

For example, in one experiment, the task was remembering pairs of cards in a memory game. One group did so in the presence of a lucky charm they had brought to the experiment; another randomly assigned group did the memory task without their lucky charm (because the experimenter had earlier removed the charm and placed it in another room). Participants also completed a measure of self-efficacy in which they rated how confident they were that they would master the memory game. Participants who had their lucky charm performed significantly better on the memory task and had higher self-efficacy than the group without their lucky charm. The researchers replicated this effect by showing that participants who had their lucky charm were more confident that they would succeed in solving an anagram puzzle (rearranging scrambled letters to make words) and, in turn, performed better on the task than the participants who did not have their lucky charm. Damisch and colleagues (2010) showed that one reason the group members who had their lucky charm performed better was that they were willing to persist longer on the task.

Finally, Damisch and colleagues (2010) tested whether *expectations* about luck could affect sports performance. They found that German students who were told that they were using a lucky golf ball performed better on a golf-putting task than did students in a control group who were not told about the lucky golf ball. The findings suggest that superstition helped participants believe they could succeed and kept them motivated to successfully complete the tasks. However, it should be noted that a recent replication of the Damisch et al. golf study failed to find that participants who were told they had a lucky golf ball putted better than the control group (Calin-Jageman & Caldell, 2014).

The results of the Damisch et al. (2010) study, as well as studies reviewed earlier, suggest that the benefits of superstitious behaviors are both motivational and emotional. Recall that engaging in superstitious behaviors may reduce the experience of stress and increase hope (Keinan, 2003). Consistent with this idea, Kay, Whitson, Gaucher, and Galinsky (2009) have proposed that people are threatened by the inherent randomness of the universe, which can arouse great uncertainty. People adopt superstitious behaviors to increase their perception of control over these essentially random events (Kay et al., 2009). For instance, after some horrific event, such as a terrorist attack or a tragic accident, people often comment that they do not understand why the event happened, but they believe that "everything happens for a reason." On one level, this response may represent an effort to maintain control in the face of senseless and unexpected random events—allowing people to go on when confronted by the stress of great uncertainty.

Nevertheless, although superstitious behaviors may help us feel better, maintain control, or even perform better, this does not imply that superstitions are true. A "lucky" rabbit's foot does not affect a person's objective chances for success, although the irrational belief that it can help may encourage the person to hope for a positive outcome and reduce the stress associated with an uncertain outcome. This raises the important question of whether we should go to the trouble of resisting superstition and magical thinking, given that these false beliefs are sometimes adaptive, have a biological basis, and may be hard to resist. Yet, even if we have a natural tendency to interpret certain events in superstitious or magical terms, this does not mean that we must inevitably be superstitious or engage in magical thinking.

A common psychological misconception about inherited traits and genetically based behaviors is that they cannot be modified, as discussed in Chapter 10. Although it is likely to take conscious effort, we do have the capacity to curtail our own unwanted behaviors and to revise our incorrect beliefs. The many examples of people who have succeeded without relying on superstition and magical thinking amply demonstrate our ability to adaptively respond to life's demands without relying on these practices.

Moreover, it seems clear that on some occasions we should resist superstition and magical thinking, especially when someone's life or well-being is threatened. A prime example is the threat posed by the persistent persecution of people as witches in some regions of the world, including parts of Brazil and much of sub-Saharan Africa. From

1991 to 2001, for example, approximately 20,000 individuals in Tanzania were accused of and executed for being witches. Many of the victims were elderly women who showed "red-eye," one of the signs a person is a witch—though this appearance is more likely a symptom of eye irritation produced by the smoke from their cooking fires.

In many of these countries, witch doctors and traditional healers use magic, sometimes for a fee, to *counteract* the magic that witches have supposedly used to harm their victims. In rural Ghana, as many as 3,000 people have been exiled to live in primitive camps with barely enough to eat because they were accused of practicing witchcraft. Often a witch doctor decides their fate by merely observing how a dying chicken falls (Figure 12.2): innocent if it falls on its back or guilty if it falls with its beak to the ground (Palmer, 2010).

Unfortunately, sick people who believe they are bewitched tend to trust traditional healers to cure them more than they trust professionals who use evidence-based medical practices (Ivey & Myers, 2008). A study of witchcraft belief in Ghana revealed another dangerous misconception: Men who tended to believe that AIDS could be acquired through witchcraft also tended not to have used a condom the last time they had sexual intercourse (Tenkorang, Gyimah, Maticka-Tyndale, & Adjel, 2011).

FIGURE 12.2 A chicken being sacrificed in West Africa, as part of a ritual to determine the fate of someone accused of witchcraft.

Eric Lafforgue/Art in All of Us/Corbis News/Getty Images

Perhaps better science education could help people understand the irrationality of such beliefs. Yet education is unlikely to eradicate superstitious belief in witchcraft in such regions because, in part, people seem capable of maintaining both scientific and superstitious beliefs at the same time (Ivey & Myers, 2008). A study of the health practices and beliefs about witchcraft in rural Tanzania found that many people believe that AIDS can result from witchcraft. Some people with AIDS went to traditional healers as well as medical practitioners for help, but stopped going to the medical facilities because they did not believe they could be cured there. Traditional healers sometimes claim to be able to cure AIDS with witchcraft, even though no real cure for AIDS exists as yet. Foregoing evidence-based treatments, such as antiretroviral medicines that can prolong the life of a person with AIDS, in favor of ineffective, superstitious, and traditional remedies is likely to have deadly consequences.

Other examples of the need to resist dangerous superstitions and magical thinking are found in Western and developed countries. For instance, the mistaken belief that AIDS is transmissible by ordinary and nonsexual contact with an infected person may lead to needless avoidance, and even ostracism, of people with AIDS.

Finally, although belief in superstition is not usually associated with psychopathology and other mental problems (Vyse, 2014), some research suggests that people with obsessive–compulsive disorder may be more prone to engage in magical and superstitious thinking than people without the disorder (Einstein, Menzies, St. Clare, Drobny, & Helgadottir, 2011; Sica, Novara, & Sanavio, 2002). Feeling compelled to practice some superstitious ritual or engage in magical thinking that causes problems indicates the need for help in using a more adaptive, evidence-based therapy for coping with stressful events.

Practice Thinking 12.3: Recognizing Thinking Errors and Magical Thinking

For each of the following situations, write the thinking error or type of magical thinking that is likely involved.

1. Nicole wore her light blue blouse the day she was elected to be vice president of the psychology club. When later running for an office in her sorority, she made sure to wear the same blue blouse on election day.

   Thinking error: _____

2. In Erica's introductory psychology class last week, the instructor had said she would randomly call on people in this week's class to answer questions about the chapter to check whether they had done the reading. Suppose Erica has *not* done the assigned reading. How likely is it that she will be called on today versus the likelihood she would have been called on if she had done the reading? Explain your answer.

   More likely than if she had done the reading _____

   Less likely than if she had done the reading _____

   Equally likely whether she had done the reading or not _____

Suppose Erica said that she thought she was more likely to be called on.

Magical thinking: _____

3. For two weeks, Hashim had been harboring negative thoughts about Renee because she had dumped him for another guy. Then Ron said, "Hey, did you hear that Renee got hurt in a car accident?" Hashim immediately felt a pang of guilt because he had been hoping something bad would happen to her and wondered if perhaps he had influenced this event.

Magical thinking: _____

4. Describe an example of magical thinking you have experienced.

Your example of magical thinking: _____

_____

SUMMARY

Superstition is a commonsense belief that is not plausible, given what we know from scientific research, but unlike pseudoscience no claims are made that superstitious ideas are scientific. Also unlike psychological misconceptions that make specific claims about behavior and mental processes, superstitions make no such specific psychological claims. Superstitious beliefs, which are associated with magical thinking, sometimes imply that people have paranormal and supernatural powers. Two fundamental laws of sympathetic magic are the law of similarity and the law of contagion. According to the law of similarity, things that resemble each other share important properties, and control can be exerted by way of this similarity. According to the law of contagion, things that come into contact may change each other for a period of time even after they are no longer in contact.

Research has shown that many people are susceptible to superstition and magical thinking, particularly people in high-risk situations. They underestimate the role of coincidence, especially coincidences that happen to them, and tend to find patterns in random data. These factors may contribute to their finding patterns in behaviors and outcomes that they attribute to luck but which are actually coincidental. Studies on operant conditioning have shown that pigeons and people can both acquire superstitious behaviors through this learning procedure, wherein behaviors are associated with randomly occurring rewards. Engaging in superstitious behaviors may help people manage stress and tension associated with uncertain outcomes; it may also sometimes improve performance.

Other research shows that people who endorse paranormal and superstitious beliefs tend to rely more on an intuitive thinking style (Type 1 thinking). The law of contagion may help explain why people want contact with objects associated with celebrities and avoid contact with objects associated with criminals and sick people. The law of contagion may have evolved through natural selection, as it increases the survival rate for individuals who avoid people who are ill.

Superstitious behavior and magical thinking are associated with thinking errors as well. Besides operant conditioning, people can come to believe that objects are lucky by means of "after this, therefore because of this" reasoning, as when they irrationally perceive the presence of some unrelated object to have increased their chances of success. The law of similarity is related to the inappropriate use of the representativeness heuristic. Research has shown that college students may commit the thinking error of apparent mental causation, wherein they believe their thoughts can directly affect other people or events without any intermediate physical mechanism. Finally, belief in tempting fate or pushing one's luck is a type of magical thinking error in which a person mistakenly believes that engaging in or not engaging in some action will lead to a negative outcome when there is no objective relation between the action and the outcome's probability.

What we decide to do about superstitions and magical thinking depends on our analysis of their costs and benefits. Although superstitious behaviors are irrational, they may actually help people reduce stress, improve performance, and do little harm in many cases. The law of contagion has probably kept many people alive over the years, by prompting the implementation of quarantines for persons with communicable diseases. Unfortunately, they can also lead to unnecessary avoidance of and discrimination against individuals, as in the case of people accused of witchcraft and the avoidance of people with AIDS. If engaging in superstitious rituals or magical thinking causes distress, prevents people from getting evidence-based treatment, or leads to the harming of others, then intervention is needed.

Practice Thinking 12.4: WHAT DO YOU THINK NOW?
Please explain how you know.

1. How much would knowing that a politician was superstitious affect your vote? Why? _____

   _____

2. Do you have a lucky shirt or some other object that brings you luck? How does something become "lucky"? _____

   _____

3. When things are going right, are you careful of what you do next so you do not tempt fate or push your luck? _____

   _____

4. Is science education reducing belief in superstition, magic, and supernatural events? _____

   _____

5. Should we try to eliminate superstition and magical thinking? Why or why not? _____

   _____

REVIEW QUESTIONS

1. What is superstition?
2. Describe some similarities and differences between superstition, pseudo-science, and psychological misconceptions.
3. How is one person's belief another person's superstition? How does this relate to arguing from a scientific perspective that some idea or practice is superstitious?

4. What is magical thinking? Which forms does it take?

   - What is the law of similarity? How is it related to the representativeness heuristic?

   - What is the law of contagion? How is it related to feelings of contamination?

5. How are superstitions acquired? Are they acquired in nonhumans the same way?

6. Explain how thinking errors can play a role in people acquiring and maintaining superstitions.

7. Which factors influence superstition?

   - What role does knowledge of probability play (e.g., estimating coincidences)?

   - How are tension, stress, and feelings of control related to superstitious rituals?

8. What is apparent mental causation?

9. What does research on "tempting fate" show?

10. Explain how magical thinking and superstitious behaviors might serve adaptive functions.

    - Explain how evolution might have contributed to the law of contagion.

    - How might the law of contagion be related to the emotion of disgust?

11. When are magical thinking and superstition dangerous?

12. What should we do when magical thinking and superstition are problematic?

13. What psychological misconceptions were discussed in this chapter?

CRITICAL THINKING IN CLINICAL REASONING AND DIAGNOSIS

LEARNING OUTCOMES

After studying this chapter, you should be able to:

1. Explain issues related to categorizing people as normal versus abnormal and as having one mental disorder versus another.

2. Evaluate the severity of psychological problems to decide whether a person has a mental disorder.

3. Use critical thinking to do a "preliminary" diagnosis of a person.

4. Recognize thinking errors in clinical diagnosis and reasoning, and understand how to deal with them.

WHAT DO YOU THINK?

Has another driver ever gotten very angry with you, perhaps cursing at you or engaging in some aggressive behavior toward you on the road? This problem, informally called *road rage,* is increasingly common. In two separate studies of Canadian drivers and U.S. drivers, approximately one-third reported that they had perpetrated road rage in the last year (Sansone & Sansone, 2010).

A personal experience of my own involved another driver jumping out of his car after we had come to a stop, screaming at me for making a driving error, and then punching me in the face. Although his anger seemed far out of proportion to the severity of the incident, I concluded that he just had a bad temper, not a mental disorder. Was my conclusion correct?

Another incident occurred one day while I was riding the subway to my part-time job as a waiter in New York City, where I was attending Columbia University. I was sitting near an elderly woman who I heard talking to someone. Generally, people do not talk much on the subway, so I looked over to see who was there—but saw only the elderly woman. She was apparently talking to a hallucination of someone. Although I knew little psychology at the time, I thought this behavior was abnormal and that she likely had a serious mental disorder. Do you think I was right?

Practice Thinking 13.1: What Do You Think?

Please explain how you know.

1. How do you know if a behavior is abnormal?

2. Why are nearly half the people in the United States diagnosed with a mental disorder at some point in their lives?

3. How should psychological assessment and diagnosis be done properly?

4. Do clinicians make the same kinds of thinking errors as people with less formal training?

5. Could a computer or statistical program diagnose mental disorders better than a trained clinician?

WHAT IS ABNORMAL BEHAVIOR?

Even with only minimal information at your disposal, you may have quickly formed opinions about the mental status of the two people in the opening vignettes, just as I did. How are we able to do this so quickly? The answer is that we use our commonsense or folk theories about abnormal behavior and the availability heuristic to judge whether behaviors are abnormal (Haslam, 2005). Recall from Chapter 11 that heuristics are cognitive shortcuts that underlie rapid

Type 1 thinking. If a behavior seems unfamiliar (unavailable), then we may judge it to be abnormal. But judging whether a person has a mental disorder is not so easy. Making the correct judgment requires careful, deliberate thinking based on a larger, more representative sample of a person's behavior, rather than simple snapshots of behavior as provided in the chapter-opening scenarios. Of course, judging whether a behavior is abnormal also depends on which norms (criteria) you use to judge. Are people's informal judgments of abnormal behavior based on the same norms as those used by professional clinicians?

This question would be easier to answer if experts agreed on how to distinguish normal from abnormal behavior—but they do not (Bartlett, 2011; McNally, 2011; Smoller, 2012; Szaz, 1974). One expert view is that abnormal behavior differs from average or typical behavior, perhaps based on the folk theory view that abnormal behavior is infrequent. Other experts have argued that using conformance with what is commonly considered to be "normal" as a standard is setting the bar too low (Bartlett, 2011). "Normal" people lie, start fights, bully others, overeat while others starve, and generally do not reach their full potential as human beings. Still others point out that what is considered "normal" is defined differently in different cultures (Smoller, 2012). In China, men sometimes seek help for a condition known as *koro*, or "shrinking penis," which involves panic and the impression that the penis is shrinking into the abdomen. *Koro* has been recognized in Chinese traditional medicine for centuries but not in the West.

Despite disagreements about how to define abnormal behavior, clinicians generally consider this standard to be important in deciding whether a person suffers from a mental disorder. Table 13.1 contains preliminary questions to help determine the severity of a problem and the possible presence of a mental

---

TABLE 13.1 Preliminary Questions to Help Decide Whether a Serious Psychological Problem Exists

Is the person's behavior

1. **Maladaptive?** Does the person's behavior bother other people, interfere with his or her functioning, or get in the way of his or her effectiveness in adaptively responding to stimuli in the environment?

2. **Abnormal?** Is the behavior very unusual, excessive, and of long duration in ways that cannot be attributed to the context in which it appears?

3. **Distressing?** Does the person find his or her behavior bothersome, making life unpleasant or troubled?

disorder. If the answer to each question is "yes," then the troubled individual is more likely to have a psychological problem warranting a diagnosis.

To help you remember the main word in each of the three questions (maladaptive, abnormal, and distressing), think of the first letter of each— *m, a, d*—to form the word *mad,* an outdated term that is still sometimes used to describe someone with a mental disorder. When you think of the word *mad,* you can decode it into the first three letters of each main word.

Applying Table 13.1 to the case of the elderly woman on the subway, her behavior seems abnormal because hallucinations are very unusual. However, if we knew her hallucination was of a loved one who had recently died, we would be less likely to consider her behavior abnormal or a sign of a mental disorder. Without knowing the frequency or length of her episodes of abnormal behavior, we cannot determine whether she has a mental disorder. We need more information about the context in which the behavior occurs if we are to interpret it correctly. For instance, when I get angry, I sometimes yell an angry epithet at no one in particular. An outside observer might interpret this behavior as my yelling at another person who is not there, but I am not hallucinating. Taking into account the context in which I am displaying anger, the fact that I do not often have these outbursts, and the knowledge that such outbursts in people are not unusual, it appears that my behavior is probably not a symptom of a mental disorder, even though it may seem somewhat maladaptive.

The answers to the questions in Table 13.1 can suggest that someone has a severe problem, but they do not help much to distinguish ordinary emotional reactions from a specific mental disorder. For example, what distinguishes major depression, a psychological disorder, from sadness, a normal emotion? A young college student might quite reasonably become sad and troubled sometimes, feeling challenged by his schoolwork, disappointed by a poor exam grade, and anxious about whether he can succeed. Many of us have felt this kind of disappointment at one time or another, and it probably should not be diagnosed as major depression.

Deciding that a person has a particular mental disorder and not some lesser problem involves a formal procedure called *diagnosis,* in which the clinician classifies a client as belonging to one diagnostic category or another. The idea of diagnosing mental disorders parallels the notion of medically diagnosing physical problems; as with medical diagnosis, correct diagnosis of a mental disorder is expected to lead to more effective treatment for it.

Clinicians frequently use the *Diagnostic and Statistical Manual of Mental Disorders—Fifth Edition* (*DSM-5*), published by the American Psychiatric

Association (APA, 2013), to help them diagnose mental disorders in their clients. The *DSM-5* is a classification system that associates certain important signs and symptoms with specific disorders. The signs and symptoms that tend to go together are expressed as criteria that must be met for a diagnosis to be made. These "collections of symptoms that tend to occur together and that appear to have a characteristic course and outcome" are called syndromes (Black & Andreasen, 2011, p. 4). Table 13.2 lists questions that refer to signs and symptoms indicating major depression based on criteria from the *DSM-5*.

TABLE 13.2	Questions to Help Diagnose Major Depression Based on the *DSM-5* Criteria

Does the person

1. Show depressed mood much of the day, on most days (for at least two weeks)?
2. Show diminished interest in pleasurable activities?
3. Show significant weight loss, not due to dieting?
4. Experience sleep disturbances (a lack of or too much sleep)?
5. Show agitation, restlessness, or slowing?
6. Show signs of fatigue or loss of energy almost every day?
7. Report feelings of worthlessness?
8. Show signs of problems in concentrating or being indecisive?
9. Have recurrent thoughts of death, suicide, or has he or she even attempted suicide?

The questions in Table 13.2 show how the diagnostic category of major depression is associated with symptoms in the *DSM-5*. When a person exhibits the specified number of symptoms (corresponding to meeting the criteria for diagnosing the disorder), then that person may be formally diagnosed with the mental disorder. For a diagnosis of major depression, for example, a person must meet either the first criterion (showing depression much of the day and on most days) or the second criterion (showing disinterest or a lack of pleasure in activities). Once either criterion 1 or 2 is satisfied, the individual must also meet four other criteria from the list to receive a diagnosis of major depression.

Further complicating the diagnosis of major depression is the fact that it is just one of several mood-related disorders in which depression occurs. For instance, depressed mood is also experienced by people with postpartum depression, dysthymic disorder, and bipolar disorder. Bipolar disorder, formerly called manic-depressive disorder, is now included in a class of disorders defined separately from depressive disorders. In bipolar disorder, depressed mood often alternates with periods of mania in which a person often shows high energy, inflated self-esteem, a flight of ideas, talkativeness, and excessive involvement in activities that can bring both pleasure and negative consequences (Black & Andreasen, 2011).

Making a *DSM-5* diagnosis of major depression or another disorder indicates the individual is categorically different from someone who is simply sad or in a temporarily depressed mood. This is a difference in kind (i.e., clinically depressed versus not depressed). But is a person who is diagnosed with a mental disorder such as depression really categorically different from someone who does not meet the criteria for it? Is a very sad or mildly depressed person categorically different from someone who is diagnosed with major depression, but of a mild variety?

Some psychologists say no, maintaining that depression should be viewed as a continuum (McNally, 2011). As shown in Figure 13.1, continuous differences

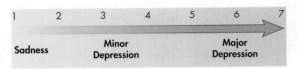

FIGURE 13.1 Depression may be viewed as existing on a continuum; notice the quantitative scale above the continuum.

vary in degree, with no sharp boundary between one thing and another. People simply fall at different points along the same dimension, with differences in depression being quantitative (i.e., differing in amount or degree). Figure 13.1 illustrates how, from a continuous perspective, an individual with major depression is just more depressed than someone who has minor depression, with no sharp distinction between the two.

One way to quantify the differences would be to say that the more symptoms of depression someone shows, the more depressed he or she is. Supporting this continuous view is the fact that the more symptoms of depression a person has, the more likely that person is to take medications for depression, seek professional help, and report that those symptoms interfere with daily life (McNally, 2011). Reporting even just one symptom is associated with greater impairment than is showing no symptoms (Kessler, Zhao, Blazer, & Swartz, 1997).

The continuous approach could be applied to other mental disorders as well, such as social anxiety disorder. An individual at the low end of the continuum might feel a little shy around other people, whereas at the high end a person would be diagnosed as having social anxiety disorder. Thus, the two cases differ in the degree of anxiety each individual exhibits when around other people.

How depression is conceived and diagnosed is important because this disorder affects so many people. Indeed, depression has been called the "common cold of mental problems." Reviewing research on its occurrence, Horwitz and Wakefield (2007) estimated that major depression afflicts approximately 10% of the U.S. population within a given year and nearly one-fifth of the population during their lifetime. From 1987 to 1997, the number of people treated for depression in U.S. outpatient settings increased by a whopping 300%. Spending on antidepressant drugs soared 600% in the 1990s alone, and overall spending on depression was more than $40 billion (Horwitz & Wakefield, 2007). The World Health Organization (2008) has estimated that by 2030 the amount of loss of life and disability that can be attributed to depression will exceed that of any other single condition, including heart disease, stroke, cancer, wars, and accidents. But why are there so many cases of depression?

CRITICISMS OF THE *DSM'S* APPROACH TO DIAGNOSING MENTAL DISORDERS

Could the *DSM* itself be contributing to the increase in the number of diagnosed cases of depression and other disorders? If so, how? Every 12 to 15 years, experts in the fields of psychiatry and psychology revise the *DSM* based largely on clinical experience and consensus of opinion—and less on research (Davies, 2013). This has resulted in the addition of many new disorders. The first edition of the *DSM*, published in 1954, ran only 126 pages with 106 disorders. By 1994, the *DSM-IV* had grown to 886 pages and 365 disorders—one for every day of the year, critics pointed out (APA, 2000; McNally, 2011). The *DSM-5* has 947 pages and approximately the same number of disorders as the *DSM-IV*, but now they can be classified by severity. This increase has made it possible to diagnose many new disorders not previously recognized.

Some critics say that the large number of people diagnosed with a mental disorder is due to the *DSM* recognizing such a large number of disorders, which allows people to fit into more categories (Davies, 2013). Although the *DSM-5* has slightly fewer diagnostic categories than the *DSM-IV*, critics have argued that the *DSM-5* has looser criteria for diagnosing some disorders, making it easier to diagnose someone incorrectly (Frances, 2013). Could the *DSM* be "pathologizing" everyday life, making normal people appear to be disordered?

An alternative interpretation is that the *DSM* is becoming a more sensitive tool that is better able to detect when people have mental disorders. Perhaps, just as medical research has identified many new physical disorders and diseases over the years, more mental disorders have actually been discovered. Just as we are not surprised when someone develops a physical disease, then maybe we should not be surprised when someone develops a mental disorder. Comparing depression to the common cold may be a more apt analogy than we thought.

The tremendous increase in autism diagnoses in recent years serves as an instructive, real-world example of the controversy surrounding diagnosis of mental disorders with the *DSM*. Perhaps the *DSM* is leading to better diagnosis of autism and it truly is on the rise, and the increase is due to some unrecognized, environmental cause. One group has vehemently insisted that the increase is due to the side effects of children receiving vaccines that contain thimerosal, a mercury compound that preserves the vaccine but becomes toxic when it accumulates after multiple vaccinations. This view initially gained support as the result of a deliberately misleading study of a few cases of autistic children in the United Kingdom (Wakefield et al., 1998). Since then, careful studies of the incidence of autism in the population in relation to the number of inoculations given have refuted this claim and the article has been retracted (Offit, 2008).

A more plausible explanation is that the *method* of diagnosis itself has resulted in the increase in the population considered to have autism. In 1994, the newly published *DSM-IV* extended the category of autism to fit in a *spectrum* of related disorders, including a newly defined disorder called Asperger's syndrome. People with Asperger's syndrome engage in repetitive behaviors and have problems with social interactions, much like autistic people; *unlike* severely autistic individuals, however, persons with Asperger's syndrome do not tend to have problems with language delay and may even have above-average intelligence. Indeed, widening the range of what could be considered autism has led to a marked increase in diagnoses of this disorder (King & Bearman, 2009). It is therefore likely that the belief that autism is occurring at epidemic proportions is a psychological misconception.

Perhaps mental disorders are being overdiagnosed. David Rosenhan (1973) published an influential study in the journal *Science* describing how he and four other mental health professionals without mental health problems presented themselves for admission at 12 different psychiatric hospitals. All initially reported they heard voices that said "thud," "empty," and "hollow," but offered no other symptoms. All five of them were admitted, and most were diagnosed with schizophrenia, a serious mental disorder that often entails auditory hallucinations. Although none of them displayed symptoms after being admitted and all claimed to have recovered, they were compelled to agree that they did indeed suffer from a mental disorder, were made to take antipsychotic drugs, and were kept in the hospitals for an average of 19 days.

As Rosenhan's study illustrates, overdiagnosis of mental disorders can have serious consequences, such as the unnecessary use of powerful mind-altering drugs, wasted time and money, and the stigma of being labeled with a psychiatric illness. All too often, people place negative labels on individuals who have been diagnosed with a mental disorder. A common misconception is that mentally ill individuals tend to be more aggressive and dangerous than "normal" people. In fact, research shows that they are generally no more prone to such problems than are undiagnosed people (Hodgins et al., 1996; Steadman, Monahan, Pinals, Vesselinov, & Robbins, 2015).

The stigma of mental illness can lead to personal doubt and discomfort as well (Corrigan & Kleinlein, 2005). Yet, it is a misconception to think that diagnostic labels are always bad. Some people like knowing what their problem is, that it has a name. Properly labeling an individual's problem may even elicit more support from other people (Wood & Valdez-Menchaca, 1996). In fact, clients who have received diagnostic labels for their mental disorders may attribute a number of the positive characteristics they exhibit—such as their creativity, insightfulness, and uniqueness—to their disorder. These positive reactions have been shown to increase after treatment (Forgeard et al., 2016).

THINKING CRITICALLY ABOUT PSYCHOLOGICAL PROBLEMS

Correctly diagnosing psychological problems requires critical thinking (CT) because clinicians must analyze and evaluate many different kinds of information from their clients. Moreover, clinicians get only a glimpse of the sample of behavior that their clients want to show them. Figuring out a person's problem is very much like putting together a 1,000-piece puzzle—but with many of the pieces missing (Dumont, 1993). Also, although the puzzle pieces may fit together neatly, the pieces of information about a person often do not—nor do they always fit neatly within the *DSM* categories.

When formulating a diagnosis, a clinician should engage in CT the same way a scientist tests a hypothesis. First, they should collect high-quality data and then carefully evaluate it to decide whether a client has one psychological disorder versus another (Snyder & Thomsen, 1988). Just as the experimental psychologist tries to find the cause of some observed behavior, so the clinician tries to eliminate alternative explanations and determine the best explanation for a client's behavior. In reality, the clinician's task is even more challenging than the experimenter's task because the experimenter can study behavior under controlled conditions.

Once a diagnosis is made, we need to think appropriately about what it means, avoiding thinking errors and misconceptions. Recall that a diagnosis is made by applying the best-fitting label for an individual's set of symptoms and behaviors. It is based on finding a syndrome or cluster of symptoms that are associated with a specific disorder. When they fail to understand that a diagnosis is simply a label for a set of symptoms, people may assume that a clinician has identified a "real" or concrete thing when making a diagnosis. For instance, they may speak of "my depression" or her "anxiety disorder" as if the disorder is a real entity that exists in the natural world, the way physical objects like arms and legs exist. Assuming that a hypothetical construct, such as a mental disorder, is a real or concrete entity rather than simply an abstract idea is a thinking error called reification. Diagnosing major depression as meeting five of nine criteria listed under that particular *DSM* category simply gives that person's behavior an operational definition—a way to define the hypothetical construct of depression in measurable, observable terms (as discussed in Chapter 4). It does not mean we have identified a concrete condition in the brain or mind.

The idea that specific mental disorders are real entities that exist in nature is easily refuted by the removal of some diagnostic labels for disorders from the *DSM* (Bartlett, 2011). The most famous example is the removal of homosexuality as a disorder when the *DSM-III* was published. Homosexuality is now considered by some to be a lifestyle choice, by others to be a biologically based predisposition, and by still others to be a bad moral choice. In any case, it is no longer considered a mental disorder.

How was it determined that homosexuality should be removed from the *DSM*? The *DSM-III* task force voted to remove it, just as they vote to add new disorders. Critics of the *DSM* have complained that such decisions are made mostly via an APA task force's consensus or occasional vote rather than being based on scientific evidence.

Indeed, in an interview, *DSM* task force member Renee Garfinkle reported that one time when the group was discussing how to specify a disorder for inclusion in the *DSM*, a member objected, "Oh no, no, we can't include that behavior as a symptom because I do that" (Davies, 2013, p. 22). The task force then decided not to include the symptom, apparently based on the objection of one member who was presumed to be normal. These examples make mental disorders seem to be less the result of scientific discoveries of real entities in the brain or mind and more the creation of labels by APA task force members to refer to hypothetical constructs. Still, despite all its problems, the *DSM* can be a useful tool; but all who use it should be aware of its limitations.

A second type of thinking error is mistakenly inferring causation from a diagnosis. Although making a sound diagnosis can help us understand a client's problem, it is not the same as identifying the cause of the problem (Gambrill, 2010; Oltmanns & Klonsky, 2007). Recall that a *DSM* diagnosis involves applying a descriptive diagnostic label to a set of symptoms; it does not identify the underlying cause of the problem that led to the symptoms. For example, concluding that a diagnosis of major depression indicates that depression is *causing* an individual's profound sadness or interpersonal difficulties is to mistakenly infer causation from a set of symptoms that are simply correlated in the individual. The more likely *cause* of the depressive symptoms is a problem with the mood regulation system in a person's brain in relation to environmental conditions.

The hope is that future research will identify the neural and psychological mechanisms that actually cause symptoms of depression and other disorders—but the diagnosis of depression does not pinpoint these mechanisms. Even so, *DSM* diagnosis is useful in helping to specify a person's problem, simplify its description, and point scientists in a direction to search for actual causes.

Practice Thinking 13.2: Thinking Critically About Psychological Disorders

1. Which view of psychological disorders do you think is best—a categorical view or a continuous view? Explain your position by citing the advantages and disadvantages of each approach.

2. Horrific, high-profile murder cases appear fairly frequently in the media and vividly portray multiple homicides by people with severe psychological problems. Examples include Andrea Yates, who murdered her children; Cho Seung-Hui, who killed 32 students at Virginia Tech; and James Holms, who killed 12 people in an Aurora, Colorado, movie theater. A review of studies showed that in approximately 75% of movies that depicted a violent character, that character had a serious mental illness (Lilienfeld, Lynn, Ruscio, & Beyerstein, 2010). Why might coverage in the media and application of one or more of the heuristics discussed in Chapter 11 contribute to the psychological misconception that people with mental disorders are more likely to commit violent crimes than people without such disorders? Explain your answer.

WHAT IS CLINICAL ASSESSMENT?

To understand a client's problem and make a sound diagnosis, a clinician must gather and interpret information from many sources in a process called **clinical assessment**. For instance, clinicians use self-reports of clients' symptoms, behavioral observations, paper-and-pencil psychological inventories or surveys, psychological interviews, client histories, and sometimes information from brain scans. Assessment results can help support a possible diagnosis and perhaps eliminate other possibilities. Clinical assessment also has many other uses besides diagnosis, such as deciding which therapy may be most effective, tracking the progress of therapy, and providing feedback to clients.

A standard part of clinical assessment is the clinical interview, wherein the clinician directs the questioning to gather certain information from the client. Important initial goals of the interview are to make the client feel comfortable; to identify the chief complaint while gathering background information on the history of the problem and any previous treatment; and to collect information on the client's family, social, and general medical history (Black & Andreasen, 2011).

To develop a general impression of the client's overall mental abilities and functioning, the clinician conducts a **mental status examination**—a comprehensive evaluation of the person's appearance, attitude, mood, motor activity, and cognition. The cognitive component of the mental status examination involves evaluation of the client's attention, perception, memory, knowledge, judgment, and basic abilities to visualize, calculate, read, write, and think abstractly.

Using information from the mental status examination and keeping in mind the initial complaint of the client, the clinician begins to develop hypotheses about the client's problem to guide the search for more specific information. Sometimes this process involves asking follow-up questions that can help determine whether information provided earlier and newly acquired information are consistent with a hypothesized diagnosis or specific *DSM* criterion. For example, if the client says she has been sad a lot lately, the clinician may follow up by asking how long she has felt that way, to see if she meets the *DSM*'s "major depression" criterion of being in a depressed mood for at least two weeks.

From the start, clinicians need to remain open to alternative hypotheses about a client's troubles, because clinicians have been observed to form a preliminary hypothesis or diagnosis too quickly (Garb, 1998). Indeed, even trained clinicians are susceptible to confirmation bias. Like a good scientist, the clinician should seek to disconfirm both the preliminary and alternative hypotheses. It is easy to ask interview questions about a preliminary diagnosis and obtain evidence to support it if one does not also gather evidence about other hypotheses that might favor them instead of the initial diagnosis.

To supplement information gleaned from the interview and to explore different hypotheses, the clinician should administer psychological tests. For instance, an instrument such as the second revision of the Minnesota Multiphasic Personality Inventory (MMPI-2) can be used to screen for specific disorders and to provide information about personality. To help test hypotheses about specific disorders, the clinician may follow up with measures designed to identify certain kinds of disorders. For example, the Beck Depression Inventory can help diagnose major depression.

According to the American Psychological Association's ethical guidelines, clinicians have a responsibility to use tests and inventories that demonstrate *reliability* and *validity.* **Reliability** refers to the consistency in the measurement of scores on a test. A test that is reliable should reveal similar scores when people take the test multiple times. Likewise, if two different people are scoring the same person on a particular measure, they should assign similar scores. In addition, if two different clinicians are reliably diagnosing the same person, they should give the same diagnosis.

In contrast, the **validity** of a test concerns whether a test or measure is actually measuring what it was intended to measure. For instance, a valid test of depression like the Beck Depression Inventory should predict things like whether admission to a mental health facility for depression is necessary and should be positively correlated with other established measures of depression.

Decisions about which assessment procedure to use may also depend on the clinician's training and theoretical perspective. On the one hand, a behavior therapist is likely to use observation of a client's problem behaviors. On the other hand, a psychoanalyst would be much more likely to use a projective technique, such as the Rorschach Inkblot Test (Figure 13.2).

The Rorschach test is based on the assumption that the client's interpretation of these ambiguous figures will reveal unconscious conflicts that should be resolved in therapy. But how good is this test? The effectiveness of the Rorschach test and its more recent interpretive method, the comprehensive system developed by Exner (1974), have not been well supported as tools for assessment (Wood, Nezworski, Lilienfeld, & Garb, 2003). Even so, the Rorschach test remains popular among clinicians due to the amazing ability of some experts to use just a few responses to the inkblots to accurately describe clients' personalities and psychological problems. It is likely that the experts' apparent accuracy depends on their ability to provide plausible, general descriptions of the people who

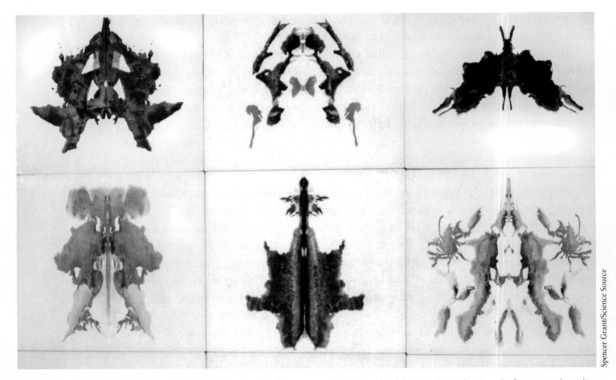

Spencer Grant/Science Source

FIGURE 13.2 A client's interpretation of an inkblot drawing (like the ones used in the Rorschach test) is assumed to reveal information about that client's personality, underlying motives, and disorder.

take this test (Wittenborn & Sarason, 1949). Yet these same experts are unable to make specific predictions about the individuals whose responses they have interpreted, suggesting that the Rorschach test lacks validity.

Further challenging the validity of the Rorschach test are studies reviewed by Wood and colleagues (2003), which showed that scores on self-report inventories thought to identify certain disorders were not related to interpretations of Rorschach responses. Other research has found that different clinicians offer markedly different interpretations of the same clients' responses to the inkblots, suggesting that the Rorschach test is subjective and not reliable. Taken together, these findings suggest that the notion that the Rorshach test can accurately tell us a great deal about an individual's personality is a misconception.

Clinicians' use of general descriptions of people in interpreting Rorschach drawings is akin to the "Barnum effect," in which people accept very general statements in their horoscopes as accurate descriptions of themselves.

Kadushin (1963) called them "Aunt Fanny descriptions"—that is, statements written so broadly that they could be true of anyone's "Aunt Fanny." In a demonstration of how little diagnostic information such case descriptions provide, Forer (1949) asked students to complete a psychological test he dubbed the "Forer Diagnostic Interest Blank." He told them that based on their test results, he would give each student an individualized diagnostic description.

In reality, each student received the exact same diagnostic description, which included general statements such as "You have a tendency to be critical of yourself" and "At times you are extroverted, affable, and sociable, while at other times you are introverted, wary, and insecure inside" (Forer, 1949, pp. 120–123). Even though they were given the same description, the students rated Forer's general assessments as very revealing of their basic personality characteristics.

Kadushin (1963) obtained similar results when he gave 60 supervisors of social work students the same diagnostic case summary. Three groups of 20 supervisors were issued the same summary for three distinct social work cases—yet the supervisors rated the quality of the diagnostic summary as equally descriptive of the three different cases. This result suggests that general case descriptions provide very little useful information for diagnosing people (Meehl, 1973). The practical implication is that clinicians who do not ask relevant, specific questions in a clinical interview will not learn the particular signs and symptoms they need to make a specific diagnosis.

MAKING A DIAGNOSIS BASED ON THE *DSM*

The *DSM-5* lists many basic groupings of mental disorders besides bipolar and depressive disorders, including anxiety disorders, obsessive–compulsive disorders, trauma- or stress-related disorders, dissociative disorders, disruptive impulse control/conduct disorders, and personality disorders. Our purpose here is not to learn about the specifics of these diagnostic categories, but rather to focus on the CT involved in formulating well-reasoned diagnoses while making sure to avoid thinking errors.

For example, a good diagnosis might show that schizophrenia is a better fit with the client's symptoms than brief psychotic disorder, major depression, or other plausible alternative diagnoses. To make this determination, the clinician would formulate a **differential diagnosis**, in which the client's signs, symptoms, and behaviors are shown to best fit the criteria for diagnosing one specific disorder (schizophrenia, in this case), while ruling out other possible disorders with criteria that do not fit as well the signs, symptoms, and behaviors observed in the client. This process requires clinicians to consider more categories of disorders than we can examine here, however.

We have already seen that the signs and symptoms of major depression might potentially be attributed to other depressive disorders. Likewise, the *DSM-5* groups other, similar disorders that share signs and symptoms. For instance, schizophrenia, a serious mental disorder, is listed under the heading "schizophrenia spectrum and other psychotic disorders"; this grouping also includes brief psychotic disorder, schizophreniform disorder, schizoaffective disorder, and substance/medication-induced psychotic disorder. Table 13.3 lists a set of questions for diagnosing schizophrenia, based on the *DSM-5* criteria.

TABLE 13.3 Questions to Help Diagnose Schizophrenia Based on *DSM-5* Criteria

Does the person

1. Show signs of psychosis and disorganized thinking, including delusions, hallucinations, disorganized/incoherent speech, disorganized or catatonic behavior, diminished emotional expression, or other negative symptom? (In the past month, the person must show at least two of these signs, of which one must be delusions, hallucinations, or disorganized speech.)

2. Show a marked disturbance in functioning in interpersonal relations, work, or self-care?

3. Show continual signs of disturbance for at least six months?

4. Show little indication of depression or mania, while the previously mentioned symptoms are active?

5. Have a history of communication disorders, such as autism with onset in childhood?

Notice that the first fundamental question in Table 13.3 asks whether the person is showing signs of psychosis. **Psychosis** refers to a serious thought disturbance, suggesting disconnection from the conventional experience of reality. It typically manifests in the form of hallucinations and delusions. The *hallucinations* experienced by people with schizophrenia often involve hearing voices that are not there. *Delusions* are fixed, false beliefs that are readily contradicted, such as the false belief that one is being observed, followed, or persecuted by some malevolent entity. All the disorders within the schizophrenia spectrum and psychotic disorders group list psychotic features as a main criterion for diagnosis. Notice also that criteria 4 and 5 in Table 13.3 help rule out depressive and communication disorders, respectively.

Sometimes, a client fits the criteria for more than one disorder, making it difficult for a clinician to rule out one disorder or the other, and suggesting that diagnosis of more than one disorder is indicated—a situation called **comorbidity**. For example, the most common secondary diagnosis to major depression is substance abuse disorder. Schizophrenia and depression often occur together as well (Buckley, Miller, Lehrer, & Castle, 2009). The *DSM-5* contains comorbidity information for most disorders (APA, 2013).

To further appreciate the complexity of diagnosis and to illustrate the two major diagnostic categories listed in Tables 13.2 and 13.3, let's examine an actual case of depression complicated by other symptoms. Andrea Yates (Figure 13.3) is notorious for having murdered all five of her children in 2001. Yates had previously attempted suicide more than once and was repeatedly hospitalized for depression beginning in 1999 (O'Malley, 2004). She was diagnosed with major depression with severe psychotic features that same year, ruling out schizophrenia. Following the birth of her fifth child at the end of November 2000 and the death of her father soon thereafter, she was hospitalized again and diagnosed with postpartum depression and recurrent major depression at the end of March 2001.

In April 2001, Yates's new psychiatrist, Mohammad Saeed, diagnosed her with major depression with psychotic features. The next month, Yates was hospitalized again, diagnosed with severe postpartum depression, and given Haldol, a drug to relieve her psychotic symptoms. In June 2001, Saeed ordered that she discontinue Haldol and did not prescribe any other antipsychotic drug as a replacement, but he kept her on Remeron, an antidepressant. On June 20, 2001, Yates drowned all five of her children, one by one, in the bathtub of her Houston, Texas, home.

Yates was charged with first-degree murder, and her defense team decided to plead "not guilty by reason of insanity." In Texas, as in many other states, a person is considered not guilty by reason of insanity if that person can demonstrate he or she did not know the difference between right and wrong at the time of the crime. Appointed as an expert witness for the defense, forensic psychiatrist Dr. Phillip Resnick interviewed Yates in jail three weeks after the murders.

FIGURE 13.3 Andrea Yates murdered her five children by drowning them in the family bathtub. She suffered for several years with various forms of depression. Later, she showed clear signs of psychosis. Her insanity defense failed in her original trial, and she was convicted of first-degree murder.

During the interview, Yates said she believed that Satan was inside of her and that she heard him tell her in a growling voice to kill her son Noah (O'Malley, 2004). She believed she was failing as a mother, that her children were not developing the way they should be in an academic and righteous sense, and that "maybe in their innocent years God would take them up." In other words, Yates believed that she could save her children from hell by killing them before they strayed further from the righteous path and that God would allow them into heaven (O'Malley, 2004, p. 152). She also believed that after killing her children, she would be executed and then Satan would die with her.

The expert psychiatrists consulting on her trial agreed that Yates had suffered a psychotic episode, but they disagreed about her specific diagnosis. Although psychosis is often associated with schizophrenia, it is also present in approximately 20% of depression cases. Lucy Puryear, another witness for the defense, thought Yates suffered from schizophrenia, while Resnick thought she had schizoaffective disorder, a mental disorder included in the same category as schizophrenia, in which the individual suffers from severe depression or mania at the same time as psychosis. Yet Yates's psychiatrist had taken her off of antipsychotics and prescribed Remeron, a powerful antidepressant, two weeks before the murders.

Another view was that Yates had bipolar disorder. Although sometimes she was catatonic, hardly speaking or moving at all, at other times she showed great surges of energy as compared to her depressed state. According to psychiatrist Deborah Sichel, Yates's competitive swimming in high school might be one example of her behavior while in a manic state—her husband said Yates once even swam around an entire island (O'Malley, 2004). If she had been misdiagnosed and still had psychosis with bipolar disorder, then discontinuing her antipsychotic medication could have led to greater disconnection from reality, and prescribing Remeron could have pushed her into a manic phase.

Despite her recurring episodes of mental disorder and hospitalizations, her suicide attempts, and the evidence of psychosis, the insanity defense failed and Yates was sent to prison. Contrary to the popular misconception that the insanity defense often succeeds, it prevails in only 15% of all cases in which this defense is mounted (Lilienfeld et al., 2010). Moreover, those who are acquitted based on this defense often spend more time in a mental institution than those who are sent to prison for their crimes (Silver, Cirincione, & Steadman, 1994).

In prison, Yates showed improvement on lithium, a drug that is effective in treating patients with schizoaffective disorder and bipolar disorder. On this basis, Puryear reconsidered her earlier diagnosis of schizophrenia and concluded that schizoaffective disorder was actually a better diagnosis. Another plausible alternative is that Yates showed comorbidity, having a dual diagnosis of schizophrenia and major depression. The difficulties in differentially diagnosing Yates may reveal underlying problems in distinguishing between these disorders. It may be that major depression, schizoaffective disorder, and bipolar disorder are related conditions showing similar patterns of dysfunction in the same underlying system.

The Andrea Yates case also raises questions about the legal plea of "not guilty by reason of insanity." In her first trial, prosecutors successfully argued that in her own statements, Yates confirmed that she knew killing her children was wrong. But recall that Yates said Satan had commanded her to kill her children. Although she knew this action was wrong, she thought she was doing the right thing by killing them so they would go to heaven. In essence, her moral judgment seems to have been compromised by her psychotic delusion. Regardless of disagreements about her diagnosis, experts agreed that Yates had a severe mental disorder involving psychosis and the inability to make good judgments based on a sense of conventional reality. When she was retried on an appeal, her insanity defense was successful and she was committed to a Texas mental institution.

 ## Practice Thinking 13.3: Identifying and Diagnosing Cases

To analyze the two hypothetical cases that follow, first use the questions from Table 13.1 to decide whether the person described has a psychological problem. Then, if a mental disorder is indicated, use the questions in Tables 13.2 and 13.3, along with other information in the book, to make a preliminary diagnosis. Rule out other possibilities as much as you reasonably can. What other information is needed to make a decision?

Case 1: "The Walls Have Earrings"

Matt, a 19-year-old English major, was referred to the college counseling center by one of his composition professors, who noticed some disturbing changes in his behavior. Matt had turned in a very unusual writing assignment, which prompted a very strange conversation with the professor after class. Matt refused to see the counselor at first, but then relented. With Matt's permission, the professor contacted the clinic after Matt had scheduled an appointment, and reported that Matt had good attendance at the beginning of the semester but attended only occasionally in the last two months.

In Matt's first clinical interview, he reported no recent changes in his physical health, nor did his psychiatrist find any unusual physical symptoms after checking Matt's health records and doing a medical screening. Matt did mention, however, that sometimes swarms of ideas would fly through his mind. He considered this a good thing because those inspirational ideas often provided material for his creative writing and poetry. Lately, though, the ideas had become more intense and distracted him so much that sometimes he could not write.

Spending more and more time by himself, supposedly focused on his creative writing, Matt frequently failed to turn in his class assignments. He said it was to help him focus on his creative writing. In fact, while he did spend much time sitting by himself, apparently absorbed in the creative process, he had difficulty concentrating on everyday matters. His recent trouble connecting with other people, including his ex-girlfriend Sara, was a major reason why she and Matt had broken up.

In addition, the words Matt used in his poems began to change. Matt claimed that he was seeking new ways to express himself, yet his unusual use of language had begun to creep into his conversations with other people. For instance, in explaining a poem to his psychiatrist, Matt said, "You know, the walls have earrings." When asked what he meant by this, he answered, "Sometimes I have a ringing in my ears. If I listen carefully, I can hear people's thoughts behind the walls. One time I heard Sara's thoughts. She was plotting to get me to fail ever since she had broken up with me." Matt felt that he was becoming increasingly sensitive to signals in the environment that other people simply overlooked.

As time went on, Matt became very unresponsive—as if an emotionless mask was covering his face. For example, at one session he told his therapist that he would have to move to another room because the thoughts coming through the wall were becoming too disturbing. However, as Matt described this disturbance, he showed no negative emotion.

Case 2: "I'm Not Ready Yet"

Ryan and Cara had been dating for a couple months at the end of her junior year and his senior year in high school. They liked each other a lot, but in two months' time Ryan would be leaving to attend college several hundred miles from their hometown. As summer vacation progressed, they saw each other more and more and were becoming increasingly intimate.

Ryan wanted to have sex, but Cara was from a traditionally religious family that discouraged premarital sex. Although she did not always agree with her family's beliefs, she respected them and did not want to disappoint her parents. Cara realized this was a problem and resolved to talk to Ryan about it.

Cara explained that she trusted Ryan, but she was inexperienced and worried about getting pregnant. Having sex with Ryan would be a big step for her. Ryan started to pressure her about the issue. She understood his feelings, but was worried about doing the "right" thing. She felt torn and began to feel anxious about it. Her friends didn't think it was a problem and urged her to have sex with Ryan; "Don't worry," they said, "because everybody does it." The more Cara thought about her dilemma, the more confused she became. Her stomach felt as if it were tied in knots. She worried that if she didn't have sex with Ryan, he would leave her for someone else at college. Her fears nagged at her. Her muscles were tense.

After three days during which she had severe headaches and trouble getting to sleep, Cara finally decided to see her physician, a female general practitioner, whom she had known for several years. The physician found no organic basis for her headaches apart from muscle tension. After listening to Cara describe the conflicts she was experiencing, her physician recommended that she talk to a psychotherapist about her problems. She also told Cara that if after thinking about the issue, she wanted a prescription for birth control pills, she would write it for her.

CHALLENGES TO CLINICAL REASONING

You probably realized from analyzing the rather simple case descriptions in the last exercise that actually diagnosing real people in the real world is a much more complex task. In an actual case, an individual's behaviors and symptoms would not be so neatly summarized. The clinician would need additional information from the client, family, and friends, as well as data from administering and interpreting inventories and tests. Only then would the clinician be able to integrate all the information and compare it with the criteria for various disorders in the *DSM*.

The characteristics of the diagnosis task itself may make it difficult to master. Shanteau (1992) has identified several task characteristics that can lead to poor performance in clinical psychologists and psychiatrists. Specifically, tasks such as diagnosis are difficult because they involve judgments about behaviors and situations that are changeable, unique, fairly unpredictable, subjective, and for which feedback about performance is often not readily available. Many times, clinical experts do not even agree on which stimuli are to be evaluated. In addition, as Dumont (1991) has pointed out, the field of psychotherapy lacks a common knowledge base, accepted by experts in the field, upon which they can make good judgments. Under these conditions, it is difficult to learn and practice using cues that would lead to reliable and accurate diagnoses (Kahneman & Klein, 2009).

Disagreements about the nature of psychological disorders and the fact that clinicians seldom get prompt, reliable feedback about whether their diagnoses are correct make it difficult for them to learn from their experience. Unlike in some fields, in which it becomes clear when a problem has been identified and solved, in psychotherapy, it is often not clear what the problem is. This ambiguity also makes it difficult for clinicians to acquire expertise. Cognitive psychologists have found that becoming an expert in a field such as physics or in a well-defined task such as playing chess, a person mostly needs to engage in a great deal of the right kind of practice (Ericsson, 2006).

In contrast, research has often shown that very experienced clinicians are no better at clinical judgment tasks than are beginner-level therapists or even much less experienced students (Garb, 1998). In fact, the experience that highly educated clinicians receive may not prevent them from making some of the same thinking errors as individuals with much less training and experience. Why would experienced clinicians show many of the same thinking errors as less experienced and less educated people? Surely, this outcome does not occur because they are not smart enough, given that clinical and counseling doctoral programs are some of the most competitive graduate programs, accepting only the best students. Instead, a key factor may be the demands made by clinical reasoning, which exceed the cognitive abilities of people to perform well on very difficult tasks.

As discussed in Chapter 6, people seem to have limited capacity for holding information in memory—estimates range from about seven chunks (Miller, 1956) to only four chunks (Cowan, 2000) at a time. Importantly, research shows that people are also limited in the number of complex relations they can handle at once (Halford, Baker, McCredden, & Bain, 2005). In Chapter 11, we saw that people have bounded rationality, in that they can behave rationally within the constraints of their limited processing resources and the task requirements. In response to tasks that demand too much of their processing resources, people behave like cognitive misers, conserving their limited cognitive resources by using cognitive shortcuts called heuristics. Unfortunately, although using heuristics and Type 1 thinking can speed up processing, it can also lead to thinking errors.

THINKING ERRORS IN CLINICAL PRACTICE

The idea that clinicians are prone to certain kinds of thinking errors may run counter to our idealized conception of them as experts, but the research clearly shows that they make many of the same thinking errors as people with less training. Reviews of research on clinical judgment have documented how clinicians make errors based on representativeness, availability, and hindsight bias, just as do people with less training (Dumont, 1991; Faust, 1986; Garb, 1998; Ruscio, 2007).

The error of rapid diagnosis occurs when clinicians make a diagnosis within just a few minutes. Gauron and Dickinson (1969) found that when psychiatrists viewed a filmed interview between therapists and clients, the psychiatrists often formed diagnostic impressions in as little as 30 to 60 seconds. Given that good differential diagnoses require collection and consideration of many different kinds of client data, this tendency suggests that clinicians who make rapid diagnoses may be jumping to hasty generalizations about their clients, prematurely drawing a conclusion before carefully considering all the relevant, available information. In fact, some early studies showed that psychiatrists sometimes made diagnoses no better than their secretaries (Goldberg, 1959; 1968).

Another reason for errors in diagnosis may be that clinicians sometimes tend to engage in too much "backward reasoning" at the expense of "forward reasoning." As Dumont (1991) has noted, clinical reasoning is much like the theory building of scientists. Clinicians engage in forward reasoning when they collect information about their clients and try to find patterns in it, forming hypotheses about possible causes of the behavior. They engage in backward reasoning when they test hypotheses using theory and their knowledge to decide whether the evidence obtained is consistent with their hypotheses concerning the client's problem.

Good reasoning depends on both forward and backward reasoning. Unfortunately, when a clinician considers only one hypothesis or is overly influenced by preconceptions, this narrow perspective can lead to excessive backward reasoning and poor diagnoses. Many studies suggest that clinicians are often biased by their background knowledge and expectations. For example, Temerlin (1968) found that clinicians who were told which diagnosis an individual had previously received from high-prestige clinicians were more likely to give that same diagnosis than clinicians who were not given that information.

Stereotypes can also induce clinicians to reason backward from unwarranted assumptions they make about clients. Garb (1997) reviewed the accuracy of clinical judgments in several studies in which bias effects were replicated. He found that Hispanics and African Americans were more often misdiagnosed with schizophrenia than were Whites in those cases in which clients had psychotic affective disorders. Consistent with gender stereotypes, males tended to be diagnosed more often with antisocial personality disorder compared to females, whereas females tended to be diagnosed more often with histrionic personality disorder (i.e., excessive displays of emotion). Finally, a bias for social class was demonstrated in the tendency of clinicians to refer more middle-class people for psychotherapy than lower-class individuals.

Preconceptions about people who seek help for psychological problems may also create expectations about the severity of those problems. The fact that someone is consulting a clinician implies that the individual has a problem or at least has symptoms that need to be explained (Ruscio, 2007), which sets in motion a search for the potential causes of the individual's symptoms. If the clinician is not wary, the human tendency to find patterns in unrelated events may lead to the erroneous conclusion that the client has a disorder, when none actually exists. Clinicians sometimes find illusory correlations in client data, finding disorders that are not there (Chapman & Chapman, 1967).

In addition, hindsight bias and knowing the outcome of a client's behavior may make a client's diagnosis appear to have been inevitable. A clinician may think, "Of course, my client has a substance abuse disorder involving alcohol. He was referred to me because he was charged with driving while intoxicated after he wrapped his car around a tree." Succumbing to these thinking errors may be partly why clinicians tend to overdiagnose their clients.

The influence of stereotypes, preconceptions, and the clinician's background knowledge in general suggest that information that can be readily accessed from a clinician's memory might lead to excessive backward reasoning. Information may be more available to a clinician because she has recently treated a number of similar cases, because she has recently read an article or attended a conference that discussed a particular disorder, or because she observes a client showing symptoms that are vivid, emotionally arousing, or memorable. Returning to the preceding drunk driving example, the clinician is likely to recall the vivid information about the car being wrapped around the tree and the passenger bleeding more readily than more pallid information such as the facts that the man's IQ is 109 and he has worked at the same place for 20 years.

Clinicians' experiences with clients who have disorders may also be more memorable than abstract facts about the base rates of the disorders gathered from research, even though the base rate information may be more predictive of a disorder's occurrence. In general, clinicians rely too much on their personal experience in making judgments (Ruscio, 2007).

It may be very difficult for trained clinicians to prevent their own experiences from affecting what they observe in a client. Philosopher of science Imre Lakatos (1970) noted that all observations are theory-laden—that is, observations are made within the context of certain assumptions and preconceptions. The more highly trained clinicians are, the more susceptible they may be to interpreting observed behavior within the bounds of their training and the theoretical framework within which they operate. The training and theoretical focus of the clinician naturally make certain patterns, associations, and schemas more accessible, and these tend to constrain the interpretation of client data. In this way, greater clinical expertise may induce inherent liabilities that incline clinicians to engage in excessive backward reasoning at the expense of forward reasoning (Dumont, 1991).

A basic assumption about expertise is that through extensive, deliberate practice in thinking about specific problems, the true expert can rapidly access knowledge, patterns, and strategies that facilitate efficient solving of similar problems (Ericsson, 2006). Because the expert perceives or knows the underlying structure or relationship in the data (essentially, the valid cues that help the expert solve the problem), he or she can automatically process relevant information without paying much attention to irrelevant information. A problem occurs with clinical expertise when the clinician reasons backward from a clinical knowledge base and a particular therapeutic orientation that do not provide valid cues that can help the clinician solve a specific clinical problem. The clinician with considerable clinical experience may actually access information that is not useful for effective thinking, even though the information is accessed and applied rapidly.

This process may partly explain why many studies have now shown that experience and training are not related to the quality of diagnoses (Witteman, Wiess, & Metzmacher, 2012) or to the outcome of psychotherapy (Beutler, 1997); see Tracey, Wampold, Lichtenberg, and Goodyear, 2014, for a review). Sometimes less experienced helpers may diagnose clients even more accurately than professionals (Witteman et al., 2012) and are rated as more effective than professionals on some measures (Hattie, Sharpley, & Rogers, 1984). Unfortunately, many clinicians may be overconfident of their abilities. In a recent study, 25% of clinicians surveyed rated themselves to be at the 90th percentile compared with their peers (Walfish, McAlister, O'Donnell, & Lambert, 2012). None of the respondents judged themselves to be below average, clearly showing the better than average effect (Walfish et al., 2012).

More evidence that clinicians may be engaging in excessive backward reasoning comes from studies showing that clinicians engage in confirmation bias (Houts & Galante, 1985; Strohmer & Shivy, 1994). In one study, a group of researchers gave experienced clinicians and less experienced clinicians the same case file of a client. In one version, a neutral fact about the client was presented early in the case description, whereas the neutral fact was mentioned later in the other version of the case description (Sladeczek, Dumont, Martel, & Karagiannakis, 2006). When the fact was presented early, experienced clinicians tended to use it in a more confirmational manner than did the less experienced clinicians.

The overemphasis on backward reasoning is also evident when clinicians engage in behavioral confirmation, wherein they send their clients signals, often inadvertently, to behave in ways consistent with the clinicians' own theoretical interpretation or preconceived notion of the client's problem (Snyder & Thomsen, 1988). Suppose, for example, that a clinician asked his anxious client about the death of her friend and then asked if she was feeling depressed about it because she was frowning. The client said that she was not feeling depressed, but as she thought about her loss, she continued to feel sad and frowned even more. When the clinician later turned the interview back to her friend's death, he observed his client frowning again. He decided that her problem was not actually anxiety, but depression.

As you can see from this example, although behavioral confirmation resembles confirmation bias, in which a person looks for evidence to confirm a favored belief, behavioral confirmation goes beyond that. More than just the selective processing of evidence, behavioral confirmation actually affects the behavioral evidence that a client produces, by eliciting behaviors that fit the expected pattern.

Another problem in diagnosing mental disorders is the failure of clinicians to use *DSM* criteria appropriately. Proponents of the *DSM* have argued that improvements in its criteria over the years should help make diagnoses more reliable and more consistent from one clinician to another. Indeed, studies have shown that clinicians who do not systematically use *DSM* criteria—and perhaps instead rely on their own beliefs, personal experiences, and other knowledge—tend to formulate inaccurate diagnoses that are less reliable (Blashfield & Herkov, 1996; Morey & Ochoa, 1989). This thinking error, referred to as inappropriate use of criteria, can result from failure to use the relevant criteria, from assigning excessive weight to certain criteria, or from use of nondiagnostic criteria. In all cases, it ultimately tends to reduce the reliability of diagnoses.

If clinicians are not using *DSM* criteria appropriately, then on what basis are they making a diagnosis? Garb (1996) described a study in which clinicians were presented with a case and were asked to rate the likelihood that the client suffered from different possible disorders. The participants also rated how typical the client was compared with other clients who had each specific disorder. The likelihood and similarity ratings were highly correlated, suggesting that the clinicians were using similarity to a prototypical person having the disorder, as happens when applying the representativeness heuristic.

Another study by Kim and Ahn (2002) found that when making a diagnosis, clinicians looked more closely at symptoms that better fit their theory of the cause of a person's problem than at other symptoms. This tendency contradicts the basic approach of the *DSM*, which expects clinicians to treat each symptom or criterion as having equal weight when making a diagnosis, without consideration of any particular theory.

Table 13.4 summarizes and organizes the various clinical thinking errors discussed so far.

TABLE 13.4 **Descriptions of Clinical Thinking Errors and Recommendations for Correcting Them**

Thinking Error	Description	How to Fix It
Reification	Assuming that a hypothetical construct, such as a mental disorder, is a real, concrete entity	Realize that a mental disorder is an operationally defined and created construct.
Mistaking diagnosis for a cause	Thinking that a diagnosis is a cause of behavior or a mental problem	Realize that a diagnosis is a label for a classification.
Forer or Barnum effect	Assuming that a general description of a person is predictive and diagnostic	Use more detailed, specific information about signs, symptoms, and behaviors.
Rapid diagnosis (hasty generalization)	Quickly diagnosing a mental disorder without considering relevant criteria and all relevant signs and symptoms	Conduct a more thorough assessment and a differential diagnosis.
Excessive backward reasoning	Relying too much on preconceptions, expectations, and stereotypes to guide reasoning	Engage in more forward reasoning, paying more attention to the data.
Behavioral confirmation (self-fulfilling prophesy)	Eliciting certain behaviors from a client that confirm the clinician's expectations about the client	Remain open to other interpretations of a client's behavior and use objective measures to assess the behavior.

Practice Thinking 13.4: Identifying Errors in Reasoning About Psychological Problems

For each of the following examples, identify the thinking error involved and then explain how to deal with it.

1. Jeremy said, "I'm glad I went to a clinical psychologist about my feelings of being uncomfortable around people. She diagnosed me as having social anxiety disorder. Now that we know the cause of my feelings, she can begin to help me get better."

   Thinking error: _____

   How to fix it: _____

   _____

2. At the beginning of Dr. Johnson's interview with his new client Maria, he asked, "Have you been feeling anxious for very long?" Maria replied that she had just begun to feel anxious. Dr. Johnson continued to ask about her anxiety, which caused Maria to show more signs of anxiety, especially during her therapy sessions. Dr. Johnson became increasingly certain that his diagnosis of anxiety disorder was correct.

   Thinking error: _____

   How to fix it: _____

   _____

3. Logue, Sher, and Frensch (1992) asked college students to read a few personality profiles of people they were told were the adult children of alcoholics. The students then rated how accurately the profiles described the adult children of alcoholics. The profiles were really based on characteristics of adult children of alcoholics found in the popular literature, with general descriptive statements such as "In times of crisis, you take care of others" and "You can be counted on to take on more than your share of work." The college students rated the

profiles as being highly descriptive of the adult children of alcoholics; they also rated a set of other general statements as highly descriptive of themselves.

Thinking error: _____

How to fix it: _____

_____

4. Freud proposed that through the defense mechanism of repression, the ego pushes unpleasant, threatening experiences outside of conscious awareness. After his theory was published, some people who misunderstood Freud or believed strongly in these ideas began to speak of the ego and the unconscious as if they were actual parts of the mind.

Thinking error: _____

How to fix it: _____

_____

5. Dr. Langston was new to her clinic and was observing her older, more experienced colleagues. She told one of these experienced psychologists that she was amazed at how quickly he could diagnose a new case. He replied that within just a couple of minutes he could accurately identify the main problem. After observing him on more cases, however, Dr. Langston came to doubt the accuracy of his diagnoses and learned that his conclusions often disagreed with earlier diagnoses reported by other clinicians in the clients' case records.

Thinking error: _____

How to fix it: _____

_____

GUIDELINES FOR IMPROVING CLINICAL REASONING

It is clear that the reasoning of clinicians is subject to many of the same errors and biases found in people with less training, but what can be done to improve it? One approach, called the "rational" approach, emphasizes improving the reasoning skills of clinicians, debiasing their judgments, and eliminating their reasoning errors. Table 13.5 summarizes some guidelines for this rational approach, based partly on recommendations from Faust (2007), Gambrill (2010), Rabinowitz and Efron (1997), and Ruscio (2007).

A second approach to improving clinical reasoning emphasizes getting support for the clinician through the use of external devices such as computers, statistical equations, and tables. Given the difficulty that clinicians have in integrating the massive amount of relevant client data they obtain, we would expect that a system that could keep track of and use all the relevant information predictive of a client's behavior would do a better job. Meehl (1954) first showed that inputting relevant, predictive information into a statistical or actuarial program yielded better diagnostic judgments than did clinicians who used their usual clinical intuitions about a client.

This mechanical approach is also sometimes called the *actuarial* or *statistical* method because it assumes that clinicians can use statistical data from tables akin to the actuarial tables that insurance companies use to make predictions about

TABLE 13.5	**General Guidelines for Improving Clinical Reasoning**
1.	Collect high-quality data on clients, using reliable and valid measures and assessments.
2.	Take into account contextual, situational, and background knowledge that might affect the collection and interpretation of client data.
3.	Generate multiple hypotheses from different perspectives about a client's problem.
4.	Avoid hindsight bias, stereotypes, preconceptions, and bias from heuristics.
5.	Use relevant base rate information and probabilities to make judgments and predictions.
6.	Test hypotheses about clients' data and seek to disconfirm them.
7.	Select the hypothesis that best fits the data, weighing intuitions and personal experience less in judgments, and accurately assessing confidence in your conclusions.
8.	Seek and use reliable and valid feedback on the quality of your reasoning and judgments.

clients. Insurance companies' actuarial tables contain statistical data about diseases, accident rates, and risk factors for health problems such as smoking, poor diet, and lack of exercise, which those companies then use to compute the risk of insuring a specific client. In the case of diagnosis of mental disorders, tables with base rate data on the incidence of symptoms, specific disorders, and other risk factors that predict psychological problems, as well as data based on empirically supported relations, might be entered into equations that predict the likelihood that an individual has one disorder versus another (Faust, 2007).

The mechanical approach is contrasted with the clinical approach, the name given to the subjective and intuitive judgments that clinicians ordinarily make as they integrate information from various sources. Given that clinicians are often subject to many of the same cognitive limitations, biases, and errors as other people, we might wonder if the mechanical approach that calculates probabilities in an unbiased way and integrates relevant, predictive information more systematically would make better judgments.

In fact, a substantial body of research supports the superiority of the mechanical approach over the clinical approach. A meta-analysis of 163 studies in the areas of human health and behavior showed that the mechanical approach was, on average, approximately 10% more accurate than the clinical approach (Grove, Zald, Lebow, Snitz, & Nelson, 2000). Specifically, in 63 of the 164 studies reviewed, the mechanical approach predicted human behavior better than the clinical approach. In only 8 of the studies was the clinical–intuitive approach better.

Gaudiano, Brown, and Miller (2011) found that clinicians who scored lower on a test of CT ability also tended to endorse a more intuitive approach to decision making, magical beliefs, and alternative approaches to health and medicine. Many studies suggest that when clinicians use a commonsense, informal, or intuitive approach, they often fail to systematically assess and consider all the relevant information about clients (Garb, 1998). This process can result in excessive reliance on intuition in making clinical judgments, as well as more errors at the expense of taking a careful, systematic, scientific approach that is likely to lead to a better outcome.

Applying both the rational and the mechanical approaches to improving clinical reasoning should help. The mechanical approach has some notable advantages over simply taking a rational approach. To some extent, it tends to more automatically overcome some initial difficulties in the diagnostic process, by forcing clinicians to use base rate data and avoid base rate neglect. It also gets around the tendency to overvalue subjective impressions and give too much weight to personal experiences.

Thus, stereotyping, representativeness, and availability are not as likely to contribute to errors in prediction.

The mechanical approach also helps clinicians avoid the cognitive limitations they face in systematically integrating large amounts of data. Unfortunately, many clinicians resist using this approach because they feel it dehumanizes the process and because they wrongly assume that a statistics-based approach relies on observations of many people that have little to do with the behavior of a specific individual (Ruscio, 2006). In fact, much of the power of the mechanical approach derives from its practice of basing predictions on the responses of many people instead of just one.

SUMMARY

Before diagnosing someone with a mental disorder, a clinician should decide whether the person's behavior is maladaptive, is abnormal, and causes distress, while considering the context of the behavior. Diagnosis based on the *DSM* criteria conceives of disordered and normal individuals as categorically different, but many clinicians view these differences as continuous or varying in degree.

The diagnosis of mental disorders is difficult because the clinician must evaluate a complex variety of symptoms and behaviors based on a limited sample of a client's behavior. Like all good scientists, good clinicians make careful observations of behavior and test hypotheses about a client's problem. This process involves conducting a clinical assessment, including a clinical interview; gathering information on the client's history; making behavioral observations; administering psychological tests; and evaluating the client's mental status. Clinicians should formulate a differential diagnosis, which shows that the signs, symptoms, and behaviors of the person fit one diagnostic category while eliminating other possible diagnoses for the same set of signs, symptoms, and behaviors. It is challenging to make an accurate diagnosis when an individual shows comorbidity, wherein the symptoms seem to fit more than one diagnostic category. Other difficulties with diagnosis involve the use of assessments with low reliability and validity and the creation of case descriptions that are too general and have little diagnostic value.

People often misinterpret the meaning of a diagnosis of a mental disorder. Although a diagnosis applies a label to describe a person's condition, people assume that the diagnostic label corresponds to an actual mental disorder that exists in nature—an error called reification. Some people may also mistakenly assume that a diagnosis means that the cause of a person's problem has been identified. Moreover, clinicians may make various judgment and reasoning errors, sometimes quite similar to those made by less well-trained people, such as being overly influenced by availability of information and vivid cases.

Another problem occurs when clinicians allow their knowledge and expectations to overly influence their evaluation of case evidence, as in excessive backward reasoning and behavioral confirmation. In general, clinicians seem to have difficulty integrating all the important information presented to them. When faced with this challenge, statistical (computer) programs have been found to perform better on clinical judgment tasks than clinicians using their intuition.

Practice Thinking 13.5: WHAT DO YOU THINK **NOW**? Please explain how you know.

1. How do you know if a behavior is abnormal? _____

_____

2. Why are nearly half the people in the United States diagnosed with a mental disorder at some point in their lives? _____

_____

3. How should psychological assessment and diagnosis be done properly?

_____

4. Do clinicians make the same kinds of thinking errors as people with less formal training? _____

_____

5. Could a computer or statistical program diagnose mental disorders better than a trained clinician?_____

_____

REVIEW QUESTIONS

1. What is abnormal behavior? How should we define it?

2. Which questions are important in deciding whether a person's behavior is abnormal and in evaluating the severity of a psychological problem?

3. What is a categorical approach to mental problems and disorders?

4. What is a continuous approach to mental problems and disorders?

5. What is the *DSM*? What approach does it take?

6. What is a syndrome? How does it relate to the *DSM*?

7. Has the increase in the number of mental disorders that can be diagnosed led to greater accuracy in diagnosing disorders or to overdiagnosis of disorders?

8. Why is the task of understanding people's problems so complex?

9. How does a clinician's process of hypothesis testing resemble the process followed by a scientist?

10. Describe some potential problems in thinking about a diagnosis.
    - What is reification?
    - What is meant by mistakenly inferring causation from a diagnosis?

11. What are the advantages and disadvantages of using diagnostic labels?

12. How does a clinician assess a client's mental status properly?
    - Which problems can arise with assessment, such as the Barnum effect and projective tests?
    - What is the reliability of a test? What is the validity of a test?

13. How does one make a differential diagnosis?
    - What is comorbidity? Why is it a problem for diagnoses based on the *DSM*?

14. How do thinking errors affect diagnosis and clinical judgment?
    - Describe bias from the representativeness heuristic and stereotyping.
    - How does the availability heuristic affect diagnosis? What about overreliance on personal experience?
    - Explain the possible effects of hindsight bias and finding causes for outcomes.

- How might hasty generalization and rapid diagnosis affect clinical judgment?
- What is excessive backward reasoning?
- What is the difference between behavioral confirmation and confirmation bias?
- What is inappropriate use of criteria?

15. How can clinical judgment be improved?

- Describe the clinical (intuitive) approach versus the mechanical (statistical) approach.

16. What are psychological misconceptions discussed in this chapter?

14

LANGUAGE, WRITING, AND CRITICAL THINKING

LEARNING OUTCOMES

After studying this chapter, you should be able to:

1. Explain the relationship between language and thinking.

2. Identify propaganda and various abuses and misuses of language and related thinking errors.

3. Use the language of argumentation appropriately to make arguments in psychology.

4. Construct a good extended argument in a critical thinking essay.

WHAT DO YOU THINK?

In this chapter, we examine the connections between language and thinking and, especially, between writing and thinking. Please complete the following rating.

How often, when you have written about an idea, did it help you think more clearly about that idea?

Never   Sometimes   Always
1------------2------------3------------4------------5------------6------------7

How did you answer? When I asked instructors and students from my department this question, they reported an average rating of 5.84. I would answer with a 6. Often, when I begin writing, my thinking seems fuzzy and unfocused, shooting off in many directions. But after I write about a topic, I think more clearly, which suggests that the act of writing may help people clarify and improve their thinking. Now suppose you wrote a paper for a course assignment that your instructor did not like. Comments on the paper included "Your thinking is unclear" and "Your reasoning is faulty." Is it fair to judge your thinking by what you have written?

Practice Thinking 14.1: What Do You Think?

Please explain how you know.

1. What is the relationship between language and thinking? Between thinking and writing?

   _____

2. How, specifically, do advertisers, politicians, and others use language to persuade you?

   _____

3. How might language be misused to produce thinking errors and impede clear thinking?

   _____

4. How might improving your critical thinking improve your writing, and vice versa?

   _____

LANGUAGE AND THINKING

Words start wars, end wars, jail defendants, free them, start relationships, end them, describe discoveries, describe the commonplace, express love, and express hate. Words are powerful because they affect our thoughts, feelings, conclusions, and actions. But their real power comes from how we use language to put ideas together. Language is a system of communication that uses symbols, such as words, and a set of rules called a *grammar* to make a practically unlimited number of meaningful statements. We combine words into phrases, phrases into sentences, and sentences into paragraphs to convey ever more complex and subtle messages. Evolutionary psychologists have argued that our amazing capacity for language is what has made humans the preeminent species on the planet (Pinker, 1994). But what makes language so powerful?

An important feature of language and thinking that enables this complexity in our communication is recursion, which is our capacity to embed one structure within another. A children's story, "The House That Jack Built," demonstrates recursion, as each sentence becomes more and more elaborate through the addition of prepositional phrases and dependent clauses. It begins as follows:

"This is the house that Jack built." [Then, a dependent clause is added:]

"This is the malt that lay in the house that Jack built." [Add another dependent clause:]

"This is the rat that ate the malt that lay in the house that Jack built." [Add another . . .]

(Corballis, 2012, p. 20)

A second powerful feature of language is its symbolic nature. We can use language to represent things that exist, that have never existed, that might exist, or that we merely wish existed. Symbols allow us to represent the world abstractly, disconnected from the objective world, which gives us the power to think in new ways. For example, when no word exists for an idea, we simply create a new word for it.

A third important feature of language is that it provides a means to make reasoned arguments. The language of argumentation includes special words and terms, allowing us to signal and clarify the meaning of the parts of arguments, as shown in the Appendix.

Language is an important way to express our thinking, but research shows that thinking does not always involve words (Terrace, 2011). People solve problems using visual imagery without the use of words. Before they learn to speak, infants as young as 3 to 4 months old think that an object in one place cannot occupy the same space as another object. Slightly older infants engage in something like counting before learning the words for numbers (Terrace, 2011).

We may not always use words to think, but we often do. Language helps us externalize our thoughts, making our otherwise invisible thinking observable. For instance, you do not know that I am thinking about having another cup of coffee, but as soon as I say it, you can understand my invisible thought. Many cognitive scientists now agree that much of our thinking and other mental processes occur outside of our conscious awareness. Language allows us to make our thinking conscious, as we externalize what we are thinking and it becomes the object of our attention (Jackendoff, 1996). We can use words to cue and direct our thinking, too.

Writing is an especially powerful tool for improving thinking because it creates a record of your externalized thoughts that you can observe later. It allows you to think about the quality of your thinking because you are able to see a representation of those otherwise invisible thoughts. Other people who read your writing can give you feedback about the thinking displayed in your writing as well. By reflecting on the arguments you have made in your writing, you can revise them, strengthen them, and make them clearer. As you improve your written products, you can observe the representation of your thinking change. Furthermore, as your writing improves, you can see your thinking improve.

PROPAGANDA, PERSUASION, AND MOTIVATED REASONING

The power of language makes inquiry and persuasion possible. At its best, inquiry is the open-minded and reasonable pursuit of knowledge and well-reasoned conclusions aimed at finding the truth in a situation. Often, however, language is used to persuade or convince someone of a particular conclusion, sometimes without much concern for the truth. **Persuasion** is the process by which a message induces a change in beliefs, attitudes, or behaviors (Myers, 2013, p. 226). Each day, we are confronted with a deluge of persuasive messages. For example, the world's businesses spend nearly $1.5 trillion on advertisements each year in an effort to persuade us to buy their products and services (Sedivy & Carlson, 2011). On a more personal level, your friends might seek to persuade you to go to a party with them. Your instructors may seek to persuade you that one idea is better than another. Job applicants try to persuade prospective employers to hire them. Biased news sources try to persuade you to interpret world events along political party lines. Sometimes, we hear people mouthing the same words as those trying to persuade them—a parroting that suggests their thinking and beliefs have taken a form that is consistent with the language used to persuade them.

Persuasion becomes dangerous when politicians use inflammatory language in the form of propaganda to whip up hatred of an enemy. They may seek to persuade ordinary citizens who have never killed another person to go to a foreign land and kill someone they do not even know. **Propaganda** is a type of persuasive communication used to make political arguments geared toward convincing a group of people to behave a certain way or adopt a certain position. When propaganda is informative and we like its message, we call it educational (Myers, 2013). But at its worst, propaganda is biased, presenting one-sided messages that are often factually inaccurate. For example, in their grab for power before

World War II, Adolf Hitler and his Nazi followers published lengthy, one-sided essays against the Jews (see Figure 14.1), undoubtedly contributing to support for the subsequent gassing and execution of 6 million Jewish men, women, and children. Commentary from *The Eternal Jew,* a Nazi anti-Semitic propaganda film, stated: "Just like rats, the Jews 200 years ago moved from the Middle East to Egypt. . . . Even then they had all the criminal traits they display today. . . ." In this way, the Nazi propagandists used language to disparage a whole group of people.

Politicians are especially fond of using **emotive language,** which consists of words and phrases with positive or negative associations that are linked to parts of arguments to sway or influence other people. Emotive language is related to how people appeal to emotions such as anger, pity, and fear when making an argument, as discussed in Chapter 9. An example of negative emotive language is demonstrated by the caustic terms Hitler and the Nazis used to refer to Jews, calling them

FIGURE 14.1 Nazi Germans during World War II used anti-Semitic essays and posters like this one for the movie, *The Eternal Jew,* as propaganda tools.

"vermin" and saying they were an enemy of Christians, almost as poisonous as the devil. In nineteenth-century America, White American settlers often referred to Native Americans as "savages," to justify their mistreatment of these peoples and their confiscation of Indian lands.

Another strategy that employs negative associations is **attacking the person,** in which an individual verbally attacks the *person* making an argument rather than countering the *content* of the argument itself to prevent serious consideration of more relevant information. For instance, a politician might say, "My opponent has taken campaign contributions from illegal sources. Therefore, his proposal is not worthy of consideration." This attack on the person seeks to deflect attention from the content of the proposal to the less relevant issue of the proposer's character. A variation of attacking the person is making it uncomfortable for the listener evaluating the argument to consider it seriously—an approach exemplified in the expression, "Only a fool or ignorant person would believe the ideas proposed by 'so-and-so.'"

Emotive language can also take a positive form in which someone seeks to persuade by expressing their ideas and claims in affirmative terms. Members of the U.S. Congress often use positive emotive language to sway opinion in favor of legislation. Following the September 11, 2001, terrorist attacks on the World

Trade Center and the Pentagon, legislators authored a bill they called the "Patriot Act," whose goal was to curb terrorism. The language they chose to title this legislation was deliberately positive. Who would dare vote against a bill that had the word *patriot* in its name, especially when patriotic feelings were running so high in the United States in the wake of the devastating attacks? Use of emotive language is an attempt to shift the focus away from the quality of the information or evidence presented, and toward the feeling associated with the emotion-laden word. This redirection can derail the process of critically evaluating the content of ideas. Thus, politicians use words with either positive or negative associations to create spin that influences the direction of an interpretation.

A similar type of positive association strategy is demonstrated when people use euphemisms to make unpleasant ideas more acceptable by substituting a positive expression for a negative one. For instance, to make the horrors of war more acceptable, the military use euphemisms such as "collateral damage" instead of "civilian casualties," "neutralize" instead of "kill" the enemy, and "soft targets" instead of "people to kill" (Vaughn, 2010). Other, more everyday examples abound: Businesspeople refer to the mass firing of employees as "downsizing"; politicians call tax increases "revenue enhancements"; and political lies are described as statements "somewhat at variance with the truth." Some euphemisms are harmless, as when garbage collectors are called "sanitary engineers." Suppose, however, that an alcoholic tells herself that she is merely a "social drinker." This euphemism could prevent her from accepting that she actually has a substance abuse disorder, discussed in Chapter 13.

Practice Thinking 14.2: Recognizing Affective Language Strategies

For each of the following examples, identify the affective language strategy used to persuade (e.g., emotive language, attacking the person, or euphemism). Then explain why it is a problem and how to deal with it.

1. A political opponent of Mr. Greene objected to one of Greene's proposals saying, "Mr. Greene has proposed that we lower taxes on all of our citizens, but Greene is known to have engaged in scandalous behavior. Why should we think his proposal is in the public interest?"

   Affective language strategy: _____

   _____

How to fix it: _____

_____

2. An advertisement for a luxury car shows an attractive woman in a sexy evening gown standing next to the car. A voiceover says, "You've worked hard—and we've worked hard to bring you a finely crafted automobile that shows your good taste. You deserve it."

Affective language strategy: _____

_____

How to fix it: _____

_____

3. Proponents of women's reproductive rights describe themselves as "pro-choice" rather than as "pro-abortion." Opponents of abortion describe themselves as "pro-life" rather than as "anti-abortion" or "anti-women's right to choose."

Affective language strategy: _____

_____

How to fix it: _____

_____

LANGUAGE THAT IMPEDES CLEAR THINKING AND COMMUNICATION

Another strategy that reflects an error in thinking is inadequate comparison, which involves not mentioning the comparison group or simply making an irrelevant or inappropriate comparison. For instance, an advertiser who claims that "Shiney-White soap is better than all other soaps of its kind" is deliberately not specifying what "of its kind" refers to or in what way Shiney-White soap is better. As another example, after the January 4, 2015, premiere of ABC's new comedy mini-series *Galavant,* the television network advertised four days later on January 8, 2015, that the show was the "number 1 comedy of the year." Did ABC mean it was the number 1 comedy of the new year *so far,* which was only 8 days old, or of the entire year *prior* to January 8, 2015? Was the new comedy number 1 in terms of the number of viewers during that time slot, or number 1 in terms of the comedies the network had recently aired? These types of inadequate comparisons contrast sharply with the clearly defined comparisons that scientists make in precisely specifying the characteristics of control and treatment groups.

Another problematic approach to clear and informative communication is the use of **weasel words** that hedge or qualify claims so much that they are empty of meaning. The term *weasel* in this case reflects the behavior of weasels in the wild: They punch holes in bird eggs and suck out the contents, leaving an egg seemingly intact to the casual observer when in reality it is empty (Bassham, Irwin, Nardone, & Wallace, 2005). In the context of persuasion, using a weasel word such as *relatively* creates a statement that lacks meaningful content. For instance, saying "The side effects of the drug are relatively harmless" may persuade someone to use a drug, but important content is missing when the statement fails to mention potentially dangerous side effects. Other weasel words and expressions include *about, approximately, by and large, in effect, more or less, occasionally, partially, practically,* and *somewhat.*

I can hear your objections now, however: "Don't scientists and critical thinkers use some of these same words to qualify their conclusions?" Indeed, such writers may qualify inductive conclusions when necessary with expressions such as "The results *suggest . . .*" or "A review of the research has *mostly* shown. . . ." Sometimes, we explicitly qualify a conclusion to indicate the limited conditions under which it is supported. Using an example from Chapter 2, "Catharsis or venting of anger as a way to reduce aggression has *generally* not been supported by research, but the venting of anger has been shown to reduce higher heart rate, a sign of anger." These examples show that we should qualify a conclusion to clarify the conditions of its acceptance. Reporters in the media who exaggerate the results of scientific research would be well advised to use more qualifying words in describing research findings, such as pointing out that the results from a correlational study do not imply that a cause has been found.

Nevertheless, Steven Pinker, an expert on language and writing, has criticized academic writers for too often hedging their statements with qualifying terms, such as *almost, apparently, nearly, partially, predominately, seemingly, somewhat, virtually, to a degree,* and *to some extent* (Pinker, 2014). He has argued that the overuse of hedge words is an example of CYA (cover your anatomy), a defensive strategy to ward off possible attacks from critics who might object to an unqualified conclusion. So what should you do in your own writing? A good rule of thumb is to qualify your words when you introduce new ideas, research findings, and conclusions and to qualify the conditions under which a theory or hypothesis is true. In contrast, when research findings and theory are clearly established, you need not use hedge words.

As with weasel words, the use of vague terms impedes clear and precise communication. **Vagueness** refers to the use of imprecise words—that is, words that do not have clear boundaries. For instance, the word *rich* specifies wealth at the high end, but is rather imprecise at lower values (Bassham et al., 2005). Most people would agree that the multibillionaires Bill Gates, Warren Buffet, and Oprah Winfrey are rich. Maybe even the plastic surgeon who makes $1 million a year is rich, but is the general practitioner in a small town who makes $200,000 a year rich? Other less well-defined words that describe measurements, such as *high, long, short, rapid, brief,* and *heavy,* are often vague as well.

Here is a quote from Deepak Chopra, the medical doctor and mystic: "Attention and intention are the mechanics of manifestation" (Pennycook, Cheyne, Barr, Koehler, & Fugelsang, 2015, p. 550). Does this statement have any special meaning for you? Sometimes, writers deliberately use vague language to make an audience believe a message is profound when it is actually bullshit. Pennycook and his colleagues define **pseudo-profound bullshit** as a statement that "may seem to convey some sort of potentially profound meaning, but is merely a collection of buzzwords put together randomly in a sentence that retains syntactic structure" (p. 549). Pennycook and colleagues found that people who have a more intuitive cognitive style and endorse more supernatural beliefs were more receptive to pseudo-profound bullshit.

A vague word can be useful, however, when we are unsure of an object's property or the accuracy of an observation. In general, though, scientists seek precision in their communications. In everyday conversation, we might say, "Jen is highly intelligent," yet a psychologist would specify that Jen has an IQ of 134 on the Wechsler Adult Intelligence Test. Chapter 5 discusses the importance of making precise predictions that can be tested and explains how those who practice pseudoscience make vague predictions that cannot be shown to be false. Chapter 4 discusses how psychologists can clarify a vague description of good memory by giving it an operational definition, such as recalling 90% of the words on a memory test. Chapter 13 discusses how terms such as *depression, anxiety,* and *abnormal behavior* tend to be vague and lack clear boundaries. To solve this problem, psychologists have created diagnostic categories with rules that establish boundaries for distinguishing between depressed and nondepressed people and between normal and abnormal behavior. Scientists value clarity in their writing and other communications, avoiding the misuses and abuses of language mentioned previously.

Another problem related to clarity of expression and thinking is the use of **ambiguous language**. Ambiguity occurs when something can be interpreted in more than one way. For example, the statement "Morgan ate the ice cream with relish" is ambiguous because the word *relish* has two meanings (Vaughn, 2010, p. 118). When we assume one sense of the word, we infer that Morgan ate the ice cream with delight or gusto. When we assume another sense, we infer that Morgan has unusual taste in ice cream toppings. Pronouns are useful because they allow us to generally refer to a noun or noun phrase mentioned earlier without the need to repeat it, but their use can lead to ambiguity if the pronoun is misplaced. For instance, consider the statement "I saw the comparative psychologists and their monkeys in the primate laboratory and left them some bananas." In this case, the pronoun *them* could refer to the comparative psychologists, the monkeys, or both.

At other times, a statement is ambiguous because a prepositional phrase or dependent clause is too far from its referent in a sentence. For example, the statement "On Monday, Professor Kraus will give a lecture on safe sex in the college auditorium" (Bassham et al., 2005, p. 68) is ambiguous because the phrase "in the college auditorium" could be interpreted either as people having safe sex in the auditorium or as the location for the lecture. The ambiguity is easily resolved by moving "in the college auditorium" to an earlier place in the sentence.

Sometimes, people equivocate to make a point, win an argument, or avoid losing one. Equivocation is an argumentation strategy in which an individual shifts from one meaning of a word to another meaning of the word in the same argument, which can thwart clarity of expression and lead to a thinking error. Suppose a student says, "The author of my social psychology textbook claims that someone who helps without concern for receiving something in return is showing altruistic behavior. But how could that argument be true if learning the term *altruistic behavior* did not help me understand it?" Here the student shifts from the meaning of the word *help*, defined as "an altruistic act," to the different meaning of *help* as "facilitating or making it easier" for the student to understand the definition. This equivocation is not relevant to determining whether the author's method of defining the term is correct. Table 14.1 summarizes equivocation and the other ways in which language can impede clear thinking and communication.

TABLE 14.1	Impediments to Clear Thinking and Communication	
Name	Description	How to Fix or Avoid It
Inadequate comparison	Failing to make a sufficient or adequate comparison when a comparison is implied	Complete a contrast or comparison with a group, person, or condition.
Weasel words	Words that qualify or hedge so much that statements lose their force or importance	Use words to describe conclusions that qualify them only as much as the strength of the evidence supports.
Vagueness	Using words that are imprecise, abstract, or too general	Use the most specific and precise words you can.
Ambiguity	Using a word or making a statement that has more than one meaning or interpretation.	Use words/statements with a single meaning in a particular context.
Equivocation	Shifting the meaning of an important word in an argument from its original meaning to a different one.	Define important terms and stick to the same meaning.

Practice Thinking 14.3: Recognizing Impediments to Clear Communication and Thinking

For each of the following examples, use complete sentences to identify the obstacle(s) to clear communication and thinking. Then explain how to fix the problem you identified.

1. When asked by the reporter if he supported the XYZ petroleum pipeline to be constructed across environmentally vulnerable lands, Senator Johnson replied, "I support the XYZ Pipeline because it is good for the country" without making any additional comments.

   Impediment: _____

   _____

   How to fix it: _____

   _____

2. Based on brain research, many neuroscientists conclude that the mind is produced through the normal functioning of the brain. Nevertheless,

I mind it when they offer such simplistic explanations. I have made up my mind that this view of the brain is wrong.

Impediment: _____

_____

How to fix it: _____

_____

3. The establishment clause of the U.S. Bill of Rights says, "Congress shall make no laws respecting an establishment of religion, or prohibiting the free exercise thereof."

Impediment: _____

_____

How to fix it: _____

_____

4. An advertisement for Easy-Does-It cleaner says, "It is highly effective."

Impediment: _____

_____

How to fix it: _____

_____

5. The car salesman said, "Our new hybrid model is so efficient it uses practically no gas."

Impediment: _____

_____

How to fix it: _____

_____

6. The clinical psychologist said, "This is one of the more effective treatments for depression."

Impediment: _____

_____

How to fix it: _____

_____

7. The modern synthesis of Darwin's evolutionary theory has been generally accepted by biologists.

Impediment: _____

_____

How to fix it: _____

_____

8. Man is a social animal. Because no woman is a man, women are not social.

Impediment: _____

_____

How to fix it: _____

_____

WHY WRITING IS IMPORTANT

Writing is an important tool of language for communicating ideas in a visual medium, usually externalized in text or script. Writing takes many forms in our lives, much of it informal, as in emails, text messages, letters, notes to yourself, lists, lecture notes, and comments made on social media. Other writing is more formal, such as essays, term papers, articles, and academic books, which require better sentence construction and grammar than informal writing. In this chapter, we focus on formal writing in psychology, wherein we display our best thinking. In particular, we focus on how to write a good critical thinking (CT) essay.

Writing skill is important to success in many fields—not just in psychology. One study showed that the average adult spends more than 2 hours per day writing and that employed people write more than those who are not employed (Cohen, White, & Cohen, 2011). Just getting a good job often requires a well-written application letter. Employers value the skill of writing, but in a national survey, 35% reported that only one-third or fewer of their new employees possessed the writing skills needed for their work (National Commission on Writing, 2003).

Results from large-scale assessments of American students suggest that the U.S. educational system may not be doing enough to prepare students to think critically through writing (e.g., Langer & Applebee, 1987; National Assessment of Educational Progress [NAEP], 1986, 2011). Although many students show general deficits in writing skill (NAEP, 2011), analytic writing that requires CT may be the most challenging (Crowhurst, 1990; Langer & Applebee, 1987). Fortunately, other studies have shown that special writing instruction can improve students' writing ability. More relevant to our specific goals, other research suggests that CT can be improved through special writing instruction (e.g., Bensley & Haynes, 1995; Butler & Britt, 2011; Roussey & Gombert, 1996; Scardamalia, Bereiter, & Steinbach, 1984; Wolfe, Britt, & Butler, 2009). To explore ways to improve CT through writing, we first examine what psychologists know about the writing process.

THE WRITING PROCESS

Many experts on writing agree that writing involves several processes: planning, translating ideas into text, and reviewing (e.g., Hayes, 1989; Hayes & Flower, 1980; Kellogg, 1988; Mayer, 2004). In practice, a writer must also collect information on a subject before trying to write about it (Kellogg, 1988). Table 14.2 describes each process and suggests strategies that might help with each component of writing.

Although writers may follow the sequence of the four processes outlined in Table 14.2, they often move around from one process to another. For example, after writing a few sentences, you might realize you want to include some more information and so return to acquire the additional material you need. Or, after reviewing what you have written, you might discover that you left out

TABLE 14.2 **Four Components of the Writing Process**

Process	Description	Strategies/Actions
Collecting information	Finding background information on the topic, recording, and summarizing it	• Read about the topic and take notes • Conduct research on the topic • Listen to lectures and other sources • Observe the writing of others
Planning	• Creating and organizing ideas • Setting goals for writing	• Organize notes • Outline important points • Write down goals
Translating ideas into text	• Generating sentences • Drafting	• Use focused rewriting • Compose a first draft
Reviewing	• Reading the text as it develops • Evaluating how well it executes the plan • Editing and revising as needed	• Read what has already been written • Compare it to the goals for the task • Edit errors in the text • Make global revisions as needed

an important idea. After adding it to your outline, you then go back to writing. The reviewing process is important for reflecting on what you have written and may lead you to return to another process, such as revising or generating a new sentence that better communicates what you intended.

Writing is a very complex process that places heavy cognitive demands on the writer. Two influential writing researchers have described the writer as "a thinker on full-time cognitive overload" (Hayes & Flower, 1980, p. 33). Successful writing involves keeping in mind background knowledge and goals for writing. The writer must compose sentences that contain the right words, are coherent, and follow the plan. In reviewing, the writer must read what has been written and compare it to the goals of his or her writing—all the while keeping in mind how the reader is likely to respond. If this seems like a lot of information to attend to at once, it is. Many studies have shown that writing makes great demands on the writer's attention (Kellogg, 1988). As discussed in Chapter 6, we have limited attentional resources. To be successful, the writer must effectively juggle the various demands of writing, dividing attention among the various parts of the task without becoming overwhelmed.

The writing task makes big demands on working memory as well. As discussed in Chapter 6, our working memory allows us to hold a limited amount of information for a brief period of time as we work on that information to do a cognitive task, such as writing.

Next, we examine each of the four processes in Table 14.2 in detail, discussing the cognitive difficulties that writers encounter, as well as ways to overcome them.

Collecting Information

For many writing assignments in psychology, such as term papers or research reports, you will first need to find out what is known about a question so that you can write an intelligent, relevant composition. When choosing your own topic, it is best to find one that interests you and about which adequate information is available. If you need help selecting a topic or focusing a question, consult one of the many books on this subject (e.g., Beins & Beins, 2012) or talk to your instructor.

Once you decide on your topic, read a relevant textbook discussion to acquaint yourself with the basic ideas. This may lead you to a literature review that analyzes the research on your question. By looking up the sources cited in the literature review's References section, you can often find many other articles that pertain to your topic. An especially good tool for finding studies, literature reviews, and books is PsycINFO, the database discussed in Chapter 8. If you are collecting material for a CT essay, be sure to search for information that disagrees with your favored position as well as information that supports it so that you can offer a well-reasoned discussion that includes counterarguments.

Planning

Organizing and deciding how to go about writing is crucial to ending up with a good product, but planning cannot proceed effectively if you do not understand the kind of writing task that is being requested by the writing prompt. Planning involves selecting the right approach to answer the question. For example, suppose you are asked to critically examine the question of whether reversing letters is the defining feature of dyslexia. If you write an essay that simply defines dyslexia as having difficulty learning to read and list the symptoms of this condition, including the reversal of letters, you have not answered the question. You may not have recognized the clues in the prompt that indicate the form of response and the type of thinking the instructor seeks.

Based on the work of Bloom (1956), Stiggins, Rubel, and Quellmalz (1988) proposed six important types of thinking tasks, commonly assessed by instructors asking essay questions: (1) knowledge, (2) comprehension, (3) application, (4) analysis, (5) synthesis, and (6) evaluation. Table 14.3 offers a guide to question prompts that may signal which type of response an instructor is seeking.

TABLE 14.3 **Common Essay Question Types and Related Prompts**

Type of Question	Description	Prompt Words
Knowledge	Asks what you remember pertaining to the question	*List, Describe, Name, Define Identify, Who, What, When*
Comprehension	Asks you to show you understand the relevant terms and concepts you remember, using your own words	*Paraphrase, Summarize, Explain, Review, Discuss, Interpret, How, Why*
Application	Use your knowledge to go beyond simple recall and understanding to solve a problem or make something	*Apply, Construct, Simulate, Employ, Predict, Show how*
Analysis	Break something down into its component parts so that it can be understood	*Classify, Distinguish, Differentiate, Compare, Contrast, Categorize, Break down*
Synthesis	Bring together different knowledge or concepts in a unified response	*Combine, Relate, Put together, Integrate*
Evaluation	Judge whether something is good or bad, true or false, or reaches some criterion	*Judge, Argue, Assess, Appraise, Decide, Defend, Debate, Evaluate, Choose, Justify*

Let's illustrate how the prompts in Table 14.3 might signal different types of writing responses for questions about dyslexia. Dyslexia is characterized as a problem in learning how to read fluently. Suppose a question asked, "What is the definition of dyslexia?" The *what* prompt and the word *definition* signal that this is a knowledge question that could be mostly answered by listing the symptoms of dyslexia—such as slow reading in a person with no other deficits in basic cognitive skills and intelligence, but often with other problems, such as poorer-than-expected spelling, difficulty sounding out the sounds that make up words, and, to a lesser extent, reversal of letters.

Now suppose a different question asked, "Compare and contrast dyslexia with expressive language disorder." This analysis question requests a breakdown of similarities and differences in the two disorders. Suppose another question asked, "Decide whether reversing letters is the principal sign of dyslexia." To adequately answer this evaluation question, you would have to do much more than simply recall and understand the facts about dyslexia and other communication problems. You would need to evaluate the evidence that agrees with as well as the evidence that disagrees with the claim to decide which position is better supported—that is, examine the arguments and counterarguments. Other evaluation prompts such as *justify, defend,* or *argue for* imply the goal of marshaling the evidence that supports a particular side of the argument.

Planning a Critical Thinking Essay

This brings up an important distinction between CT and persuasive essays. If you are prompted to take a position and justify it, your goal is to convince the reader to accept your position—that is, to persuade the reader. All too often, when writing this kind of persuasive essay, writers do not carefully examine the evidence on all sides of the question. This book has emphasized that critical thinkers should evaluate *all* the relevant evidence (or at least evidence representative of the available relevant evidence). In contrast to persuasive writing, academic writing is more focused on inquiry, with the goal of examining the evidence that supports different sides or positions. This is the goal of the critical thinking essay—to evaluate and present all the relevant evidence supporting the different sides of an argument in written form so as to draw the best inductive conclusion. Common prompts in CT essay questions include "Analyze and evaluate the evidence . . ." "Draw a well-reasoned conclusion from the evidence . . ." and "What is the best conclusion . . . ?"

Practice Thinking 14.4: Identifying Kinds of Questions

For each of the following essay question prompts, label which type of essay response is being sought. Then describe how you would go about writing your response to that type of question.

1. Distinguish between Type 1 and Type 2 thinking. _____

_____

2. Explain how heuristics (Chapter 11) are related to judgment errors.

_____

3. Decide whether people who watch violence on television are more likely to behave aggressively than those who do not, and justify your answer.

   _____

4. Compare and contrast hypnosis with psychological states, such as sleep, drug-induced states, and emotional states. Is hypnosis a different state of consciousness? _____

   _____

5. Show how you could use what you have learned about memory and the writing process to advise a student on how to study for an essay exam.

   _____

6. Combine what you know about critical reading with what you know about critical writing to show how the two processes are related.

   _____

7. What is repressed memory? _____

   _____

To write a CT essay, the writer gathers and organizes the evidence relevant to *all* sides of the question, evaluates that evidence including counterarguments, and then is led to and writes a conclusion that is consistent with the evidence. This process exemplifies CT in the form of writing. Writing a critical essay is obviously a complex task to plan and execute. Research suggests that constructing an outline before beginning to write can improve the quality of writing (Kellogg, 1988). Other research shows that relying on a schema or strategy for organizing your writing can improve it, too (McCutchen, Teske, & Bankston, 2008). Table 14.4 provides a general outline schema that you could use to organize an essay and draw a well-reasoned inductive conclusion in a literature review that examines the evidence supporting the different sides of an extended argument.

Take a close look at the general outline structure in Table 14.4. Parts of it should seem familiar, because they are similar to the ideas about critical reading discussed earlier in the book. Chapter 3 began the discussion of how to analyze and evaluate

TABLE 14.4	**Outline Structure for Planning and Writing a Critical Thinking Essay**

I. Introduction of the basic problem or question

    A. Purpose in writing the paper

    B. How the problem will be discussed in the paper (What are the sides of the question?)

    C. Definition of relevant terms

II. Development of the discussion of the problem

    A. Evidence supporting a position, claim, or hypothesis

        1. Specific bit of evidence supporting one aspect of the claim (What is its quality?)

        2. Specific bit of evidence supporting another aspect of the claim (What is its quality?)

        3. Additional evidence (What is its quality?)

        4. Response to rebuttals and criticisms of evidence presented

    B. Evidence against or supporting a rival position, claim, or hypothesis

        1. Specific bit of evidence supporting one aspect of the rival claim (What is its quality?)

        2. Specific bit of evidence supporting another aspect of the rival claim (What is its quality?)

        3. Additional evidence (What is its quality?)

        4. Response to rebuttals and criticisms of evidence supporting the rival claim

III. Conclusion

    A. Evaluation of the quality and quantity of the evidence on each side

    B. Drawing a well-reasoned inductive conclusion from the review and evaluation of the evidence

critical reading essays to draw a well-reasoned inductive conclusion from a literature review, but now your task is to organize the evidence for a literature review that you are writing. Tables 3.1 and 4.3 summarize the strengths and weaknesses of different types of evidence to help you evaluate the quality of the evidence presented, but now you will provide information about the quality of the evidence you include in your critical writing essay. The literature reviews for the critical reading exercises in Chapters 6, 7, 9, and 10 provide examples of how evidence is organized and analyzed. Table 14.4 provides a framework for planning and organizing your CT essay, to help you prepare to translate your thoughts into sentences for critical evaluation.

As with the critical reading passages that earlier presented evidence on both sides of an extended argument, the writing schema in Table 14.4 requires you to evaluate evidence on all sides of an argument. This process should help you avoid myside bias, or the tendency to provide only the evidence consistent with the side that you favor. Studies have often documented that students tend to show myside bias in their writing (e.g., Baron, 1995; Perkins, 1985). Using a CT writing schema, such as the one in Table 14.4, should help you plan and organize the evidence for a critical writing essay (Bensley & Haynes, 1995) so that you avoid myside bias in your writing (Wolfe et al., 2009).

Your outline should follow the basic structure presented in Table 14.4, but the details of your outline, such as the particular bits of evidence, will be specific to the content of your paper. To help you learn how to construct this kind of outline, complete the exercise in Practice Thinking 14.5. To make the task more manageable, I have provided the title of the essay ("Is Reversing Letters the Defining Feature of Dyslexia?") and the evidence supporting each side.

Practice Thinking 14.5: Making an Outline for a Critical Writing Essay

Following are several bits of evidence concerning the question, "Decide whether reversing letters is the defining feature of dyslexia." Your task is to use the basic outline structure of Table 14.4 to organize an essay you will write on this question. In filling in part I, Introduction, your purpose is to discuss the question. Briefly describe how you will reach a well-reasoned conclusion. Next, define the most important terms relevant to the question. Then, for parts IIA and IIB, correctly fill in the brief descriptions of evidence that go under one side of the argument versus the other. You will need to add places for additional evidence, as shown in parts A3 and B3.

Evidence related to the question

1. In one study, 70% of educators, including speech therapists and special education teachers, considered that reversing letters was the defining feature of dyslexia (Wadlington & Wadlington, 2005).

2. U.S. neurologist Samuel Orton (1925), writing in the prestigious journal *Archives of Neurology and Psychiatry,* proposed that reversing letters was the most important symptom of dyslexia.

3. Dyslexic children make many mistakes (e.g., spelling errors) that are sometimes as common as or more common than reversing letters (Guardiola, 2001).

4. Perhaps a subset of dyslexics are deficient in visual processing along with processing sounds (phonemes), but this remains controversial (Badian, 2005).

5. Dyslexic children generally have worse spelling skills than non-dyslexic children, but teachers of dyslexic children cannot distinguish between the spelling of dyslexic and non-dyslexic children (Cassar, Treiman, Moats, Pollo, & Kessler, 2005).

6. Dyslexics have trouble "sounding out words," which suggests that the problem may be something other than reversing visually read letters.

7. The media have often depicted the reversal of letters in movies and in news programs as a symptom of dyslexia. In the 2001 movie *Pearl Harbor,* actor Ben Affleck plays an army captain supposedly suffering from dyslexia. He tells the nurse testing his vision that he sometimes cannot read the letters because he turns the letters around. In a National Public Radio program on dyslexia, a commentator said, "The simplest explanation, I suppose, is you see things backward" (Lilienfeld, Lynn, Ruscio, & Beyerstein, 2010).

8. A defining feature of a category is one that must be present for an example to be classified as part of a category. For example, if letter reversal is a defining feature of dyslexia, then a person who reverses letters is classified as dyslexic. Reversing letters, then, would be regarded as a core feature that distinguishes dyslexics from non-dyslexics.

9. When children are first learning to spell and write, many show letter reversals and backward writing, such as writing *b* for *d,* or vice versa. Although the problems decrease in both dyslexics and non-dyslexics over time, they decrease more slowly in dyslexics.

10. The fact that many people make jokes about letter reversals in dyslexics and not about other aspects of dyslexia suggests this is a common belief about dyslexia. For instance, did you hear about the dyslexic who answers the phone, "O hell," instead of "Hello?" (Lilienfeld et al., 2010).

11. The observation that dyslexics reverse the letters in reading is often hypothesized to be a visual problem.

12. Much research on dyslexia has led many experts in the field to view dyslexia as a phonological problem. Dyslexics have more difficulty in decoding phonemes, the basic sound units that distinguish one word from another. For example, they may have difficulty distinguishing words, such as *cat* versus *sat* or *dim* versus *vim.* They also have more trouble filling in missing phonemes in text (Farquharson, Centanni, Franzluebbers, & Hogan, 2014).

13. In a study of German children, Wimmer (1996) observed dyslexic children with a variety of phonological problems, including the inability to blend phonemes into pronounceable words, poor decoding, and trouble in assembling phonemes. This study provided good evidence supporting the phonological hypothesis, as well as evidence *against* the visual hypothesis, because German is a language for which it is easier to decode phonological features.

Translating Ideas Into Text

Having a solid outline should help you write your essay. Your focus for this draft should be on writing clearly and coherently in your own words for a psychologically literate audience. Writing clearly means constructing sentences that can be understood by your audience, which consists of people who are psychology majors and are familiar with basic ideas in psychology. To write clearly, you need not use "big" words that show off your vocabulary. Rather, use the simplest, relevant words conventionally used by psychologists to convey your idea. Avoid ambiguous words and expressions, and instead use the most specific, relevant terms you can.

Clarify the way your essay will approach the question by explicitly stating the question and the positions taken to address it, which will be discussed in your essay. Another good strategy is to define terms that will be important to your discussion early in the essay to help the reader understand what your essay is about.

Looking at how psychologists use words and terms in writing about your topic might help you learn more about writing clearly, but there is a danger in borrowing too much from other sources. It is very easy to plagiarize someone else's writing. Plagiarism is a form of intellectual dishonesty in which an individual behaves as if someone else's ideas or work are his or her own or fails to give adequate credit to the author of some idea or work. In psychology and other fields, we are often called upon to summarize someone else's ideas. If we are not careful, we may commit unintentional plagiarism by taking those ideas and forgetting to give the original authors credit or by using too many of their words. In the worst cases, people *intentionally* pretend that all or part of another person's work is their own.

Whether intentional or unintentional, plagiarism can have serious consequences. Students have been known to fail a course or even be kicked out of school for plagiarizing. Jayson Blair lost his job as a reporter for *The New York Times* when the paper discovered he had plagiarized several articles. Other people have been sued for plagiarism.

In academic writing, we should cite the author or authors who originated the work being discussed to give them credit for their contributions. For example, we may cite Kellogg (1988) by listing his name followed by the year of publication of his research article to credit him with the finding that an outline can improve the quality of writing and reduce the load on working memory. Citing the author of a research study also increases the support for and credibility of an argument we are making.

Plagiarists are not just doing a disservice to the people whose work they have taken without due credit—they are also doing a disservice to themselves. The purpose of writing assignments is to improve the important skills of writing and thinking. Often when people plagiarize, they are not learning how to summarize and paraphrase other people's ideas in their own words. They are not getting the practice they need to improve their writing. Table 14.5 lists four ways that people often commit plagiarism. See also the writing textbook by Beins and Beins (2012) for a similar list to help you recognize plagiarism and avoid it in your own writing.

TABLE 14.5 Four Common Forms of Plagiarism You Must Avoid

1. You fail to cite someone else's idea you are using.

2. You use someone else's exact words without citing them.

3. You use someone else's exact words without putting the words in quotation marks (even if you cited them).

4. You pretend that you are the author of some work that was actually created by someone else.

Practice Thinking 14.6: Avoiding Plagiarism When Generating Sentences

Here is a passage from Chapter 7 about testing the reality of an out-of-body experience (OBE), followed by a summary of it. Compare the summary to the original passage and use Table 14.5 to decide in which ways the summary plagiarizes the original text, underlining the parts that are plagiarized. Then label the form of plagiarism according to Table 14.5. Finally, explain how you would rewrite the plagiarized portions.

Original: Olaf Blanke and his colleagues (2002) have used ESB to produce a more convincing OBE in a 43-year-old epileptic woman. While trying to find the focus of her brain damage, they stimulated points in the right angular gyrus within the temporal parietal junction (TPJ), shown in Figure 7.4. This stimulation produced various disturbances in the perception of her body. When stimulated at different intensities, the woman reported feeling that she was "sinking into the bed," "falling from a height," and seeing parts of her body shorten (p. 269). At one point, she had an OBE in which she saw her trunk and legs from above—the same portion of her body she had felt when stimulated before. However, when Blanke and his colleagues stimulated the epileptic focus in her temporal lobe more than 5 cm away from the angular gyrus in the TPJ, the woman did not have an OBE.

Summary: Olaf Blanke and his colleagues produced an OBE and other distortions in the perception of the body in an epileptic woman by stimulating her brain as she was being operated on for epilepsy. When they stimulated her brain at different intensities, she reported various disturbances in the perception of her body, such as the impression that she was falling from a height and seeing parts of her body shortening. When at one point they stimulated the right angular gyrus within the TPJ, she reported that she had an OBE. When Blanke and his colleagues stimulated her epileptic focus in her temporal lobe more than 5 cm away from the TPJ, the woman did not have an OBE.

Even when people follow the rules and put quotation marks around the exact words of another person and cite the author with the year of publication and page number for the quotation, they may still not be writing well. I have received many papers that followed these rules but that disappointingly used far too many quotations from other people. These papers showed that the writers knew *how to cite* quotations properly, but not that they knew how to *summarize* the ideas of others. In essence, they relied on someone else's writing, rather than creating their own. Quotations should be used sparingly, with at most only one or two included in an essay. You should quote when an author is known for saying something a certain way, when certain technical terms must be used, or to state a standard definition—not to avoid summarizing the work of others.

When writing a summary of a study, cite the author(s) and year of publication in parentheses following the author's last name, using the format guidelines developed by the American Psychological Association (2010).

If possible, identify which kind of study it was, such as a case study, correlational study, or experiment. For example, you might write, "Johnson (2007) conducted an experiment showing. . . ." Make it clear to the reader what was tested, what was found, and which side of the argument is supported. Note any strengths or weaknesses of the study. If you find a problem with a study offered as evidence, you may wish to comment on that issue or write a brief rebuttal statement. You may explain why the study does not offer strong support or even sometimes how the study might be reinterpreted to support the other side of the argument. Readers value the counterarguments offered in rebuttals, and a good counterargument can weaken support for one side of an argument in favor of the other side.

Your counterargument can also be a good way to introduce the evidence on the opposing side (listed in Table 14.4 under "B. Evidence against or not supporting a position, claim, or hypothesis"). If a good second counterargument can be offered to rebut the counterargument offered against the one side, then readers may be persuaded to accept this rebuttal, thereby strengthening the first side (Wolfe et al., 2009).

Good writing is coherent, in that the ideas in an essay are logically connected and the reader can follow the reasoning and arguments made by the author. You can improve the coherence of your writing by signaling to the reader how ideas are related and fit together. Ask yourself, "Can my reader follow my argument?" Separating different ideas into paragraphs can help the reader see the organization of your ideas. The first sentence in a paragraph is often the topic sentence, a general statement to which all the other sentences in the paragraph are related.

The Appendix offers ways to improve the coherence of the sentences you are writing from your outline. It shows how to use transition words to connect ideas and paragraphs so that the discussion of the evidence will flow more smoothly. For example, to signal that you are offering more evidence to support a side, you might say, "*Another* experiment supporting the hypothesis that . . . by Authors (year) showed that. . . ." To signal that you are describing a study offering a rebuttal, you might use the word *however* or *nevertheless,* as in "*However,* an experiment by Author (year) obtained the opposite result, showing . . . ," or state the contradictory evidence more bluntly, as in "Author (year) failed to replicate the original finding."

The Appendix also offers words that signal the parts of the extended argument you are making. For instance, "*Because* Author (year) found . . ." signals evidence in support of a claim made in the essay. Alternatively, you might use the word *suggests* to signal a tentative, inductive conclusion, as in "The results of several large experiments *suggest* that. . . ." Consult the Appendix for other ideas about how to indicate transitions and signal parts of arguments.

Practice Thinking 14.7: Drafting the Critical Writing Essay

Your task is to use the outline you developed for Practice Thinking 14.4 and the information about the evidence in that exercise to write a draft of your essay. Follow your outline, but revise it if you can think of ways to improve it. Begin with a paragraph that introduces the question, states how it will be discussed, and defines key terms. Translate as many of the relevant pieces of evidence into your own words as you can, organizing them under the side of the argument each supports. Use the Appendix to help you communicate clearly and coherently and to signal the parts of your discussion and extended argument.

Reviewing and Revising

What is the most important difference between a good writer and a poor writer? The answer is *revision*. Good writers successfully review and effectively revise what they have written before they submit it. Unfortunately, Pianko (1979) found that college freshmen, when asked to write an essay, spent less than 10% of their total writing time reading and revising what they had written. Even if you have planned your essay well and kept your goals in mind as you generated sentences, your essay may still contain errors. If you do not fix them, they will severely detract from the finished product. The good writer reviews what has been written and finds problems to be fixed. Then, he or she selects a better word, connects ideas together to improve transition, reorganizes the information, and fixes any other errors observed.

Writing experts have noted that reviewing requires critical reading, which places a big load on working memory (Hayes, 1996; McCutchen et al., 2008). To help manage this load when reviewing, you may find it helpful to print out your draft and write notes to yourself about problems to be fixed. In reviewing, first focus on coherence and clarity without much concern for grammar, punctuation, and spelling. Ask yourself, "Have I accomplished my goals and followed my revised outline?" Only after you have clearly and coherently expressed your ideas should you check your writing for spelling, punctuation, and grammatical errors.

SUMMARY

Language is a powerful tool for communication because it can symbolize and connect many ideas while providing the means to externalize thoughts so they can be inspected and modified in the form of verbal expressions. Language is used to persuade and propagandize, but it can also be misused when propaganda takes the form of one-sided, political statements designed to harm other people. Often, people make positive and negative associations with ideas that they want others to accept or reject, such as attacking a person instead of challenging the person's ideas, using emotive language that distracts from the critical evaluation of ideas, or using euphemisms to make arguments. Other problematic uses of language impede the clarity of communication and thinking, as when a person makes inadequate comparisons, uses weasel words, vague expressions, ambiguous references, and equivocation.

Writing is a complex cognitive task that demands considerable cognitive resources. The writing process involves collecting information, planning, translating ideas into text, and reviewing and revising. Writing can be improved by reducing the cognitive resources required during writing (e.g., taking notes when collecting information), identifying the goals for writing, making an outline while keeping in mind the goals for writing, and using the outline as you translate ideas into text. The CT essay examines evidence on all sides of a question and draws a well-reasoned conclusion based on the quality and quantity of the evidence presented. When translating ideas into words, it is important to summarize other people's ideas in your own words as much as possible and to give them credit for their ideas and work. Finally, writers should strive for logical coherence and revise their writing as needed.

Practice Thinking 14.8: WHAT DO YOU THINK **NOW**?
Please explain how you know.

1. What is the relationship between language and thinking? Between thinking and writing? _____

_____

2. How, specifically, do advertisers, politicians, and others use language to persuade you? _____

_____

3. How might language be misused to produce thinking errors and impede clear thinking? _____

_____

4. How might improving your critical thinking improve your writing, and vice versa? _____

_____

REVIEW QUESTIONS

1. How is language related to thinking? How can language be used to improve thinking?

2. What is persuasion? How is it related to propaganda?

3. In what ways are emotion and affect used when making arguments?
   - How is emotive language used to persuade?
   - What is attacking the person?
   - What is euphemism and how is it related to spin?

4. In what ways can clear communication and thinking be impeded?
   - What is inadequate comparison?
   - What are weasel words?
   - What is vagueness?
   - How is pseudo-profound bullshit related to vagueness and a failure to think critically?
   - What is ambiguity?
   - What is equivocation?

5. What is writing? Why is it such a challenging task?

6. What are the basic steps in writing?

7. What is involved in collecting information for an essay?

8. What is involved in planning to write an essay?

9. How does your purpose for writing affect what you write?

10. Which clues indicate that you are being asked to answer a knowledge, comprehension, application, synthesis, or evaluation question?
    - How is a CT essay different from some persuasive essays?
    - What can you do to better organize your writing?
    - What are the basic parts of the outline for a CT essay?

11. What is involved in translating ideas into text?
    - Why and how should you avoid plagiarism?

12. What is involved in reviewing and revising what you have written?

13. What should you keep in mind about your audience as you write?

14. What psychological misconceptions did this chapter discuss?

COMMON EXPRESSIONS FROM THE LANGUAGE OF ARGUMENTATION AND DISCUSSION

LANGUAGE FOR DEFINING, SPECIFYING, AND QUALIFYING

The terms and expressions in this section are commonly used to help define and fill in an extended argument with specifics, to make fine points, and to clarify by filling in the blanks with specific content. They can be used when the topic of the discussion is first introduced but also as it is developed, as well as in the conclusion statement.

All or some _____
Although _____ ,
Assuming that _____ ,
Defining _____
Distinguish between _____
_____ is different from _____
For example, _____ or For instance, _____
In comparison to _____
In contrast to _____
In particular, _____
_____ is really; or _____ is actually
_____ is like or similar to _____
Seeing that _____
Specifically, _____
Supposing that _____
To clarify, _____
Unlike _____
While _____

LANGUAGE THAT SIGNALS A NON-CAUSAL RELATIONSHIP

The blanks indicate where variables are filled in to state a specific non-causal relationship, such as a correlation. Use of these terms can help make it clear that an association between variables exists and not a causal relationship.

_____ decreases as _____ increases (significant negative correlation)

_____ increases as _____ increases (significant positive correlation)

_____ is associated with _____

_____ is connected to _____

_____ is correlated with _____

_____ is linked to _____

_____ is related to _____

LANGUAGE THAT SIGNALS A CAUSAL RELATIONSHIP

The blanks can be filled in with a variable name that is either a cause or an effect of another variable. The direction of this relation indicates in parentheses following the blank whether what fills the blank functions as a cause or effect. Use of these terms and expressions is reserved for identifying a causal relationship, such as the results of a well-conducted true experiment or true experiments that have confirmed a causal relationship exists.

_____ (some cause) causes _____ (some effect)

_____ (some cause) contributes to _____ (some effect)

_____ (some effect) depends on _____ (some cause)

_____ (some effect) is due to _____ (some cause)

_____ (some cause) is the reason that _____ (some effect occurs)

_____ (some cause) leads to _____ (some effect)

_____ (some cause) produces _____ (some effect)

_____ (some effect) results from _____ (some cause)

LANGUAGE USED IN MAKING A CLAIM

When filled in, the following blanks indicate specifically what is being claimed; the various terms illustrate the variety of forms that the claims can take.

argue that _____

assert that _____

claim that _____
expect that _____
hypothesize that _____
predict that _____
propose that _____
suggest that _____
theorize that _____
think that _____

LANGUAGE SIGNALING THAT EVIDENCE IS PROVIDED

The following terms and expressions are commonly used to signal that reasons or evidence is being offered. Some of the terms and expressions also suggest whether that evidence offers support for or against a claim. However, the content of the information filling the blanks must be considered in relation to the term or expression to determine which side of an argument is supported or opposed.

On account of _____
_____ argues against _____
_____ argues for _____
Because _____
_____ is consistent with _____
_____ is inconsistent with _____
_____ contradicts _____
_____ demonstrates that _____
_____ disagrees with _____
_____ does not support _____
_____ is evidence that _____
The fact that _____
_____ is reason to think _____
_____ shows that _____
Since _____
_____ suggests that _____
_____ supports the claim that _____

WORDS THAT SIGNAL DIFFERENT SIDES OR POSITIONS

The following terms and expressions are commonly used to signal that one side is making an argument versus another. Paying attention to these cues can help keep the arguments organized under the side each pertains to, as well as distinguishes one side from the other.

_____ assumes, but _____ assumes _____
On the one hand _____ argues; on the other hand _____
One side proposes/argues _____ while the other side _____
_____ takes the position that _____
_____ thinks _____; in contrast, _____ thinks _____
Contrary to _____, _____ thinks/believes that _____

WORDS THAT SUGGEST KINDS OF EVIDENCE

The following terms and expressions are commonly used to signal kinds of evidence offered as support. Paying attention to the use of this language can assist in evaluating the quality of the evidence provided and the strength of a conclusion that can be drawn.

After reviewing the evidence, [name] concluded _____ (Expert authority)
The case of _____ (Case study or perhaps anecdotal)
For example, _____; For instance, _____ (Often anecdotal)
They found _____ (Research study)
He compared _____ (Either quasi- or true experiment)
A significant effect of _____ (True experiment)
They found that as _____ increased, _____ increased (Correlation)

DRAWING A CONCLUSION

The following terms and expressions are commonly used to signal that a conclusion follows. Note that using them does not mean the conclusion logically follows or is well-reasoned.

Accordingly, _____
Consequently, _____
_____ conclude _____; In conclusion, _____
_____ deduce that _____

_____found _____
Hence, _____
_____ infer that _____
It follows that _____
The implication is _____
_____ indicated that _____
leads one to think that _____
Logically, _____
reasoned that _____
A reasonable evaluation of the evidence suggests that _____
A review of the evidence suggests that _____
_____ has been shown that _____
In summary, _____ (Used to summarize evidence before drawing a conclusion)
It stands to reason that _____
So, _____
Then, _____
Therefore, _____
Thus, _____

WORDS THAT SIGNAL TRANSITIONS

The following terms and expressions are commonly used to provide coherence in the presentation of ideas and arguments, signaling how ideas are similar, how they differ, and how they are related in specific ways. These expressions signal transition from one idea to another, from one side's evidence to another side's, and from one paragraph to another. As such, they usually appear at the beginning of a sentence or paragraph and often signal that the direction of the discussion and extended argument is continuing in the same way or is about to change.

Additionally, _____ (To signal other similar evidence or information to be provided)

Also, _____ (To signal other similar information to be provided)

Although _____ (Granting some truth or fact, something else is true)

Anyhow, _____ (Signaling that no matter what the situation, something else is true)

At any rate, _____ (To shift to another topic after drawing a general inference when something contradictory or diverging from the main thread of the discussion has been considered)

As discussed previously, _____ (To signal that some new idea to be considered extends or expands upon information already provided)

At the same time, _____ (To signal that some related idea is to be pondered along with something already considered)

However, _____ (To signal a contrary or qualifying idea is to be considered)

In addition, _____ (To signal other similar evidence or information to be provided)

In spite of (or despite) _____ (To signal something is still true in spite of information just considered—see "Nevertheless")

Moreover, _____ (To signal other similar and often better evidence or information is to be provided)

Nevertheless or nonetheless _____ (To signal something is still true despite other information or putting aside other information already considered)

Notwithstanding, _____ (To signal something is still true in spite of information just considered)

GLOSSARY

affect The many different shades of mood, feeling, and evaluative experience related to emotion.

altruism Helping another person or other people without the expectation of receiving any benefit in return.

ambiguous language Words and expressions that can be interpreted in more than one way.

anchoring and adjustment heuristic The rule of thumb in which one makes a judgment by starting with some arbitrary value when lacking good information upon which to base a decision, and then insufficiently adjusts from that point.

anchoring effect The tendency to be overly influenced by a starting value or information provided before making a judgment, even if that information is not useful for the judgment.

anecdotes Examples, cases, or stories used to illustrate a point and support a claim, but which are often unique, not repeatable, and difficult to authenticate.

apparent mental causation A type of thinking error in which a person believes that merely having a thought can affect objective reality, akin to the paranormal ability of telekinesis.

appraisal The interpretation or evaluation of a situation that leads one to experience an affective state, such as a mood or emotion.

argument A reason or evidence in support of a claim or conclusion.

argument from ignorance or possibility A type of thinking error violating the basic rule that a person should argue from true statements, from knowledge the person possesses, and from high-quality evidence to draw well-reasoned conclusions.

assumption A premise that is omitted and is taken for granted as true.

attacking the person The practice of verbally targeting the person making an argument rather than countering the content of the argument itself, typically in an effort to prevent serious consideration of more relevant information.

availability heuristic The rule of thumb assuming that events that come readily to mind are more frequent; it can be influenced by how vivid and how recent the events are in memory and so lead to judgment errors in estimating the probability of events.

base rate The known probability or rate of an event; the known value that a variable typically takes on.

base rate neglect The probability judgment error in which a person bases his or her estimates on details of an example and the created expectations, ignoring the more predictive base rate.

behavior therapy A type of psychotherapy that approaches the treatment of psychological problems by helping clients develop more adaptive behaviors.

behavioral confirmation A practice similar to confirmation bias in which clinicians send their clients signals, often inadvertently, to behave in ways consistent with the clinician's own theoretical interpretation or preconceived notion of the client's problem.

belief bias A thinking error in which one uses prior knowledge or belief rather than logic to draw a conclusion.

belief perseverance The refusal to reject or revise one's faulty belief when confronted with evidence that clearly refutes that belief.

better than average effect A form of the self-serving bias in which individuals have the tendency to judge themselves as better than the average person in their peer group on positive and socially valued traits.

bias A tendency to judge unfairly with a preference not based on objective evidence; judgments that differ from the prescriptions of probability theory.

bias blind spot A pervasive lack of awareness of one's own biases.

black-and-white thinking A type of thinking error in which only two extreme positions or options are offered when others could be considered, also called *either-or thinking*. See also *false dilemma* and *false dichotomy*.

bounded rationality The view that people have limited cognitive resources, such that complex judgment tasks place great demands on the cognitive system.

case study A research study consisting of a detailed description of part of usually a single individual's life, often documenting the person's abilities, traits, symptoms, behaviors, and treatment.

cause An event that precedes another event and produces an effect in the second event; it meets all three criteria for showing causation.

change blindness An effect related to inattentional blindness that occurs when a person misses a change from one scene to the next.

change blindness blindness A label that describes the metacognitive error in which a person is unaware of, or blind to, his or her inability to detect change.

circular reasoning A type of reasoning and argumentation in which the conclusion returns to the initial premise, restating in the conclusion what was initially asserted or stated as a reason.

claim A statement asserting that someone or something has a particular characteristic or property.

clinical approach A method of clinical reasoning in which clinicians make subjective and intuitive judgments as they integrate information from various sources.

clinical assessment The process in which a clinician gathers and interprets information from multiple sources so as to make a sound diagnosis of a client's problem.

cognitive dissonance theory The concept that when a prophesy or some other belief fails to be true, a believer will experience an intense state of discomfort until the discrepancy with the belief is resolved.

cognitive errors Errors the mind makes as it processes information (e.g., perceptual, attentional, and memory errors).

cognitive load The amount of information that is held or manipulated in working memory as a task is completed.

coherent Being logically connected, such that one can follow the reasoning and arguments presented.

commonsense belief Informal beliefs that are commonly assumed to be true and which are offered as evidence; however, what many people believe may not be true.

commonsense psychology The use of personal, informal, and often inaccurate commonsense or folk "theories" to explain behavior and mental events.

comorbidity A situation in which a client fits the criteria for more than one disorder, suggesting diagnosis of more than one disorder in the same person.

conclusion A claim that has been accepted as true; an inference drawn from reasons.

conditional (if–then) argument Reasoning traditionally presented in three statements in which the first two statements set the conditions for the third statement, or conclusion, to be true.

confirmation bias A type of thinking error in which one tends to attend to, seek, and give more weight to evidence that supports one's favored position rather than evidence that could disconfirm it.

confounding An undesirable situation in which an extraneous variable varies along with the independent variable and could also plausibly account for the changes in the dependent variable, thereby threatening the internal validity of the study.

confusing correlation with causation A type of thinking error in which one infers that one of two correlated variables is the cause of the other.

confusing familiarity with truth A type of memory error in which familiarity is mistaken for truth.

conjunction fallacy A type of error associated with the representativeness heuristic in which one judges that someone or something is more likely to belong in a category that includes two or more features, rather than deciding that the person or item belongs to a category that includes only one of the same features.

consciousness A person's current, subjective state of awareness.

conspiracy theory An alternative explanation offered in place of a conventional understanding of events.

correlational study A kind of research study that can show a quantitative relationship or association between variables but which cannot show a causal relationship.

counterargument A claim and any corresponding evidence that run counter to or disagree with a previous claim or argument.

creative thinking A type of thinking that requires approaching a problem in new ways to produce a useful solution.

criteria for establishing causation Three conditions that must be met to show something is a cause: (1) covariation, (2) time order, and (3) elimination of plausible alternative explanations.

critical thinking dispositions Attitudes, traits, thinking styles, and motives that make a person more likely to think critically, such as open-mindedness and a skeptical attitude.

critical thinking essay A paper written to evaluate and present all relevant evidence supporting the different sides of an argument so as to draw the best inductive conclusion.

cross-race effect The ability to better identify the face of someone of one's own race than the face of a person of a different race; also called *own race bias*.

debiasing The act of reducing the biasing effects from the inappropriate use of a heuristic; more generally, acting to reduce judgment or decision error.

decision making The act of evaluating options and then selecting a course of action.

deductive reasoning A type of formal reasoning in which one often argues from a general theory or principle to a specific case.

dependent variable The measured variable within an experiment.

diagnosis Classifying a person as having one condition or disorder versus another; putting a person into one clinical category versus another.

differential diagnosis A type of clinical analysis in which a client's signs, symptoms, and behaviors are shown to best fit the diagnostic criteria of one specific disorder, while ruling out other possible disorders with criteria that do not fit as well as those observed in the client.

efficacy The effectiveness of treatments demonstrated by clinical research studies.

egoism Selfishness or the tendency to not help another in need of help.

electroencephalography (EEG) A technique for studying brain activity that measures the electrical activity in large groups of neurons and plots it in brain-wave form.

electrostimulation of the brain (ESB) A technique for studying the brain in which minute amounts of electricity are sent to specific cells or small groups of cells.

emotion A mental state elicited by an event that a person has appraised as relevant to fulfilling his or her needs, and that motivates behavior to fulfill those needs and reach the individual's goals.

emotive language Words and phrases with positive or negative associations that are linked to parts of arguments to sway or influence other people.

empirical approach An approach to inquiry that relies on carefully made observations; for example, researchers in science take an empirical approach.

equivocation A strategy often used to win or avoid losing an argument by shifting the meaning of an important word to have a different meaning in the argument.

euphemisms Alternative, positive expressions used to make negative, unpleasant ideas more acceptable.

evidence The reasons supporting one conclusion versus another. Evidence comes in various forms, such as the opinions of experts, informal observations, personal experience, and the results of scientific research studies.

evidence-based treatments (EBTs) Treatments for problems and disorders whose effectiveness is validated through high-quality scientific research.

excessive backward reasoning Reasoning about clients' problems in which a clinician is overly influenced by preconceptions, perhaps considering only one hypothesis.

excessive reliance on intuition A thinking error in which a clinical assessment is based on common sense or intuition instead of systematic assessment of all the relevant information about a client.

extraneous variables Variables that are outside of the intended focus of a study and that could provide alternative explanations for research findings when not controlled.

Facilitated Communication (FC) A method of communication in which a facilitator is purported to help an autistic person communicate through a special keyboard; however, it is widely considered to be pseudoscientific.

fallacy A reasoning error, typically associated with deductive reasoning that leads to an invalid argument.

false memory An error in which one mistakenly remembers something that was not seen, heard, or otherwise experienced.

falsifiable A condition whereby a hypothesis, theory, or claim can be shown to be false; good hypotheses are falsifiable.

field studies Studies in which researchers collect data in the natural environment, often using naturalistic observation.

forward reasoning The practice of collecting information about clients to try and find patterns in it, forming hypotheses about possible causes of the behavior.

framing effect A judgment resulting from the use of words that bias the way in which a comparison is made or some other choice options are evaluated.

Freudian psychoanalysis The psychodynamic approach to the mind and psychotherapy developed by Sigmund Freud.

functional magnetic resonance imaging (fMRI) A type of magnetic resonance imaging in which the subject's brain activity is monitored while he or she is engaged in some task or mental activity.

functionalist A scientist who regards mental states and processes as something to be explained in their own right, and who assumes that mental processes serve certain functions.

fundamental attribution error A thinking error based on the self-serving bias in which people attribute their success to their possession of positive traits and skills and blame their failures on situational factors.

gambler's fallacy The judgment error in which a person mistakenly expects the probability of one independent trial to affect the outcome of another independent trial.

groupthink A thinking error involving overconfidence in a decision that occurs when group members know of a leader's preference for a decision option and dissent is suppressed, with group members conforming to the leader's opinion.

hallucination A cognitive error in which a person experiences something as if it were perceived, even though nothing in the environment directly corresponds to it.

hasty generalization A thinking error in which one rapidly generalizes from the evidence, not considering all of it or only superficially analyzing and evaluating it before drawing a conclusion.

heuristics Rules of thumb that serve as cognitive shortcuts to simplify judgment and decision making but that do not guarantee a good judgment or decision.

hindsight bias A type of metacognitive error in which people are overconfident of what they knew about an event before it actually occurred.

hot-hand illusion The mistaken perception that a set of random events predicts the outcome of the next independent event, as in the belief in streak shooting.

hypothesis The predicted relationship between two or more variables.

illusory correlation A thinking error in which one mistakenly perceives a correlation or relationship between two variables when none exists.

inadequate comparison The act of not mentioning the comparison group or the act of making an irrelevant or inappropriate comparison.

inappropriate use of criteria A thinking error in which one fails to use relevant criteria due to the practice of assigning excessive weight to certain criteria or using nondiagnostic criteria.

inattentional blindness An error in which one does not see a part of a display that is within the field of view when paying attention to another part.

independent The condition of a trial in which the outcome of one trial is separate from and does not affect the outcome of another trial.

independent variable The manipulated variable within an experiment.

inductive reasoning A type of reasoning in which one often argues from a specific case to a general principle, such as a theory or hypothesis; a generalization from bits of evidence.

internal validity The degree to which it can be said that the independent variable and no other variable had an effect on the dependent variable.

intuitive-experiential An approach to thinking characterized by rapid responses to questions and reliance on knowledge of patterns and experience, instead of careful deliberation; it is associated with Type 1 thinking.

law of contagion The principle, based on sympathetic magic, that things that come into contact may change each other for a period of time, even after they are no longer in contact.

law of large numbers The principle that the larger the size of a randomly selected sample, the more closely it will tend to approximate the actual percentage of some characteristic in the population.

law of similarity The principle, based on sympathetic magic, that things that resemble each other share important properties.

law of small numbers The pervasive tendency of people to make judgments that ignore sample size and rely too heavily on small samples.

literature review A summary and analysis of research studies on a particular subject, often organizing the studies according to the hypotheses or theories that they support or do not support.

localization of function An approach that focuses on locating specific areas of the brain that become activated or are related to particular functions, behaviors, and mental states.

M–B (mind–brain) dualism A position which assumes that the mind and body are two different entities.

magical thinking A kind of thinking that makes supernatural and paranormal assumptions about the workings of the world, especially attributing paranormal powers to oneself or to others (e.g., apparent mental causation).

magnet therapy A type of therapy in which a magnet is placed on or near the body to promote health or well-being; it is widely considered to be pseudoscientific.

materialism A form of monism that assumes the world is physical and thus the mind and brain are both fundamentally physical entities.

mechanical approach A method of clinical reasoning in which clinicians use statistical data from tables similar to insurance companies' actuarial tables to make predictions about clients.

mental status examination A comprehensive evaluation of a person's appearance, attitude, mood, motor activity, and cognition as part of clinical assessment.

mesmerism A pseudoscience involving the influencing of another person's behaviors and experiences; it resembles the modern technique of hypnosis.

mind–brain (M–B) question The perplexing question of how the mind is related to the brain.

misinformation effect A situation in which a biased or incorrect memory is produced after encountering misleading information of an event.

mistakenly inferring causation from a diagnosis A thinking error in which a diagnosis is incorrectly identified as the cause of a problem.

monism The position that the mind and brain are really all one thing.

motivated reasoning Reasoning that is driven to reach specific goals, such as to be accurate or to maintain preexisting beliefs.

myside bias A thinking error similar to confirmation bias in which thinking is one-sided and neglectful of the information and evidence that support the other side of a question.

naive realism An approach to personal experience in which one believes that what one perceives corresponds directly to reality and that one's experience is accurate; it is associated with errors in perception and memory.

naturalistic observation The collection of data in the natural environment used to observe behavior in natural settings but which cannot show causation.

normal distribution A probability distribution that serves as a model for how the values of different random variables are expected to occur by chance. When plotted, scores are distributed in a bell-shaped curve, with most of the scores clustering around the mean in the middle.

nudge theory A theory assuming that, by manipulating the way in which options are framed and the context in which they are presented, people can be prodded to improve their decisions without reducing their freedom of choice.

operational definition Defining a hypothetical construct in terms of the methods and procedures that make it possible to study it in observable form (e.g., memory is defined as the number of words recalled).

paranormal Any phenomenon that is beyond ordinary experience and cannot be explained by conventional science.

parsimony The preference for the simplest theories, hypotheses, and explanations that can still account for data.

participant–observer A type of field study in which a researcher infiltrates a group to study it without the participants knowing they are being studied.

peer review of research The process in which research submitted for publication is reviewed by experts on the subject, who evaluate the quality of the research and look for problems and ways the researcher's conclusions could be false.

perspective The way a person views or approaches a question, providing a framework within which to think and a set of assumptions within which to operate.

perspective taking An active process of trying to look at a question from another person's viewpoint.

persuasion The sending of messages intended to change other people's opinions, beliefs, attitudes, or behaviors.

phrenology A pseudoscience in which the study of the bumps and indentations on one's skull was thought to indicate one's specific characteristics and abilities.

placebo A fake treatment; it is commonly used in science as a control for the effects of expecting to receive an active treatment.

plagiarism A form of intellectual dishonesty in which an individual behaves as if someone else's ideas or work are his or her own, or fails to give adequate credit to the author of some idea or work.

plausible Considered to be reasonable given what is already known; e.g., in psychological science, what is reasonable given what is known about science and human behavior.

population All the possible observations on some variable, behavior, or characteristic that could be made.

post hoc reasoning A thinking error in which a person infers that some event that occurred before a second event was the cause of the second event; shortened from *post hoc ergo propter hoc* ("after this, therefore because of this").

primary source An original study of research or authored work.

probability The likelihood that some event of interest will occur, ranging from 0.00 (not at all) to 1.00 (certain to occur).

problem A situation in which a person encounters an obstacle and lacks the knowledge or strategy that would enable him or her to move from this initial state to a goal state.

propaganda A type of persuasive communication used to make political arguments geared toward convincing a group of people to behave a certain way or adopt a certain position.

prosocial behavior Any behavior that is focused on benefiting others or society at large.

pseudo-profound bullshit A type of vague expression that may sound profound but is actually composed of imprecise words and buzzwords that, although they retain syntactic structure, lack precise meaning.

pseudoscience An approach that masquerades as real science, but makes false claims that are not supported by scientific research and does not conform to good scientific method.

psychological misconceptions Firmly held, commonsense beliefs about behavior and mental processes that are not supported by psychological research.

psychosis A serious thought disturbance indicating a disconnection from conventional reality.

qualified conclusion A conclusion that is true under certain conditions.

quantity of evidence A measure of how much evidence is offered to support a claim; it is assumed that having more evidence is better than having less, all things being equal.

quasi-experiments A type of experiment in which there is no true manipulation of an independent variable through random assignment to treatment conditions.

randomized-trial experiment A kind of true experiment used in clinical science in which experimenters randomly assign subjects to one of multiple groups: at least one that receives a treatment expected to be effective in treating a condition, and one that serves as a control group, often receiving a *placebo*.

rapid diagnosis A diagnostic error in which clinicians make a diagnosis within just a few minutes; compare with *hasty generalization*.

rational-analytic An approach to thinking characterized by deliberate analysis and reasoning of the information presented; associated with Type 2 thinking.

reappraisal The reevaluation of a situation so as to look for other possible interpretations that may lead to experiencing a different emotion and a different response to the situation.

reconstructive memory Memory in which one uses prior knowledge and other available information to actively search for material that fills in the gaps in one's memory, which may result in inaccurate memory.

recursion The capacity to embed one structure within another.

red herring fallacy The thinking error in which one's attention is diverted from the question at hand by irrelevant evidence and information from an arguer hoping to win by creating a smoke screen.

reductionist A materialist who assumes that scientific research will ultimately be able to explain all mental states in physical terms when relevant biochemical and other physical changes within the nervous system are understood.

regression toward the mean A pattern of results in which the results of a test, when measured again, tend to be less extreme, or closer to the mean.

reification A thinking error in which a hypothetical construct is assumed to be a real or concrete entity rather than simply an abstract idea.

relationship The connection or correlation between two variables such that changes in one variable occur consistently in relation to the other variable.

reliability The consistency of scores obtained on a test or other measure.

replication Repeating methods and observations under similar or identical conditions to see if previously obtained findings will be duplicated.

representative sample A sample characterized by having the same characteristics, in the same proportion, as found in the population.

representativeness heuristic A heuristic in which a person reasons that "like goes with like"; when applied inappropriately, it produces a judgment error.

reproductive memory A view of memory which assumes that what one remembers is reproduced exactly from what occurs as if memory is a copy made on a video recorder; compare with *naive realism.*

sample A subset of a population used to represent that population.

schema A knowledge structure that organizes prior knowledge and can help us acquire new information but which can have selective effects on learning and memory.

scientific standards of evidence Rules and principles used to determine higher- versus lower-quality scientific evidence.

secondary source A study in which the author summarizes, interprets, or comments on the original research done by someone else.

self-correcting The property of science by which it can revise and refine its own premises and assumptions.

self-serving bias A tendency to evaluate oneself favorably.

shifting the burden of proof A problem in argumentation that arises when a person makes a new or poorly supported claim but does not assume the responsibility to present evidence in support of it and instead redirects that responsibility to the better-supported position; it often occurs with arguing from ignorance.

sound A deductive argument that is valid or follows correct logical form and has a true conclusion when all of the premises are true.

source forgetting A type or memory error in which a person attributes some memory or knowledge to the wrong source.

spontaneous remission A situation in which a person recovers from a problem unexpectedly over time without the aid of a treatment.

statements of authority A type of evidence based on the statements made by someone presumed to have special knowledge or expertise, offered in support of an argument; the strength of the authoritative statements depends on the relevant knowledge and expertise of the presumed authority.

statistically significant The minimal criterion that a result would occur by chance fewer than 5 times out of 100.

status quo bias The pervasive tendency for people to stay with their initial response.

superstition A commonsense belief that is not plausible, given what is known from scientific research and rational principles. It is frequently associated with rituals and practices for promoting positive outcomes and preventing negative ones. Such beliefs are often thought to be the faulty beliefs of people not in one's own group and not the unsubstantiated beliefs of one's own group.

survey research A study conducted by asking participants multiple questions.

sweeping generalization A conclusion that is too broad or goes beyond an appropriate conclusion based on the evidence presented.

syndrome A set of signs or symptoms that go together and correspond to a specific diagnostic category.

theory A set of general principles that attempts to explain and predict behavior or other phenomena.

thinking errors Mistakes in judgment, decision making, and reasoning, including cognitive errors, logical fallacies, and incorrect use of rules for estimating probabilities.

Thought Field Therapy (TFT) A power therapy that claims it is fast-acting and highly effective—claims that are likely pseudoscientific.

transcranial magnetic stimulation (TMS) A technique for studying the brain in which a magnetic pulse is applied to the scalp over the brain region to be stimulated; it sets up tiny electric currents that can briefly disrupt or enhance function of that region.

true experiment A method that compares treatment conditions by manipulating an independent variable to examine its possible effect on a dependent (or measured) variable while controlling other variables through random assignment and other means, allowing causation to be inferred under the right conditions.

unwarranted assumption A notion in which something is implied to be true but has not been justified or supported by good reason.

vagueness The use of imprecise words, or words that do not have clear boundaries.

valid An argument that follows correct logical form, such as one that asserts the antecedent in a conditional deductive argument.

valid cue Evidence that provides information that is predictive of a good judgment or decision.

validity The degree to which a test or measure actually measures what it was intended to measure.

variable A characteristic or event of interest that can take on different values.

weapon focus An effect influencing the ability of eyewitnesses to process context in which the presence of a weapon increases the witnesses' stress and arousal levels, riveting their attention to the weapon and not the event.

weasel words Words that hedge or qualify claims so much that they are empty of meaning.

web-based Information that is based on the Internet, such as databases delivered via the Internet and updated and maintained by professional scholars and librarians; it tends to be more reliable and of higher quality than web-placed information.

web-placed Information placed on various websites for differing purposes, typically by individuals, groups, or organizations to promote their own ideas, products, and/or services.

REFERENCES

Abrami, P. C., Bernard, R. M., Borokhovski, E., Wade, A., Surkes, M. A., Tamim, R., & Zhang, D. (2008). Instructional interventions affecting critical thinking skills and dispositions: A stage 1 meta-analysis. *Review of Educational Research, 4,* 1102–1134.

Albas, D., & Albas, C. (1989). Modern magic: The case of examinations. *Sociological Quarterly, 30,* 603–613.

Alcock, J. E. (1987). Parapsychology: Science of the anomalous or search for the soul? *Behavioral and Brain Sciences, 10,* 553–565.

Alcock, J. (2011). Back to the future: Parapsychology and the Bem affair. *Skeptical Inquirer, 35,* 31–39.

Aleman, A., & Laroi, F. (2008). *Hallucinations: The science of idiosyncratic perception.* Washington, DC: American Psychological Association.

Aleman, A., & Vercammen, A. (2013). The "bottom-up" and "top-down" components of the hallucinatory phenomenon. In R. Jardri et al. (Eds.), *The neuroscience of hallucinations* (pp. 107–121). New York, NY: Springer.

Alicke, M. D., & Govorun, O. (2005). The better-than-average effect. In M. Alicke, D. Dunning, & J. Krueger (Eds.), *The self in social judgment* (pp. 85–106). New York, NY: Psychology Press.

Alvarado, C. S. (2000). Out-of-body experiences. In E. Cardena, S. J. Lynn, & S. Krippner (Eds.), *Varieties of anomalous experiences: Examining the scientific evidence* (pp. 183–218). Washington, DC: American Psychological Association.

American Psychiatric Association (2000). *Diagnostic and statistical manual of mental disorders* (Fourth ed.) (*DSM-IV-TR*). Washington, DC: Author.

American Psychiatric Association. (2013). *Diagnostic and statistical manual of mental disorders* (Fifth ed.) (*DSM-5*). Washington, DC: Author.

American Psychological Association. (2002). Ethical principles for psychologists and code of conduct. *American Psychologist, 57,* 1060–1073.

American Psychological Association. (2004). *2004 Graduate study in psychology.* Washington, DC: Author.

American Psychological Association. (2010). *Publication manual of the American Psychological Association.* Washington, DC: Author.

Anderson, C. A. (2007). Belief perseverance. In R. F. Baumeister & K. D. Vohs (Eds.), *Encyclopedia of social psychology* (pp. 109–110). Thousand Oaks, CA: Sage.

Anderson, C. A., Benjamin, A. J., & Bartholow, B. D. (1998). Does the gun pull the trigger? Automatic priming of weapon pictures and weapon names. *Psychological Science, 9,* 308–314.

Anderson, C. A., & Bushman, B. J. (2002). Human aggression. *Annual Review of Psychology, 53,* 27–51.

Anderson, C. A., Shibuya, A., Ihori, N., Swing, E. L., Bushman, B. J., Sakamoto, A., . . . Saleem, M. (2010). Violent video game effects on aggression, empathy, and prosocial behavior in Eastern and Western countries: A meta-analytic review. *Psychological Bulletin, 136,* 151–173.

Ariely, D., Loewenstein, G., & Prelec, D. (2003). Coherent arbitrariness: Stable demand curves without stable preferences. *Quarterly Journal of Economics, 118,* 73–106.

Arkes, H. R. (1991). Costs and benefits of judgment errors: Implications for debiasing. *Psychological Bulletin, 110,* 486–498.

Arms, R. L., Russell, G. W., & Sandlands, M. L. (1979). Effects on the hostility of spectators of viewing aggressive sports. *Social Psychology Quarterly, 42,* 275–279.

Arnold, J. M., & Jayne, E. A. (2003). Putting the web in context. In T. Jacobson (Ed.), *Critical thinking and the web: Teaching users to evaluate Internet resources* (pp. 15–17). Pittsburgh, PA: Library Instruction Publications.

Asch, S. E. (1951). Effects of group pressures upon the modification and distortion of judgments. In H. Guertzkow (Ed.), *Groups, leadership, and men* (pp. 177–190). Pittsburgh, PA: Carnegie Press.

Asimov, I. (1989). The relativity of wrong. *Skeptical Inquirer, 14,* 35–44.

Auerbach, L. (1986). *ESP, hauntings, and poltergeists: A parapsychologist's handbook.* New York, NY: Warner Books.

Auerbach, R. P., Webb, C. A., Gardiner, C. K., & Pechtel, P. (2013). Behavioral and neural mechanisms underlying cognitive vulnerability models of depression. *Journal of Psychotherapy Integration, 23,* 222–225.

Baars, B. J., & Gage, N. M. (2010). *Cognition, brain, and consciousness: Introduction to cognitive neuroscience* (2nd ed.). Boston, MA: Academic Press.

Baddeley, A. (2012). Working memory, theories, models, and controversies. *Annual Review of Psychology, 63,* 1–29.

Baddeley, A., Eysenck, M. W., & Anderson, M. C. (2015). *Memory* (2nd ed.). New York, NY: Psychology Press.

Badian, N. (2005). Does a visuo-orthographic deficit contribute to reading disability? *Annals of Dyslexia, 55,* 28–52.

Bailey, J. F. (1979). The effects of an instructional paradigm on the development of critical thinking of college students in an introductory botany course (Doctoral dissertation, Purdue University). *Dissertation Abstracts International, 39,* 480A.

Baker, L. (1989). Metacognition, comprehension monitoring, and the adult reader. *Educational Psychology Review, 1,* 3–38.

Baker, T. B., McFall, R. M., & Shoham, V. (2009). Current status and future prospects of clinical psychology. *Psychological Science in the Public Interest, 9,* 67–103.

Balance, C. T. (1977). Students' expectations and their answer-changing behavior. *Psychological Reports, 41,* 163–166.

Balch, R. W. (1993). Waiting for the ships: Disillusionment and the revitalization of faith in Bo and Peep's UFO cult. In J. R. Lewis (Ed.), *The gods have landed: New religions from other worlds* (pp. 137–166). Albany, NY: State University of New York Press.

Balch, R. W., & Taylor, D. (1977). Seekers and saucers: The role of the cultic milieu in joining a UFO cult. *American Behavioral Scientist, 20,* 839–860.

Bandura, A. (1977). *Social learning theory.* Englewood Cliffs, NJ: Prentice Hall.

Bandura, A., & Walters, R. H. (1959). *Adolescent aggression.* New York, NY: Ronald Press.

Baron, J. (1995). Myside bias in thinking about abortion. *Thinking and Reasoning, 1,* 221–235.

Baron, J. (2008). *Thinking and deciding* (4th ed.). Cambridge, UK: Cambridge University Press.

Barrett, L. F. (2015). Ten common misconceptions about psychological construction theories of emotion. In L. F. Barrett & J. A. Russell (Eds.), *The psychological construction of emotion* (pp. 45–79). New York, NY: Guilford.

Barrett, T. R., & Etheridge, J. B. (1992). Verbal hallucinations in normals, I: People who hear "voices." *Applied Cognitive Psychology, 6,* 379–387.

Bartholomew, R. E., & Goode, E. (2000). Mass delusions and hysterias: Highlights from the past millennium. *Skeptical Inquirer, 24.* Retrieved from http://www.csicop.org/si/show/mass_delusions_and_hysterias_highlights_from_the_past_millennium

Bartlett, F. C. (1932). *Remembering: A study in experimental and social psychology.* Cambridge, UK: Cambridge University Press.

Bartlett, S. J. (2011). *Normality does not equal mental health.* Santa Barbara, CA: Praeger.

Bassham, G., Irwin, W., Nardone, H., & Wallace, J. M. (2005). *Critical thinking: A student's introduction* (2nd ed.). Boston, MA: McGraw-Hill.

Batson, C. D. (1990). Affect and altruism. In B. Moore & A. Isen (Eds.), *Affect and social behavior* (pp. 89–125). Cambridge, UK: Cambridge University Press.

Batson, C. D. (2011). *Altruism in humans.* New York, NY: Oxford University Press.

Batson, C. D., Bolen, M. H., Cross, J. A., & Neuringer-Benefiel, H. E. (1986). Where is the altruism in the altruistic personality? *Journal of Personality and Social Psychology, 50,* 212–220.

Baumann, J., & DeSteno, D. (2012). Context explains divergent effects of anger on risk taking. *Emotion, 12,* 1196–1199.

Baumeister, R. F., DeWall, C. N., & Zhang, L. (2007). Do emotions improve or hinder the decision-making process? In K. D. Vohs, R. F. Baumeister, & G. Loewenstein (Eds.), *Do emotions help or hurt decision making? A hedgfoxian perspective* (pp. 11–31). New York, NY: Russell Sage Foundation.

Baumeister, R. R., & Bushman, B. J. (2008). *Social psychology and human nature.* Belmont, CA: Thomson Wadsworth.

Baumeister, R. R., Campbell, J. D., Krueger, J. J., & Vohs, K. D. (2008). Exploding the self-esteem myth. In S. O. Lilienfeld, J. Ruscio, & S. J. Lynn (Eds.), *Navigating the mindfield: A user's guide to distinguishing science from pseudoscience in mental health* (pp. 575–587). Amherst, NY: Prometheus Books.

Beaman, A., Barnes, P., Klentz, B., & McQuirk, B. (1978). Increasing helping rates through information dissemination: Teaching pays. *Personality and Social Psychology Bulletin, 4,* 406–411.

Beck, A. T. (1963). Thinking and depression. *Archives of General Psychiatry, 9,* 324–333.

Beck, A. T. (2005). The current state of cognitive therapy: A 40-year retrospective. *Archives of General Psychiatry, 62,* 953–959.

Beckman, V. E. (1956). An investigation of the contributions to critical thinking made by courses in argumentation and discussion in selected colleges (Doctoral dissertation, University of Minnesota). *Dissertation Abstracts International, 16,* 2551A.

Beecher, H. (1955). The powerful placebo. *Journal of the American Medical Association, 159,* 1602–1606.

Beins, B. C., & Beins, A. M. (2012). *Effective writing in psychology: Papers, posters, and presentations* (2nd ed.). Walden, MA: Wiley-Blackwell.

Beloff, J. (1989). Dualism: A parapsychological perspective. In J. R. Smythies & J. Beloff (Eds.), *The case for dualism.* Charlottesville, VA: University Press of Virginia.

Bem, D. J. (2011). Feeling the future: Experimental evidence for anomalous retroactive influences on cognition and affect. *Journal of Personality and Social Psychology, 100,* 407–425.

Bem, D. J., & Honorton, C. (1994). Does psi exist? Evidence for an anomalous process of information transfer. *Psychological Bulletin, 115,* 4–18.

Benjamin, L. T., Cavell, T. A., & Shallenberger, W. R., III. (1984). Staying with initial answers on tests: Is it a myth? *Teaching of Psychology, 11,* 133–141.

Bensley, D A. (1998). *Critical thinking in psychology: A unified skills approach.* Belmont, CA: Brooks/Cole.

Bensley, D. A. (2002). Science and pseudoscience: A primer in critical thinking. In M. Shermer (Ed.), *The skeptic encyclopedia of pseudoscience* (pp. 195–203). Santa Barbara, CA: ABC-CLIO.

Bensley, D. A. (2003). Can minds leave bodies? A cognitive science approach. *Skeptical Inquirer,* 34–39.

Bensley, D. A. (2006). Why great thinkers sometimes fail to think critically. *Skeptical Inquirer, 30,* 47–52.

Bensley, D. A. (2010). A brief guide to teaching and assessing critical thinking in psychology. *APS Observer, 23,* 49–53.

Bensley, D. A. (2011). Rules for reasoning revisited: Toward a scientific conception of critical thinking. In C. P. Horvath & J. M. Forte (Eds.), *Critical thinking* (pp. 1–35). Hauppauge, NY: Nova Science Publishers.

Bensley, D. A., Crowe, D. S., Bernhardt, P., Buckner, C., & Allman, A. L. (2010). Teaching and assessing critical thinking skills for argument analysis. *Teaching of Psychology, 37,* 91–96.

Bensley, D. A., & Haynes, C. (1995). The acquisition of general purpose strategic knowledge for argumentation. *Teaching of Psychology, 22,* 41–45.

Bensley, D. A., & Lilienfeld, S. O. (2015). What is a psychological misconception? Moving towards an empirical answer. *Teaching of Psychology, 42,* 282–292.

Bensley, D. A., & Lilienfeld, S. O. (2017). Psychological misconceptions: Recent scientific advances and unresolved issues. *Current Directions in Psychological Science, 26,* 377–382.

Bensley, D. A., Lilienfeld, S. O., & Powell, L. A. (2014). A new measure of psychological misconceptions: Relations with academic background, critical thinking, and acceptance of paranormal and pseudoscientific claims. *Learning and Individual Differences, 36,* 9–18.

Bensley, D. A., & Murtagh, M. P. (2012). Taking a scientific approach to critical thinking assessment: Guidelines for psychology programs. *Teaching of Psychology, 37,* 5–16.

Bensley, D. A., Rainey, C., Bernhardt, P. C., Grain, F., & Rowan, K. (2017). How can thinking be both better and worse than average? Testing the hard–easy effect in the metacognitive monitoring of critical thinking. (Manuscript in preparation)

Bensley, D. A., Rainey, C., Lilienfeld, S. O., & Kuehne, S. (2016). What do psychology students know about what they know in psychology? *Scholarship of Teaching and Learning in Psychology, 1,* 283–297.

Bensley, D. A., Rainey, C., Murtagh, M. P., Flinn, J. A., Maschiocchi, Bernhardt, P. C., & Kuehne, S. (2016). Closing the assessment loop on critical thinking: The challenges of multidimensional testing and low test-taking motivation. *Thinking Skills and Creativity, 21,* 158–168.

Bensley, D. A., & Spero, R. A. (2014). Improving critical thinking skills and metacognitive monitoring through direct infusion. *Thinking Skills and Creativity, 12,* 55–68.

Benson, H. (1975). *The relaxation response.* New York, NY: Morrow.

Berenbaum, H., & Boden, M. T. (2014). In I. Blanchette (Ed.), *Emotion and reasoning* (pp. 65–83). New York, NY: Psychology Press.

Berkowitz, L. (1972). Social norms, feelings, and other factors affecting helping and altruism. In L. Berkowitz (Ed.), *Advances in experimental social psychology* (Vol. 6, pp. 435–436). New York, NY: Academic Press.

Best, M., Neuhauser, D., & Slavin, L. (2003). Evaluating mesmerism, Paris, 1784: The controversy over the blinded placebo controlled trials has not stopped. *Quality and Safety in Health Care, 12,* 232–233.

Beutler, L. E. (1997). The psychotherapist as a neglected variable in psychotherapy: An illustration by reference to the role of therapist experience and training. *Clinical Psychology: Science and Practice, 4,* 44–52.

Beutler, L. E. (2000). Empirically based decision making in clinical practice. *Prevention & Treatment, 3* (Article 27). Retrieved from http://journals.apa.org/prevention/volume3/pre0030027a.html

Beyer, B. K. (1995). Critical thinking. *Fastback* series, no. 385, 7–33. Bloomington, IN: Phi Delta Kappa Educational Foundation.

Black, D. W., & Andreasen, N. C. (2011). *Introductory textbook of psychiatry.* Washington, DC: American Psychiatric Publishing.

Blackmore, S. J. (1982). Parapsychology: With and without the OBE? *Parapsychology Review, 13,* 1–7.

Blackmore, S. J. (1987). Where am I? Perspectives in imagery and the out-of-body experience. *Journal of Mental Imagery, 11,* 53–66.

Blackmore, S. J. (1992a). *Beyond the body: An investigation of out-of-body experiences* (rev. ed.). Chicago, IL: Academy Chicago Publishers.

Blackmore, S. J. (1992b). Psychic experience: Psychic illusions. *Skeptical Inquirer, 16,* 367–376.

Blanchette, I. (2014). Does emotion affect reasoning? Yes, in multiple ways. In I. Blanchette (Ed.), *Emotion and reasoning* (pp. 1–21). New York, NY: Psychology Press.

Blanchette, I., Gavigan, S., & Johnston, K. (2014). Does emotion help or hinder reasoning? The moderating role of relevance. *Journal of Experimental Psychology: General, 143,* 1049–1064.

Blanchfield, B., Bensley, D. A., Hierstetter, J., Mahdavi, A., & Rowan, V. (2007, March). *Reported OBE occurrence: Be careful how you ask.* Poster presented at the annual meeting of the Eastern Psychological Association, Philadelphia, PA.

Blanke, O., Mohr, C., Michel, C. M., Pasucal-Leone, A., Brugger, P., Seeck, M., . . . Thut, G. (2005). Linking out-of-body experience and self-processing to mental own-body imagery at the temporoparietal junction. *Journal of Neuroscience, 25,* 550–557.

Blanke, O., Ortigue, S., Landis, T., & Seeck, M. (2002). Stimulating illusory own-body perceptions. *Nature, 419,* 269–270.

Blanke, O., & Thut, G., (2007). Inducing out-of-body experiences. In S. Della Sala (Ed.), *Tall tales about the mind and brain* (pp. 425–439). New York, NY: Oxford University Press.

Blashfield, R. K., & Herkow, M. J. (1996). Investigating clinician adherence to diagnosis by criteria: A replication of Morey and Ochoa (1989). *Journal of Personality Disorders, 10,* 219–228.

Blitz, D. (1991). The line of demarcation between science and nonscience: The case for psychoanalysis and parapsychology. *New Ideas in Psychology, 9,* 163–170.

Bloom, B. S. (1956). *Taxonomy of educational objectives: The classification of educational goals.* Harlow, UK: Longman Group.

Bloom, P. (2004). *Descartes' baby: How the science of child development explains what makes us human.* New York, NY: Basic Books.

Boden, M. T., Berenbaum, H., & Gross, J. J. (2016). Why do people believe what they do? A functionalist perspective. *Review of General Psychology.* Retrieved from PsycINFO: http://dx.doi.org/10.1037/gpr0000085

Bok, B. J. (1975). A critical look at astrology. In B. J. Bok & L. Jerome (Eds.), *Objections to astrology* (pp. 21–33). Buffalo, NY: Prometheus Books.

Bonto, M. A., & Payne, D. G. (1991). Role of environmental context in eyewitness memory. *American Journal of Psychology, 104,* 117–134.

Boudry, M., & Braekman, J. (2012). How convenient! The epistemic rationale of self-validating systems. *Philosophical Psychology, 25,* 341–364.

Bouzar, D. (2016, May/June). Escaping radicalism. *Scientific American Mind,* 41–43.

Boysen, S. (2012). *The smartest animals on the planet.* Buffalo, NY: Firefly Books.

Bradfield, A. L., Wells, G. L., & Olson, E. A. (2002). The damaging effect of confirming feedback on the relation between eyewitness certainty and identification accuracy. *Journal of Applied Psychology, 87,* 112–120.

Bransford, J., & Johnson, M. K. (1972). Contextual prerequisites for understanding: Some investigations of comprehension and recall. *Journal of Verbal Learning & Verbal Behavior, 11,* 717–726.

Brevers, D., Dan, B., Noel, X., & Nils, F. (2011). Sport superstition: Mediation of psychological tension on non-professional sportsmen's superstitious rituals. *Journal of Sport Behavior, 34,* 3–24.

Brewer, W. F., & Treyans, J. C. (1981). Role of schemata in memory for places. *Cognitive Psychology, 13,* 207–230.

Broca, P. (1966). Paul Broca on the speech center. In R. Herrnstein & E. Boring (Eds.), *A source book in the history of psychology* (pp. 223–228). Cambridge, MA: Harvard University Press.

Brook, A., & Stainton, R. J. (2000). *Knowledge and mind: A philosophical introduction.* Cambridge, MA: MIT Press.

Brown, L. T. (1983). Some more misconceptions about psychology among introductory psychology students. *Teaching of Psychology, 10,* 207–210.

Brown, W. A. (2013). *The placebo effect in clinical practice.* New York, NY: Oxford University Press.

Brownell, C. A., Svetlova, M., & Nichols, S. (2009). To share or not to share: When do toddlers respond to another's needs? *Infancy, 14,* 117–130.

Bruce, V., Henderson, Z., Greeenwood, K., Hancock, P., Burton, A. M., & Miller, P. (1999). Verification of face identities from images captured on video. *Journal of Experimental Psychology: Applied, 5,* 339–360.

Bryan, J. H., & Test, M. A. (1967). Models and helping: Naturalistic studies in aiding behavior. *Journal of Personality and Social Psychology, 6,* 400–407.

Buck, R. (1988). *Human motivation and emotion* (2nd ed.). New York, NY: John Wiley.

Buckley, P. F., Miller, B. J., Lehrer, D. S., & Castle, D. J. (2009). Psychiatric comorbidities and schizophrenia. *Schizophrenia Bulletin, 35,* 383–402.

Bunge, M. (1984). What is pseudoscience? *Skeptical Inquirer, 9,* 36–46.

Burnstein, E., Crandall, C., & Kitayama, S. (1994). Some neo-Darwinian decision-rules for altruism: Weighing cues for inclusive fitness as a function of biological importance of the decision. *Journal of Personality and Social Psychology, 67,* 773–789.

Bushman, B. J., Baumeister, R. F., & Stack, A. D. (1999). Catharsis, aggression, and persuasive influence: Self-fulfilling or self-defeating prophesies. *Journal of Personality and Social Psychology, 76,* 367–376.

Butler, J. A., & Britt, M. A. (2011). Improving instruction for improving revision of argumentative essays. *Written Communication, 28,* 70–96.

Byford, J. (2011). *Conspiracy theories: A critical introduction.* New York, NY: Palgrave Macmillan.

Byrne, D. (1971). *The attraction paradigm.* New York, NY: Academic Press.

Byrnes, J. P., & Dunbar, K. N. (2014). The nature and development of critical-analytic thinking. *Educational Psychology Review, 26,* 477–493.

Calin-Jageman, R. J., & Caldell, T. L. (2014). Replication of the superstition and performance study by Damisch, Stroberock, and Mussweiler (2010). *Social Psychology, 45,* 239–245.

Callahan, R. (1997). Thought field therapy: The case of Mary. *Traumatology, 3,* 1. doi: 10.1177/153476569700300105

Carlsen, E. R. (1995). Evaluating the credibility of sources: A missing link in the teaching of critical thinking. *Teaching of Psychology, 22,* 39–41.

Carlson, J. A., & Russo, K. E. (2001). Biased interpretation of evidence by mock jurors. *Journal of Experimental Psychology: Applied, 7,* 91–103.

Carnevale, P. J. D., & Isen, A. M. (1986). The influence of positive affect and visual access on the discovery of integrative solutions in bilateral negotiation. *Organizational Behavior and Human Decision Processes, 37,* 1–13.

Carr, N. (2010). *The shallows: What the Internet is doing to our brains.* New York, NY: W. W. Norton.

Carrera, P., Oceja, L., Caballero, A., Munoz, D., López-Pérez, B., & Ambrona, T. (2012). I feel so sorry: Tapping the joint influence of empathy and personal distress on helping behavior. *Motivation and Emotion, 37,* 335–345.

Cassar, M., Treiman, R., Moats, L., Pollo, T. C., & Kessler, B. (2005). How do the spellings of children with dyslexia compare with those of nondyslexic children? *Reading and Writing, 18,* 27–49.

Chambless, D. L., & Ollendick, T. H. (2001). Empirically supported psychological interventions: Controversies and evidence. *Annual Review of Psychology, 52,* 685–716.

Chapman, L. J., & Chapman, J. P. (1967). Genesis of popular but erroneous psychodiagnostic observations. *Journal of Abnormal Psychology, 72,* 193–204.

Chen, Z., & Cowan, N. (2009). Core verbal working-memory capacity: The limit in words retained without covert articulation. *Quarterly Journal of Experimental Psychology, 62,* 1420–1429.

Cheyne, J. A., & Girard, T. A. (2009). The body unbound: Vestibular–motor hallucinations and out-of-body experiences. *Cortex, 45,* 201–215.

Cheyne, J. A., Rueffer, S. D., & Newby-Clark, I. R. (1999). Sleep paralysis and associated hypnogogic and hypnopompic hallucinations during sleep paralysis. *Consciousness and Cognition, 8,* 319–337.

Cialdini, R. B., Baumann, D. J., & Kenrick, D. T. (1981). Insights from sadness: A three-step model of the development of altruism as hedonism. *Developmental Review, 1,* 207–223.

Cialdini, R. B., Schaller, M., Houlihan, D., Arps, K., Fultz, J., & Beaman, A. (1987). Empathy-based helping: Is it selflessly or selfishly motivated? *Journal of Personality and Social Psychology, 52,* 749–758.

Clancy, S. A. (2005). *Abducted: How people come to believe they were kidnapped by aliens.* Cambridge, MA: Harvard University Press.

Cohen, D. J., White, S., & Cohen, S. B. (2011). A time use diary: Study of adult everyday writing behavior. *Written Communication, 28,* 3–33.

Coirier, P., & Golder, C. (1993). Writing argumentative text: A developmental study of the acquisition of supporting structures. *European Journal of Psychology of Education, 8,* 116–180.

Coke, J. S., Batson, C. D., & McDavis, K. (1978). Empathic mediation of helping: A two-stage model. *Journal of Personality and Social Psychology, 36,* 752–766.

Cook, J., Oreskes, N., Doran, P. T., Anderegg, W. R. L., Verheggen, B., Maibach, E. W., . . . Green., S. A. (2016). Consensus on consensus: A synthesis of consensus estimates on human-caused global warming. *Environmental Research Letters, 11*(4).

Coppinger, R., & Coppinger, L. (2002). A startling new understanding of canine origin, behavior, and evolution. *Animal Behavior, 64,* 511–512.

Corballis, M. C. (2012). *The recursive mind: The origins of human language, thought, and civilization.* Princeton, NJ: Princeton University Press.

Corrigan, P. W., & Kleinlein, P. (2005). The impact of mental illness stigma. In P. W. Corrigan (Ed.), *On the stigma of mental illness: Practical strategies for research and social change* (pp. 11–44). Washington, DC: American Psychological Association.

Coscarelli, W. C., & Schwen, T. M. (1979). Effects of three algorithmic representations on critical thinking, laboratory efficiency, and final grade. *Educational Communication & Technology, 27,* 58–64.

Cowan, N. (2000). The magical number 4 in short-term memory: A reconsideration of mental storage capacity. *Behavioral and Brain Sciences, 24,* 87–185.

Coyne, J. (2009). *Why evolution is true.* New York, NY: Penguin.

Crossley, R. (1992). Getting the words out: Case studies in facilitated communication training. *Topics in Language Disorders, 12,* 46–59.

Crowe, R. A. (1990). Astrology and the scientific method. *Psychological Reports, 67,* 163–191.

Crowhurst, M. (1990). Teaching and learning the writing of persuasive/argumentative discourse. *Canadian Journal of Education, 15,* 348–359.

Damasio, A. R. (1994). *Descartes' error: Emotion reason and the human brain.* New York, NY: G. P. Putnam.

Damasio, H., Grabowski, T., Frank, R., Galaburda, A. M., & Damasio, A. R. (1994). The return of Phineas Gage: The skull of a famous patient yields clues about the brain. *Science, 264,* 1102–1105.

Damisch, L., Stroberock, B., & Mussweiler, T. (2010). Keep your fingers crossed! How superstition improves performance. *Psychological Science, 21,* 1014–1020.

Dansereau, D., McDonald, B., Collins, K., Garland, J., Holley, C., Diekhoff, G., & Evans, S. (1979). Evaluation of a learning strategy system. In H. O'Neil & C. Spielberger (Eds.), *Cognitive and affective learning strategies.* New York, NY: Academic Press.

Darley, J., & Latané, B. (1968). Bystander intervention in emergencies. *Journal of Personality and Social Psychology, 8,* 377–383.

Davies, G., & Hine, S. (2007). Change blindness and eyewitness testimony. *Journal of Psychology: Interdisciplinary and Applied, 14,* 423–434.

Davies, G., & Thomson, D. (1988). *Memory in context: Context in memory.* Oxford, UK: John Wiley.

Davies, J. (2013). *Cracked: The unhappy truth about psychiatry.* New York, NY: Pegasus Books.

Davis, D., Loftus, E. F., Vanous, S., & Cucciare, M. (2008). "Unconscious transference" can be an instance of "change blindness." *Applied Cognitive Psychology, 22,* 605–623.

Davis, M. D., Luce, C., & Kraus, S. J. (1994). The heritability of characteristics associated with dispositional empathy. *Journal of Personality, 62,* 369–391.

Dawkins, R. (1989). *The selfish gene* (2nd ed.). Oxford, UK: Oxford University Press.

Dawkins, R. (2009). *The greatest show on earth: The evidence for evolution.* New York, NY: Free Press.

Deffenbacher, K. A., Bornstein, B. H., Penrod, S. D., & McGorty, E. K. (2004). A meta-analytic review of the effects of high stress on eyewitness memory. *Law and Human Behavior, 28,* 687–706.

De Ridder, D., Van Laere, K., Dupont, P., Menovsky, T., & Van De Heyning, P. (2007). Visualizing out-of-body experience in the Brain Brief Report. *New England Journal of Medicine, 357,* 1829–1833.

Descartes, R. (1999). *Discourse on method and related writings,* trans. by Desmond M. Clarke. London, UK: Penguin.

DeWaal, F. (2005). *Our inner ape.* New York, NY: Penguin Books.

Djamasbi, J. (2007). Does positive affect influence effective usage of a decision support system? *Decision Support Systems, 43,* 1707–1717.

Domonoske, C. (2016, November, 23). Students have "dismaying" inability to tell fake news from real, study says (National Public Radio interview with Sam Wineburg). Retrieved from http://www.npr.org/sections/thetwo-way/2016/11/23/503129818/

Donaldson, S. (1988, May 8). Excerpts from a discussion on Reagan and astrology, *This Week with David Brinkley,* ABC Television.

Dovidio, J. F., Allen, J. L., & Schroeder, D. A. (1990). The specificity of empathy-induced helping: Evidence for altruism. *Journal of Personality and Social Psychology, 59,* 249–260.

Dumont, F. (1991). Expertise in psychotherapy: Inherent liabilities of becoming experienced. *Psychotherapy, 28,* 422–428.

Dumont, F. (1993). Inferential heuristics in clinical problem formulation: Selective review of their strengths and weaknesses. *Professional Psychology: Research and Practice, 24,* 196–205.

Dumont, F., & Lecomte, C. (1987). Inferential processes in clinical work: Inquiry into logical errors that affect diagnostic judgments. *Professional Psychology: Research and Practice, 18,* 433–438.

Dunbar, K., & Fugelsang, J. (2005). Scientific thinking and reasoning. In K. Holyoak & R. Morrison (Eds.), *The Cambridge handbook of thinking and reasoning* (pp. 705–725). New York, NY: Cambridge University Press.

Dunlosky, J., & Lipko, A. R. (2007). Metacomprehension: A brief history and how to improve its accuracy. *Current Directions on Psychological Science, 16,* 228–232.

Dunning, D., Griffin, D. W., Milojkovic, J. D., & Ross, L. (1990). The overconfident effect in social prediction. *Journal of Personality and Social Psychology, 58,* 568–581.

Dunning, D., Johnson, K., Ehrlinger, J., & Kruger, J. (2003). Why people fail to recognize their own incompetence. *Current Directions in Psychological Science, 12,* 83–87.

Ebbesen, E. B., Duncan, B., & Konecni, V. J. (1975). Effects of content of verbal aggression on future verbal aggression: A field experiment. *Journal of Experimental Social Psychology, 11,* 192–204.

Ehrsson, H. H. (2007). The experimental induction of out of body experiences. *Science, 317,* 1048.

Eilan, N., Mareel, A., & Bermudez, J. (1995). Self-consciousness and the body: An interdisciplinary introduction. In J. Bermudez, A. Marcel, & N. Eilan (Eds.), *The body and the self* (pp. 1–28). Cambridge, MA: MIT Press.

Einstein, D. A., Menzies, R. G., St. Clare, T., Drobny, J., & Helgadottir, F. J. (2011). The treatment of magical ideation in two individuals with obsessive compulsive disorder. *Behaviour Therapist, 4,* 16–29.

Eisenberg, N., & Fabes, R. A. (1990). Empathy: Conceptualization, measurement, and relation to prosocial behavior. *Motivation and Emotion, 14,* 131–149.

Eisner, D. A. (2000). *The death of psychotherapy: From Freud to alien abduction.* Westport, CT: Praeger.

Ekman, P. (1994). Strong evidence for universals in facial expressions: A reply to Russell's mistaken critique. *Psychological Bulletin, 115,* 268–287.

Ekman, P., & Friesen, W. V. (1975). *Unmasking the face.* Englewood Cliffs, NJ: Prentice Hall.

Ekroll, V., Sayim, B., & Wagemans, J. (2017). The other side of magic: The psychology of perceiving hidden things. *Perspectives on Psychological Science, 12,* 91–106.

Ellis, A. (1977a). The basic clinical theory of rational-emotive therapy. In A. Ellis & R. Geiger (Eds.), *Handbook of rational emotive therapy.* New York, NY: Springer.

Ellis, A. (1977b). Research data supporting the clinical and hypotheses of RET and other cognitive-behavior therapies. In A. Ellis & R. Geiger (Eds.), *Handbook of rational emotive therapy.* New York, NY: Springer.

Ellsworth, P. C. (2013). Appraisal theory: Old and new questions. *Emotion Review, 5,* 125–131.

Englich, B., Mussweiler, T., & Strack, F. (2006). Playing dice with criminal sentences: The influence of irrelevant anchors on experts' judicial decision making. *Personality and Social Psychology Bulletin, 32,* 188–200.

Ennis, R. H. (1987). A taxonomy of critical thinking dispositions and abilities. In J. Baron & R. Sternberg (Eds.), *Teaching thinking skills: Theory and practice* (pp. 9–26). New York, NY: W. H. Freeman.

Epley, N., & Gilovich, T. (2006). The anchoring and adjustment heuristic: Why the adjustments are insufficient. *Psychological Science, 17,* 311–318.

Epstein, S. (2008). Intuition from the perspective of cognitive-experiential self-theory. In H. Plessner, C. Betsch, & T. Betsch (Eds.), *Intuition in judgment and decision making* (pp. 23–37). New York, NY: Erlbaum.

Ericsson, K. A. (2006). *The Cambridge handbook of expertise and expert performance.* New York, NY: Cambridge University Press.

Evans, J. St. B. T. (2008). Dual-processing accounts of reasoning, judgment and social cognition. *Annual Review of Psychology, 59,* 255–278.

Evans, J. St. B. T., & Stanovich, K. E. (2013). Dual-process theories of higher cognition: Advancing the debate. *Perspectives on Psychological Science, 8,* 223–241.

Exner, J. E. (1974). *The Rorschach: A comprehensive system: Vol. 1.* New York, NY: Wiley.

Falk, R. (1989). Judgment of coincidences: Mine versus yours. *American Journal of Psychology, 102,* 477–493.

Farquharson, K., Centanni, T. M., Franzluebbers, C. E., & Hogan, T. P. (2014). Phonological and lexical influences on phonological awareness in children with specific language impairment and dyslexia. *Frontiers in Psychology, 5,* 1–10.

Faust, D. (1986). Research on human judgment and its application to clinical practice. *Professional Psychology: Research and Practice, 17,* 420–430.

Faust, D. (2007). Decision research can increase the accuracy of clinical judgment. In S. O. Lilienfeld & W. T. O'Donohue (Eds.), *The great ideas of clinical science* (pp. 49–76). New York, NY: Routledge.

Fawkes, D. (2003). Reliance on indicator terms is not critical thinking. *Inquiry: Critical Thinking, 21,* 7–14.

Ferguson, C. J. (2015). Do angry birds make for angry children? A meta-analysis of video game influences on children's and adolescents' aggression, mental health, prosocial behavior, and academic performance. *Perspectives on Psychological Science, 10,* 646–666.

Fernandez, C., Pascual, J. C., Soler, J., Elices, M., Portella, M. J., & Ferndandez-Abascal, E. (2012). Physiological responses induced by emotion-eliciting films. *Applied Physiological Biofeedback, 37,* 73–79.

Festinger, L., Riecken, H. W., & Schacter, S. (1956). *When prophesy fails.* New York, NY: Harper Torchbooks.

Feynman, R. (1985). *Surely you're joking, Mr. Feynman: Adventures of a curious character.* New York, NY: W. W. Norton.

Fischhoff, B. (1975). Hindsight is not equal to foresight: The effect of outcome knowledge on judgment under uncertainty. *Journal of Experimental Psychology: Human Perception and Performance, 1,* 288–299.

Fisher, M., Goddhu, M. K., & Keil, F. C. (2015). Searching for explanations: How the Internet inflates internal knowledge. *Journal of Experimental Psychology: General, 144,* 674–687.

Flamm, B. L. (2006). Magnet therapy: A billion dollar boondoggle. *Skeptical Inquirer, 30,* 26–28.

Fong, G. T., Krantz, T. H., & Nisbett, R. E. (1986). The effects of statistical training on thinking about everyday problems. *Cognitive Psychology, 18,* 253–292.

Forer, B. R. (1949). The fallacy of personal validation: A classroom demonstration of gullibility. *Journal of Abnormal and Social Psychology, 44,* 118–123.

Forgeard, M. J., Pearl, R. L., Cheung, J., Rifkin, L. S., Beard, C., & Bjorgvinsson, T. (2016). Positive beliefs about mental illness: Associations with sex, age, diagnosis, and clinical outcomes. *Journal of Affective Disorders, 204,* 197–204.

Forsyth, D. R., Lawrence, N. K., Burnette, J. L., & Baumeister, R. F. (2007). Attempting to improve the academic performance of struggling college students by bolstering their self-esteem: An intervention that backfired. *Journal of Social and Clinical Psychology, 26,* 447–459.

Fox, L., Marsh, G., & Crandall, J. (1983). *The effect of college classroom experiences on formal operational thinking.* Annual Convention of the Western Psychological Association in San Francisco, CA, April 30, 1983.

Frances, A. (2013). *Essentials of psychiatric diagnosis: Responding to the challenge of DSM-5.* New York, NY: Guilford Press.

Franz, C. M. (2006). I am being fair: The bias blind spot as a stumbling block to seeing both sides. *Basic and Applied Social Psychology, 28,* 157–167.

Frazer, J. G. (1996). *The illustrated golden bough: A study in magic and religion.* New York, NY: Simon and Schuster. (Abridged by R. K. G. Temple; original work published 1890.)

Freidrich-Cofer, L., & Huston, A. C. (1986). Television viewing and aggression: The debate continues. *Psychological Bulletin, 100,* 364–371.

Fukaya, T. (2013). Explanation generation, not explanation expectancy improves metacomprehension. *Metacognition and Learning, 8,* 1–18.

Fultz, J., Batson, C. D., Fortenbach, V., McCarthy, P., & Varney, L. (1986). Social evaluation and the empathy–altruism hypothesis. *Journal of Personality and Social Psychology, 50,* 761–769.

Galak, J., LeBoeuf, R. A., Nelson, L. D., & Simmons, J. P. (2012). Correcting the past: Failures to replicate PSI. *Journal of Personality and Social Psychology, 103,* 933–948.

Gallup Poll. (1997). Black/White relations in the U.S. Retrieved from http://www.gallup.com/poll/9874/blackwhite-relations-united-states

Gambrill, E. (2010). Critical thinking *in clinical practice: Improving the quality of judgments and decisions.* Hoboken, NJ: Wiley.

Garb, H. N. (1989). *Studying the clinician: Judgment research and psychological assessment.* Washington, DC: American Psychological Association.

Garb, H. N. (1996). The representativeness and past-behavior heuristics in clinical judgment. *Professional Psychology: Research and Practice, 27,* 272–277.

Garb, H. N. (1997). Race bias, social class bias, and gender bias in clinical judgment. *Clinical Psychology: Science and Practice, 4,* 99–120.

Garb, H. N. (1998). *Studying the clinician: Judgment research and clinical assessment.* Washington, DC: American Psychological Association.

Garcia, J., Kimeldorf, D. J., & Koelling, R. A. (1955). Conditioned aversion to saccharin resulting from exposure to gamma radiation. *Science, 122,* 157–158.

Garnham, A., & Oakhill, J. (1994). *Thinking and reasoning.* Oxford, UK: Blackwell.

Garrett, R. K. (2009). Politically motivated reinforcement seeking: Reframing the selective exposure debate. *Journal of Communication, 59,* 676–699.

Garrett, R. K., & Stroud, N. J. (2015). Partisan paths to exposure diversity: Differences in pro- and counterattitudinal news consumption. *Journal of Communication, 64,* 680–701.

Gaudiano, B. A., Brown, L. A., & Miller, I. W. (2011). Factors associated with critical thinking abilities in psychotherapists. *Cognitive Behaviour Therapy, 40,* 137–146.

Gaudiano, B. A., Dalrymple, K. L., Weinstock, L. M., & Lohr, J. M. (2015). The science of psychotherapy: Developing, testing, and promoting evidence-based treatments. In S. O. Lilienfeld, S. J. Lynn, & J. M. Lohr (Eds.), *Science and pseudoscience in clinical psychology* (2nd ed., pp. 155–190). New York, NY: Guilford Press.

Gauron, E. F., & Dickinson, J. K. (1969). The influence of seeing the patient first on diagnostic decision making in psychiatry. *American Journal of Psychiatry, 126,* 199–205.

Gauthier, I., Tarr, M. J., Anderson, A., Skudlarski, P., Gore, J. C. (1999). Activation of the middle fusiform "face area" increases with expertise in recognizing novel objects. *Nature Neuroscience, 6,* 568–573.

Geen, R. G., Stonner, D., & Stope, G. L. (1975). The facilitation of anger by aggression: Evidence against the catharsis hypothesis. *Journal of Personality and Social Psychology, 31,* 721–726.

Geiger, M. (1996). On the benefit of changing multiple-choice answers: Student perception and performance. *Journal of Experimental Education, 6,* 49–60.

Gelman, S. A. (2011). When worlds collide—or do they? Implications of explanatory coexistence for conceptual development and change. *Human Development, 54,* 185–190.

Gendin, S. (1981). ESP: A conceptual analysis. *Skeptical Inquirer, 5,* 367–376.

Gilovich, T. (1991). *How we know what isn't so: The fallibility of human reason in everyday life.* New York, NY: Free Press.

Gilovich, T. (1997). Some systematic biases of everyday judgment. *Skeptical Inquirer, 21,* 31–35.

Gilovich, T., & Savitsky, K. (1996). Like goes with like. *Skeptical Inquirer, 20,* 34–40.

Gilovich, T., Vallone, R., & Tversky, A. (1985). The hot hand in basketball: On the misperception of random sequences. *Cognitive Psychology, 17,* 295–314.

Glaser, E. M. (1985). Critical thinking: Educating for responsible citizenship in a democracy. *National Forum, 65,* 24–27.

Glick, P., Gottesman, D., & Jolton, J. (1989). The fault is not in our stars: Susceptibility of skeptics and believers in astrology to the Barnum effect. *Personality and Social Psychology Bulletin, 15,* 572–583.

Glickson, J. (1990). Belief in the paranormal and subjective paranormal experience. *Personality and Individual Differences, 11,* 675–683.

Gold, P. E., Cahill, L., & Wenk, G. L. (2002). Ginkgo biloba: A cognitive enhancer? *Psychological Science in the Public Interest, 3,* 2–11.

Goldberg, L. R. (1959). The effectiveness of clinicians' judgments: The diagnosis of organic brain damage from the Bender–Gestalt test. *Journal of Consulting Psychology, 23,* 25–33.

Goldberg, L. R. (1968). Simple or simple processes: Some research on clinical judgments. *American Psychologist, 23,* 483–496.

Goldman, A. (2016). The Comet Ping Pong gunman answers our reporter's questions. *New York Times.* Retrieved from http://www.nytimes.com/2016/12/07/us/edgar-welch-comet-pizza-fake-news.html

Gould, E., Beylin, A., Tanapat, P., Reeves, A., & Shors, T. J. (1999). Learning enhances adult neurogenesis in the hippocampal formation. *Nature Neuroscience, 2,* 260.

Gould, S. J. (2002). *The structure of evolutionary theory.* Cambridge, MA: Harvard University Press.

Gow, K., Lang, T., & Chant, D. (2004). Fantasy proneness, paranormal beliefs, and personality features in out-of-body experiences. *Contemporary Hypnosis, 21,* 107–125.

Grace, R. C. (2001). On the failure of operationalism. *Theory & Psychology, 11,* 5–33.

Green, G. (2002). Facilitated communication. In M. Shermer (Ed.), *The skeptic encyclopedia of pseudoscience* (Vol. 1, pp. 344–346). Santa Barbara, CA: ABC-CLIO.

Greenspan, S. (2009). Fooled by Ponzi: How Bernard Madoff made off with my money, or why even an expert on gullibility can get gulled. *Skeptic, 14,* 20–25.

Greenwald, A. G., Spangenberg, E. R., Pratkanis, A. R., & Eskenazi, J. (1991). Double-blind tests of subliminal self-help audiotapes. *Psychological Science, 2,* 119–122.

Grosso, M. (1976). Some varieties of out-of-body experience. *Journal of the American Society for Psychical Research, 70,* 179–193.

Grove, W. M., Zald, D. H., Lebow, B. S., Snitz, B. E., & Nelson, C. (2000). Clinical versus mechanical prediction: A meta-analysis. *Psychological Assessment, 12,* 19–30.

Grusec, J. E. (1991). The socialization of altruism. In M. S. Clark (Ed.), *Review of personality and social psychology: Vol. 12: Prosocial behavior* (pp. 9–33). Newbury Park, CA: Sage.

Grusec, J. E., & Redler, E. (1980). Attribution, reinforcement, and altruism: A developmental analysis. *Developmental Psychology, 16,* 525–534.

Guardiola, J. G. (2001). The evolution of research on dyslexia. Retrieved from http://ibgwww.colorado.edu/-gayan/ch1.pdf

Guo, L., Trueblood, J. S., & Diederich, A. (2017). Thinking fast increases framing effects in risky decision making. *Psychological Science, 28,* 530–543.

Gutierrez-Garcia, J. M., & Tusell, T. (1997). Suicides and the lunar cycle. *Psychological Reports, 80,* 243–250.

Gvion, Y., & Apter, A. (2011). Aggression, impulsivity, and suicide behavior: A review of the literature. *Archives of Suicide Research, 15,* 93–112.

Haidt, J. (2001). The emotional dog and its rational tail: A social intuitionist approach to moral judgment. *Psychological Review, 108,* 814–834.

Haidt, J. (2012). *The righteous mind: Why good people are divided by politics and religion.* New York, NY: Vintage Books.

Halford, G. S., Baker, R., McCredden, J. E., & Bain, J. D. (2005). How many variables can humans process? *Psychological Science, 16,* 70–76.

Halpern, D. F. (1993). Assessing the effectiveness of critical thinking instruction. *Journal of General Education, 42,* 238–254.

Halpern, D. F. (1998). Teaching critical thinking for transfer across domains: Dispositions, skills, structure training, and metacognitive monitoring. *American Psychologist, 53,* 449–455.

Halpern, D. F. (2014). *Thought and knowledge: An introduction to critical thinking* (5th ed.). Hillsdale, NJ: Erlbaum.

Han, D. H., Hwang, J. W., & Renshaw, P. F. (2011). Bupropion sustained release treatment decreases craving of video games and cue-induced brain activity in patients with Internet video game addiction. *Psychology of Popular Media Culture, 1,* 108–117.

Harambam, J., & Aupers, S. (2017). "I am not a conspiracy theorist": Relational identifications in the Dutch conspiracy milieu. *Cultural Sociology, 11,* 113–139.

Harris, R. (1997). Evaluating Internet research sources. Retrieved from http://www.virtualsalt.com/evalu8it.htm

Harris, R. (2000). *Webquester: A guidebook to the web.* Guilford, CT: Dushkin/McGraw-Hill.

Harris Polls. (2013). Americans' belief in God, miracles, and heaven decline. Retrieved from http://www.harrisinteractive.com/Newsroom/HarrisPolls/tabid/447/ctl/ReadCustom

Haslam, N. (2005). Dimensions of folk psychiatry. *Review of General Psychology, 9,* 35–47.

Hattie, J. A., Sharpley, C. F., & Rogers, H. J. (1984). Comparative effectiveness of professional and paraprofessional helpers. *Psychological Bulletin, 95,* 534–541.

Hayes, J. R. (1989). Writing research: The analysis of a very complex task. In D. Klahr & K. Kotovsky (Eds.), *Complex information processing* (pp. 209–234). Hillsdale, NJ: Erlbaum.

Hayes, J. R. (1996). A new framework for understanding cognition and affect in writing. In C. M. Levy & S. Ransdell (Eds.), *The science of writing* (pp. 1–27). Mahwah, NJ: Erlbaum.

Hayes, J. R., & Flower, L. S. (1980). Identifying the organization of writing processes. In L. W. Gregg & E. R. Steinberg (Eds.), *Cognitive processes in writing* (pp. 3–30). Hillsdale, NJ: Erlbaum.

Heider, F. (1958). *The psychology of interpersonal relations.* New York, NY: Wiley.

Hendry, A. (1979). *The UFO handbook.* Garden City, NY: Doubleday.

Herbert, J. D. (2003). The concept of pseudoscience as a pedagogical heuristic. *Scientific Review of Mental Health Practice, 2,* 102–104.

Herbert, J. D., Sharp, I. R., & Gaudiano, B. A. (2002). Separating fact from fiction in the etiology and treatment of autism: A scientific review of the evidence. *Scientific Review of Mental Health Practice, 1,* 23–43.

Hergenhahn, B. R. (1992). *An introduction to the history of psychology* (2nd ed.). Belmont, CA: Wadsworth.

Herrnstein, R. J., Nickerson, R. S., de Sanchez, M., & Swets, J. A. (1986). Teaching thinking skills. *American Psychologist, 11,* 1279–1289.

Hill, A. (2011). *Paranormal media: Audiences, spirits, and magic in popular culture.* New York, NY: Routledge.

Hines, T. (2003). *Pseudoscience and the paranormal* (2nd ed.). Amherst, NY: Prometheus Books.

Hodgins, S., Mednick, S., Brennan, P. A., Schulsinger, F., & Engberg, M. (1996). Mental disorder and crime: Evidence from a Danish birth cohort. *Archives of General Psychiatry, 53,* 489–496.

Hoffman, M. L. (1981). Is altruism part of human nature? *Journal of Personality and Social Psychology, 40,* 121–137.

Holmes, D. (1995). The evidence for repression: An examination of sixty years of research. In J. L. Singer (Ed.), *Repression and dissociation: Implications for personality theory, psychopathology, and health* (pp. 85–102). Chicago, IL: University of Chicago Press.

Hood, B. M. (2009). *The science of superstition: How the developing brain creates supernatural beliefs* (rev. ed.). New York, NY: Harper Collins.

Horwitz, A. V., & Wakefield, J. C. (2007). *The loss of sadness.* Oxford, UK: Oxford University Press.

Houts, A. C., & Galante, M. (1985). The impact of evaluative disposition and subsequent information on clinical impressions. *Journal of Social and Clinical Psychology, 3,* 201–212.

Hunsley, J., & Di Giulio, G. (2002). Dodo bird, phoenix, or urban legend? The question of psychotherapy equivalence. *Scientific Review of Mental Health Practice, 1,* 11–22.

Hutton, R. (1999). *The triumph of the moon: A history of modern pagan witchcraft.* Oxford, UK: Oxford University Press.

Innocence Project. (2017). Retrieved from https://www.innocenceproject.org/

Institute for the Advancement of Philosophy for Children. (n.d.). *Research in philosophy for children.* Upper Montclair, NJ: Montclair State College. Retrieved from https://www.montclair.edu/cehs/academics/centers-and-institutes/iapc/research/

Irwin, H. J. (1985). *Flight of mind: A psychological study of the out-of-body experience.* Metuchen, NJ: Scarecrow Press.

Isen, A. M., & Daubman, K. A. (1984). The influence of affect on categorization. *Journal of Personality and Social Psychology, 47,* 1206–1217.

Isen, A. M., Johnson, M., Mertz, E., & Robinson, G. (1985). The influence of positive affect on the unusualness of word associations. *Journal of Personality and Social Psychology, 48,* 1413–1426.

Isen, A. M., & Levin, P. F. (1972). Effect of feeling good on helping: Cookies and kindness. *Journal of Personality and Social Psychology, 21,* 384–388.

Isen, A. M., & Means, B. (1983). The influence of positive affect on decision-making strategy. *Social Cognition, 2,* 18–31.

Isen, A. M., & Patrick, R. (1983). The effect of positive feeling on risk taking: When the chips are down. *Organizational Behavior and Human Performance, 31,* 194–202.

Isikoff, M., & Corn, D. (2006). *Hubris: The inside story of spin, scandal, and selling of the Iraq War.* New York, NY: Crown.

Ivey, G., & Myers, T. (2008). The psychology of bewitchment (Part I): A phenomenological study of the experience of bewitchment. *South African Journal of Psychology, 38,* 54–74.

Izard, C. E. (2007). Basic emotions, natural kinds, emotion schemas, and a new paradigm. *Perspectives on Psychological Science, 2,* 260–280.

Jackendoff, R. (1996). How language helps us think. *Pragmatics & Cognition, 4,* 1–34.

Jacobsen, E. (1929). *Progressive relaxation.* Oxford, UK: University of Chicago Press.

Janis, I. L. (1972). *Victims of groupthink: A psychological study of foreign-policy decisions and fiascoes.* Oxford, UK: Houghton Mifflin.

Jansen, K. (1997). The ketamine model of the near-death experience: A central role for the N-methyl-D-aspartate receptor. *Journal of Near Death Studies, 16,* 5–26.

Johnson, E. J., & Tversky, A. (1983). Affect, generalization, and the perception of risk. *Journal of Personality and Social Psychology, 45,* 20–31.

Johnson, M., & Pigiliucci, M. (2004). Is knowledge of science associated with higher skepticism of pseudoscientific claims? *American Biology Teacher, 66,* 536–548.

Johnson, M. L. (1995). Incarnate mind. *Minds and Machines, 5,* 533–545.

Johnson, R. C., Danko, G. P., Darvill, T. J., Bochner, S., Bowers, J. K., Huang, Y., & Pennington, D. (1989). Cross-cultural assessment of altruism and its correlates. *Personality and Individual Differences, 10,* 855–868.

Johnson-Laird, P. N., & Oatley, K. (1992). Basic emotions, rationality, and folk theory. *Cognition and Emotion, 6,* 201–223.

Kadushin, A. (1963). Diagnosis and evaluation for (almost) all occasions. *Social Work, 8,* 12–20.

Kahneman, D. (2011). *Thinking fast and slow.* New York, NY: Farrar, Straus, and Giroux.

Kahneman, D., & Klein, G. (2009). Conditions for intuitive expertise: A failure to disagree. *American Psychologist, 64,* 515–526.

Kahneman, D., & Tversky, A. (1972). Subjective probability: A judgment of representativeness. *Cognitive Psychology, 3,* 430–454.

Kahneman, D., & Tversky, A. (1973). On the psychology of prediction. *Psychological Review, 80,* 237–251.

Kalal, D. M. (1999). Critical thinking in clinical practice: Pseudoscience, fad psychology, and the behavioral therapist. *Behavior Therapist, 22,* 81–84.

Kang, C., & Goldman, A. (2016, December 6). In Washington pizzeria attack, fake news brought real guns. *New York Times*. Retrieved from http://nyti.ms/2h8nPmp

Kapoun, J. (1998). Teaching undergrads web evaluation: A guide for library instruction. *College & Research Libraries News, 59,* 522–523.

Kassin, S. M., Tubb, V. A., Hosch, H. M., & Memon, A. (2001). On the "general" acceptance of eyewitness testimony research. *American Psychologist, 56,* 405–416.

Kay, A. C., Whitson, J. A., Gaucher, D., & Galinsky, A. D. (2009). Compensatory control: Achieving order through the mind, our institutions, and the heavens. *Current Directions in Psychological Science, 18,* 264–268.

Keeley, S. M. (1992). Are college students learning the critical thinking skill of finding assumptions? *College Student Journal, 26,* 316–322.

Keeley, S. M., Browne, M. N., & Kreutzer, J. S. (1982). A comparison of freshmen and seniors on general and specific essay tests of critical thinking. *Research in Higher Education, 17*(2), 139–154.

Keinan, G. (1987). Decision making under stress: Scanning of alternatives under controllable and uncontrollable threats. *Journal of Personality and Social Psychology, 52,* 639–644.

Keinan, G. (2003). Magical thinking as a way of coping with stress. In R. Jacoby & G. Keinan (Eds.), *Between stress and hope: From a disease-centered to a health-centered perspective* (pp. 123–138). Westport, CT: Praeger.

Kellogg, R. T. (1988). Attentional overload and writing performance: Effects of rough draft and outline strategies. *Journal of Experimental Psychology: Learning, Memory, and Cognition, 14,* 355–365.

Kelly, I. W. (1997). Modern astrology: A critique. *Psychological Reports, 81,* 1035–1066.

Kenrick, D. T. (1989). Selflessness examined: Is avoiding tar and feathers nonegoistic? *Behavioral and Brain Sciences, 12,* 711–712.

Kessler, R. C., Zhao, S., Blazer, D. G., & Swartz, M. (1997). Prevalence, correlates, and course of minor depression and major depression in the national comorbidity survey. *Journal of Affective Disorders, 45,* 19–30.

Kida, T. (2006). *Don't believe everything you think: The six basic mistakes we make in thinking.* Amherst, NY: Prometheus.

Kim, N. S., & Ahn, W. (2002). Clinical psychologists' theory-based representations of mental disorders predict their diagnostic reasoning and memory. *Journal of Experimental Psychology: General, 131,* 451–476.

Kim, Y., & Stevens, J. H. (1987). The socialization of prosocial behavior in children. *Childhood Education, 63,* 200–206.

King, M., & Bearman, P. (2009). Diagnostic change and increased prevalence of autism. *International Journal of Epidemiology, 38,* 1224–1234.

Klahr, D., Matlen, B., & Jirout, J. (2013). Children as scientific thinkers. In G. J. Feist & M. E. Gorman (Eds.), *Handbook of the psychology of science* (pp. 223–247). New York, NY: Springer.

Klimoski, R. J. (1992). Graphology and personnel selection. In B. L. Beyerstein & D. F. Beyerstein (Eds.), *The write stuff* (pp. 232–268). Amherst, NY: Prometheus.

Klingberg, T. (2009). *The overflowing brain: Information overload and the limits of working memory.* New York, NY: Oxford University Press.

Klingner, J. K., Morrison, A., & Eppolito, A. (2011). Metacognition to improve reading comprehension. In R. E. O'Connor & P. F. Vadasy (Eds.), *Handbook of reading interventions* (pp. 220–253). New York, NY: Guilford Press.

Knoblich-Westerwick, S., Mothes, C., Johnson, B. K., Westerwick, A., & Donsbach, W. (2015). Political online information searching in Germany and the United States: Confirmation bias, source credibility, and attitude impacts. *Journal of Communication, 65,* 489–511.

Kohn, A. (1990). *You know what they say.* New York, NY: Harper Collins.

Kolb, B., & Whishaw, I. Q. (1990). *Fundamentals of human neuropsychology.* New York, NY: W. H. Freeman.

Koole, S. L. (2009). The psychology of emotion regulation: An integrative review. *Cognition and Emotion, 23,* 4–41.

Kopko, K. C., Bryner, S. K., Budziak, J., Devine, C. J., & Nawarra, S. P. (2011). In the eye of the beholder? Motivated reasoning in disputed elections. *Political Psychology, 33,* 271–290.

Kosova, W., & Wingert, P. (2009, June 8). Crazy talk: Oprah, crazy cures & you. *Newsweek,* pp. 53–62.

Krebs, D. L. (1991). Altruism and egoism: A false dichotomy? *Psychological Inquiry, 2,* 137–139.

Kruger, J., & Dunning, D. (1999). Unskilled and unaware of it: How difficulties in recognizing one's own incompetence lead to inflated self-assessments. *Journal of Personality and Social Psychology, 77,* 1127–1134.

Kuhn, D. (1993). Connecting scientific and informal reasoning. *Merrill-Palmer Quarterly, 39,* 74–103.

Kuhn, D., Weinstock, M., & Flaton, R. (1994). How well do jurors reason? Competence dimensions of individual variation in a juror reasoning task. *Psychological Science, 5,* 289–296.

Kuhn, G., Amiani, A. A., & Rensink, R. A. (2008). Towards a science of magic. *Trends in Cognitive Science, 12,* 349–354.

Kunda, Z. (1990). The case for motivated reasoning. *Psychological Bulletin, 108,* 480–498.

Kung, S., & Mrazek, D. A. (2005). Psychiatric emergency room visits on full moon nights. *Psychiatric Services, 56,* 221–222.

Kyle, R. (1995). *The New Age movement in American culture.* Lanham, MD: University Press of America.

LaCapria, K. (2016, December 4). Comet Ping Pong Pizzeria home to child abuse sex ring led by Hillary Clinton. Retrieved from http://www.snopes.com/pizzagate-conspiracy/

Ladavas, E., Zelon, G., & Farne, A. (1998). Visual peripersonal space centered on the face in humans. *Brain, 121,* 2317–2326.

Lakatos, I. (1970). Falsification and the methodology of scientific research programs. In I. Lakatos & A. Musgrave (Eds.), *Criticism and the growth of knowledge* (pp. 91–195). Cambridge, UK: Cambridge University Press.

Lamm, C., Batson, C. D., & Decety, J. (2007). The neural substrate of human empathy: Effects of perspective-taking and cognitive appraisal. *Journal of Cognitive Neuroscience, 19,* 42–58.

Lampinem, J. M., Neuschatz, J. F., & Cling, A. D. (2012). *The psychology of eyewitness identification.* New York, NY: Psychology Press.

Laney, C. (2013). The sources of memory errors. In D. Reisberg (Ed.), *The Oxford handbook of cognitive psychology* (pp. 232–242). New York, NY: Oxford University Press.

Langer, J. A., & Applebee, A. N. (1987). *How writing shapes thinking: A study of teaching and learning.* Urbana, IL: National Council of Teachers of English.

Larrick, R. P. (2004). Debiasing. In D. J. Koehler & N. Harvey (Eds.), *Blackwell handbook of judgment and decision making* (pp. 316–337). Malden, MA: Blackwell.

Latane, B., & Nida S. (1981). Ten years of research on group size and helping. *Psychological Bulletin, 89,* 308–324.

Laurence, J. R., & Perry, C. W. (1983). Hypnotically created memories among highly hypnotizable subjects. *Science, 222,* 523–524.

Leahey, T. H., & Leahey, G. E. (1983). *Psychology's occult doubles: Psychology and the problem of pseudoscience.* Chicago, IL: Nelson Hall.

Lee, Y.-S., & Waite, L. J. (2005). Husbands' and wives' time spent on housework: A comparison of measures. *Journal of Marriage and Family, 67,* 328–336.

Lefford, A. (1946). The influence of emotional subject matter on logical reasoning. *Journal of General Psychology, 34,* 127–151.

Lehman, D. E., & Nisbett, R. E. (1990). A longitudinal study of the effects of undergraduate training on reasoning. *Developmental Psychology, 26,* 952–960.

Leigh, R., Oishi, K., Hsu, J., Linquist, M., Gottesman, R., Jarso, S., & Hillis, A. E. (2013). Acute lesions that impair affective empathy. *Brain: Journal of Neurology, 136,* 2539–2549.

Lench, H. C., Flores, S. A., & Bench, S. W. (2011). Discrete emotions predict changes in cognition, judgment, experience, behavior, and physiology. *Psychological Bulletin, 137,* 834–855.

Lenggenhager, B., Tadi, T., Metzinger, T., & Blank, O. (2007). Video ergo sum: Manipulating bodily self-consciousness. *Science, 317,* 1096–1099.

Leon, M. R., & Revelle, W. (1985). Effects of anxiety on analogical reasoning: A test of three theoretical models. *Journal of Personality and Social Psychology, 49,* 1302–1315.

Levin, D. T., Momen, N., Drivdahl, S. B., & Simons, D. J. (2000). Change blindness: The metacognitive error of overestimating change-detection ability. *Visual Cognition, 7,* 397–412.

Levine, R. V. (2003). The kindness of strangers. *American Scientist, 91,* 226–233.

Levine, R. V., Reysen, S., & Ganz, E. (2008). The kindness of strangers revisited: A comparison of 24 U.S. cities. *Social Indicators Research, 85,* 461–469.

Lewak, R. W., Wakefield, J. A., & Briggs, P. F. (1985). Intelligence and personality in mate choice and marital satisfaction. *Personality and Individual Differences, 4,* 471–477.

Lewandowsky, S., Gignac, G. E., & Oberauer, K. (2013). The role of conspiracist ideation and worldviews in predicting rejection of science. *CPLOS One, 8,* 1–11. Retrieved from http://www.plosone.org

Lewandowsky, S., & Oberauer, K. (2016). Motivated rejection of science. *Current Directions in Psychological Science, 25,* 217–222.

Leyans, J., & Dunand, M. (1991). Priming aggressive thoughts: The effect of the anticipation of a violent movie upon the aggressive behavior of the spectators. *European Journal of Social Psychology, 21,* 507–516.

Lilienfeld, S. O. (1998). Pseudoscience in contemporary clinical psychology: What it is and what we can do about it. *Clinical Psychologist, 51*(4), 3–9.

Lilienfeld, S. O. (2007). Psychological treatments that cause harm. *Perspectives on Psychological Science, 2*(1), 53–70.

Lilienfeld, S. O., Ammirati, R., & Landfield, K. (2009). Giving debiasing away: Can psychological research on correcting cognitive errors promote human welfare? *Perspectives in Psychological Science, 4,* 390–398.

Lilienfeld, S. O., Fowler, K. A., Lohr, J. M., & Lynn, S. J. (2005). Pseudoscience, nonscience, and nonsense in clinical psychology: Dangers and remedies. In R. H. Wright & N. A. Cummings (Eds.), *Destructive trends in mental health: The well-intentioned path to harm* (pp. 187–217). New York, NY: Routledge.

Lilienfeld, S. O., Lynn, S. J., & Lohr, J. M. (2015). *Science and pseudoscience in clinical psychology* (2nd ed.). New York, NY: Guilford.

Lilienfeld, S. O., Lynn, S. J., Ruscio, J. & Beyerstein, B. L. (2010). *50 great myths of popular psychology.* Chichester, UK: Wiley-Blackwell.

Lindeman, M., & Aarnio, K. (2006). Superstitious, magical, and paranormal beliefs: An integrative model. *Journal of Research in Personality, 41,* 731–744.

Lindquist, K. A., Siegel, E. H., Quigley, K. S., & Barrett, L. F. (2013). The hundred-year emotion war: Are emotions natural kinds or psychological constructions? Comment on Lench, Flores, and Bench (2011). *Psychological Bulletin, 139,* 255–263.

Linn, M., Bell, P., & Hsi, S. (1999). Using the Internet to enhance student understanding of science: The knowledge integration environment. *Interactive Learning Environments, 1,* 4–38.

Lipman, M. (1991). *Thinking in education.* Cambridge, UK: Cambridge University Press.

Litvak, P. M., Lerner, J. S., Tiedens, L. Z., & Shonk, K. (2010). Fuel in the fire: How anger impacts judgment and decision making. In M. Potegal & G. Stemmler (Eds.), *International handbook of anger* (pp. 287–309). New York, NY: Springer Science+Business Media.

Loftus, E. F. (1992). When a lie becomes a memory's truth: Memory distortions after exposure to misinformation. *Current Directions in Psychological Science, 13,* 145–147.

Loftus, E. F., & Bernstein, D. (2005). Rich false memories: The royal road to success. In A. Healy (Ed.), *Experimental cognitive psychology and its applications* (pp. 101–113). Washington, DC: American Psychological Association.

Loftus, E. F., Coan, J., & Pickrell, J. E. (1996). Manufacturing false memories using bits of reality. In L. M. Reder (Ed.), *Implicit memory and metacognition* (pp. 195–220). Mahwah, NJ: Erlbaum.

Loftus, E. F., Donders, K., & Hoffman, H. G. (1989). Creating new memories that are quickly accessed and confidently held. *Memory & Cognition, 17,* 607–616.

Loftus, E. F., Loftus, G. R., & Messo, J. (1987). Some facts about "weapon focus." *Law and Human Behavior, 11,* 55–62.

Loftus, E. F., & Palmer, J. C. (1974). Reconstruction of automobile destruction: An interaction of language and memory. *Journal of Verbal Learning and Verbal Behavior, 13,* 585–589.

Loftus, E. F., & Zanni, G. (1975). Eyewitness testimony: The influence of the wording of a question. *Bulletin of the Psychonomic Society, 5,* 86–88.

Logue, M. B., Sher, K. J., & Frensch, P. A. (1992). Purported characteristics of adult children of alcoholics: A possible "Barnum effect." *Professional Psychology: Research and Practice, 23,* 226–232.

Lord, C. G., Ross, L., & Lepper, M. R. (1979). Biased assimilation and attitude polarization: The effects of prior theories on subsequently considered evidence. *Journal of Personality and Social Psychology, 37,* 2098–2109.

Lorenz, K. (1966). *On aggression.* New York, NY: Harcourt, Brace, and World.

Losh, S. C., Tavani, C. M., Njoroge, R., Wilke, R., & McAuley, M. (2003). What does education really do? Educational dimensions and pseudoscience support in the American general public, 1979–2001. *Skeptical Inquirer, 27*(5), 30–35.

Mack, A., & Rock, I. (1998). *Inattentional blindness.* Cambridge, MA: MIT Press.

Mahoney, M. J. (1977). Publication prejudices: An experimental study of confirmatory bias in the peer review system. *Cognitive Therapy and Research, 1,* 161–175.

Mandler, J. M. (1987). On the psychological reality of story structures. *Discourse Processes, 10,* 1–29.

Maner, J. K., & Gailliot, M. T. (2007). Altruism and egoism: Prosocial motivations for helping depend on relationship context. *European Journal of Social Psychology, 37,* 347–358.

Manning, R., Levine, M., & Collins, A. (2007). The Kitty Genovese murder and the social psychology of helping: The parable of the 38 witnesses. *American Psychologist, 62,* 555–562.

Marcus, G. (2004). *The birth of the mind: How a tiny number of genes creates the complexities of human thought.* New York, NY: Basic Books.

Marin, L. M., & Halpern, D. F. (2011). Pedagogy for developing critical thinking in adolescents: Explicit instruction produces greatest gains. *Thinking Skills and Creativity, 6,* 1–13.

Marks, G., & Miller, N. (1987). Ten years of the false-consensus effect: An empirical and theoretical review. *Psychological Bulletin, 102,* 72–90.

Marsh, A. A. (2016). Neural, cognitive, and evolutionary foundations of human altruism. *WIREs Cognitive Science, 7,* 59–71.

Matlin, M. (1994). *Cognition* (3rd ed.). Fort Worth, TX: Harcourt Brace.

Matthews, K. A., Batson, C. D., Horn, J., & Rosenan, R. H. (1981). The heritability of empathic concern for others. *Journal of Personality, 49,* 237–247.

Mayer, R. E. (2004). Teaching of subject matter. *Annual Review of Psychology, 55,* 715–744.

McCaffrey, P. (2012). Preface: Categorizing conspiracy theories. In P. McCaffrey (Ed.), *Conspiracy theories* (pp. ix–xii). Ipswich, MA: H. W. Wilson.

McCutchen, D., Teske, P., & Bankston, C. (2008). Writing and cognition: Implications of the cognitive architecture for learning to write and writing to learn. In C. Brazerman (Ed.), *Handbook of research on writing: History, society, school, individual, text* (pp. 451–470). New York, NY: Routledge.

McCutcheon, L. E. (1991). A new test of misconceptions about psychology. *Psychological Reports, 68,* 647–653.

McCutcheon, L. E., Apperson, J. M., Hanson, E., & Wynn, V. (1992). Relationships among critical thinking skills, academic achievement, and a misconceptions test about psychology. *Psychological Reports, 71,* 635–639.

McKinnon, J. W., & Renner, J. W. (1971). Are colleges concerned with intellectual development? *American Journal of Psychology, 39,* 1047–1052.

McMackin, J., & Slovic, P. (2000). When does explicit justification impair decision making? *Applied Cognitive Psychology, 14,* 527–541.

McNally, R. J. (2011). *What is mental illness?* Cambridge, MA: Harvard University Press.

Meehl, P. E. (1954). *Clinical versus statistical prediction: A theoretical analysis and review of the evidence.* Minneapolis, MN: University of Minnesota Press.

Meehl, P. E. (1973). Why I do not attend case conferences. In P. E. Meehl (Ed.), *Psychodiagnosis: Selected papers* (pp. 225–302). Minneapolis: University of Minnesota Press.

Meijsing, M. (2000). Self-consciousness and the body. *Journal of Consciousness Studies, 7,* 34–52.

Mentkowski, M., & Strait, M. J. (1983). *A longitudinal study of student change in cognitive development, learning styles, and generic abilities in an outcome-centered liberal arts curriculum* (Final Report to the National Institute of Education: Research Report Number Six). Milwaukee, WI: Alverno College, Office of Research and Evaluation (NIE-G-77-0058).

Mercer, J. (2014). Attachment therapy. In S. O. Lilienfeld, S. J. Lynn, & J. M. Lohr (Eds.), *Science and pseudoscience in clinical psychology* (2nd ed., pp. 466–499). New York, NY: Guilford.

Mezulis, A. H., Abramson, L. Y., Hide, J. S., & Hankin, B. L. (2004). Is there a universal positivity bias in attributions? A meta-analytic review of individual, developmental, and cultural differences in the self-serving attributional bias. *Psychological Bulletin, 130,* 711–747.

Midlarsky, E., & Bryan, J. H. (1972). Affect expressions and children's imitative altruism. *Journal of Experimental Research in Personality, 6,* 195–203.

Miller, G. (1956). The magical number 7 plus or minus 2: Some limits on our capacity for processing information. *Psychological Review, 63,* 81–97.

Milton, J., & Wiseman, R. (1999). Does psi exist? Lack of replication of anomalous information transfer. *Psychological Bulletin, 125,* 387–391.

Mohammed, S. N. (2012) *The (Dis)Information Age: The persistence of ignorance.* New York, NY: Peter Lang.

Moody, R. A. (1976). *Life after life.* Harrisburg, PA: Stackpole Books.

Mook, D. G. (1991). Why can't altruism be selfish? *Psychological Inquiry, 2,* 139–140.

Moons, W. G., & Mackie, D. M. (2007). Thinking straight while seeing red: The influence of anger on information processing. *Personality and Social Psychology Bulletin, 33,* 706–720.

Moore, D. W. (2005). Three in four Americans believe in paranormal. Gallup News Service. Retrieved from http://www.gallup.com/poll/16915/three-four-americans-believe-paranormal.aspx

Morey, L. C., & Ochoa, E. S. (1989). An investigation of adherence to diagnostic criteria: Clinical diagnosis of the *DSM-III* personality disorders. *Journal of Personality Disorders, 3,* 180–192.

Morrot, G., Brochet, F., & Dubourdieu, D. (2001). The color of odors. *Brain and Language, 79,* 309–320.

Mostert, M. P. (2001). Facilitated communication since 1995: A review of published studies. *Journal of Autism and Developmental Disorders, 31*(3), 287–313.

Myers, A., & Hansen, C. (2012). *Experimental psychology* (7th ed.). Belmont, CA: Wadsworth-Cengage.

Myers, D. G. (2013). *Social psychology* (11th ed.). Boston, MA: McGraw-Hill.

Nathan, P. E., & Gorman, J. E. (2007). *A guide to treatments that work* (3rd ed.). New York, NY: Oxford University Press.

National Assessment of Educational Progress. (1986). *The writing report card: Writing achievement in American schools.* Princeton, NJ: Educational Testing Service. Retrieved from http://www.writingcommission.org/prod_downloads/writingcom/neglectedr.pdf

National Assessment of Educational Progress. (2011). The nation's report card: Writing 2011: Executive summary. Retrieved from nces.ed.gov/nationsreportcard/pubs/main2011/2012470

National Center for Educational Statistics. (2003). The nation's report card: Reading 2002. Retrieved from http://nces.ed.gov/nationsreportcard/pubs/main2002/2003521.asp

National Center for Educational Statistics. (2009). Science in action: Hands-on and interactive computer tasks from the 2009 Science Assessment National Assessment of Educational Progress at Grades 4, 8, and 12. Retrieved from https://nces.ed.gov/nationsreportcard/pdf/main2009/2012468.pdf

National Commission on Terrorist Attacks upon the United States. (2004). The 9/11 Commission report. Retrieved from http://govinfo.library.unt.edu/911/report/911Report.pdf

National Commission on Writing. (2003, April). The neglected "R": The need for a writing revolution. Retrieved from https://www.nwp.org/cs/public/print/resource/2523

Neimark, E. D. (1987). *Adventures in thinking.* San Diego, CA: Harcourt Brace Jovanovich.

Neisser, U. (1993). The self perceived. In U. Neisser (Ed.), *The perceived self* (pp. 3–21). Cambridge, UK: Cambridge University Press.

Nemeroff, C., & Rozin, P. (2000). The makings of the magical mind: The nature and function of sympathetic magical thinking. In K. S. Rosengren, C. N. Johnson, & P. L. Harris (Eds.), *Imagining the impossible: Magical, scientific, and religious thinking in children* (pp. 1–34). New York, NY: Cambridge University Press.

Newell, A., & Simon, H. A. (1972). *Human problem solving.* Englewood Cliffs, NJ: Prentice Hall.

Newport, F., & Strausberg, M. (2001). *America's belief in psychic and paranormal phenomena is up over last decade.* Princeton, NJ: Gallup News Service.

Nickerson, R. S. (1998). Confirmation bias: A ubiquitous phenomenon in many guises. *Review of General Psychology, 2,* 175–220.

Nickerson, R. S. (2002). The production and perception of randomness. *Psychological Review, 109,* 330–357.

Nieto, A. M., & Saiz, C. (2008). Evaluation of Halpern's "structural component" for improving critical thinking. *Spanish Journal of Psychology, 11*(1), 266–274.

Nisbett, R. E., Krantz, D. H., Jepson, C., & Kunda, Z. (1983). The use of statistical heuristics in everyday inductive reasoning. *Psychological Review, 90,* 339–363.

Nisbett, R. E., & Ross, L. (1980). *Human inference: Strategies and shortcomings of social judgment.* Englewood Cliffs, NJ: Prentice Hall.

Nisbett, R. E., & Wilson, T. D. (1977). Telling more than we can know: Limitations on verbal reports of mental processes. *Psychological Review, 84,* 231–259.

Noice, H., & Noice, T. (2006). What the studies of actors and acting can tell us about memory and cognitive functioning. *Current Directions in Psychological Science, 15,* 14–18.

Northcraft, G. B., & Neale, M. A. (1987). Experts, amateurs, and real estate: An anchoring-and-adjustment perspective on property pricing decisions. *Organizational Behavior and Human Decision Processes, 39,* 84–97.

Novella, S. (2012). *Your deceptive mind: A scientific guide to critical thinking skills* (Course guidebook). Chantilly, VA: Great Courses.

Oatley, K. (1990). Do emotional states produce irrational thinking? In K. Gilhooly, M. Keane, R. Logie, & G. Erdos (Eds.), *Lines of thinking* (pp. 121–131). West Sussex, UK: John Wiley.

Odinot, G., Wolters, G., & van Koppen, P. J. (2009). Eyewitness memory of a supermarket robbery: A case study of accuracy and confidence after 3 months. *Law and Human Behavior, 33,* 506–514.

Offit, P. A. (2008). *Autism's false prophets: Bad science, risky medicine, and the search for a cure.* New York, NY: Columbia University Press.

Olatunji, B. O., Parker, L. M., & Lohr, J. M. (2005). Pseudoscience in contemporary psychology: Professional issues and implications. *Scientific Review of Mental Health Practice, 4*(2), 97–101.

Oltmanns, T. F., & Klonsky, E. D. (2007). Critical thinking in clinical inference. In R. J. Sternberg, H. J. Roediger, & D. F. Halpern (Eds.), *Critical thinking in psychology* (pp. 196–215). New York, NY: Cambridge University Press.

O'Malley, S. (2004). *Are you there alone? The unspeakable crime of Andrea Yates.* New York, NY: Simon & Schuster.

Ono, K. (1987). Superstitious behavior in humans. *Journal of the Experimental Analysis of Behavior, 47,* 261–271.

Orosz, G., Kreko, P., Paskuj, B., Toth-Kiraly, I., Bothe, B., & Roland-Levy, C. (2016). Changing conspiracy beliefs through rationality and ridiculing. *Frontiers in Psychology, 7,* 1–9. Retrieved from http://www.frontiersin.org

Orton, S. T. (1925). "Word blindness" in school children. *Archives of Neurology and Psychiatry, 14,* 581–615.

Osis, K., & McCormick, D. (1980). Kinetic effects as the ostensible location of an out-of-body projection during perceptual testing. *Journal of the American Society for Psychical Research, 74,* 319–329.

Osis, K., & Mitchell, J. L. (1977). Physiological correlates of reported out-of-body experiences. *Journal of the Society for Psychical Research, 49,* 525–536.

Overgaard, M., Nielsen, J. F., & Fuglsang-Frederiksen, A. (2004). A TMS study of the ventral projection from V1 with implications for the finding of neural correlates of consciousness. *Brain and Cognition, 54,* 58–64.

Owens, M., & McGowan, I. W. (2006). Madness and the moon: The lunar cycle and psychopathology. *German Journal of Psychiatry.* Retrieved from http://www.gypsy.uni-goettingen.de/gjp-article-owens.pdf

Pacini, D., & Epstein, S. (1999). The relation of rational and experiential information processing styles to personality, basic beliefs, and the ratio-bias phenomenon. *Journal of Personality and Social Psychology, 76,* 972–987.

Pagnin, D., DeQueroz, V., Pini, S., & Cassano, G. B. (2004). The efficacy of ECT in depression: A meta-analytic review. *Journal of ECT, 20,* 13–20.

Palfai, T. P., & Salovey, P. (1993). The influence of depressed and elated mood on deductive and inductive reasoning. *Imagination, Cognition, and Personality, 13,* 57–71.

Palmer, D. (2009). *Evolution: The story of life.* Berkeley, CA: University of California Press.

Palmer, K. (2010). *Spellbound: Inside West Africa's witch camps.* New York, NY: Free Press.

Palmer, S. J. (1975). The effects of contextual scenes on the identification of objects. *Memory & Cognition, 3*, 519–526.

Park, R. L. (2008). *Superstition: Belief in the age of science.* Princeton, NJ: Princeton University Press.

Parnia, S. (2006). *What happens when we die? A groundbreaking study into the nature of life after death.* Carlsbad, CA: Hay House.

Parra, A. (2009). Out-of-body experiences and hallucinatory experiences: A psychological approach. *Imagination, Cognition, and Personality, 29*, 211–223.

Parrott, W. G. (1995). But emotions are sometimes irrational. *Psychological Inquiry, 6*, 230–232.

Pascarella, E. T., & Terrenzini, P. T. (1991). *How college affects students: Findings and insights from twenty years of research.* San Francisco, CA: Jossey-Bass.

Pascarella, E. T., & Terrenzini, P. T. (2005). *How college affects students: Volume 2: A third decade of research.* San Francisco, CA: Jossey-Bass.

Paul, G. L. (2007). Psychotherapy outcome can be scientifically studied. In S. O. Lilienfeld & W. T. O'Donohue (Eds.), *The great ideas of clinical science* (pp. 119–147). New York, NY: Routledge.

Paul, R. (1984). Critical thinking: Fundamental to education for a free society. *Educational Leadership, 42*, 4–14.

Paul, R. (1993). *Critical thinking: Fundamental to education for a free society.* Santa Rosa, CA: Foundation for Critical Thinking.

Peale, N. V. (1952). *The power of positive thinking.* Upper Saddle River, NJ: Prentice Hall.

Penfield, W. (1955). The role of the temporal cortex in certain psychic phenomena. *Journal of Mental Science, 101*, 451–465.

Pennycook, G., Cheyne, J. A., Barr, N., Koehler, D. J., & Fugelsang, J. A. (2015). On the reception and detection of pseudo-profound bullshit. *Judgment and Decision Making, 10*, 549–563.

Perkins, D. N. (1985). Postprimary education has little impact on informal reasoning. *Journal of Educational Psychology, 77*, 562–571.

Perkins, D. N., Jay, E., & Tishman, S. (1993). Beyond abilities: A dispositional theory of thinking. *Merrill-Palmer Quarterly, 39*, 1–21.

Persinger, M. (1995). Out-of-body experiences are more probable in people with elevated complex partial epileptic-like signs during periods of enhanced geomagnetic activity: A nonlinear effect. *Perceptual and Motor Skills, 80*, 563–569.

Peterson, M. A. (2007). The piecemeal, constructive, and schematic nature of perception. In M. Peterson, B. Gillam, & H. A. Sedgwick (Eds.), *In the mind's eye: Julian Hochberg on the perception of pictures, films, and the world* (pp. 419–428). New York, NY: Oxford University Press.

Petry, N. M. (2005). Gamblers anonymous and cognitive-behavioral therapies for pathological gamblers. Journal of Gambling Studies, 21, 27–33.

Peverly, S. T., & Sumowski, J. F. (2001). What variables predict quality of text notes and are text notes related to performance on different types of tests? *Applied Cognitive Psychology, 26*, 104–117.

Pew Research Center. (2013). Online dating. Retrieved from http://www.pewinternet. org/2013/10/21/online-dating-2/

Pezdek, K., Whetstone, T., Reynolds, K., Askari, N., & Dougherty, T. (1989). Memory for real-world sciences: The role of consistency with schema expectation. *Journal of Experimental Psychology: Learning, Memory, and Cognition, 15,* 587–595.

Pianko, S. (1979). A description of the composing process of college freshmen writers. *Research in Teaching English, 13,* 5–22.

Pigliucci, M., & Boudry, M. (2013). *Philosophy of pseudoscience: Reconsidering the demarcation problem.* Chicago, IL: University of Chicago Press.

Piliavin, J. A. (2008). Altruism and helping: The evolution of a field. *Social Psychology Bulletin, 72,* 209–225.

Pinker, S. (1994). *The language instinct.* New York, NY: William Morrow.

Pinker, S. (2014). *The sense of style: The thinking person's guide to writing in the 21st century.* New York, NY: Viking.

Piolat, A., Olive, T., & Kellogg, R. T. (2005). Cognitive effort during note taking. *Applied Cognitive Psychology, 19,* 291–312.

Plato. (1956). *Great dialogues of Plato.* Trans. by W. H. D. Rouse. New York, NY: New American Library.

Plous, S. (1993). *The psychology of judgment and decision making.* New York, NY: McGraw-Hill.

Polk, C., & Postow, E. (1996). *Handbook of biological effects of electromagnetic fields.* Boca Raton, FL: CRC Press.

Popper, K. R. (1959). *The logic of scientific discovery.* New York, NY: Basic Books.

Popper, K. R., & Eccles, J. C. (1980). *The self and its brain: An argument for interactionism.* New York, NY: Routledge.

Posey, T. B., & Losch, M. E. (1983). Auditory hallucinations of hearing voices in 375 normal subjects. *Imagination, Cognition, and Personality, 3,* 99–113.

Posner, M. I., & Raichle, M. E. (1994). *Images of mind.* New York, NY: W. H. Freeman.

Preston, S. D. (2013). The origins of altruism in offspring care. *Psychological Bulletin, 139,* 1305–1341.

Preston, S. D., & de Waal, F. (2002). Empathy: Its ultimate and proximate bases. *Behavioral and Brain Sciences, 25,* 1–71.

Pronin, E., Gilovich, T., & Ross, L. (2004). Objectivity in the eye of the beholder: Divergent perceptions of bias in self versus others. *Psychological Review, 111,* 781–799.

Pronin, E., Lin, D. Y., and Ross, L. (2002). The bias blind spot: Perceptions of bias in self versus others. *Personality and Social Psychology Bulletin, 28,* 369–381.

Pronin, E., Wegner, D. M., McCarthy, K., & Rodriguez, S. (2006). Everyday magical powers: The role of apparent mental causation in the overestimation of personal influence. *Journal of Personality and Social Psychology, 91,* 218–231.

Prothero, D. (2013). The holocaust denier's playbook and the tobacco smokescreen. In M. Pigliucci & M. Boudry (Eds.), *Philosophy of pseudoscience* (pp. 341–358). Chicago, IL: University of Chicago Press.

Purves, D., Brannon, E. M., Cabeza, R., Huettel, S., LaBar, K. S., Platt, M. L., & Woldorff, M. G. (2008). *Principles of cognitive neuroscience.* Sunderland, MA: Sinauer.

Quirk, J., Likhtik, E., Pelletier, J. G., & Pare, D. (2003). Stimulation of medial prefrontal cortex decreases the responsiveness of central amygdala output neurons. *Journal of Neuroscience, 23,* 8800–8807.

Rabinowitz, J., & Efron, N. J. (1997). Diagnosis, dogmatism, and rationality. *Journal of Mental Health Counseling, 19,* 40–57.

Radford, B. (2012, April 12). Airplane, UFO, or Venus: A strange celestial optical illusion involving Venus explains some UFO reports. Retrieved from http://www.seeker.com/airplane-ufo-or-venus-1765746736.html

Raimy, V. (Ed.). (1950). *Training in clinical psychology.* New York, NY: Prentice Hall.

Ramachandran, V. S., & Hirstein, W. (1998). The perception of phantom limbs. *Brain, 121,* 1603–1630.

Rand, A., & Branden, N. (1964). *The virtue of selfishness: A new concept of egoism.* New York, NY: Signet.

Randi, J. (1977). The media and reports on the paranormal. *The Humanist, 37,* 45–47.

Rapoport, A. (1991). Ideological commitments in evolutionary theories. *Journal of Social Issues, 47,* 83–99.

Rayner, K., White, S. J., Johnson, R. L., Liversedge, S. P. (2006). Raeding wrods with jubmled lettres: There is a cost. *Psychological Science, 17,* 192–195.

Redelmeier, D. A., & Tibshrani, R. J. (1997). Association between cellular-telephone calls and motor vehicle collisions. *New England Journal of Medicine, 306,* 453–458.

Redlawsk, D. P., Civettini, A. J., & Emmerson, K. M. (2010). The affective tipping point: Do motivated reasoners ever "get it"? *Political Psychology, 31,* 563–593.

Reese, W. L. (1980). *Dictionary of philosophy and religion.* Atlantic Highlands, NJ: Humanities Press.

Regan, D. T. (1988). *For the record.* San Diego, CA: Harcourt Brace Jovanovich.

Reicher, S. D., & Haslam, S. A. (2016, May/June). Fueling extremes. *Scientific American Mind,* 36–39.

Reyes, R. M., Thomspon, W. C., & Bower, G. H. (1980). Judgmental biases resulting from differing availabilities of arguments. *Journal of Personality and Social Psychology, 39,* 2–12.

Rhine, J. B. (1947). *The reach of the mind.* New York, NY: William Sloane Associates.

Rind, B., Bauserman, R., & Tromovitch, P. (1998). A meta-analytic study of assumed properties of child sexual abuse using college samples. *Psychological Bulletin, 124,* 22–53.

Rips, L. J., & Conrad, F. G. (1989). Folk psychology of mental activities. *Psychological Review, 96,* 187–207.

Risen, J. (2016). Believing what we do not believe: Acquiescence to superstitious beliefs and other powerful intuitions. *Psychological Review, 123,* 182–207.

Risen, J., & Gilovich, T. (2007). Informal logical fallacies. In R. Sternberg, H. Roediger, & D. Halpern (Eds.), *Critical thinking in psychology* (pp. 110–130). New York, NY: Cambridge University Press.

Robinson, D. B. (1981). *An intellectual history of psychology* (rev. ed.). New York, NY: Macmillan.

Roediger, H. L., III. (1996). Memory illusions. *Journal of Memory and Language, 35,* 76–100.

Roediger, H. L., III, & McDermott, K. B. (1996). Creating false memories: Remembering words not presented in lists. *Journal of Experimental Psychology: Learning, Memory, and Cognition, 21,* 803–814.

Roese, N. J., & Vohs, K. D. (2012). Hindsight bias. *Perspectives on Psychological Science, 7,* 411–426.

Rogo, D. S. (1978). Research on some deathbed experiences: Some contemporary and historical perspectives. *Parapsychology Review, 9,* 20–27.

Rogo, D. S. (1984). Researching the out-of-body experience: The state of the art. *Anabiosis: The Journal of Near-Death Studies, 4,* 21–49.

Rogo, D. S., & Bayless, R. G. (1979). *Phone calls from the dead: The results of a two-year investigation into an incredible phenomenon.* Upper Saddle River, NJ: Prentice Hall.

Romanczyk, R. G., Arnstein, L., Soorya, L. V., & Gillis, J. (2003). The myriad of controversial treatments for autism: A critical evaluation of efficacy. In S. O. Lilienfeld, S. J. Lynn, & J. M. Lohr (Eds.), *Science and pseudoscience in clinical psychology* (pp. 363–395). New York, NY: Guilford.

Romer, D., Gruder, C. L., & Lizardo, T. (1986). A person–situation approach to altruistic behavior. *Journal of Personality and Social Psychology, 51,* 1001–1012.

Roseman, I. J., Wiest, C., & Swartz, T. S. (1994). Phenomenology, behaviors, and goals differentiate discrete emotions. *Journal of Personality and Social Psychology, 67,* 206–221.

Rosen, G. M., Barrera, M., & Glasgow, R. E. (2008). Good intentions are not enough: Reflections on past and future efforts to advance self-help. In P. L Watkins & G. A. Clum (Eds.), *A handbook of self-help therapies* (pp. 25–39). New York, NY: Routledge.

Rosen, G. M., Glasgow, R. E., & Barrera, M. (1976). A controlled study to assess the efficacy of totally self-administered systematic desensitization. *Journal of Consulting and Clinical Psychology, 44,* 208–217.

Rosen, G. M., Glasgow, R. E., Moore, T. E., & Barrera, M. (2014). Self-help therapy: Recent developments in the science and business of giving psychology away. In S. O. Lilienfeld, S. J. Lynn, & J. M. Lohr (Eds.), *Science and pseudoscience in clinical psychology* (2nd ed., pp. 245–274). New York, NY: Guilford.

Rosenhan, D. (1973). On being sane in insane places. *Science, 179,* 250–258.

Ross, B., Chuchmach, M., & Hill, A. M. (2012, April 17). Sleepy pilot mistakes planet for oncoming plane, sends passenger jet into dive. Retrieved from http://abcnews. go.com/Blotter/sleepy-pilot-mistakes-planet-venus-oncoming-plane/story?id=16158107

Ross, L., & Ward, A. (1996). Naïve realism: Implications for social conflict and misunderstanding. In T. Brown, E. Reed, & E. Turiel (Eds.), *Values and knowledge* (pp. 103–135). Hillsdale, NJ: Erlbaum.

Rotton, J., & Kelly, I. (1985). Much ado about the full moon: A meta-analysis of lunar-lunacy research. *Psychological Bulletin, 97,* 286–306.

Roussey, J., & Gombert, A. (1996). Improving argumentative writing skills: Effect of two types of aids. *Argumentation, 10,* 283–300.

Rozin, P., Markwith, M., & MacCauley, C. R. (1994). The nature of aversion to indirect contact with another person: AIDS aversion as a composite of aversion to strangers, infection, moral taint and misfortune. *Journal of Abnormal Psychology, 103,* 495–504.

Rozin, P., & Nemoroff, C. (1990). The laws of sympathetic magic: A psychological analysis of similarity and contagion. In J. Stigler, R. A. Shweder, & G. Herdt (Eds.), *Cultural psychology: Essays of comparative human development* (pp. 205–232). Cambridge, UK: Cambridge University Press.

Ruscio, J. (2006). *Critical thinking in psychology: Separating sense from nonsense* (2nd ed.). Belmont, CA: Thomsen-Wadsworth.

Ruscio, J. (2007). The clinician as subject. In S. O. Lilienfeld & W. T. O'Donohue (Eds.), *The great ideas of clinical science* (pp. 29–47). New York, NY: Routledge.

Russell, B. (1972). *History of western philosophy.* New York, NY: Touchstone.

Russell, G. W., & Dua, M. (1983). Lunar influences on human aggression. *Social Behavior and Personality, 11,* 41–44.

Sacks, O. (2012). *Hallucinations.* New York, NY: Alfred A. Knopf.

Sagan, C. (1996). *The demon-haunted world: Science as a candle in the dark.* New York, NY: Ballantine Books.

Sagi, A., & Hoffman, M. L. (1976). Empathic distress in the newborn. *Developmental Psychology, 12,* 175–176.

Salamé, P., & Baddeley, A. D. (1989). The effects of background music on phonological short-term memory. *Quarterly Journal of Experimental Psychology A: Human Experimental Psychology, 41,* 107–122.

Saleem, M., Anderson, C. A., & Gentile, D. A. (2012). Effects of prosocial, neutral, and violent games on children's helpful and hurtful behaviors. *Aggressive Behavior, 38,* 281–287.

Salerno, S. (2005). *Sham: How the self-help movement made America helpless.* New York, NY: Crown.

Salter, D., MacMillan, D., Richards, M., Talbot, T., Hodges, J. Bentovim, A., . . . Skuse, D. (2003). Development of sexually abusive behavior in sexually victimized males: A longitudinal study. *Lancet, 361,* 471–476.

Sanna, L. J., Schwarz, N., & Stocker, S. L. (2002). When debiasing backfires: Accessible content and accessibility experiences in debiasing hindsight. *Journal of Experimental Psychology: Learning, Memory, and Cognition, 28,* 497–502.

Sansone, R. A., & Sansone, L. A. (2010). Road rage: What's driving it? *Psychiatry, 7,* 14–18.

Saxe, L., Dougherty, D., & Cross, T. (1985). The validity of polygraph testing: Scientific analysis and public controversy. *American Psychologist, 40,* 335–366.

Scardamalia, M., Bereiter, C., & Steinbach, R. (1984). Teachability of reflective processes in written composition. *Cognitive Science, 8,* 173–190.

Schacter, D. (2001). *The seven sins of memory: How the mind forgets and remembers.* New York, NY: Houghton Mifflin.

Schaefer, C. E., & Mattei, D. (2005). Catharsis: Effectiveness in children's aggression. *International Journal of Play Therapy, 14,* 103–109.

Schank, R. C., & Abelson, R. P. (1977). *Scripts, plans, and goals and understanding: An inquiry into human knowledge structures.* Hillsdale, NJ: Erlbaum.

Scherer, K. R. (1984). On the nature and function of emotion: A component process approach. In K. Scherer & P. Ekman (Eds.), *Approaches to emotion* (pp. 293–317). Hillsdale, NJ: Erlbaum.

Schirmer, A. (2015). *Emotion.* Los Angeles, CA: Sage.

Schroeder, D. A., Penner, L. A., Dovidio, J. F., & Piliavin, J. A. (1995). *The psychology of helping and altruism: Problems and puzzles.* New York, NY: McGraw-Hill.

Schuman, H., & Presser, S. (1981). *Questions and answers in attitude surveys.* New York, NY: Academic Press.

Schwarz, N. (2007). Evaluating surveys and questionnaires. In R. J. Sternberg, H. L. Roediger, & D. F. Halpern (Eds.), *Critical thinking in psychology* (pp. 54–74). New York, NY: Cambridge University Press.

Schwarz, N., & Bless, H. (1991). Happy and mindless, but sad and smart? The impact of affective states on analytic reasoning. In J. Forgas (Ed.), *Emotion and social judgments* (pp. 55–71). Oxford, UK: Pergamon Press.

Sedivy, J., & Carlson, G. (2011). *Sold on language: How advertisers talk to you and what this says about you.* Chichester, UK: Wiley-Blackwell.

Semmler, C., Brewer, N., & Douglass, A. B. (2012). Jurors believe eyewitnesses. In B. L. Cutler (Ed.), *Conviction of the innocent: Lessons from psychological research* (pp. 185–209). Washington, DC: American Psychological Association.

Shanteau, J. (1992). The psychology of expertise: An alternative view. In G. Wright & F. Bolger (Eds.), *Expertise and decision support* (pp. 11–23). New York, NY: Plenum Press.

Shatz, M. A., & Best, J. B. (1987). Students' reasons for changing answers on objective tests. *Teaching of Psychology, 14,* 241–242.

Shaughnessy, J. J., & Vander Stoep, S. W. (1997). Taking a course in research methods improves reasoning about real-life events. *Teaching of Psychology, 24,* 122–124.

Shaw, J. S., III. (1996). Increases in eyewitness confidence from post-event questioning. *Journal of Experimental Psychology: Applied, 2,* 126–146.

Shaw, J., & Porter, S. (2015). Creating rich false memories of committing crime. *Psychological Science, 26,* 291–301.

Shermer, M. (1997). *Why people believe weird things.* New York, NY: W. H. Freeman.

Shermer, M. (2001). *The borderlands of science: Where sense meets nonsense.* Oxford, UK: Oxford University Press.

Shermer, M. (2011). *The believing brain.* New York, NY: Time Books.

Shiels, D. (1978). A cross-cultural study of belief in out-of-body experiences, waking and sleeping. *Journal of the Society for Psychical Research, 49,* 697–741.

Shriver, E. R., Young, S. G., Hugenberg, K., Bernstein, M. J., & Lanter, J. R. (2008). Class race and the face: Social context modulates the cross-race effect in face recognition. *Personality and Social Psychology Bulletin, 34,* 260–274.

Sibicky, M. E., Schroeder, D. A., & Dovidio, J. F. (1995). Empathy and helping: Considering the consequences of intervention. *Basic and Applied Social Psychology, 16,* 435–453.

Sica, C., Novara, C., & Sanavio, E. (2002). Culture and psychopathology: Superstition and obsessive–compulsive cognitions and symptoms in a non-clinical Italian sample. *Personality and Individual Differences, 32,* 1001–1012.

Silver, E., Cirincione, C., & Steadman, H. J. (1994). Demythologizing the insanity defense. *Law and Human Behavior, 18,* 63–67.

Simon, H. (1990). Invariants of human behavior. *Annual Review of Psychology, 41,* 1–19.

Simons, D. J., & Chabris, C. F. (1999). Gorillas in our midst: Sustained inattentional blindness for dynamic events. *Perception, 28,* 1059–1074.

Simons, D. J., & Levin, D. T. (1998). Failure to detect changes to people during a real-world interaction. *Psychonomic Bulletin and Review, 5,* 644–649.

Simmons, J., LeBeouf, R., & Nelson, L. (2010). The effect of accuracy motivation on anchoring and adjustment: Do people adjust from provided anchors? *Journal of Personality and Social Psychology, 99,* 917–932.

Skinner, B. F. (1948). Superstition in the pigeon. *Journal of Experimental Psychology, 38,* 168–172.

Skurnik, I., Yoon, C., Park, D. C., & Schwarz, N. (2005). How warnings about false claims become recommendations. *Journal of Consumer Research, 31,* 713–723.

Sladeczek, I. E., Dumont, F., Martel, C., & Karagiannakis, A. (2006). Making sense of client data: Clinical experience and confirmation sim revisited. *American Journal of Psychotherapy, 60,* 375–391.

Slovic, P., Fischhoff, B., & Lichtenstein, S. (1976). Cognitive processes in societal risk taking. In J. Carroll & J. Payne (Eds.), *Cognition and societal behavior* (pp. 165–184). Hillsdale, NJ: Erlbaum.

Small, G. W., Moody, T. D., Siddarth, P., & Brookheimer, S. Y. (2009). Your brain on Google: Patterns of activation during Internet searching. *American Journal of Geriatric Psychiatry, 17,* 116–126.

Smedsland, J. (1978). The concept of correlation in adults. *Scandinavian Journal of Psychology, 4,* 165–173.

Smith, A. M., & Messier, C. (2014). Voluntary out-of-body experience: An fMRI study. *Frontiers in Human Neuroscience, 8,* 1–10.

Smith, L., Glass, G. V., & Miller, T. I. (1980). *The benefits of psychotherapy.* Baltimore, MD: Johns Hopkins University Press.

Smith, M. L., & Glass, G. V. (1977). Meta-analysis of psychotherapeutic outcome studies. *American Psychologist, 32,* 752–760.

Smoller, J. (2012). *The other side of normal: How biology is providing the clues to unlock the secrets of normal and abnormal behavior.* New York, NY: William Morrow.

Snyder, M., & Thomsen, C. J. (1988). Interactions between therapists and clients: Hypothesis testing and behavioral confirmation. In D. Turk & P. Salovey (Eds.), *Reasoning, inference, and judgment in clinical psychology* (pp. 124–151). New York, NY: Free Press.

Solon, T. (2007). Generic critical thinking infusion and course content learning in introductory psychology. *Journal of Instructional Psychology, 34,* 972–987.

Sporer, S. L., Penrod, S. D., Read, D., & Cutler, B. (1995). Choosing, confidence, and accuracy: A meta-analysis of the confidence–accuracy relation in eyewitness identification studies. *Psychological Bulletin, 118,* 315–327.

Standing, L., Conezio, J., & Haber, R. N. (1970). Perception and memory for pictures: Single-trial learning of 2500 visual stimuli. *Psychonomic Science, 19,* 73–74.

Stanovich, K. E. (1989). Implicit philosophies of mind: The dualism scale and its relation to religiosity and belief in extrasensory perception. *Journal of Psychology, 123,* 5–23.

Stanovich, K. E. (1994). Reconceptualizing intelligence: Dysrationalia as an intuition pump. *Educational Researcher, 22,* 11–21.

Stanovich, K. E. (2010). *How to think straight about psychology* (9th ed.). Boston, MA: Allyn & Bacon.

Stanovich, K. E. (2011). *Rationality and the reflective mind.* Oxford, UK: Oxford University Press.

Stanovich, K. E., & West, R. F. (2000). Individual differences in reasoning: Implications for the rationality debate? *Behavioral and Brain Sciences, 23,* 645–726.

Stanovich, K. E., West, R. F., & Toplak, M. E. (2013). Myside bias, rational thinking, and intelligence. *Current Directions in Psychological Science, 22,* 259–264.

Steadman, H. J., Monahan, J., Pinals, D. A., Vesselinov, R., & Robbins, P. C. (2015). Gun violence and victimization of strangers by persons with a mental illness: Data from the MacArthur violence risk assessment study. *Psychiatric Services, 66,* 1238–1241.

Stiggins, R. J., Rubel, E., & Quellmalz, E. (1988). *Measuring thinking skills in the classroom* (rev. ed.). Washington, DC: National Education Association.

Strayer, D. L., & Johnston, W. A. (2001). Driven to distraction: Dual-task studies of simulated driving and conversing on a cellular telephone. *Psychological Science, 12,* 462–466.

Strohmer, D. C., & Shivy, V. A. (1994). Bias in counselor hypothesis testing: Testing the robustness of counselor confirmatory bias. *Journal of Counseling and Development, 73,* 191–197.

Suksringarm, P. (1976). An experimental study comparing the effects of BSCS and the traditional biology on achievement understanding of science, critical thinking ability, and attitude towards science of first-year students at the Sakon Nakorn Teachers College, Thailand (Doctoral dissertation, Pennsylvania State University). *Dissertation Abstracts International, 37,* 2764A.

Sutherland, R., & Hayne, H. (2001). Age-related changes in the misinformation effect. *Journal of Experimental Child Psychology, 79,* 388–404.

Swami, V., Voracek, M., Stieger, S., Tran, U. S., & Furnham, A. (2014). Analytic thinking reduces belief in conspiracy theories. *Cognition, 133,* 572–585.

Sweller, J. (2011). Cognitive load theory. In J. P. Mestre & B. H. Ross (Eds.), *The psychology of learning and motivation: Cognition in education* (Vol. 55, pp. 37–76). San Diego, CA: Elsevier Academic Press.

Swenson, D. X. (1999). Thought field therapy. *Skeptic, 7,* 60–65.

Szaz, T. (1974). *The myth of mental illness: Foundations of a theory of personal conduct* (rev. ed.). New York, NY: Harper & Row.

Tabacyk, J., & Mitchell, T. (1987). The out-of-body experience and personality adjustment. *Journal of Nervous and Mental Disease, 175,* 367–369.

Tart, C. T. (1968). A psychophysiological study of out-of-the-body experience in a selected subject. *Journal of the American Society for Psychical Research, 62,* 3–27.

Tart, C. T. (1998). Six studies of out-of-body experience. *Anabiosis: The Journal of Near-Death Studies, 17,* 73–99.

Taube, K.T. (1997). Critical thinking ability and disposition as factors of performance on a written critical thinking test. *Journal of General Education, 46,* 129–164.

Tavris, C. (2003). Mind games: Psychological warfare between therapists and scientists. *Chronicle Review, 49,* B7.

Taylor, A. K., & Kowalski, P. (2004). Naïve psychological science: The prevalence, strength, and sources of misconceptions. *Psychological Record, 54,* 15–25.

Tellegen, A., & Atkinson, G. (1974). Openness to absorbing and self-altering experiences: ("Absorption"), a trait related to hypnotic susceptibility. *Journal of Abnormal Psychology, 83,* 268–277.

Temerlin, M. K. (1968). Suggestion effects in psychiatric diagnosis. *Journal of Nervous and Mental Disorders, 147,* 349–353.

Tenkorang, E. Y., Gyimah, S. O., Maticka-Tyndale, E., & Adjel, J. (2011). Superstition, witchcraft and HIV prevention in sub-Saharan Africa: The case of Ghana. *Culture, Health, & Sexuality, 13,* 1001–1014.

Terhune, D. B. (2009). The incidence and determinants of visual phenomenology during out-of-body experiences. *Cortex, 45,* 236–242.

Terrace, H. S. (2011). Thinking without language. In M. Gernsbacher, R. Pew, L. Hough, & J. Pomerantz (Eds.), *Psychology and the real world* (pp. 99–106). New York, NY: Worth.

Tetlock, P. E., & Kim, J. I. (1987). Accountability and judgment processes in a personality prediction task. *Journal of Personality and Social Psychology, 52,* 700–709.

Thalbourne, M. (1999). Dualism and the sheep–goat variable: A replication and extension. *Journal of the Society for Psychical Research, 63,* 213–216.

Thaler, R. H., & Sunstein, C. R. (2008). *Nudge: Improving decisions about health, wealth, and happiness.* New Haven, CT: Yale University Press.

Thompson-Cannino, J., Cotton, R., & Torneo, E. (2000). *Picking cotton: Our memoir of injustice and redemption.* New York, NY: St. Martin's Press.

Thorne, S. B., & Himelstein, P. (1984). The role of suggestion in the perception of satanic messages in rock-and-roll recordings. *Journal of Psychology: Interdisciplinary and Applied, 116,* 245–248.

Thornton, D. J. (2011). *Brain culture: Neuroscience and popular media.* New Brunswick, NJ: Rutgers University Press.

Thurs, D. P. (2007). *Science talk: Changing notions of science in American popular culture.* New Brunswick, NJ: Rutgers University Press.

Todd, A. R., Forstmann, M., Burgmer, P., Brooks, A. W., & Galinsky, A. (2015). Anxious and egocentric: How specific emotions influence perspective taking. *Journal of Experimental Psychology: General, 144,* 374–391.

Tomlinson-Keasey, C., & Eisert, D. (1977). Second year evaluation of the ADAPT program. In *Multidisciplinary Piagetian-based programs for college freshmen: ADAPT.* Lincoln, NE: University of Nebraska.

Tomlinson-Keasey, C., Williams, V., & Eisert, D. (1977). Evaluation report of the first year of the ADAPT program. In *Multidisciplinary Piagetian-based programs for college freshmen: ADAPT.* Lincoln, NE: University of Nebraska.

Toplak, M. E., Liu, E., Macpherson, R., Toneatto, T., & Stanovich, K. E. (2007). The reasoning skills and thinking dispositions of problem gamblers: A dual-process taxonomy. *Journal of Behavioral Decision Making, 20,* 103–124.

Tourouteglou, A., Lindquist, K. A., Dickerson, B. C., & Barrett, L. F. (2015). Intrinsic connectivity in the human brain does not reveal networks for "basic" emotions. *Scan, 10,* 1257–1265.

Tracey, J. G., Wampold, B. E., Lichtenberg, J. W., & Goodyear, R. K. (2014). Expertise in psychotherapy: An elusive goal? *American Psychologist, 69,* 218–229.

Trivers, R. L. (1971). The evolution of reciprocal altruism. *Quarterly Review of Biology, 46,* 35–57.

Tuckey, M. R., & Brewer, N. (2003). The influence of schemas, stimulus ambiguity, and interview schedule on eyewitness memory over time. *Journal of Experimental Psychology: Applied, 9,* 101–118.

Tversky, A., & Kahneman, D. (1971). Belief in the law of small numbers. *Psychological Bulletin, 76,* 105–110.

Tversky, A., & Kahneman, D. (1974). Judgment under uncertainty: Heuristics and biases. *Science, 185*(4157), 1124–1131.

Tversky, A., & Kahneman, D. (1981). The framing of decisions and the psychology of choice. *Science, 211*(4481), 453–458.

Tversky, A., & Kahneman, D. (1982). Judgments of and by representativeness. In D. Kahneman, P. Slovic, & A. Tversky (Eds.), *Judgment under uncertainty: Heuristics and biases* (pp. 84–98). Cambridge, UK: Cambridge University Press.

Tylor, E. B. (1974). *Primitive culture: Researches into the development of mythology, philosophy, religion, art and custom.* New York, NY: Gordon Press. (Original work published 1871.)

Tyson, G. A. (2001). Occupation and astrology or season of birth: A myth? *Journal of Social Psychology, 110,* 73–78.

U.S. Census Bureau. (2016). Quarterly retail e-commerce sales: 3rd quarter 2016. Retrieved from http:www.census.gov/estats

Valentine, T., Pickering, A., & Darling, S. (2003). Characteristics of eyewitness identification that predict the outcome of real lineups. *Applied Cognitive Psychology, 17,* 969–993.

Vallone, R. P., Griffin, D. W., Lin, S., & Ross, L. (1990). Overconfident prediction of future actions and outcomes by self and others. *Journal of Personality and Social Psychology, 58,* 582–592.

Van Prooijen, J. (2017). Why education predicts decreased belief in conspiracy theories. *Applied Cognitive Psychology, 31,* 50–58.

Van Rillaers, J. (1991). Strategies of dissimulation in the pseudosciences. *New Ideas in Psychology, 9,* 235–244.

Vaughn, L. (2010). *The power of critical thinking* (3rd ed.). New York, NY: Oxford University Press.

Velten, E. (1968). A laboratory task for the induction of mood. *Behaviour Research and Therapy, 6,* 473–482.

Verona, E., & Sullivan, E. A. (2008). Emotional catharsis and aggression revisited: Heart rate reduction following aggressive responding. *Emotion, 8,* 331–340.

Vogt, W. P. (1993). *Dictionary of statistics and methodology.* Newbury Park, CA: Sage.

Voss, J. F., & Means, M. L. (1991). Learning to reason via instruction in argumentation. *Learning and Instruction, 1,* 337–350.

Vrij, A. (2008). *Detecting lies and deceit: Pitfalls and opportunities.* New York, NY: Wiley.

Vyse, S. (2014). *Believing in magic: The psychology of superstition.* Oxford, UK: Oxford University Press.

Wade, C., & Tavris, C. (1993). *Critical and creative thinking: The case of love and war.* New York, NY: Harper Collins.

Wadlington, E. M., & Wadlington, P. L. (2005). What educators really believe about dyslexia. *Reading Improvement, 42,* 16–33.

Wagner, G. A., & Morris, E. K. (1987). "Superstitious" behavior in children. *Psychological Record, 37,* 471–488.

Wakefield, A. J., Murch, S. H., Anthony, A., Linnell, J., Casson, D. M., Malik, M., . . . Walker-Smith, J. A. (1998). Ileal-lymphoid nodular hyperplasia, non-specific colitis, and pervasive developmental disorder in children. *Lancet, 351,* 637–641.

Walfish, S., McAlister, B., O'Donnell, P., & Lambert, M. J. (2012). An investigation of self-assessment bias in mental health providers. *Psychological Reports, 110,* 639–644.

Walker, W. R., Hoekstra, S. J., & Vogl, R. J. (2002). Science education is no guarantee of skepticism. *Skeptic, 9,* 24–27.

Wann, D. L., Carlson, J. D., Holland, L. C., Jacobs, B. E., Owens, D. A., & Wells, D. D. (1999). Beliefs in symbolic catharsis: The importance of involvement with aggressive sports. *Social Behavior and Personality, 27,* 155–164.

Wargo, E. (2008). The many lives of superstition. *APS Observer, 21,* 18–24.

Warneken, F., & Tomasello, M. (2006). Altruistic helping in human infants and young chimpanzees. *Science, 311*(5765), 1301–1303.

Watkins, P. L. (2008). Self-help therapies: Past and present. In P. L. Watkins & G. A. Clum (Eds.), *Handbook of self-help therapies* (pp. 1–24). New York, NY: Routledge.

Watkins, P. L., & Clum, G. A. (2008). Self-help therapies: Retrospect and prospect. In P. L. Watkins & G. A. Clum (Eds.), *A handbook of self-help therapies* (pp. 419–436). New York, NY: Routledge.

Weisberg, R. W. (2006). *Creativity: Innovation in problem solving, science, invention, and the arts.* New York, NY: Wiley.

Wells, G. L. (1993). What do we know about eyewitness identification? *American Psychologist, 48,* 553–571.

West, R. F., Toplak, M. E., & Stanovich, K. E. (2008). Heuristics and biases as measures of critical thinking: Associations with cognitive ability and thinking dispositions. *Journal of Educational Psychology, 100,* 930–941.

Westen, D., Blagov, P. S., Harenski, K., Kilts, C., & Hamaan, S. (2006). Neural bases of motivated reasoning: An fMRI study of emotional constraints on partisan political judgment in the 2004 U.S. presidential election. *Journal of Cognitive Neuroscience, 18,* 1947–1958.

Wilford, M., Chan, J. C. K., & Tuhn, S. J. (2014). Retrieval enhances eyewitness suggestibility to misinformation in free and cued recall. *Journal of Experimental Psychology: Applied, 20,* 81–93.

Willingham, D. T. (2007, Summer). Critical thinking: Why is it so hard to teach? *American Educator,* 8–19.

Wilson, T. D., & Schooler, J. W. (1991). Thinking too much: Introspection can reduce the quality of preferences and decisions. *Journal of Personality and Social Psychology, 60,* 181–192.

Wimmer, H. (1996). The early manifestation of developmental dyslexia: Evidence from German children. *Reading and Writing: An Interdisciplinary Journal, 8,* 171–188.

Wise, R. A., & Safer, M. A. (2004). What U.S. judges know and believe about eyewitness testimony. *Applied Cognitive Psychology, 18,* 427–443.

Witteman, C. L., Weiss, D. J., & Metzmacher, M. (2012). Assessing diagnostic expertise of counselors using the Cochran–Weiss–Shanteau (CWS) index. *Journal of Counseling & Development, 90,* 30–34.

Wittenborn, J. R., & Sarason, S. B. (1949). Exceptions to certain Rorschach criteria of pathology. *Journal of Consulting Psychology, 13*, 21–27.

Wixted, J. T., Mickes, L., Clark, S. E., Gronlund, S. D., & Roediger, H. L. (2015). Initial eyewitness confidence reliably predicts eyewitness identification accuracy. *American Psychologist, 70*, 515–526.

Wolfe, C. R., Britt, M. A., & Butler, J. A. (2009). Argumentation schema and the myside bias in written communication. *Written Communication, 26*, 183–209.

Wolpe, J. (1958). *Psychotherapy by reciprocal inhibition.* Stanford, CA: Stanford University Press.

Wood, E., Zicakova, L., Gentile, P., Archer, K., De Pasquale, D., & Nosko, A. (2012). Examining the impact of off-task multi-tasking with technology on real-time classroom learning. *Computers & Education, 58*, 365–374.

Wood, J. M., Nezworski, M. T., Lilienfeld, S. O., & Garb, H. N. (2003). *What's wrong with the Rorschach: Science confronts the controversial inkblot test.* San Francisco, CA: Jossey-Bass.

Wood, M., & Valdez-Menchaca, M. C. (1996). The effect of diagnostic label of language delay on adults' perceptions of preschool children. *Journal of Learning Disabilities, 29*, 582–588.

Wootton, D. (2016). *The invention of science: A new history of the scientific revolution.* New York, NY: Harper Collins.

World Health Organization. (2008). *The global burden of disease: 2004 update.* Geneva, Switzerland: Author.

Wylie, R. C. (1979). *The self-concept: Vol. 2: Theory and research on selected topics.* Lincoln, NE: University of Nebraska Press.

Yama, H., & Adachi, K. (2011). A cross-cultural study of hindsight bias and conditional probabilistic reasoning. *Thinking and Reasoning, 16*, 346–371.

Yates, J. F. (1990). *Judgment and decision making.* Englewood Cliffs, NJ: Prentice Hall.

Young, M. J., Tiedens, L. Z., Jung, H., & Tsai, M.-H. (2011). Mad enough to see the other side: Anger and the search for disconfirming information. *Cognition and Emotion, 25*, 10–21.

Yuille, J. C., & Cutshall, J. L. (1986). A case study of eyewitness memory of a crime. *Journal of Applied Psychology, 71*, 291–301.

Zaki, J., & Mitchell, J. P. (2013). Intuitive prosociality. *Current Directions in Psychological Science, 22*, 466–470.

Zaroff, C. M., & Uhm, S. Y. (2012). The prevalence of autism spectrum disorders and influence of country or measurement and ethnicity. *Social Psychiatry and Psychiatric Epidemiology, 47*, 395–398.

Zechmeister, E. B., & Johnson, J. E. (1992). *Critical thinking: A functional approach.* Pacific Grove, CA: Brooks/Cole.

Zeidner, M. (2007). Test anxiety in educational contexts: Concepts, findings, and future directions. In P. A. Shutz & R. Pekrun (Eds.), *Emotion in education* (pp. 165–184). New York, NY: Elsevier.

NAME INDEX

SUBJECT INDEX

Page numbers followed by *f* indicate figures; those followed by *t* indicate tables.